INTERTWININGS

INTERTWININGS

*Interdisciplinary Encounters
with Merleau-Ponty*

Edited by
Gail Weiss

State University of New York Press

Published by
State University of New York Press, Albany

© 2008 State University of New York

All rights reserved

Printed in the United States of America

No part of this book may be used or reproduced in any manner whatsoever without written permission. No part of this book may be stored in a retrieval system or transmitted in any form or by any means including electronic, electrostatic, magnetic tape, mechanical, photocopying, recording, or otherwise without the prior permission in writing of the publisher.

For information, contact State University of New York Press, Albany, NY
www.sunypress.edu

Production by Diane Ganeles
Marketing by Michael Campochiaro

Library of Congress Cataloging-in-Publication Data

Intertwinings : interdisciplinary encounters with Merleau-Ponty / edited by Gail Weiss.
   p. cm.
   Includes bibliographical references and index.
   ISBN 978-0-7914-7589-8 (hardcover : alk. paper)
   ISBN 978-0-7914-7590-4 (pbk. : alk. paper)
 1. Merleau-Ponty, Maurice, 1908–1961. I. Weiss, Gail, 1959–

B2430.M3764I58 2008
194—dc22

                          2007049730

10 9 8 7 6 5 4 3 2 1

Contents

Acknowledgments   ix

Introduction   1
   Gail Weiss

Part I
Ontological and Developmental Concerns: Difference and the Other

1. Merleau-Ponty, Bergson, and the Question of Ontology   13
   Elizabeth Grosz

2. Elemental Alterity: Levinas and Merleau-Ponty   31
   Lawrence Hass

3. The Developing Body: A Reading of Merleau-Ponty's Conception of Women in the Sorbonne Lectures   45
   Talia Welsh

Part II
Feminist Possibilities: Reading Irigaray, Reading Merleau-Ponty

4. Phenomenology in the Feminine: Irigaray's Relationship to Merleau-Ponty   63
   Annemie Halsema

5. The Language of the Lips, Merleau-Ponty and Irigaray: Toward a Culture of Difference   85
   Bruce Young

Part III
Literary Enactments: Merleau-Ponty, Proust, and Stein

6. Among the Hawthorns: Marcel Proust and
   Maurice Merleau-Ponty 99
   Patricia M. Locke

7. "Mixing the Outside with the Inside": Interior Geographies
   and Domestic Horizons in Gertrude Stein 111
   Justine Dymond

Part IV
Ethical Challenges: Recognition, Reciprocity, Violence, and Care

8. Beyond Recognition: Merleau-Ponty and an Ethics of Vision 131
   Kelly Oliver

9. Ethical Reciprocity at the Interstices of Communion
   and Disruption 153
   Sally Fischer

10. Merleau-Ponty, Reciprocity, and the Reversibility
    of Perspectives 169
    Greg Johnson

11. Entering the Place We Already Live: A Phenomenology of
    Female Voice 189
    Janice McLane

12. Resources for Feminist Care Ethics in Merleau-Ponty's
    Phenomenology of the Body 203
    Maurice Hamington

Part V
Sedimented Meanings: Conservation and Transformation

13. Can an Old Dog Learn New Tricks? Habitual Horizons in
    James, Bourdieu, and Merleau-Ponty 223
    Gail Weiss

14. The Borderlands of Identity and Culture 241
    Rashmika Pandya

15. Entwining the Body and the World: Architectural Design
    and Experience in the Light of "Eye and Mind" 265
    Rachel McCann

List of Contributors 283

Index 287

Acknowledgments

Edited volumes are always collaborative efforts and I am very grateful to *Intertwinings*' contributors for their assistance in putting this collection together. They have been patient with the inevitable delays and prompt when quick responses were called for; it has been a pleasure to work with each and every one of them. Each of the contributors has presented papers at one or more Merleau-Ponty Circle annual conferences and I would be remiss if I did not acknowledge the crucial role the Circle has played in bringing together a diverse group of increasingly interdisciplinary scholars who share a serious interest in Merleau-Ponty's philosophy, particularly its emphasis on the primacy of embodied experience. I would like to thank The George Washington University for allowing me to host the 2000 meeting of the Merleau-Ponty Circle on the theme, "Merleau-Ponty, Feminism, and Intersubjectivity" since the idea for this volume initially arose out of the topic for that conference. Jane Bunker, senior editor at SUNY Press, has been enthusiastic about this project from the outset; it has been delightful to have the privilege of working with her a second time on a wonderful anthology. The anonymous reviewers provided extremely helpful recommendations that have strengthened the volume as a whole, and I'm indebted to them for their crucial, behind-the-scenes contributions. I am deeply appreciative of the excellent work done by *Intertwinings*' copyeditor and the SUNY production staff as they shepherded the volume through the various stages of the pre-publication process. Valerie Hazel has done a terrific job with the index for this book just as she has for so many others, and her expertise, calm, cheerfulness, and dependability always make this part of the final production stage go incredibly smoothly. My family has supported me throughout my work on this volume. I cannot imagine accomplishing any of the things I have done without them.

Introduction

GAIL WEISS

Although he was formally trained as a philosopher, Merleau-Ponty, who occupied the chair of child psychology at the Sorbonne at the time of his death in 1961, would himself be considered an interdisciplinary scholar by contemporary standards. Neurophysiology, gestalt and developmental psychology, political theory, literary and aesthetic theory, anthropology, and linguistics were familiar terrains that he actively drew upon in developing his phenomenological descriptions of perception, language, political life, art, literature, and history, all of which elaborated, in excitingly original and different ways, the primacy of the lived body in our everyday experience. For this reason, it should not surprise us that the philosophy of Merleau-Ponty has had a profound influence not only upon continental philosophers, but also upon literary theorists, cognitive scientists, architects, anthropologists, feminist theorists, psychoanalytic theorists, critical race theorists, and cultural theorists, some of whose work is included in this volume. For Merleau-Ponty, as for his teacher Edmund Husserl, the attempt to provide a comprehensive description of any given phenomenon leads one inevitably outside of the domain of philosophy proper to all the other disciplines that can help us to understand the "what" of its appearance. As Merleau-Ponty observes in the preface to his *Phenomenology of Perception*: "philosophy itself must not take itself for granted, in so far as it may have managed to say something true . . . (xiv)" and he argues that philosophy, the sciences, and all other disciplines, depend upon a prereflective embodied experience that provides the basis for all human inquiry. The essays that follow take up Merleau-Ponty's Husserlian challenge to "return to that world which precedes knowledge, of which knowledge always *speaks*" (1962: ix) and they enter into dialogue with Merleau-Ponty through a variety of disciplinary avenues to explore the intertwinings that dynamically join us to the shared world of our concern.

In part I: "Ontological and Developmental Concerns: Difference and the Other," Elizabeth Grosz, Lawrence Hass, and Talia Welsh advance our understanding of how Merleau-Ponty's ontology, his view of alterity, and his conception of human development can meaningfully address the always shifting boundaries between self and other, as well as between bodies and the world they inhabit. In "Merleau-Ponty, Bergson, and the Question of Ontology," Grosz reveals fundamental affinities between Merleau-Ponty's ontological conception of the flesh and Henri Bergson's ontology of becoming. Regarding the feminist implications of their work, Grosz argues that:

> Merleau-Ponty and Bergson, while being unable to account for or elaborate new concepts of woman or the feminine, may nevertheless prove indispensable in helping to formulate how we might know differently, how we might challenge and replace binarized models (of subject and object, self and object, consciousness and matter, nature and culture) with concepts of difference, what the objects of our representational and epistemological practices might be if they were undertaken with this concept of difference, the difference in being that is becoming, the difference in subjectivity that is biological openendedness, this difference in the world that is life, were a guiding principle. (26)

By tracing the enduring influence of Bergson on Merleau-Ponty, and by emphasizing their relevance for theorizing difference as becoming, biological openendedness, and life, Grosz brings both authors into a twenty-first-century conversation about difference that has only just begun.

Lawrence Hass engages Merleau-Ponty in a productive dialogue with another of his French interlocutors, namely, Emmanuel Levinas. In Hass's essay, the notorious "problem of the other," a problem that has haunted philosophy at least since the Ancient Greeks but which has been an especially salient concern for phenomenologists, is addressed through an exploration of the productive tensions in Levinas's and Merleau-Ponty's respective views of the ontological and ethical implications of intersubjective existence. Both Levinas and Merleau-Ponty, Hass argues, have creative and substantive contributions to make to our understanding of the complex relationships we sustain with others: "Levinas," he claims:

> teaches of the binding of these relationships, of the responsibility that flows toward others from our shared mortality, of the myriad ways our ipseity is called into question by the frank regard and appeal of others. He stresses the distance between self and other that cannot be consumed, and so illuminates the very nature of generosity and respect. And yet Merleau-Ponty reminds us of another binding: that the self and others are intervolved in living experience through the interanimation of flesh and behavior. These "intersubjective" relations aren't the stuff of totality and they don't eliminate the differences between us. They are, instead, the very possibility of contact and community, the opening approach to transcendent others who live and breathe, suffer and perish in their bodies and not outside of them. (40–41)

While both Hass and Grosz's essays reveal, albeit in different ways, the continued importance of Merleau-Ponty's work for contemporary scholars who are committed to an ontology of difference and becoming, Talia Welsh's essay, which concludes part I, turns directly to the question of gendered bodies, specifically Merleau-Ponty's discussion of female embodiment and development in his 1949–1952 Sorbonne lectures in psychology. Welsh seeks to address persistent feminist criticisms of Merleau-Ponty's allegedly masculinist account of human embodiment and to show how the complex intertwining of physiological factors with cultural norms and stereotypes must be acknowledged and addressed in accounting for the specificity of gendered corporeal experience. Drawing directly upon Merleau-Ponty's insights, Welsh writes: "To live is to breathe, to eat, to move. Through these behaviors we are drawn again and again into a life much larger than our own and required for our own personal flourishing. Pregnancy might be the ultimate reminder of this connection" (56).

In part II, Annemie Halsema takes up this theme of being connected through one's gendered body, to "something that is larger than oneself, being part of a community" through a close analysis of the profound resonances between Irigaray's and Merleau-Ponty's thought (72). Despite Irigaray's very critical response to Merleau-Ponty's work in her chapter, "The Intertwining-The Chiasm" in *An Ethics of Sexual Difference*, Halsema argues that Irigaray offers a "phenomenology in the feminine," a gendered phenomenology that builds upon, rather than opposes, Merleau-Ponty's own phenomenology of the body. Irigaray's phenomenology of sexual difference, Halsema suggests, is not so much a phenomenology of the female body as distinguished from the male body, but rather "a phenomenology that reflects on being two, on relating to the other, in short: a phenomenology that is intersubjective" (76). Halsema shows how Irigaray's understanding of the "negative" dimensions of sexual difference not only serves as the basis for an intersubjective ethics but can also be utilized productively to develop phenomenologies of other embodied differences, thereby helping to combat the charge of essentialism that has so often been leveled against Irigaray for privileging sexual difference.

Bruce Young introduces the term "subject-being" in his discussion of Merleau-Ponty and Irigaray, "to designate not the self but a matrix wherein self is related to what is other than it and indeed is constituted in relation to this relation" (85). There are not one but many ways to be related to otherness, Young continues, and "these constitute different forms of subject-being, each of which opens up different possible ways of being a self" (85). Young argues that fear of otherness constitutes the dominant form of subject-being in contemporary Western culture and he creatively demonstrates how the "ontology of noncoincidence" Merleau-Ponty develops in his later work offers a positive, alternative conception of otherness that provides the foundation for Irigaray's own "language of the lips." According to Young, the symbolic that Irigaray proposes "within which it becomes possible to 'speak (as a) woman' is not a semantics private to women, but a syntax that facilitates a dialogue of noncoincidence—that is, effective and articulate interaction between people who are different" (92). By illustrating the close connection between Merleau-Ponty's and Irigaray's projects, despite the latter's privileging of sexual difference and the former's lack of attention to its corporeal significance, both Halsema and Young provide us with new ways of thinking about the ethical implications of the differences that serve to distinguish self from other.

The two chapters that comprise part III of this volume explore the ways in which Marcel Proust and Gertrude Stein respectively enact, through their literature, the chiasmatic relationships Merleau-Ponty describes between the visible and the invisible, and the inside and the outside. Patricia Locke, in "Among the Hawthorns: Marcel Proust and Merleau-Ponty," closely examines Proust's leitmotif of the hawthorns, which first make their appearance at the outset of Volume One of *Remembrance of Things Past, Swann's Way*, "to show how nature gives itself to Marcel as artful, as a living church, as a symbol of life in death, and as an impetus to sexual awakening" (107). Locke eloquently traces the ways in which the visibility of the hawthorns evokes, for the young narrator, the intangible invisibles that are central to his own existence. Chief among these latter is the very movement of temporality itself, the dynamic ways in which the rhythms of the past are taken up in the present and call forth the future; indeed, in homage to Proust, Merleau-Ponty declares: "the *true* hawthorns are the hawthorns of the past" (Merleau-Ponty 1968: 243, quoted in Locke: 107). For Locke, both Proust and Merleau-Ponty reveal that "the truth in art is necessarily screened and partial. It is a wounding that comes from life experiences, but it restores life in an aesthetic transfiguration" (106).

Justine Dymond offers us another means of literary access to the "wounding that comes from life experiences," namely via a journey through several of Gertrude Stein's writings. In the process, she explores both the promise as well as the limits of Stein's own linguistic experiments. Drawing upon Merleau-Ponty's understanding of subjective experience as always informed by the intersubjective horizons out of which it arises, Dymond reveals how Stein disrupts these familiar horizons in her work. More specifically, by reading the "inside" through the "outside," detaching the signifier from the signified, and destabilizing our customary referential assumptions in the process, Stein makes us more aware of the presuppositions that we are continuously making about language, meaning, and the social world in our everyday lives. Dymond uncovers a tension in Stein's work, however, between her attempt to unmoor language and meaning from their sedimented histories so as to produce new interpretative possibilities that are nonheteronormative, and Stein's repeated invocation of racial stereotypes that produce (over)determined and fixed meanings that reinforce the degradation of the racialized other. As Toni Morrison suggests in *Playing in the Dark: Whiteness and the Literary Imagination*, foregrounding and deconstructing an author's uncritical use of racist stereotypes is essential to understanding the continuing pervasiveness and power of such imagery in the western literary tradition. Through Dymond's own recontextualization of Stein's work, we can see how, "Stein's narrators and her formal experimentation cannot fully undo the racially embedded meanings of modernity's racializing legacy" (125). This, in turn, exposes the perils of reifying "the constitutive power of language to construct subjectivity as an inside created by an *othered* outside" (125).

The essays that comprise part IV, "Ethical Challenges: Recognition, Reciprocity, Violence, and Care," are directly concerned with an implicit question raised by Dymond's critical analysis, namely, the extent of our individual and collective responsibility for the types of relationships we sustain with others. Kelly Oliver's chapter, "Beyond Recognition: Merleau-Ponty and an Ethics of Vision," counterposes Merleau-Ponty's view of the chiasmatic relationship between vision and visibility to several of his intellectual interlocutors' view of the gaze and its implications for both subjectivity and intersubjectivity, including Sartre, Hegel, Descartes, Freud, Lacan, Levinas, and Irigaray. Oliver also allows several other voices to enter the conversation, theorists and practitioners who share Merleau-Ponty's "insistence on embodied subjectivity" (175) including J. J. Gibson with his ecological optics, Emile Durkheim and his understanding of social energy, and Dori Laub who introduces the notion of the "inner witness" that developed out of her therapeutic work with other Holocaust survivors. Weaving central insights from these various theorists together, Oliver shows how they help to explain and affirm our infinite "response-ability" not only to other human beings but also to other animals and our environment. Ultimately, Oliver argues for an "ethics of vision" that moves "beyond recognition," beyond the conflictual understandings of the relations between self and other that have marked the phenomenological, existential, and psychoanalytic traditions, thereby opening Merleau-Ponty's own work up to "its own most promising engagements with otherness, and in the spirit of his double-vision, we see that subjectivity itself is necessarily both political and ethical" (149).

Merleau-Ponty, Sally Fischer argues, "has been able to deconstruct the notion of the human being as a transhistorical metaphysical constant, and has opened up an understanding of the body-subject that leaves room for different bodies, or different bodily styles of existence, variously inscribed" (153). She views Merleau-Ponty's conception of the body-subject to be particularly useful for feminist theorists' attempts to move beyond oppressive sex and gender binaries that presume that there are only two possible forms that bodies may take and two possible styles that they can and should embody. Despite the fact that Merleau-Ponty never published a formal ethics, Fischer claims that "his phenomenology of embodied intersubjectivity . . . can serve as a fruitful ground from which to build an ethics of interpersonal relations" (153). Her chapter focuses on how Merleau-Ponty's understanding of the embodied self as decentered from herself and from others generates, through dialogue, an "ethical pact with the other." This pact, Fischer concludes, "requires that we keep the dialogical circle open to the disruptions of our own perspective by the other, and at the same time, aim to facilitate a non-totalizing dialogical communion in which we can dwell in our sensuous everyday existence" (164).

Greg Johnson shares both Oliver's and Fischer's emphases upon the ethical importance of keeping dialogue open through an acknowledgment of the otherness of the other, and he argues that Merleau-Ponty's concept of reversibility offers an optimal framework for accomplishing this goal. Through a critical examination of the well-known debates between Seyla Benhabib and Iris Marion Young concerning reversibility and reciprocity, Johnson highlights the importance of avoiding the Scylla of solipsism on the one hand (where I am forever trapped within my own perspective), and the Charybdis of a false universality on the other hand (where I presuppose the transparency of others' perspectives and, ultimately, their reducibility to the understanding that I have of them). Ultimately, Johnson argues that an ethic of reciprocity, in a Merleau-Pontian sense, is founded upon a primary relationship of reversibility between myself and the other, and that the latter, as Merleau-Ponty depicts it, and, as feminist philosophers have shown us, "does not assume a completely mutual understanding but recognizes the other in a way that can understand their sufferings so that in our response we can choose to recognize this otherness and not eradicate it" (184–185).

The focus of chapter 11 by Janice McLane is on the ways in which the reciprocity Johnson describes is rendered impossible for women through their active silencing in patriarchy. This produces what McLane calls an "existential stutter," a woman's lived experience of "distance from herself, from other persons, and the world" (194, 198). She distinguishes this oppressive patriarchal silencing of women from the "fecund" silence Merleau-Ponty discusses in *The Visible and the Invisible*, "the silence from which language arises" (200). This latter silence, she argues, requires that we "enter more fully into reversibility, the doubled nature of a self connected to others" (200). Women can achieve this goal, McLane suggests, by "entering the place we already live," that is, by mining the expressive possibilities latent in gendered experience, thereby reclaiming women's voices.

Maurice Hamington shows us how the intertwinings of our bodies with the world and with other bodies, as described by Merleau-Ponty throughout his work, is an indispensable resource for contemporary feminist ethics of care. More specifically, Hamington argues that Merleau-Ponty's corporeal-centered epistemology itself reveals "the embodied basis of care" (204). By examining closely four key features of this epistemology that Merleau-Ponty discusses in depth, namely, perception, foreground-background focus phenomena, habit, and the flesh, Hamington shows how "Merleau-Ponty's philosophy of the body provides an epistemological foundation for an embodied notion of care" (216). In so doing, Hamington's work complements and adds to the critical insights of Oliver, Fischer, Johnson, and McLane, persuasively demonstrating the important contributions both Merleau-Ponty's earlier as well as his later work can collectively make to contemporary ethical theorizing and praxis.

Part V, "Sedimented Meanings: Conservation and Transformation" focuses on the diverse social forces that help to constitute the meaning of the habits we have formed, our individual and cultural identities, and the buildings whose bodies shelter our own. My chapter, "Can an Old Dog Learn New Tricks? Habitual Horizons in James, Bourdieu, and Merleau-Ponty," explores these authors' oftentimes ambivalent accounts of habit as both necessary to preserve social stability (i.e., maintaining the status quo) and as an equally crucial ingredient in achieving genuine individual and social change. Opening with a passage from Proust in which he identifies habit as a "skilful but slow-moving arranger," I argue that Merleau-Ponty's emphasis on the intersubjective, embodied dimensions of habit offers "a way of accounting for the creative aspects of habit that cannot be done justice to by either James or Bourdieu" (233). And yet, both James and Bourdieu's emphases on habit as a class-based phenomenon enrich Merleau-Ponty's view of the habit-body to give us a more comprehensive picture of how habits function to consolidate as well as potentially transform the meaning of individual, cultural, and social existence.

Rashmika Pandya considers how the meaning of our experience is continually transformed as we become habituated to our world. Following Merleau-Ponty, she describes how stylistic differences among individuals with varying cultural experiences are expressed as unique ways of "singing" the world. Pandya critically analyzes Merleau-Ponty's claim that "one never does belong to two worlds at once" (1962: 187) from an autobiographically informed perspective and argues that it is through the unity of narrative that we construct our identities, identities that perpetually negotiate and integrate cultural differences (without erasing them) into a coherent whole. Influenced by anthropologist Arjun Appadurai's concept of "imaginary identities" that "suggest a space created between cultures and traditions," she argues that "this space is not only apparent in those of us who have left our ancestral homes to create new homes elsewhere but is increasingly the state of all of us in a global world" (243). Pandya offers a close reading of Merleau-Ponty's gestural theory of speech in order to show how the "expressive function of language always transcends the purely structural aspects of a language" (258). The "'oblique passage' from one language to another," she suggests, "opens the possibility that we may be able to incorporate various worlds in our notion of self" (259).

Rachel McCann's "Entwining the Body and the World: Architectural Design and Experience in the Light of 'Eye and Mind'" is the concluding chapter of the volume and it eloquently reveals the ways in which architects inhabit the (imaginary) spaces they design, integrating past, present, and future, self and other, vision and movement, body and world. McCann cites Merleau-Ponty's reference to painting in "Eye and Mind" as a "carnal echo, a formulation that locates generative power within the active and intersubjective relationship between human beings and the surrounding world" (266) and shows us how architecture itself functions as a carnal echo of our embodied experience in the world, an echo that is differentially repeated across subjects and across time and that reverberates in turn in the durative, dynamic quality of buildings themselves. By creatively extending Merleau-Ponty's insights regarding painters and painting, vision and visibility to architecture, McCann is also able to counter the criticisms of theorists such as Irigaray who take Merleau-Ponty to task for allegedly privileging vision over the other senses. This is because architecture provides a kinaesthetic experience of the building's own depth, its multidimensionality that we access directly not only through vision but through the very movement of our bodies in space, integrating all of our senses and entwining our bodies with the space we inhabit. As McCann illustrates, the carnal echo we experience as we move through the space of the building allows us to interrogate simultaneously "the larger world and the recesses of the self" (265).

As I hope to have demonstrated throughout this introduction, despite the diversity of approaches and themes taken up by the authors in this collection, there are also important resonances that unite the various chapters together. Most notable among them, I would argue, is the importance of Merleau-Ponty's intersubjective ontology as a foundation for contemporary theorizing about bodies, their complex interrelationships with other bodies, and with the world(s) that we jointly (yet differentially) inhabit. The chapters in this volume reveal the enduring influence of Merleau-Ponty's thought not only upon philosophy but also upon feminist theory, literary theory, psychoanalytic theory, cultural studies, and architectural theory and practice. Each essay, in the spirit of Merleau-Ponty's own work, opens up new problems that cannot be anticipated or resolved in advance, but which are dynamically enacted in and through the acts of writing and reading. These interdisciplinary encounters will hopefully find their own "carnal echo" in the reader's experience, revealing the depth and complexity of the "wild being" that, for Merleau-Ponty, unites us to one another in the flesh of the world.

Works Cited

Merleau-Ponty, Maurice (1962). *Phenomenology of Perception*. London: Routledge & Kegan Paul.

Morrison, Toni (1990). *Playing in the Dark: Whiteness and the Literary Imagination*. Cambridge: Harvard University Press.

PART I

Ontological and Developmental Concerns: Difference and the Other

CHAPTER 1

Merleau-Ponty, Bergson, and the Question of Ontology

ELIZABETH GROSZ

Far from being concerned with solutions, truth and falsehood primarily affect problems. A solution always has the truth it deserves according to the problem to which it is a response, and the problem always has the solution it deserves in proportion to *its own* truth or falsity ... (Deleuze, *Difference and Repetition*, Trans. Paul Patton, London: Columbia University Press, 1994: 158–159)

The relation of the philosopher to being is not the frontal relation of the spectator; it is a kind of complicity, an oblique and clandestine relation.

—Merleau-Ponty, *Signs*, 15

Ontologies of Becoming

Instead of the more pressing feminist questions directed to political and ethical concerns, to guaranteeing a specific mode and direction of change in the world, I want to step back to take up a position of greater distance and abstraction, a position where the solution has no place, but where the question must be raised as such: to ontology and thus, ultimately, to metaphysics, that much reviled and undecidable arena where feminism is required to turn, in spite of itself, in reformulating questions of subjectivity, intersubjectivity, body and matter that are so central to the long-term development of its political and intellectual projects.[1] To turn away from feminism, at least to turn away from it directly, only in order to be able to see it more indirectly and thus less instrumentally, we must return, as Merleau-Ponty did, to the question of 'wild being,' to the question of the substance of the world, to the relations between mind and matter and the centrality of perception to conceptualizing their interface, a concern that occupied all of his work, and became the enigmatic focus of his final writings.

These questions of mind, matter, things—the provocation of the world, the entwinement of the thing with the subject and the subject with the thing, that is, ontological differences—are contemporary reformulations of metaphysics, the ways it has transformed the intractable metaphysical problems of classical philosophy into the most fundamental questions of experience, its frame and horizon, in the present. I want to celebrate the investment of knowledges in metaphysical and ontological commitments, and to discuss without defensiveness the metaphysics of Merleau-Ponty, its often neglected relations to a philosophy of process and action developed early in the twentieth century and thus, indirectly, the necessity of a return to the ontological as a question by and for feminist theory.

In this chapter, I would like to throw Merleau-Ponty's writings into another context than that in which they are commonly placed: instead of within his own self-consciously acknowledged lineage of phenomenological thinkers, from Hegel through Husserl to Heidegger and Sartre, I will place his work in a less understood and examined context, still well-documented in his own writings, of the philosophy of nature, of biology, and of movement developed since the mid-nineteenth century, and particularly since the provocations of Darwin, whose work on the active dynamism of the natural world, and thus on the active thing and the active subject it generates, not only transformed the biological sciences, which Merleau-Ponty, more than most, addresses but also changed the very task and image of philosophy itself. Philosophy after Darwin could no longer justifiably devote itself to the classical contemplation of an eternal and unchanging existence, but had to convert itself into something like an attunement to the particular and its history. It is required henceforth, as Merleau-Ponty's work testifies, to take seriously the immersion of consciousness in life, and the immersion of life in time and matter that Darwinism entails but has left underdeveloped and has thus left as a question, a gift, to philosophy that follows. In particular, I would like to counterpose Merleau-Ponty's work, not with Darwin himself, though that would be an interesting project, but with the most Darwinian of philosophers (Daniel Dennett notwithstanding!), Merleau-Ponty's own predecessor (literally, in the Chair of Philosophy at the College de France), Henri Bergson. Instead of comparing and contrasting them, I want to look only at the ways in which Merleau-Ponty addresses Bergson's work, at Merleau-Ponty's complex and changing relations with Bergsonism and with Bergson's concern with an ontology of becoming.

In establishing his own phenomenology of perception, one in which perception is understood as intermediary between mind and matter, Merleau-Ponty retains a peculiar ambivalence to Bergson's writings, while remaining tantalizingly close to his position. He insists, in ways that are not entirely fair or accurate, that Bergson be positioned within the vitalist tradition that he counterposes with mechanism, though Bergson himself remains highly critical of vitalism. Bergson too eschewed any superadded integrity, unity, or telos to organic existence and instead sought out the latent forces, impulses that lie behind not only life in its specificity but in the material world from which life emerges and against and within which it develops. One suspects that in the too rapid dismissal of Bergson's key concepts—intuition, duration, intellection, and in the accusations of mysticism and a lack of interest in history—there is an anxiety of influence, which has often been noted.[2]

In this chapter, I intend to deal with two well-known papers Merleau-Ponty devotes to Bergson's work and its impact on the philosophy that followed: his inaugural lecture at the College de France, presented in 1953, and published as a long section called "Bergson" in part 2 of *In Praise of Philosophy*; and "Bergson in the Making," a lecture presented in May 1959 for the Centenary of Bergson's birth, translated in *Signs*. There is scarcely a text in which Bergson's name is not mentioned in passing: the trace of Bergsonism is faint, though ineradicable and it returns to haunt Merleau-Ponty's writings until the end. The texts Merleau-Ponty devotes directly to Bergson explicitly honor him; yet there is a reluctant subtext, in which he attempts to establish as much distance as possible, to characterize Bergson with little generosity in elaborating his position.[3] In his earliest paper on Bergson, Merleau-Ponty explicitly welcomes Bergson's openness to the questions of life and the living, his refusal to tie the study of life to the protocols of either the natural sciences, academic philosophy or institutionalized religion:

> If we have recalled these words of Bergson, not all of which are in his books, it is because they make us feel that there is a tension in the relation of the philosopher with other persons or with life, and that this uneasiness is essential to philosophy. We have forgotten this. (*In Praise of Philosophy*: 33)

Merleau-Ponty seeks to return to the freshness of things in the making (including philosophy itself), rather than things made, seeing in Bergson an opponent of the trends that followed, describing as Bergsonian a continuous grasping for the new and the unthought, the disquieting and the unsettling in philosophical and scientific systems. The Bergson Merleau-Ponty admires cannot be identified with either his earlier or later periods, but with a spirit and intellect than remains consistently committed in all his works to the refusal to accept what is given without submitting it to the exigencies of an analysis of its role in experience, in lived reality, with submitting it to intensity:

> The truth is that there are two Bergsonisms. There is that audacious one, when Bergson's philosophy fought and . . . fought well. And there is that

other one after the victory, persuaded in advance about what Bergson took a long time to find, and already provided with concepts while Bergson himself created his own. When Bergsonian insights are identified with the vague cause of spiritualism or some other entity, they lose their bite; they are generalized and minimized. What is left is only a retrospective or external Bergsonism. . . . Established Bergsonism distorts Bergson. Bergson disturbed; it reassures. Bergson was a conquest; Bergsonism defends and justifies Bergson. Bergson was in contact with things; Bergsonism is a collection of accepted opinions . . . (Merleau-Ponty, *Signs*: 182–183)

In spite of his reluctant openness to Bergson himself, what marks these early papers is his refusal of Bergsonism in the derivative sense. Especially after World War I, Bergsonism became more and more attenuated from its roots in both the history of philosophy and in the natural sciences, became more orthodox and dogmatic, as is the tendency with all discursive positions that gain a certain level of popularity and/or notoriety (we have witnessed it ourselves more directly with the rise and fall of various figures—Sartre, Althusser, Lacan, Derrida, and so on). Merleau-Ponty quite justifiably remains wary of what he calls Bergsonism while embracing elements of Bergson's own writings. He aspires to a Bergsonism in the first sense, while attempting to distance himself from it in the second sense.

Resonances

In spite of his reluctance to be too closely identified with Bergsonism, nevertheless, in a less doctrinaire sense of the word, Merleau-Ponty can be understood as Bergsonian.[4] There are a number of apparent homologies or close resemblances between their respective positions, which I will simply indicate:

1. Like Bergson, Merleau-Ponty is committed to the primacy of perception (though unlike Bergson, for whom it is fundamentally connected to the practically oriented intellect and thus to action, for Merleau-Ponty perception is our living immersion in matter, a synthetic, additive rather than an analytic, subtractive ability. Perception synthesizes our relations with a world, projecting onto the world its status as milieu or horizon, rather than reduces and simplifies, silhouettes, a world). Perception remains, for both, the active energy of labor that brings together the living and the human with the resources of the nonliving;

2. Bergson's understanding of the convergence of matter with memory in action and intuition, like Merleau-Ponty's understanding the relations of subject and object as a shared self-enfolding flesh, moves toward a fundamental

ontology of difference, in which there are not two binarized or opposed identities, mind and matter, subject and object, consciousness and world, but a relation of emergence (and thus debt) from the one to the other, a relation in which one (mind, subject, consciousness) emerges and establishes a relation of differentiation from the other (body, object, and world). This relation is not a reciprocity of two terms, the mutual embrace of equivalents, but a relation of debt and belonging that one term owes but cannot acknowledge to the other;

3. Nature is not understood as passive inertia, Cartesian substance, fixed immanence, on which mind imposes its categories, its designs and plans, but is conceived as a dynamic and productive set of forces in which the constraints of determinism in the nonliving world, and the more complex constraints of biological regulation in the living world do not clash or complement each other but differentiate out of one another, and thus merge by degrees from certain points of view and levels of explanation.[5] Nature is that which is both within and without us, a non-normative order that suffuses but never fixes us, which always places us within its constraints and requirements;

4. The subject is neither a free consciousness, existing independent of perception and action (as Sartre suggests), nor a being immersed in mere reaction to the world but fully corporeal, a being whose corporeality extends it indefinitely out into the world, through its projects, its possible and real actions. The subject's freedom is not simply given or reflective but acted. These are not just subjects in the world, they are subjects for whom perception, proprioception, and comportment, the configuration of the senses that constitute the human, provide limits and directions within which there is immense flexibility for production and innovation, for newness. Where Merleau-Ponty posits a certain indetermination in the subject's perceptual rendering of the world, Bergson positions this indetermination in the interval or gap between stimulus and reaction, within the nervous system and the ramifying structures of neuronal organization. This indetermination is for both the site of a freedom to elaborate and invent;

5. The subject is not a subject because of a particular consciousness but rather because of a particular biology and bodily constitution. Where for Bergson it is primarily creative evolution, for Merleau-Ponty it is phylogenetic development that brings this subject into being: but for both, the subject is not a divergence from biological or bodily processes but the consequence of a particular and concrete bodily configuration. Hence neither Bergsonism nor phenomenology in Merleau-Ponty's terms retains a trace of hostility toward biological, physiological, or natural science, which marks much of metaphysics and most of phenomenology. Each remains avidly interested in the empirical formulations offered by scientific observation and speculation. Biological and physiological discourses provided data to be used rather than refuted, tools for speculation and conjecture, which are elaborated in and as experience, lived reality;

6. For both, the body-subject is the site of an inherent doubling: for Bergson the body is simultaneously the locus of a geometrical, spatial, material calculation, and the site of consciousness with its own complexity and corporeal parameters: these are not two bodies or two locations but one that is both fully spatial, occupying all of space, and another that is always and only localized and concerned with the practice of its desires and needs, a vast body and a local, small body, depending on where it is focused and whether it functions through intuition or perception:

> For if our body is the matter to which our consciousness applies itself it is coextensive with our conscious, it comprises all we perceive, it reaches to the stars. But this vast body is changing continually, sometimes radically, at the slightest shift of one part of itself which is at its centre and occupies a small fraction of space. This inner and central body, relatively invariable, is ever present. It is not merely present, it is operative: it is through this body and through it alone, that we can move parts of the larger body. And, since action is what matters, since it is an understood thing that we are present where we act, the habit has grown of limiting consciousness to the small body and ignoring the vast one . . . the surface of all our actual movement, our huge inorganic body is the seat of our potential or theoretically possible actions. (Bergson, *The Two Sources of Morality and Religion*: 258)

The vast and small body is given its scope and constraints through degrees of contraction and dilation, relations of proximity and possible effect: the smaller body is the center of directed action, the larger body the locus of theoretical, possible or virtual action.[6] For Merleau-Ponty too, the body is always doubled, reduplicated either in the form of a corporeal schema, which re-presents its organic capacities in a psychical and signifying mapping of the body, producing a ghostly and relatively autonomous spectral representation in his earlier writings,[7] or of an enfolding, intertwining of living and nonliving bodies, the seer doubled up in the seen in his later writings:

> We say there that our body is a being of two leaves, from one side a thing among other things and otherwise what sees and touches them; we say, because it is evident, that it unites these two properties within itself and its double-belongingness to the order of the 'object' and the order of the 'subject' reveals to us quite unexpected relations between the two orders. It cannot be an incomprehensible accident that the body has this double reference. (Merleau-Ponty, "The Intertwining—The Chiasm." *The Visible and the Invisible*: 136)

This duplicity of the body—its simultaneous orientation to the world and its own inner states, to space and to duration—is necessary to account for its complex emergence from the world and its capacity to live in and remake the world; and

7. Both Bergson and Merleau-Ponty situate the living being in its corporeal locatedness as both a world in itself, and a small participant in a larger world, a being who lives in a world but relocates and resignifies a transcribed world of relevance within itself. For Bergson, it is our participation in our own individual duration, in the specific movements as we live them in their unity and simplicity that necessarily place us within the more cosmological universal duration. Each duration forms a continuity, a single, indivisible movement; and yet, there are many simultaneous durations, which implies that all durations participate in a generalized or cosmological duration, which allows them to be described as simultaneous. For Merleau-Ponty too, our smallness, our concrete locatedness in our bodies directly yields for us the larger world, a greater context, out of which the living are produced. The 'fundamental narcissism of all vision' as he describes it ("The Intertwining," 139) entails that we find in ourselves the very substance of the world; from within our selves we have presented to us the world we live in, as our condition of living in it.[8]

Complexity

Most significantly, what Merleau-Ponty and Bergson share is an ontology of becoming, an ontology in which consciousness and life, respectively, do not find themselves in a world but make themselves subjects, and make the world into things, objects, entities through their activity, their engagement, their labor. Active becoming is emergent. It elaborates itself from and on a field of active forces as their contingent frame. Instead of a being dictated by the world, or at the mercy of other subjects (as Sartre hypothesized), both speculate that the living and the human, perceptual beings, are simultaneously dynamic sites of unpredictable productivity; and systems of coherence, both organic and conceptual unities drawn from fields of disparity, which integrate and locate what is fundamentally a mode of difference, the being's difference from itself, its inherent orientation to the future, to what it is becoming, to what does not yet exist.

Merleau-Ponty recognizes in Bergson's heritage this affinity of life with matter, the ways in which matter induces in life, in consciousness, a kind of elevation of itself as well as a sharing, a coexisting temporality between the living and the nonliving:

> We are not this pebble, but when we look at it, it awakens resonances in our perceptive apparatus; our perception appears to come from it. That is to say our perception of the pebble is a kind of promotion to (conscious) existence

for itself; it is our recovery of this mute thing which, from the time it enters our life, begins to unfold its implicit being, which is revealed to itself through us. What we believe to be coincidence is coexistence. (Merleau-Ponty, *Signs*: 17)

It is perhaps Bergson's fascination with the question, the problem, and the provocation that matter and the event hold as the resource and resistance necessary for life and for thought that most attracts Merleau-Ponty to him; and his recourse to God and to the apparent mysticism that surrounds his understanding of intuition as a direct communion with things that repel him. But this hypothesis remains unclear, for the animus to Bergson's earlier writings, and especially *Matter and Memory*, erupts at virtually every opportunity—generally in the form of elaborate, detailed, and often gratuitous footnotes.

To highlight the general thrust of Merleau-Ponty's critical remarks, I will simply indicate the tenor of charges and criticisms he levels at Bergson. Virtually all of Merleau-Ponty's claims here seem to be based on a misreading or a misunderstanding of Bergson's position. The criticisms he levels at Bergson nevertheless are worth exploring:

1. Bergson remains, in spite of the complexity of his position, a vitalist, with all the idealist and preformist resonances this term has. Merleau-Ponty suggests that Bergson leaves untouched the mechanism of bodily processes. His vitalism is a form of irrational mysticism, and leaves him open to a surreptitious mechanism as well. In spite of himself, Bergson reintroduces the mind/ body split:

> The relation of the vital élan to that which it produces is not conceivable, it is magical. Since the physico-chemical reactions of which the organism is the seat cannot be abstracted from those of milieu, how can the act which creates an organic individual be circumscribed in this continuous whole and where should the zone of influence of the vital élan be limited? It will indeed be necessary to introduce an unintelligible break here. (Merleau-Ponty, "The Physical Order; The Vital Order; The Human Order" *The Structure of Behavior*: 158)

2. Merleau-Ponty claims that retaining the mind/body dualism infects Bergson's understanding of duration, which is thereby fissured into a fixed divide between a continuous, snowballing present—the experience of the body—and a permanent and fixed past—the world of mind or memory such that this ruptures the very cohesion and continuity of duration Bergson seeks to elucidate:

Generally speaking, Bergson saw that the body and the mind communicate with each other through the medium of time, that to be a mind is to stand above time's flow and that to have a body is to have a present. The body, he says, is an instantaneous section made in the becoming of consciousness (*Matière et Mémoire*, p. 150). But the body remains for him what we have called the objective body; consciousness remains knowledge; time remains a successive 'now,' whether it 'snowballs upon itself' or is spread as spatialized time, Bergson can therefore only compress or expand the series of 'present moments'; he never reaches the unique movement whereby the three dimensions of time are constituted, and one cannot see why duration is squeezed into a present, or why consciousness becomes involved in a body and a world. (Merleau-Ponty, *Phenomenology of Perception*: fn, 78–79)

3. Bergson too directly equates the epistemological with the ontological, collapsing our knowledge of a thing with its being. This slippage between what I know and what there is conflates the subject with the object, and epistemic with ontological concerns. This conflation is the consequence of Bergson's problematic understanding of intuition as the coincidence of the subject with the fullness or plenitude of the object, indeed, in Merleau-Ponty's terms, the reflection of the object in the subject:

> Bergson's mistake consists in believing that the thinking subject can become fused with the object thought about, and that knowledge can swell and be incorporated into being. The mistake of reflective philosophies is to believe that the thinking subject can absorb into its thinking or appropriate without remainder the object of its thought, that our being can be brought down to our knowledge. (Merleau-Ponty, *Phenomenology of Perception*: 62); and

4. Although Bergson's understanding of duration revolutionized the way in which time could be philosophically conceptualized, his conception nevertheless, in spite of its claims to a fundamental fluidity (Bergson describes it as a liquid conception of time), is an arresting and freezing of time, the rendering of either a completing merging of past, present and future or their absolute isolation from each other:

> If, in virtue of the principle of continuity, the past still belongs to the present and the present already to the past, there is no longer any past or present. If consciousness snowballs upon itself, it is, like the snowball or everything else, wholly in the present. If the phases of movement gradually merge into one another, nothing is anywhere in motion. (fn, *Phenomenology*: 276)

Each of these claims, if it is accurate, constitutes a devastating criticism, which, taken together, would be enough to convince the average reader to believe Merleau-Ponty had repudiated the value of Bergsonism. But nothing is further from the truth. The more critical Merleau-Ponty becomes, the more he (unconsciously?) seems to absorb a more accurate Bergsonism and the more his own writings become Bergsonian. What is striking about his last writings, in *The Visible and the Invisible*, is the remarkable convergence of his conception of the flesh of the world with the Bergsonian understanding of the becoming of being.

The Flesh of the World

Merleau-Ponty's posthumously published text, *The Visible and the Invisible*, as is well-known, presents a breathtaking departure from the more structural and structured writings before. In the chapter "The Intertwining—the Chiasm," as well as in the detailed working notes published in that collection, he turns to a new ontology and a new conception of the relations between mind and matter, subject and object, consciousness and the world. While this vision remains both highly suggestive and largely underdeveloped, it harkens back more to the writings of Bergson than it does to the tradition of phenomenology.

Where in his earlier works Merleau-Ponty stresses the fundamental interimplication of the subject in the object and the object in the subject and the necessary integration of the visual in the tactile and vice-versa,[9] in his last writings, he explores the interrelations of the inside and the outside, the subject and object, one sense and another, in a common flesh—which he describes as the "criss-crossing" of the seer and the visible, of the toucher and the touched, the indeterminacy of the "boundaries" of each of the senses, their inherent transposability, their refusal to submit to the exigencies of clear-cut separation or logical identity.[10] The flesh is the term Merleau-Ponty uses to designate being, not as plenitude, self-identity or substance, but as divergence (écart), noncoincidence, or difference. For him, the notion of the flesh is no longer associated with a privileged (animate) category, but is being's most elementary level. Flesh is being as reversibility, its capacity to fold in on itself, its dual orientation inward and outward, its openness to the world.

In these last works, Merleau-Ponty gestures toward a conception of the univocity of being, a single flesh that includes, as its two surfaces or planes, the world of inert objects, matter, and the world of living beings, consciousness. No longer are the subject and the object two separate, other-affirming self-identical entities, no longer does consciousness bestow signification on the world of the in-itself: the in-itself and the for-itself are melded into a single, self-enfolded flesh, a single substance with a conscious reverse and a material obverse:

There is here no problem with the *alter ego* because it is not *I* who sees, not *he* who sees, because an anonymous visibility inhabits both of us, a vision in general, in virtue of that primordial property that belongs to the flesh, being here and now, of radiating everywhere and forever, being an individual, of being also a dimension and a universal. ("The Intertwining": 142)

Merleau-Ponty suggests a notion of flesh as a designation of the world's capacity to turn in on itself, to cycle itself through the living and the nonliving as modes of their mutual entwinement and necessary interlinkage.[11] The flesh of the world does not just clothe subjects, objects, and their relations with its touch; it doubles back on itself as the invisible underside of the visible, the push, in Bergsonian terms, of the virtual on the actual, the clothing of all materiality with an inner lining of ideality, of potentiality to transmute itself, through a potential or virtual reversibility, into the substance of beings and things:

> ... [O]nce we have entered into this strange domain [of the flesh], one does not see how there could be any question of *leaving* it. If there is an animation *of* the body; if vision and the body are tangled up in one another; if ... the surface of the visible, is doubled over its whole extension with an invisible reserve; and if finally, in our flesh as in the flesh of things, the actual empirical, ontic visible, by a sort of folding back, invagination, or padding, exhibits a visibility, a possibility that is not the shadow of the actual but is its principle, that is not the proper contribution of a 'thought' but is its condition—then (the immediate and dualist distinction between the visible and the invisible, between extension and thought, [is] impugned, not that extension be thought and thought be extension, but because they are the obverse and the reverse of one another, and the one forever behind the other). (*The Visible*: 152)

Merleau-Ponty presents a vision of the malleability of substance, its capacity to redouble itself, to invaginate itself, without actually detailing it. He presents a picture of a vast, dynamic, universe, which provides itself with a mode of reflection in the form of the perceptual agents that are both part of it and are capable of provisionally seeing it from a point of view, framing it, acting within and with it. It is only this fundamental belonging together of consciousness to the complexity of the world that enables consciousness to know, to have language, to represent and reflect as well as to act. Flesh brings to the world the capacity to turn the world back on itself, to induce its reflexivity, to fold over itself, to introduce that fold in being in which subjectivity is positioned as a perceiving, perspectival frame. The flesh is composed of "leaves" of the body and "leaves" of the world: it is the chiasm linking and separating the one from the other, the "pure difference" whose play generates subjects and things, and their belonging together. Things solicit the flesh just as the flesh beckons to and as an object for things. Perception is the flesh's reversibility, the flesh touching, seeing, perceiving itself, one fold provisionally catching the other in its own self-embrace.

It is of some significance that in his final notes he explicitly refers to Bergson's account of a universal movement toward complexity, a movement in which no object is capable of anything but a pragmatic separation from the rest of being, and in which the subject has no sovereignty or control but functions as an element or factor. It seems clear from the fragments that are published that he intended to further elaborate this understanding of a wild being in part through a return to, and hopefully a reevaluation of, Bergson's most central precepts regarding memory, the past, perception, things, and subjectivity:

> I said: the openness to the world such as we rediscover it in ourselves and the perception we divine within life (a perception that at the same time is spontaneous being (thing) and being-self ('subject')—Bergson once explicitly said . . . that there is a consciousness that is at the same time spontaneous and reflected) intertwine, encroach upon, or cling to one another.
> Make clear what that means.
> That evokes, beyond the 'point of view of the object' and the 'point of view of the subject,' a common nucleus which is the 'winding,' being as a winding (what I called 'modulation of the being in the world'). It is necessary to make understood how that . . . is a perception 'being formed in things.' This is still only an approximate expression, in the subject-object language (Wahl, Bergson) of what there is to be said. That is, that the things have us, and that it is not we who have the things. That the being that has been cannot stop having been. The 'Memory of the World.' That language has us and it is not we who have language. That it is being that speaks within us and not we who speak of being. ("Working Notes," May 20, 1959, *The Visible and the Invisible*: 193–194)

Is the flesh of the world Merleau-Ponty's mode of reformulating what Bergson understands as creative evolution? Is Merleau-Ponty more Bergsonian than he would like? Or has he reviewed his earlier opinion of Bergson's writings and seen them in a more positive light?

> In reality, life is a movement, materiality is the inverse movement, and each of these two movements is simple, the matter that forms a world being an undivided flux, and undivided also the life that runs through it, cutting out in it living beings all along its track. Of these two currents the second runs

counter to the first, but the first obtains, all the same, something from the second. There results between them a *modus vivendi*, which is organization. (Bergson, *Creative Evolution*: 249–250)

The striking resonances between this difference that constitutes a world-becoming in Bergson and that constitutes flesh in Merleau-Ponty point to an opening up of Merleau-Ponty to the metaphysical questions so powerfully posed by Bergson.

Ontologies of the Question

I began this chapter by asserting that ontology, repressed for nearly a century, addresses the real, that which provokes, incites, and induces, a real that is one of the objects of political struggle but has never been adequately addressed in ontological terms. The ontological has been reduced bit by bit to the epistemological, to the representational, and to the reflective, but it remains an abiding, indeed an intractable, commitment that politics, ethics, aesthetics—the realm of the intersubjective and the collective more generally—make in spite of their intention to leave it behind. The crucial questions of subjectivity and intersubjectivity to which feminist theory has addressed itself have an unacknowledged underside: the subjective, the intersubjective, the human, must be positioned in a context in which the subhuman, the extra-human and the nonhuman play a formative but not a determining role, in which the human emerges from and functions within the natural, technological, and social orders in which it finds itself placed as event and advent rather than as agent.

What Merleau-Ponty gestured toward, throughout his writings, was a way of understanding our relation to the world, not as one of merger or oneness, or of control and mastery, but a relation of belonging to and of not quite fitting, a never-easy kinship, a given tension that makes our relations to the world hungry, avid, desiring, needing, which makes us need a world as well as desire to make one, which makes us riven through with the very nature, materiality, worldliness that our conception of ourselves as pure consciousness, a for-itself, an agent, daily belies.

What has this to do with feminist theory? Why are these abstract, nonpractical questions of any relevance to feminist or other political concerns? Because they are irreducible questions, because we make assumptions about the real, about nature (our own and the world's), about matter, whenever we act: all our actions presuppose a world in which those actions are both viable and capable of signification. As Bergson makes clear, and Merleau-Ponty affirms, it is the resistance of the world to the immediacy of human wishes, its capacity to make us wait, that makes us produce and invent, that makes us human, conscious beings. It is because we cannot but be beings who deal with and through matter, objects, things, that we invent, imagine, and use the world to live in. It is the adversity of matter itself, just as it is adversity of political and social kinds, that generates problems, and frames the inventions that act as their solutions. The task facing feminist theory, in this moment of its maturing, is to provide the formulation of those kinds of questions that will generate inventiveness, new models, frameworks, tools, for new activities:

> ...The truth is that in philosophy and even elsewhere it is a question of *finding* the problem and consequently of *positing* it, even more than of solving it ... stating the problem is not uncovering, it is inventing. Discovery, or uncovering, has to do with what already exists actually or virtually; it was therefore certain to happen sooner or later. Invention gives being to what did not exist; it might never have happened. Already in mathematics and still more in metaphysics, the effort of invention consists most often in raising the problem, in creating the terms in which it will be stated. (Bergson, *Creative Mind*: 58–59)

Bergson may well have stated the most succinct formula for politics in articulating his metaphysics: politics, as much as life itself, is that which "gives being to what did not exist." This too is the task of feminist politics and feminist knowledges: to give being to that which may become, to explore openly that which we do not yet know, to expand on what which we might come to know and on our ways of knowing. This expansion of feminist theory— beyond feminism's common focus on dealing with empirical women as its objects, and beyond its analysis of (the repression or expression of) femininity and its representations within the patriarchal order, to raise new questions about materiality, cosmology, the natural order, about how we know and what are the limits, costs, and underside of our knowledge—is necessary in order to develop new ideals, new forms of representation, new types of knowledge, and new epistemological criteria. Merleau-Ponty and Bergson, while being unable to account for or elaborate new concepts of woman or the feminine, may nevertheless prove indispensable in helping to formulate how we might know differently, how we might challenge and replace binarized models (of subject and object, self and object, consciousness and matter, nature and culture) with concepts of difference, what the objects of our representational and epistemological practices might be if they were undertaken with this concept of difference, the difference in being that is becoming, the difference in subjectivity that is biological openendedness, this difference in the world that is life, were a guiding principle. What would a feminism that is attuned to the materiality of nature and the physical world look like, a feminism that fascinated itself as much with natural as with cultural forces? What would a feminism that is concerned not just with relations between men and women, or between sexes and races, but between these relations and a territory or milieu, a space and a temporality address, question, invent? What would a feminist cosmology or a feminist biology look like? A feminism of difference, no longer restricted to sexual difference, but based upon it, may find its intellectual predecessors in the provocative writings of those (male) philosophers whose own openness to difference has given hints of how far sexual difference can go: to the furthest reaches of the cosmos, and into every form of knowledge.

Notes

1. An earlier version of this paper was published in my book, *Time Travels. Feminism, Nature, Power* (Duke University Press, 2005).

2. Bergson had long been out of fashion and discredited as a metaphysician by the generation before Merleau-Ponty. The works of Bergson, alongside of the pragmatism of William James, and the process philosophy of Alfred North Whitehead were one strand of influence on Merleau-Ponty but were largely overpowered by the influence of Husserl, coupled with Kojève's reading of Hegel, at least in his earlier writings. Perhaps there had not yet been enough time between them for Merleau-Ponty to accept their evolutionary relation, Merleau-Ponty's inheritance of a Bergsonism in spite of himself, the line of descent with modification that weaves itself through his work as well.

3. Merleau-Ponty has two other papers dealing directly with Bergson's work, which will not be dealt with here, in *La Nature*, chapter three; and L'Union de l'âme et du corps chez Malebranche. Biran et Bergson. Notes prise au cours de Maurice Merleau-Ponty à l'École normales supérieure (1947–1953) recueillies et rédigées par Jean Deprun, Paris: Libraires Philosophiques J. Vrin, 1968.

4. Edward Casey: "Bergson is often the most effective escort into Merleau-Pontian reflection on many subjects" (1984: 283); see also Scharfstein (1955); André Clair (1996); and John C. Mullarkey (1994) on the connections between Bergson and Merleau-Ponty.

5. Cf "It is inconceivable—this is the mechanist argument—that an existing physical or chemical action not have its real conditions in other physical or chemical actions. But—this is the vitalist argument—since each constant chemical reaction in the organism (for example, the fixation of oxygen on the hemoglobin of the blood) presupposes a stable context, which itself presupposes another one, the physico-chemical explanation always seems deferred (Merleau-Ponty, *The Structure of Behavior*, 1983: 158).

6. . . . . [T]his special image which persists in the midst of others, and which I call my body, constitutes at every moment . . . a selection of the universal becoming. It is then *the place of passage* of the movements received and thrown back, a hyphen, a connecting link between the things which act upon one and things upon which one acts (Bergson *Matter and Memory*: 151).

7. *The Structure of Behavior, Phenomenology of Perception, Primacy of Perception.*

8. If it [the body] touches and sees, this is not because it would have the visibles before itself as objects; they are about it, they even enter into its enclosure, they are within it, they line its looks and its hands inside and outside. If it touches them and sees them, this is only because, being of their family, itself visible and tangible, it uses its own being as a means to participate in theirs, because each of the two beings is an archetype for the other, because the body belongs to the order of the things as the world is universal flesh (Ibid.: 137).

9. In the *Phenomenology*, the senses interact, form a union and yield access to a singular world. Sight and touch are able to communicate with each other because they are the senses of one and the same subject, operating simultaneously in a single world. The senses not only communicate with each other, adding to and enriching each other, they are transposable, at least within certain limits, onto each other's domains, although they remain irreducible in their differences. Sight, touching, hearing, smell, function contemporaneously and are cumulative in their effects. The senses are transposable only because each lays claim to a total world, a world defining the subject's sensory relations, each of which is able to mesh with, be gridded in terms of, other 'sensory worlds':

> The senses communicate with each other. Music is not in visible space, but it besieges, undermines and displaces that space.... The two spaces are distinguishable only against the background of a common world and can compete with each other only because they both lay claim to total being.
>
> The sight of sounds and the hearing of colors comes about in the same way as the unity of the gaze through the two eyes: in so far as my body is not a collection of adjacent organs, but a synergic system, all the functions of which are exercised and linked together in the general action of being in the world, in so far as it is the congealed face of existence.... When I say that I see a sound, I mean that I echo the vibration of the sound with my whole sensory being, and particularly with the sector of myself which is susceptible to colors. (1962, 232–234)

10. We must habituate ourselves to think that every visible is cut out in the tangible, every tactile being in some manner promised to visibility, and that there is encroachment, infringement, not only between the tangible and the visible, which is encrusted in it, as, conversely, the tangible in itself is not a nothingness of visibility, is not without visual existence. Since the same body sees and touches, visible and tangible belong to the same world.... Every vision takes place somewhere in the tactile space. There is a double and crossed situating of the visible; the two maps are complete and yet they do not merge into one. The two parts are total parts and yet are not superposable (1968, 134).

11. What we are calling flesh, this interiorly worked-over mass, has no name in philosophy. As the formative medium of the object and the subject, it is not an atom of being, the hard in itself that resides in a unique place and movement: one cannot say that it is here or now in the sense that objects are; and yet my vision does not soar over

them, it is not the being that is wholly knowing, for it has its own inertia, its ties. We must not think the flesh starting out from the substances, from body and spirit—for then it would be the union of contradictories—but we must think it ... as an element, as the concrete emblem of a general manner of being (147).

References

Bergson, Henri (1921). *Mind-Energy*. trans. H. Wildon Carr, London: MacMillan.

——— (1944). *Creative Evolution*. trans. Arthur Mitchell. New York: Random House.

——— (1977). *The Two Sources of Morality and Religion*. trans. R. Ashley Audra and Cloudesley Brereton. Notre Dame, Indiana: Notre Dame Press.

——— (1988). *Matter and Memory*. trans. N. M. Paul and W. S. Palmer. New York: Zone Books.

——— (1992). *The Creative Mind. An Introduction to Metaphysics*. trans. Mabelle L. Andison. New York: Citadel Press.

Casey, Edward S. (1984). "Habitual Body and Memory in Merleau-Ponty" *Man and World*, 17, 279–297.

Clair, André (1996). "Merleau-Ponty Lecteur et Critique de Bergson. Le Statut Bergsonien de l'Intuition" *Archives de Philosophie* 59, 203–218.

Deleuze, Gilles and Félix Guattari (1994). *What is Philosophy?* trans. Hugh Tomlinson and Graham Burchell. New York: Columbia University.

Merleau-Ponty, Maurice (1962). The Phenomenology of Perception, trans. C. Smith. London: Routledge and Kegan-Paul.

——— (1964). *Signs*, trans. R. C. McCleary. Chicago: Northwestern University Press.

——— (1968). "The Intertwining—the Chiasm" *The Visible and The Invisible*. trans. A. Lingis. Chicago: Northwestern University Press, 130–155.

——— (1970). *In Praise of Philosophy and Other Essays*. trans. J. Wild, J. Edie and J. O'Neill. Chicago: Northwestern University Press.

——— (1983). *The Structure of Behavior*, trans. A. L. Fisher. Pittsburgh: Duquesne University Press.

Mullarkey, John C. (1994). "Duplicity in the Flesh. Bergson and Current Philosophy of the Body" *Philosophy Today*, Winter 1994, 339–355.

Olkowski, Dorothea E. (2000). "The End of Phenomenology: Bergson's Interval in Irigaray" *Hypatia* 15.3, 79–98.

Scharfstein, Ben-Ami (1955). "Bergson and Merleau-Ponty: A Preliminary Comparison" *Journal of Philosophy*, 52, 380–386.

CHAPTER 2

Elemental Alterity: Levinas and Merleau-Ponty

LAWRENCE HASS

> The face of another is a surface of the elemental, the place where the elemental addresses, appeals and requires the involution in enjoyment which makes my eyes luminous, my hands warm, my posture supportive ... my face ardent.
> —Alphonso Lingis

A most compelling aspect of Merleau-Ponty's philosophy is its power to address a host of traditional philosophical problems. In the explicit arguments of his major works, or the direct implications of those arguments, one can find promising solutions to familiar, even perennial difficulties: for instance, the mind-body problem, the problems of skepticism and idealism, the problem of universals, and the so-called problem of other minds. With regard to this last—the problem of our confidence that solipsism is not true—Merleau-Ponty argues that our knowledge of other perceiving selves is not based on an inference (by analogy or to "the best explanation"). Nor is it based, as in Sartre, on the dialectical experience of becoming objectified by "the gaze." Instead, inspired by ideas from Scheler and Husserl, drawing on the developmental research of Piaget and Wallon, he argues that the self knows and engages others through the reciprocity of behavior.[1] More specifically, in one's carnal power to adopt and adapt behavior, one encounters other beings who also caress the things of the world, who have hands not unlike one's own, who can take up and prolong one's intentions, who address one with gleaming eyes. Reflexively, in the flow of life, I extend my corporeal schema and perceptual abilities to these other behaving beings; I extend my *self* to them and they respond in kind. For Merleau-Ponty, this reciprocal intersubjectivity—which he later refers to as "reversibility"—is explicitly not a synthesis or fusion of self and other, but rather a *syncresis*: an overlapping or enjoining or coming together of distinct selves that is exemplified in play or conversation. Evident in infants as young as six weeks, Merleau-Ponty argues that this "syncretic sociality" underlies and informs our concepts of self, and it also explains why we are so confident that solipsism cannot be true. Indeed, even framing the possibility that "I" am the only self, using language, attests to a sociality older than and beyond me that cannot legitimately be doubted.

In its full details, this view is a compelling solution to the traditional problem of other minds. However, since the time of Merleau-Ponty's writings, a new philosophical problem about otherness has emerged. This problem is not about the status of our knowledge that other selves exist, but rather about the precise nature of the ontological relation between self and others. Indeed, can I even have *relations* with others? Or is rather the otherness of the other beyond all relation, all interaction? Do our efforts toward and talk of "interrelations" and "intersubjectivity" actually keep us from the shock of exposure to the radical alterity of the other? Are those efforts and ways of speaking subtle ways for the ego to mitigate that shock and the ethical encumbrances that come with it, ways of "reducing the other to the same"? While these questions have inspired a wide array of postmodern thought (including Derrida's ethical turn), it is well known that they derive from the striking work of Emmanuel Levinas. For Levinas, most philosophers who develop views on the self-other relation believe that their accounts open us to the other, but in fact, typically end up effacing the other's transcendence in the name of some totality. This violence to the other, he argues, is exemplified by Hegel's thought—where the other is treated as an antithetical object through which "I," the subject, can synthesize toward a higher possibility. But he says it is also deeply there in Heidegger, for whom particular beings, particular existents (which includes people), are typically passed over on "the Way to Being." And Levinas implies that Merleau-Ponty is in a similar position, that his phenomenology of reciprocal or reversible intersubjectivity gathers the other into a totality, a system of indifferent exchange that ends up "reducing the other to the same."[2] Levinas argues that we need a radically different way of understanding our relations with others: the other, in its infinite otherness, is experienced prior to such systematic relations; the other is never "given," never here, but always transcendent, beyond any image or presentation. In a phrase, the other is "not-present" in "the face" of language—the language that asserts the other, that questions me, that appeals to me for bread.

Having said this much, the new problem of alterity is starting to emerge. For the great challenge after Levinas is to understand and evaluate his remarkable arguments that the fundamental relationship with the other is not a phenomenon, not empirically present to us. The other, he insists, is not present but "absolutely transcendent." My relationship to the other is not a totality, but infinity—a unique relation that reveals the limits of my self and its finite relations. But how can we grasp the infinite? How can we understand a relationship the very character of which is to not-be-in relation, which is, Levinas suggests, beyond the living body and its relations? And what does this view imply for Merleau-Ponty's account of intersubjectivity through the flesh of behavior? Is Merleau-Ponty's account justly depicted as a totalizing system that effaces alterity?

The truth is that the relationship between these two thinkers is complex and contestable, as Levinas himself seems well aware.[3] In what follows then I will endeavor to sort through and adjudicate some of the complexities; I will show some great advantages in Levinas' account, but also some unhappy baggage that Merleau-Ponty's philosophy can help unload. The result will be an attempt to do justice to the best of each thinker, to begin rendering an account of alterity that remains firmly *elemental*, that is, one that respects the irreducible otherness of others while remaining rooted in the elements of flesh, animality, and nature.[4]

It is important, I think, to begin by noting another complexity, and this is the fact that Levinas' two major works are themselves in tension on several important points. It is quite clear that Levinas partially intends *Otherwise than Being* to repair problems in *Totality and Infinity* on central themes—the nature of sensibility, the univocity of expression, the formation of the ego—and so there is not just *one* "Levinas" with which we must contend. Thus I will start with *Totality and Infinity*, with an aspect of its argument that is particularly compelling: Levinas' deep insight that the other *interrupts* my living experience, my projective organizations of the world—that the other puts me and my ideas in *question*. We have already briefly seen that for Merleau-Ponty the relation between self and other is about interacting through behavior. It is about distinct embodied selves coming together in syncretic overlapping as in a conversation or handshake. I have suggested that this is a promising account of how we know and engage one another in the flesh. But, I hasten to add, it isn't *all* that happens at the fundamental level of those relations. For we are also, otherwise, challenged by others, thrown into question by them. To be sure, we can be *arrested* in our subjectivity, called into question by the other's face, behavior, or criticism. As Levinas puts it:

> Critique does not reduce the other to the same ... but calls into question the exercise of the same.... We name this calling into question of my spontaneity by the presence of the Other ethics. The strangeness of the Other, his irreducibility to the I, to my thoughts and my possessions, is precisely accomplished as a calling into question of my spontaneity, as ethics. (1969: 43)

Indeed, there I am soaring through the world, organizing it through my living body, projecting myself and my intentions, greeting others, thinking, opining in conversation, when suddenly, *wham*: the other forgoes "niceties" and suggests that I am mistaken. My flowing self is arrested; my intellectual command is shattered—I am put in question. Or there I am on the way to work and this person in the street appeals to me with an open hand, hungry, holding her child. The woman is not seeking a handshake or dialogue, but rather seeking *me* to give of myself to her. The moment puts me in question: "Why don't I give her more?" "Why did I try to look away?" "Am I really so insensitive and selfish?" On this score, Levinas is spot-on correct: the disruption of my stability and self-command is a fundamental way others are experienced, and the self takes shape through this experience and sets up egoistic defenses against it.

It is important to see here that Levinas is not talking about the Sartrean notion of "being objectified." On the contrary, Levinas is clear that "being called into question" is not a process of objectification, but one of *subjectification*, of being thrown back into oneself, of being exposed as an ego who assumes too much in its joyous possession of the world. As Robert Bernasconi has argued on Levinas' behalf, this relation is not one of reciprocity in the sense of exchange; rather it is a one-way street with the traffic heading toward me as a *subject*.[5] Having said that, it isn't at all clear that this shattering encounter is the one and only primary relation, the *only* fundamental—a critical matter we are not able to pursue here.[6] But it is at least a primary way the self encounters others, and Merleau-Ponty doesn't recognize it. Being called into question by the other: this basic experience illuminates several ethical dimensions of living experience. It begins to illuminate—at the heart of everyday life—the birth of responsibility, the inescapability of conscience, and our resistance to the ethical. These are aspects of our social life that Merleau-Ponty's account of intersubjectivity does not explicitly address.

Thus, I see Levinas' account of the "one-way" encounter with the other, marked by the breach of the same, as a great strength of *Totality and Infinity*. The interruption of the self by the other *happens* and it must be acknowledged as another way "other minds" are experienced and known. But there are also some elements of Levinas' argument that I am sure Merleau-Ponty would have strongly contested, some things in this text *he* would have "called into question." A first of these might well be called the book's "problem of sensibility." For in *Totality and Infinity* Levinas depicts the sensible, sensitive body as essentially consumptive and possessive. For Levinas, the eye, by nature, is "avid," hungry, totalizing.[7] The hand, in its "proper nature," he says, is grasping, clutching: "Possession is ... the destiny of the hand. The hand is the organ of grasping and taking, the first and blind grasping in the teeming mass: it relates to me, to my egoist ends, things drawn from the element" (1969: 159). Indeed, for Levinas, the body and its sensibility is a "regime" of enjoyment that "overcomes" the alterity of the Other.

However, Merleau-Ponty's philosophy of the living body calls these explicitly Platonic allegations into doubt. The hand "takes," yes, but only in one of its modalities. For it is also the hand that caresses the child to sleep, that gestures to others, that surrenders to the textures of the world. And while the gaze that Sartre depicts is an objectifying one, it is important to appreciate that for Merleau-Ponty vision is "more dispossession than possession" (1964b: 170). It is, he says in *Phenomenology of Perception*, "literally a form of communion." Consider the passage that accompanies this expression:

> The relations of sentient to sensible are comparable with those of the sleeper to his slumber.... *I* am breathing deeply and slowly in order to summon sleep, and suddenly it is if my mouth were connected to some great lung outside myself which alternately calls forth and forces back my breath.... In the same way I give ear, or look ... and suddenly the sensible takes possession of my ear or my gaze, and I surrender a part of my body, even my whole body, to this particular manner of vibrating and filling space known as blue or red. (Merleau-Ponty 1962: 212)

Whatever else one wants to say about it, this is an account of sensibility that is not totalizing consumption, an account that stresses sensibility as a surrender, fascination, or communion with what is *not* me. While much could be developed about this account, particularly drawing on *Eye and Mind* and *The Visible and the Invisible*, it is not really controversial to assert that Merleau-Ponty's work offers a deep challenge to the Platonic view of sensibility as essentially consumptive and possessive. Contrary to those notions, Merleau-Ponty argues that sensibility is better grasped as an *overture, opening, l'ouverture au monde*: our access to an overspilling world, our greeting approach to other selves who he insists are not present but transcendent, "certain absences" traced out by their behavior (Merleau-Ponty 1964b: 170).

However, in *Totality and Infinity* there is no place for this understanding of sensibility as *communion*, and no understanding of communion that isn't *totality*. Instead, the logic of this text is a series of equivalences that Levinas seems content to affirm: *relation* equals *possession* equals *consumption* equals *the reduction of the Other to the Same*.[8] But this basic premise is flawed: not only does it obscure important differences between these terms, but it fails to engage Merleau-Ponty's challenging insight that sensibility is precisely a relation that does not equal possession. And with this insight comes sharper understanding of Merleau-Ponty's sense of the reciprocity between self and other. Indeed, for him, this "reciprocity" does not denote an *exchange* that goes out and back with systematic equality and indifference. Instead, as we saw at the outset, reciprocity is about *extending oneself* to another through the overlapping flesh of our behavior. It is about acknowledging the other and *responding* to them as another *self*, or *person*. It is about the intertwining of selves that are irreducibly different. This is not to say that Merleau-Ponty unpacks or even appreciates the ethical dimensions of this encounter—the sheer *responsibility* of it—for I don't believe he does. But Levinas' tendency is to treat the language of reciprocity, reversibility, and interrelation as inescapably, essentially, totalizing systematics, as though these words *could only possibly mean* totality, and this is to ignore the transcendence Merleau-Ponty builds into these concepts.

So there is this Platonic baggage in *Totality and Infinity*, this dubious view of sensibility and the body—a view with which Levinas will himself become uncomfortable. But there is another problem of the body in his early book, what I think of as its "struggle with dualism." I want to be careful here, because it is not unusual to hear Levinas' thought rather quickly dismissed as "a retreat to dualism" and that is too unsubtle. For *Totality and Infinity* contains important passages that strongly suggest Levinas is not proposing a dualistic relationship between the self and the body. For example:

> Enjoyment accomplishes the . . . separation, which is not a cleavage made in the abstract, but the existence at home with itself of the autochthonous I. . . . [The soul] to be sure dwells in what is not itself, but it acquires its own identity by dwelling in the "other" (and not logically, by opposition to the other). (1969: 115)

Elsewhere, Levinas is clear to refer to the relation of self to body as a "terrestrial" one, not a dichotomy or a dualism, but precisely a "separation." However, the problem or "struggle" is that Levinas says at least as much in this book to drive the difference all the way to opposition and dichotomy. Thus my concern here is not that Levinas' view *is* dualistic, but that he substantially equivocates on the matter.

There is no question in this essay of doing the close textual work required to expose this problem in all its details, but I hope to say enough to show there is a problem. Part of the complexity is that this equivocation is closely intertwined with another one that mars some of Levinas' argument: his sliding use of negation, of the "not," to mean both interruption and opposition. On one hand, he uses negation to mean "interrupt" or "break up" or "breach," as in: "The psychic life . . . does *not* exhibit itself in history . . . it *interrupts* historical time" (1969: 158–159, emphases added). This is, in my view, an important innovation—a radical and original way to redeploy negation, one that has had tremendous influence on contemporary thought. But Levinas also uses negation to *oppose* ontology, to place his ethics *outside* ontology, so far outside of ontology that ethics is *prior* to ontology. Clearly negation as interruption is not the same sense as oppositional priority, even though Levinas frequently treats them the same or slides back and forth indiscriminately.

A similar problem—perhaps a permutation of the same problem—happens with the separation relation between the self and the body, and the self and the other. On one hand, as suggested above, Levinas refers to the relation not as an opposition or a dichotomy, but as an "interruption" of enjoyment. Yet he also slides to formulations that cast the separation in strictly oppositional terms. Some of this oppositional dualism is implicit, such as when Levinas refers to the flesh of the face as a "plastic image," or the skin as a covering that dissimulates and deforms the Other. Or when he argues that the Other cannot be murdered, suggesting the Other is so removed from their body that they are beyond violence. However, some of this dualism is utterly explicit, such as when Levinas insists that ethics is *opposed to* sensibility and *overcomes* it, when he says that the facing position, the moral summons, is "opposition par excellence" (1969: 196–197). Thus, what we see is a struggle, an equivocation, a temptation to dualism that writes its way rather deeply into the text and which, from Merleau-Ponty's perspective, must be challenged.

The third major problem of *Totality and Infinity* that I want to address here is what I think of as its "problem of nature": Levinas' insistence that the ethical is *not* continuous with the natural world, that it is "outside" nature, that it *breaks* with nature. For Levinas, nature is the principle of mystification, it separates us from the infinite, and has nothing to do with the ethical-theological relation that is delivered in the face through *language*. Indeed, language is defined as the very power to break the continuity of nature and being.[9] One difficulty immediately arises: is that definition of language really true? Is language really, as Levinas puts it, a "magical act" outside of nature? Doesn't contemporary work in cognitive development show us that language *is* a natural phenomenon, that it is quite powerfully understood in terms of brain structures and neural capacities that have evolved in nature? In the early twenty-first century, can we really, plausibly deny this? But there is a second difficulty about nature, and it rests in Levinas' claims about the specific modalities of language that demarcate the ethical: speaking, thematizing, stating, proposing, questioning. As he insists: "Signification arises from the other stating or understanding the world, which precisely is thematized in his language" (1969: 97). What then is Levinas to say about animals? Precisely nothing. Not only does his account of language as thematic spoken discourse preclude our being in ethical relations with animals, but Levinas repeatedly affirms that transcendence is only possible between humans. For two examples: "It is our relations with men . . . that give to theological concepts the sole signification they admit of," and "only man . . . could be absolutely foreign to me."[10] What seems evident then is that Levinas' ethics, his eschatology in *Totality and Infinity*, represents a dramatic break with nature, a break with animals, a break with our animal nature, and it becomes quite puzzling what sense he could make of, say, "environmental ethics" or "the *ethical* treatment of animals."

This is, I believe, a serious difficulty in the book. Levinas has cast the ethical relationship through thematic language so specifically, so intellectually, so oppositionally that it seems impossible to reconcile it with our natural life and natural history. As noncontinuous with nature, as a radical break with the elemental, Levinas' notion of transcendence is, in a significant sense, *supernatural*. But one of the great strengths of Merleau-Ponty's account of carnal intersubjectivity is that you don't have to go so far: you can have transcendence *within* nature, you can have contact and interaction with the irreducibly other through our behavior—human and nonhuman animals alike. We have already seen that this is not a collapse into totality, not a "reduction of other to the same"; we have seen that this kind of criticism is based on a flawed understanding of the sensible.

In all this we approach that familiar question about whether Levinas is a transcendental philosopher. The key term, of course, derives from Kant who defined "transcendental" in radical distinction to the empirical, meaning something like *empiricism*. But perhaps two hundred years later, now after Darwin, we should give this question a new sense: Are Levinas' theories of the self and the other compatible and in continuity with the facts of *evolution*, with the evolutionary development of consciousness and language, with the organic animality we share with the creatures around us? Based exclusively on the views in *Totality and Infinity*—Levinas' break with nature, his driving alterity outside of animal nature, his critique of the elemental, his equivocal dualism—I would have to say "no."

However, an extraordinary thing about Levinas is that, in *Otherwise than Being*, he ameliorates some of these difficulties: while the basic project and intention remains the same (to reveal the fundamentality and transcendence of the ethical relation), he develops new positions and reformulates some old ones. The results, I think, are more compelling in several respects and they move toward a picture of alterity as an elemental relation. The two most important changes to note here are that Levinas: 1) deepens his treatment of responsibility, and 2) substantially revises his understanding of sensibility, the flesh, and their role in the ethical relation. In fact, these two developments are intimately related. With regard to the first, Levinas is clearer in this book that the encounter with the other is not just a "break up" of the self and Being, but also a *binding*.[11] Indeed, the encounter with the other does not simply put me in question, but actively limits my free-play in the world. It binds me to the other in responsibility. And it does so, he argues, not *outside* of sensibility, but precisely *through* it. For, he now says, it is in the flesh, not merely thematic language or "the said," that the self and other are in "proximity." It is through our living bodies where selves experience "the painfulness of pain," "the malignity of illness," and "the adversity of fatigue."[12] Pain, fatigue, susceptibility: these are the lassitudes of corporeality that binds self to other, manifest in the inescapable diachrony of the living body that Levinas calls *ageing*:

> Temporalization as lapse, the loss of time, is neither the initiative of an ego, nor a movement toward ... action. The loss of time is not the work of a subject. ... Time passes. This synthesis which occurs *patiently* ... is ageing. It breaks up under the weight of years and is irreversibly removed from the present. ... Subjectivity in ageing is unique, irreplaceable, me and not another. ... Temporality as ageing and death of the unique one signifies an obedience where there is no desertion. (Levinas 1998: 51)

This passage is both beautiful and moving: the responsibility at the center of our lives, that is experienced "despite oneself," the binding of oneself to others, happens through what might be called our shared mortality. This sensible encounter, this "allegiance," Levinas argues, is less a "shock" than a *vulnerability*: an exposure of ourselves to the vulnerability of others, a wounding in the face of the other's wounds. As Levinas puts it: the response of responsibility for the neighbor resounds in our vulnerability (1998: 15).

I must say that I find this notion utterly compelling. I am bound to others, responsible to them, through the lassitudes of embodied life and the possibility of suffering. In our mortality, I am bound to them, bound to give of my bread to them. Through the flesh I am vulnerable to others' vulnerability; I am traumatized by my susceptibility to them, and we no doubt expend a great deal of psychic energy trying *not* to feel, trying to make ourselves "invulnerable." In all this I am reminded of my trip to Ethiopia to trace back the path of our adopted daughter. We often talk about "culture shock," but I think this misses the vulnerability that irrupts in such travels. The Ethiopian people I met and with whom I spoke were so dignified, so warm in the immediacy of their relations, so generous to give of their bread and coffee to me. But of course this is a country where polio rages unchecked, where the exigencies of daily life are met through great hardship and suffering, where medical care is shockingly scarce and prohibitively expensive, where people don't know, upon parting, if they will see their friends and family again. I was utterly overwhelmed. My senses came alive. Aware of the fragility of life, the mortal flesh, I saw the faces of the people around me—their beauty beyond aesthetics, the lines and wrinkles of their daily struggles; I was drawn out of myself toward these others, full of respect for them. It was the overture of approach, yes, but also the passion of a wound, and I leaked strange emotions that remain with me still: a sharper feeling for contingency, a keener sense of the binding, a greater generosity. To be sure, while Merleau-Ponty's philosophy powerfully explores the nature and virtue of *receptivity*, Levinas's revision of sensibility in *Otherwise than Being* promises more toward a phenomenology of *giving*.

And yet, this book too is not without its difficulties. For while the above account of the ethical relation with alterity, in terms of the lassitudes and mortality of the flesh, does not systematically exclude animals and need not be "outside" nature, still oppositional dualism surges up. This is clear, for one example, when Levinas says that the animating psyche and the body "mark two Cartesian orders . . . which have no common space where they can touch" (1998: 70). And still in this book the other is beyond the skin altogether, more nude than nudity, "without complexion" (49). Still, once again, erotic life is cast as "Luciferian" (123). Still the terms to describe the other are nearly suffocating in their negativity: the other is poverty, withdrawal, abyss, experienced as immolation, abandonment, utter loss.

Here, once again, Merleau-Ponty's thought can inspire us differently: the other is other *in* the flesh; the other transcends us *in* their living carnality. The "in" here is not a reduction of the self or psyche to the body, but a "beyond" that is not allergic to the flesh and desire, that does not drive it to despair. The radically other, I would insist, is not "without complexion," but lived in and through complexion. For instance, my daughter is here, *present, but beyond*, in her soft smooth skin, the incessant bounce in her step, and the smell of her neck. My son is here, *present, yet beyond*, in the slope of his posture, the ruffle of his hair, and the joy of his laughter. Indeed, corporeal *style*—so familiar to dancers, actors, athletes—is the trace of the other in their bodies, and there is no *behavior* at all if alterity is outside it. Further there is no sufficient reason to cast transcendence exclusively in terms of loss, suffering, and negation, for it is also warmth, excitement, approach, and love. To be sure, while Levinas is evocative of the pain of exposure, he simply cannot appreciate the soaring joy we find in our living relations. Finally, with Merleau-Ponty you find an explicit language that is noticeably missing from both *Totality and Infinity* and *Otherwise than Being*: the language of *community*. As we have already seen, for Merleau-Ponty communion is not about fusion or synthesis, not about totalizing systematics, but rather a "coming together" between people who are irreducibly different through interanimate behavior and conversation. While the interruption of the self, being questioned, and vulnerability are fundamental aspects of our relations, so too indeed are the communities, the living bonds, we find and forge as elemental beings.

So where then do we stand on the problem of alterity? No place secure, it would seem. For although the arguments of this essay are only the beginning of a detailed, critical exchange between Levinas and Merleau-Ponty, it should be reasonably clear that neither philosopher alone expresses the full nature and range of our relationships with others. Levinas, I think, teaches of the binding of these relationships, of the responsibility that flows toward others from our shared mortality, of the myriad ways our ipseity is called into question by the frank regard and appeal of others. He stresses the distance between self and other that cannot be consumed, and so illuminates the very nature of generosity and respect. And yet Merleau-Ponty reminds us of another binding: that the self and others are intervolved in living experience through the interanimation of flesh and behavior. These "intersubjective" relations aren't the stuff of totality and they don't eliminate the differences between us. They are, instead, the very possibility of contact and community, the opening approach to transcendent others who live and breathe, suffer and perish in their bodies and not outside of them. Indeed, it is imperative to remember that kindness and violence are actions performed on others *in* the flesh and nowhere else.

But perhaps, in the end, someone will still object to that preposition "in" and insist that if alterity is not *outside* the flesh of behavior and nature, then it is a "reduction of the other to the same." No doubt, this kind of argument has been tempting to contemporary thinkers and is often present in Levinas' writings. However, by now it should be clear that this is really an a priori approach to alterity that trades on conceptual dichotomy (inside/outside) when instead the task is to become alive, sensitive, and vulnerable to the multi-faceted, transcendent relations we have with others in the flesh. What I have attempted to establish in this essay is that this task must be pursued between Levinas and Merleau-Ponty, beyond them both and perhaps with other thinkers, as we seek to understand our alterity relations in ways that remain thoroughly elemental.

Notes

The central arguments of this essay are excerpted from chapter 4 of my book *Merleau-Ponty's Philosophy*.

1. Merleau-Ponty's account of reciprocal intersubjectivity is most fully developed in the chapter of *Phenomenology of Perception* entitled "Other Selves and the Human World." His other most important discussions on the topic are found in "The Child's Relations with Others" (Merleau-Ponty 1964), "The Philosopher and His Shadow" (Merleau-Ponty 1964b), and *The Visible and the Invisible* (Merleau-Ponty 1968).

2. As Levinas puts it in *Totality and Infinity* (with Merleau-Ponty clearly implied): "The [self] and the other do not constitute a simple correlation which would be reversible. The reversibility of a relation where the terms are indifferently read from left to right and from right to left would couple them the *one* to the *other*; they would complete one another in a system visible from the outside. The intended transcendence would thus be reabsorbed into the unity of the system, destroying the radical alterity of the other" (1969: 35–36).

3. Levinas' critique of Merleau-Ponty is rarely explicit; mostly it is implied in the margins of his two main works *Totality and Infinity* and *Otherwise than Being*. More explicit engagement with Merleau-Ponty's views can be found in "Meaning and Sense" (Levinas 1987) and "Two Texts on Merleau-Ponty" (Levinas 1990).

4. Besides Merleau-Ponty and Levinas, work relevant to an account of elemental alterity can be found in Elizabeth Grosz, *Volatile Bodies*, Luce Irigaray, *An Ethics of Sexual Difference*, and Alphonso Lingis, *Sensation: Intelligibility in Sensibility* and *The Community of Those Who Have Nothing in Common*.

5. "One-Way Traffic: "The Ontology of Decolonization and its Ethics" (Bernasconi 1990).

6. This comment touches on a very large issue that goes beyond the limits of this present discussion: the difficult question of what "priority" means in Levinas (as in the "priority of ethics to ontology"), and whether or not he fully earns that claim. In my view, a first difficulty is that his use of "priority" seems to waffle between two senses that are not obviously commensurable: the sense of "prior" as temporally *before*, and the sense of it as a "breach," as interrupting the flow of time. We will show some problems in certain related equivocations below. But secondly, in cases where temporal priority is clearly intended, some of Levinas' claims seem empirically false. Indeed, developmental research does not support the claim that the most basic sense of self, desire, and pleasure is *wholly derivative* upon the shocking experience of alterity, but rather that those senses are rooted in the infant's experience of his/her body in relation to others (playing, contact, and eating). For a synthesis of the contemporary medical and scientific research to this effect see Stanley Greenspan, *Building Healthy Minds*, chapter 4. For a look at what happens to the infant's sense of self and sense of other when that physical engagement and reciprocity is missing, see Jay Belsky, Kate Rosenberger, and Keith Crnic, "The Origins of Attachment Security: Classical and Contextual Determinants."

7. For one example, see Levinas 1969, 50.

8. See, for instance, Levinas 1969, 158–159.

9. See Levinas 1969, 195.

10. The first of these quotes is from 1969, 79; the second is from 1969, 73. There is a deep question about how literally we are to read Levinas' use of "men" here, for in an infamous late section of *Totality and Infinity*, "Phenomenology of Eros," he clearly distinguishes "the feminine" from the ethical. Indeed, he argues at some length that the feminine is "seduction" "the insignificant," a "regime of tenderness," while the ethical domain belongs to "male civilization," "fathers and sons." This is a shocking development, for all along it has seemed that Levinas' ethics of the face has been universalizable, when in fact women have been systematically excluded; in short, he commits what Irigaray calls "the fallacy of the masculine universal." Levinas seems to recant this sexism in *Otherwise than Being*, but there are still problems. For while he there identifies our ethical vulnerability in the flesh as the *maternal*, this language rather abruptly disappears for that of the *fraternal*. In the end, Levinas' philosophy seems to leave woman as either Mother or Whore, one of the oldest tropes of sexist oppression. For discussion of some of this problem in Levinas see Luce Irigaray, "Questions to Emmanuel Levinas: On the Divinity of Love" (Irigaray 1991).

11. As Levinas puts it in *Otherwise than Being*: "The Infinite is non-thematizable, gloriously exceeds every capacity and manifests . . . its exorbitance in the approach

of the neighbor, obedient to its measure.... It is the breaking-point, but also the binding place ..." (1998: 12).

12. Levinas 1998, 51.

References

Belsky, Jay. Kate Rosenberger, and Keith Crnic (1995). "The Origins of Attachment Security: Classical and Contextual Determinants." In *Attachment Theory*, eds. Susan Goldberg, Roy Muir, and John Kerr. Hillsdale, NJ: Analytic Press.

Bernasconi, Robert (1990). "One-Way Traffic: The Ontology of Decolonization and its Ethics." In *Ontology and Alterity in Merleau-Ponty*, eds. Galen A. Johnson and Michael B. Smith. Evanston, IL: Northwestern University Press, 67–80.

Greenspan, Stanley (2000). *Building Healthy Minds*. Cambridge, MA: Perseus Publishing.

Grosz, Elizabeth (1994). *Volatile Bodies*. Bloomington: Indiana University Press.

Hass, Lawrence (2008). *Merleau-Ponty's Philosophy*. Bloomington: Indiana University Press.

Irigaray, Luce (1991). "Questions to Emmanuel Levinas: On the Divinity of Love." Trans. Margaret Whitford. In *Re-Reading Levinas*, eds. Robert Bernasconi and Simon Critchley. Bloomington: Indiana University Press.

——— (1993). *An Ethics of Sexual Difference*. Trans. Carolyn Burke and Gillian C. Gill. Ithaca, NY: Cornell University Press.

Levinas, Emmanuel (1969). *Totality and Infinity*. Trans. Alphonso Lingis. Pittsburgh: Duquesne University Press.

——— (1987). "Meaning and Sense." In *Collected Philosophical Papers*, trans. Alphonso Lingis. Dordrecht: Martinus Nijhoff.

——— (1998). *Otherwise than Being*. Trans. Alphonso Lingis. Pittsburgh: Duquesne University Press.

——— (1990). "Two Texts on Merleau-Ponty." Trans. Michael B. Smith. In *Ontology and Alterity in Merleau-Ponty*, eds. Galen A. Johnson and Michael B. Smith. Evanston, IL: Northwestern University Press.

Lingis, Alphonso (1994). *The Community of Those Who Have Nothing in Common*. Bloomington: Indiana University Press.

——— (1996). *Sensation: Intelligibility in Sensibility*. Atlantic Highlands, NJ: Humanities Press.

Merleau-Ponty, Maurice (1962). *Phenomenology of Perception*. Trans. Colin Smith, with translation revisions by Forrest Williams and David Guerrière. New York: Routledge.

——— (1964). "The Child's Relations with Others." Trans. William Cobb. In *The Primacy of Perception*, ed. James M. Edie. Evanston, IL: Northwestern University Press.

——— (1964b). "The Philosopher and His Shadow." In *Signs*, trans. Richard C. McCleary. Evanston, IL: Northwestern University Press.

——— (1968). *The Visible and the Invisible*. Ed. Claude Lefort. Trans. Alphonso Lingis. Evanston, IL: Northwestern University Press.

CHAPTER 3

The Developing Body: A Reading of Merleau-Ponty's Conception of Women in the Sorbonne Lectures

TALIA WELSH

Introduction

Although Maurice Merleau-Ponty's celebrated discussion of embodiment in the *Phenomenology of Perception* and other texts continues to provoke thought and inspire research, his thoughts have also drawn fire. Shannon Sullivan argues that Merleau-Ponty, along with other phenomenologists, fails to accurately portray our true existential condition since he describes the body in "neutral" terms. The body appears to be a kind of universal body, a "one size fits all" characterization, which harkens back to the entire Western tradition of universalizing experience and passing over difference. Merleau-Ponty's body is an anonymous body. Sullivan claims that Merleau-Ponty's body passes over the determining effects of "gender, sexuality, class, race, age, culture, nationality, individual experiences and upbringing, and more" (Sullivan 1997: 1). Despite a gesture toward grounding our experience in the lived world, Merleau-Ponty's neutral body ends up being a "solipsistic subject's monologue" (Sullivan 1997: 1).

Sullivan claims that when Merleau-Ponty overlooks the importance of gender and upbringing in explaining bodily behavior and interpersonal relationships, he implicitly assumes that one can approach embodiment with a "pre-gender" and "pre-upbringing" analysis (Sullivan 1997: 7). In so doing, Sullivan charges Merleau-Ponty with completely misunderstanding the nature of our bodies. For instance, Sullivan discusses how she will physically retreat from her male friend's enthusiastic gesticulations due to a long history of enculturation. The norm of women being demure, contained, and ladylike as well as the education that possible violence might lurk behind men's behavior has caused many women to find expressive gestures intrusive and threatening.

Without a discussion of respective gender roles, culture, and upbringing, this common type of everyday interpersonal interaction would be passed over for a "general" analysis of gesture.

I disagree that Merleau-Ponty is ignorant of, or passes over, such aspects of our embodied condition in the *Phenomenology*. Merleau-Ponty is careful to acknowledge the determining and transformative effects of our situation—in its physical, historical, cultural, and personal aspects. I believe it is clear in his theory that any sufficient phenomenological account would have to address these differences. Silvia Stoller makes this point succinctly in her response to Sullivan's objections (Stoller 2000). Merleau-Ponty does acknowledge that any person's lived experience is reflective of a particular socio-historical milieu. Hence, feminist theorists like Iris Marion Young, Gail Weiss, and Susan Bordo—to name a few—extend Merleau-Ponty's theory in discussing gender specific analyses without any theoretical contradiction (Bordo 1993; Young 1990; Weiss 1999).

Yet, it is true that often when Merleau-Ponty speaks of the body, he does not analyze the body in gendered terms. One might conclude that even though he allows for gendered responses, his analysis is remarkably bereft of such descriptions. An actual description of how gender, class, history, and culture affect an individual's embodied life is barely touched in the *Phenomenology*. It remains only the description of the effect of radical physical injury, Schneider's brain damage, which garners a full phenomenological description. Indeed, considering Merleau-Ponty's texts, it is fair to acknowledge that he spends scant attention to describing gender differences even though he does address class, nationality, history, and, of course, physiological/psychopathological differences. This is frustrating considering how his notion of the body as neither simply a cultural object subject to the whims of society nor as a static set of physical givens is a particularly appropriate vehicle with which to address gender.

In this chapter, I wish to draw attention to his analysis of the development of women in his Sorbonne lectures in psychology. Therein, Merleau-Ponty does spend time considering female embodiment and development. Although Merleau-Ponty does not systematically analyze gender, he does provide us with an interesting set of discussions surrounding the interplay of physical development and cultural conditioning.

Merleau-Ponty's first university appointment was a chair of child psychology at the Sorbonne (1949–1952). This position, later occupied by the famous child psychologist Jean Piaget, has been immortalized in a series of lecture notes taken by his students (Merleau-Ponty 1949–1952/1988). It is important to underline when referring to these lectures that they were preparatory courses for psychology students. In other words, Merleau-Ponty was not free to teach any material he chose. However, the interpretation and stress he places on the material is very much his own. What Merleau-Ponty can also be lauded for in these lectures is how often he was the first to bring groundbreaking work to a general audience.

Although Merleau-Ponty acknowledges the transformative effect of physical development and physical injury (or disease) upon the individual, he is also careful to acknowledge that our study of these transformations is itself always located, and, therefore, it is always a culturally determined study. Looking for a more dynamic and integrative approach to human development, Merleau-Ponty works against materialistic or intellectualist accounts in his Sorbonne lectures—a theme consistent with the rest of his texts. For Merleau-Ponty, any psychology is always a human endeavor and, as such, is always interpretative rather than universal.

The status of female development is particularly interesting to consider in terms of its interplay of cultural norms and physiological development. As an oppressed group, cornered into narrow definitions of normal female behavior, women are transformed not just by their bodies, but also they are significantly affected by cultural norms. A phenomenological exploration of female embodiment is needed to find to what degree Merleau-Ponty's theory is sufficiently sensitive to gender differences. In this chapter, I explore a Merleau-Ponty more directly engaged with female embodiment: the Merleau-Ponty of the Sorbonne lectures. First, I discuss Merleau-Ponty's focus upon sexual stereotypes and gender roles. Second, I examine how Merleau-Ponty's analysis of the onset of menstruation is an example of the nexus of forces that play out differently in each individual woman. Third, I address his thought-provoking discussion of how pregnancy impacts female embodiment. Finally, I conclude by indicating how contemporary work on pregnant embodiment perfectly extends some of Merleau-Ponty's own thesis, in particular the work of Carol Bigwood, Iris Marion Young, and Gail Weiss.

Stereotypes and Science

The first line of Merleau-Ponty's 1951–1952 lecture at the Sorbonne "The Question of Method in Child Psychology" reads: "In child psychology (as in psychopathology, the psychology of primitives, and the psychology of women), the situation of the object of study is so different from that of the observer that it cannot be grasped on its own terms"[1] (Merleau-Ponty 1949–1952/1988: 465). This introduction is troubling. Does Merleau-Ponty really want to group "primitives," "women," "children," and "mentally disturbed individuals" as similar? Who is the observer? Does he mean to suggest only a man could be a psychologist?

Merleau-Ponty discusses women as a group because the limiting stereotypes placed upon them isolates and normalizes them. This is not to say that women are all completely determined by social standards, but to acknowledge that to say someone is a "woman" is to already know a great deal about her situation, her possibilities, and her likely expectations. In 1950s France, *woman* was an occupation—mother, wife, daughter. One would only need to distinguish the woman as being an individual in the case where she lived outside these norms, for instance, "she has a career," "she never married." Otherwise, "woman" would be sufficiently explanatory. The reverse does not hold true for men. To what class does he belong? What is his occupation? What did his parents expect of him? Thus, we can consider a "psychology of women" in the sense that we can analyze the stereotypes of women and how they affect individual women. At the same time, any psychology of women has to question its, perhaps unconscious, absorption of stereotypes.

Before we can assess a psychology of women, we must question the status of psychology as a "science." Psychology, by the mid-twentieth century, was increasingly distancing itself from its philosophical roots and endeavoring to become an experimental science to be housed alongside biology and physics. In its liberation from philosophy, a scientific psychologist might conclude that it would be philosophy that would be likely to import stereotypes, since its metaphysical speculations are not subject to an analysis of observable facts. Psychology, as an experimental science, simply examines the facts without prejudice. Merleau-Ponty's earliest theoretical interests are occupied with the interplay of science and its "view from nowhere" interpretation of human experience.[2] Such a concern underlies his life-long interest in perception. Merleau-Ponty worries that traditional scientific attempts to explain perception end up blind to the true manner in which we perceive. Merleau-Ponty takes up a critical stance toward science in the preface to the *Phenomenology of Perception*, writing: ". . . Husserl's first directive to phenomenology, in its early stages, to be a 'descriptive psychology,' or to return to the 'things themselves,' is from the start a foreswearing of science" (Merleau-Ponty 1945/1996: viii). Merleau-Ponty goes on to note that "Science has not and never will have, by its nature, the same significance qua form of being as the world which we perceive, for the simple reason that it is a rationale or explanation of the world" (Merleau-Ponty 1945/1996: viii). However, this critique is directed at scientism—undefended faith in the claims of science—as any reader of the rest of the *Phenomenology* will quickly appreciate. The text is full of psychological examples and references, indicating that by "foreswearing" science, Merleau-Ponty in no way meant to reify philosophy into a solely metaphysical discussion.

Qualifying the role of science set the ground for Merleau-Ponty's critique of scientific psychology in the Sorbonne lectures. The point is not to jettison the scientific aspirations of psychology, but to make sure that any particular claim looks to the child's development as a whole: the child as a cultural, historical, living being, not as a series of isolatable motor skills and stages—"at one year," "able to manipulate objects." Merleau-Ponty's focus upon fully describing experience and, importantly, describing a variety of studies—anthropological, psychological, physiological, not to mention the manifold set of authors he cites—makes the Sorbonne lectures truly powerful. Jean Laplanche speaks highly of Merleau-Ponty's perceptive powers. He notes that Merleau-Ponty does not shy away from clinical and empirical observations—"My second digression is intended to point out how much we can learn from Merleau-Ponty's lecture notes [the Sorbonne lectures]. A philosopher who is willing to observe! A philosopher who is interested in clinical observation, in very concrete experiments involving children, and in the observations of an anthropologist" (Laplanche 1989: 92). Merleau-Ponty observes both the effect of stereotypes on the subjects of psychology as well as the influence they have upon psychology's practitioners.

In Merleau-Ponty's eyes, the largest false assumption of psychology is that the scientific observer and his or her class play no role in his or her investigations.[3] The first step must not arise from an unquestioned belief in the truths of scientific studies, but in an examination from the psychologist's own relationship to the patient and the "class" that the patient belongs to in society. In child psychology, it will not be enough to just examine how one perceives this particular child who is in front of the observer. One must also examine how one perceives children generally. What attitude is taken toward children in one's society? What is expected of them?[4]

One of Merleau-Ponty's enduring interests in his lectures on child psychology is anthropology. The studies of "primitive" peoples indicate to him the malleability of parent-child relationships. The mother remains central in most of the studies, but the manner in which children are expected to behave and, thus, do behave, varies greatly. Likewise, Merleau-Ponty argues that it is society that creates the sense that women are a category separate from "normal," that is, male. This categorization does not just indicate certain prejudices of the psychologists, it also naturally affects women. In their development, women are so narrowly defined that they often realize the stereotypes. Quoting Stendhal, Merleau-Ponty lectures, "Stendhal has shown that the traits of the feminine 'nature' are the result of the history and the style of education under which women have been subjected. . . . 'All the geniuses who are born women are lost to humanity'" (Merleau-Ponty 1949–1952/1988: 471). The impact of this inequality between the sexes goes far beyond the negative impact it has upon female development. It affects the entire culture.

The masculine-feminine relationship is, for Merleau-Ponty, a universal dichotomy around which society builds itself, as it constructs itself upon other interpersonal relations. Why masculine-feminine? Due to the obvious physiological differences we will inevitably develop symbolic systems around gender difference. However, Merleau-Ponty is not a biological essentialist in that he necessarily thinks the physiological differences must account for our conception of "masculine" and "feminine" differences. The fact that sex difference will be constitutive for any society's norms is universally given. The form of those norms is contingent. If we look at Merleau-Ponty's analysis of Margaret Mead's anthropological studies we discover a "multicultural" approach.[5] Each native society has its own ways of explaining sexual difference and justifying gender roles. We find that all societies react to sexual difference in particular ways (with various notions of what a woman "is"), but that they all maintain a masculine-feminine dichotomy, "As we find in this society, the relations between mother and child, between self and stranger, and in general the inter-human relations all are part of the tissue in which we find the masculine-feminine relation" (Merleau-Ponty 1949–1952: 495). Stereotypes are reflections of the manner in which particular civilizations take up gender difference: they do not reveal essential traits—"We have no grounds to speak of "the" masculine and "the" feminine since each civilization, according to its mode of existence, elaborates a certain type of masculinity in correlation to a certain type of femininity. But within any given society one finds *sexual stereotypes*" (Merleau-Ponty 1949–1952: 495). Stereotypes founded in physical differences are the norm, but the particular manifestation of stereotypes is flexible. Thus, a psychological experiment that "discovers" women are afraid of angry gesticulations has not necessarily discovered that women are weaker or more easily threatened due to the fact they are physiologically women. We have to ask if the stereotype of the role women are expected to play has caused the behavior or if we can really conclude that the behavior is caused by the individual's physical nature.

If we accept that stereotypes are inevitable, does this mean that we are unable to free ourselves from them? Does such a characterization lead to relativism? What grounds do we have to assert one stereotype is better or worse than another? Merleau-Ponty considers certain stereotypes to be truly limiting. If inequality exists between sexes, the society fundamentally is set askew for all further relationships are modeled upon the paradigm of the sexual relationship. What has occurred in Merleau-Ponty's society is that women are denied the possibility of healthy development. Healthy development is characterized as the ability to psychologically adjust to physical changes. Women in their transformation from childhood to adulthood are set upon a narrow path toward a narrow definition of what it is to be an adult woman. Thus, individual manners of adjusting to personal physiological and psychological change are not available. As such, Merleau-Ponty argues that many girls rebel and reject physical transformation. Merleau-Ponty asserts that social acceptance of one's development (both physical and psychical) is a necessary part of healthy development. Since we are always already inserted into a social world, we cannot "choose" our own stereotype. Nonetheless, physical transformation occurs independently of a social norm. Below, I discuss two physical transformations unique to women, and how Merleau-Ponty interprets the relationship between them for individual expression, cultural imposition, and physical determinism.

The Passage to Womanhood—Menstruation

"The fragile woman," Merleau-Ponty lectures, "is a fact of culture and not of nature" (Merleau-Ponty 1949–1952/1988: 470). Given that anthropology reveals to us a diversity of attitudes toward women's strength, our own tendency to view women as physically inferior quickly shows itself to be a prejudice. How, then, do we assess what aspects of sexual difference might be essential? Are all stereotypes false? Are some more "true" than others? Obviously, men and women have different bodies and this would seem to play some role in experience. Merleau-Ponty agrees by saying that, "[m]ethodologically, there is no point in denying psychological differences between men and women which arise from biological differences" (Merleau-Ponty 1949–1952: 470). In order to approach difference more accurately, we must throw away our own notions of what constitutes an appropriate female or male behavior—"The only way in which to know whether, and to what extent, such differences exist is to get rid of notions of a 'feminine nature' and of a 'masculine nature'" (Merleau-Ponty 1949–1952: 470). We must direct our attention toward physical change and behavior without assuming that a necessary connection exists between them. Instead, we must allow the observation to speak for itself.

An example to illustrate this point is Merleau-Ponty's reception of an example drawn from Hélène Deutsch. One obvious, and much discussed, physical change in women is menstruation. This is considered by some to be the passage into heterosexual, adult "womanhood." Merleau-Ponty disagrees: "*Heterosexuality is not directly related to the physiological phenomenon of menstruation.* Hélène Deutsch cites the case of Evelyne, who began menstruating at the age of twelve, in which menstruation had had no direct influence on her mode of sexuality" (Merleau-Ponty 1949–1952/1988: 502). Merleau-Ponty does not question the assumption that the transformation to "womanhood" is a transformation to "heterosexuality." Merleau-Ponty's lectures are not free from his own cultural prejudices. Perhaps it is the case that his lack of gender-analysis in his other texts is indicative of a certain unconscious sexism.

One example of how his prejudices, perhaps despite himself, surface is that although he asserts above that the "object" of a psychology of women—that is, women—is so different from the observer—that is, the male psychologist—that it cannot be grasped on its own terms, Merleau-Ponty commences to speak authoritatively on female psychology from a neutral, ideal observer position. Nonetheless, Merleau-Ponty's *method* of acknowledging the importance of physical development while continuing to allow for individual differences remains a trenchant analysis. For Merleau-Ponty, Evelyne's body does not decide for her—she too must play a role in development.—"There had been no psychological assimilation of the physiological event" (Merleau-Ponty 1949–1952/1988: 502).[6] According to Merleau-Ponty, menstruation appears before the girl is ready for her new physical abilities. Such discordance between the physical and psychical inevitably causes turmoil. If protracted, the subject will form pathological symptoms. These problems are compounded by the overwhelming push by society to conform to a certain model of womanhood, which often causes great resentment and anxiety in the young girl. The manner in which someone adjusts to physical development is individual, but the narrower the "normal" category of development, the more problems the girl will face. Merleau-Ponty discusses how families can either aid or further hinder a girl in her development by loosening or strengthening the expectation to live up to social norms.

Merleau-Ponty argues that the psychological series of developments a young girl goes through before and after menstruation are *related* to the actual commencement of menstruation. As in the discussion of sexual stereotyping above, the physical body does determine our conceptions. Evelyne is not free to decide *any* mode of relating to her body. Yet, the particular mode in which she takes up her embodiment is itself not determined. For Merleau-Ponty, development is flexible, but, it is not, therefore, without any necessary structure—"development follows certain lines all the same; the possibilities of aberration are not infinite. This order, as entirely contingent as it may be, must surge forth spontaneously from prior states, from materials that it is going to utilize" (Merleau-Ponty 1949–1952/1988: 505). Evelyne must adapt to the possibilities of her new body in some manner; she cannot reject development without personal (not just social) problems. "The individual must take up again what the present bodily state has rendered possible"[7] (Merleau-Ponty 1949–1952: 505). Obviously, social norms can negatively influence our attitudes toward our bodies (take the preponderance of eating disorders in our society for instance). But, Merleau-Ponty also notes in his discussion how the body's transformations in-themselves can be a source of negative energy and resentment. The question remains unanswered whether or not the negative transference upon one's physical development is created solely by social norms, and, thus, in an ideal world one's physical development would be without internal conflict.

Pregnancy and Contemporary Research

Pregnancy, for Merleau-Ponty, possesses precisely this same ambiguity about the body's transformations but it is more extensive in its general philosophical implications. Merleau-Ponty indicates that the developing body in pregnancy carries with it a tie to a primordial, presubjective existence. In this section, I consider his description of the ambivalent embodiment in pregnancy, his discussion of the pregnant "order of life," and, finally, I conclude by discussing how some contemporary research inspired by Merleau-Ponty completes his thoughts on pregnancy.

Pregnancy is obviously a time of great physical change and transformation. However, unlike the case of menstruation, it is not a question of adapting to a new stage of *individual* physical development. Although "womanhood" might be defined inappropriately by society, a menstruating body is indeed a different body and carries with it different demands and a different lifestyle. Evelyne must "catch up" in a certain sense, to her body. In an ideal society, once she grows accustomed to menstruation, she might very well experience a harmonious interaction between her psychical states and her physical state. It might also be the case that in an unhealthy society, no woman can ever feel entirely at ease with her body. However intricately physical and psychological development occurs, it remains the case that change plays out within the individual human subject.

Pregnancy is entirely different because it does not just concern the nexus of social forces, personal upbringing, physical development, and psychological states—it concerns another being entirely. The physical change is not just an individual process. Merleau-Ponty lectures that the developing presence of another body causes the mother to be alienated from her body—"She feels her own body to be alienated from her" (Merleau-Ponty 1949–1952: 101). For each woman, this sense of alienation is naturally different given the context of her pregnancy, her physiology, and her psychical state; however, it is similar in all women given the presence of this alien being.

Merleau-Ponty adds that this alienation is not just about the physical challenges of pregnancy: the heaviness of pregnancy, the discomfort, and awkwardness. It is also about being tied into another manner of living. The mother lives her pregnancy in a *primitive* manner—"The woman with child lives her pregnancy in a primitive manner" (Merleau-Ponty 1949–1952/1988: 101). Pregnancy's "primitiveness" is a participation in an "anonymous process" that is ambivalent precisely because it is not just about the mother's decisions, her relationship with society, her desires, and complexes: "Her own pregnancy is not for her an act like others she accomplishes with her body. It is more an anonymous process that takes place through her and of which she is only the seat (*siège*)" (Merleau-Ponty 1949–1952/1988: 101). The mother is taken outside of her own experience of her body as belonging to her.

This is not to say that the mother's experience of being alienated from her body is necessarily a negative experience. It is, rather, a sense of going beyond her personal embodiment to a far greater sensation of life. Merleau-Ponty calls this a "mystery" surrounding "the order of life"—"On the one hand, her own body escapes her, but, on the other hand, the infant which is to be born is an extension of her own body. During the entirety of her pregnancy, the woman is living a major mystery, which is neither the order of matter nor the order of the mind, but, rather, *the order of life*" (Merleau-Ponty 1949–1952/1988: 101). What is the "order of life"? It appears in these comments to be a tie into the primordial aspect of life itself: a possession of no "one" body but comprising all living bodies. This discussion is very akin to Merleau-Ponty's exploration of infant experience in the Sorbonne lectures; he often describes infancy as a kind of oneness or wholeness with the mother. The infant finds the development of personal identity to be a break with this fleshly immersion in life itself. Is Merleau-Ponty's characterization of pregnancy pointing toward a much larger philosophical discussion of embodiment in general, not just a discussion of female psychological and physiological development?

Merleau-Ponty's extremely suggestive discussion brings much to more contemporary work in embodiment and pregnancy, which does not cite the Sorbonne lectures but certainly shares theoretical sympathy with them. It also furthers some of the tentative philosophical suggestions present in the Sorbonne lectures. Carol Bigwood's piece "Renaturalizing the Body (with the help of Merleau-Ponty)" calls for a "world-earth-home" to provide a model of the body that reaches beyond cultural and material terminology. "We need a new model of the body that leads neither to biological determinism nor to gender skepticism and cultural relativism" (Bigwood 1991: 57). Her notion of "world-earth-home" is similar to Merleau-Ponty's idea above about the "order of life." Bigwood wants to incorporate embodiment as not just the living body qua individual Leib, but something much greater and more expansive. "My term 'world-earth,' by contrast, reminds us that we are here with other animals and on an earth that gives rise to a myriad of life that, unfortunately, has become marginal to our human world" (Bigwood 1991: 57). Pregnancy perfectly shows our insertion in this much larger sense of life that exceeds a single body. Such work also helps make sure that the focus on the body in contemporary phenomenology does not become equated with a kind of materialist monism—where instead of seeing ourselves as individual isolated minds, we are but individual isolated lived-bodies.

It is particularly interesting to consider the small vignettes Bigwood has inserted in her article about her own pregnancy in reference to Merleau-Ponty's thought. One finds the alienation Merleau-Ponty refers to—"This weight. It is not a weight that I willfully bear with muscular strength like a pack on my back. It is a weight that I live with, that has slowly entered into every aspect of my bodily being" (Bigwood 1991: 59). For Bigwood, the demands of the pregnant body would be unbearable if it were a project one embarked upon, rather than a bodily experience which does frustrate her, but also continues her, takes her beyond her body, just as Merleau-Ponty lectures above.

The ambiguity of pregnancy is also discussed by Iris Marion Young. She calls what Merleau-Ponty terms "alienation," a "splitting" that occurs in pregnancy. Describing the splitting that occurs within the first sensations of pregnancy, Young writes, "The first movements of the fetus produce this sense of the splitting subject; the fetus's movements are wholly mine, completely within me, conditioning my experience and space" (Young 1990/1998: 276). Young continues to note that the splitting causes not only socially determined senses of alienation (i.e., how pregnant women are objectified), but also that pregnancy also interferes with one's basic bodily constitution. Young argues that pregnancy disrupts our typical sense of "bodily integrity" in splitting:

> This integrity of my body is undermined in pregnancy not only by this externality of the inside, but also by the fact that the boundaries of my body are themselves in flux. In pregnancy I literally do not have a firm sense of where my body ends and the world begins. My automatic body habits become dislodged; the continuity between my customary body and my body at this moment is broken. (Young 1990/1998: 277)

Returning to Merleau-Ponty's assessments of the transformations of the body on the self, we find a characterization where basic physical experience causes rupture and discord. Whether or not society embraces and celebrates pregnancy, Young's work seems to suggest there would still be a radical alienation from one's natural embodiment.

Could we interpret pregnant experience in another manner? Must being drawn into the "order of life" be negative since it includes a departure from one's everyday embodied life? Might the problem be the notion of "integrity" and "selfhood"? To some degree, Bigwood already promises a solution. Her thoughts on "world-earth-home" seem to suggest an embodied experience which expands the notion of body.

Gail Weiss carries this thought even further. Commenting on Young's piece, Weiss asks if it is Young's sense of "integrity" that must be challenged:

> Thinking back to my own pregnancies, my changing bodily experiences did not so much undermine as *resignify* bodily integrity; newly emerging bodily rhythms, the temporality Young identifies with process and growth gave both consistency and insistency to even the most unsettling and disruptive aspects of my pregnant existence. (Weiss 1999: 53)

Weiss' description suggests that perhaps pregnancy expands integrity into a new sphere (perhaps the "world-earth-home" of Bigwood). Weiss notes that pregnancy disintegrates typical notions of what bodily (as enclosed) experience is: "Fluidity and expansiveness, rather than the myths of wholeness and closure (which I don't believe any of us, male or female, ever truly experience) were the tangible signs of this newly discovered bodily integrity" (Weiss 1999: 53). Her critique is to suggest not just that pregnancy's "splitting" or "alienation" might be positively viewed, but perhaps that the radicalness of pregnancy indicates that the primitive order of life is something that undergirds all bodily experience:

> This is not to say that pregnancy is the only way to achieve the kind of bodily integrity I am talking about here. Rather, what I would argue is that bodily integrity is created through developing a greater sensitivity to one's bodily changes, capacities, movements, and gestures, whether these latter involve the more noticeable changes of pregnancy, childbirth, and lactation, or the daily changes that all bodies (even those of adult males who are not yet old) continually undergo. (Weiss 1999: 53)

One can also not help but have Merleau-Ponty's ever-suggestive work in *The Visible and the Invisible* on "flesh" come to mind when considering these themes. The "order of life" in the Sorbonne lectures, the "world-earth-home" of Bigwood, and Weiss's discussion of bodily integrity as being inclusive of all life draw us back to the late Merleau-Ponty. In "The Intertwining—The Chiasm," he writes, "Where are we to put the limit between the body and the world, since the world is flesh? . . . The world seen is not 'in' my body, and my body is not 'in' the visible world ultimately: as flesh applied to a flesh, the world neither surrounds nor is surrounded by it" (Merleau-Ponty 1964/1995: 138). So, too, is the fetus not merely "in" the mother and the mother "in" the world like a series of Russian dolls all neatly capable of being taken apart and put back together. To even think of human life as somehow separate from the world is also incomprehensible. To live is to breathe, to eat, to move. Through these behaviors we are drawn again and again into a life much larger than our own and required for our own personal flourishing. Pregnancy might be the ultimate reminder of this connection.

In conclusion, these remarks of Merleau-Ponty's need much more consideration than the short attention I have given them here. The reader must decide whether or not Merleau-Ponty's violation of his own principle that no philosopher or psychology can be a neutral, objective observer in his descriptions of pregnant embodiment is too significant to take his descriptions seriously. Additionally, we need to consider a series of tensions. First, what is the role between unjust stereotyping of "normal" development and "normal" embodiment and real healthy embodied experience? Are the frustrations we experience with our changing bodies due largely to social norms, which, in principle, could be changed, or, are some of those discordances part and parcel of embodied life? As a subject keen to organize my experiences around my sense of self, will I inevitably be frustrated by my body which often changes without my consent? Or, is this simply a product of a false manner of conceiving myself? In the discussion of the anonymous, primitive, "order of life" experienced in pregnancy, we find another tension between the self-conscious subject and life broadly construed. Again, the question arises whether "alienation" or "splitting" is something essential to the experience of pregnancy or if this very sensation is a product of a narrowly conceived conception of body, self, and integrity. I believe it is the latter suggestion which remains the most promising and the one future work inspired by Merleau-Ponty will undoubtedly continue to explore.

Notes

1. All translations are mine. Page numbers refer to the French text.

2. As early as 1933, Merleau-Ponty writes, "It has seemed to me that in the present state of neurology, experimental psychology (particularly psychopathology), and philosophy, it would be useful to take up again the problem of perception, and particularly perception of one's own body" (Merleau-Ponty 1933/1996: 74).

3. The impact of Edmund Husserl's *Crisis* is evident. Husserl criticizes the sciences for thinking that their foundation and access to truth is guaranteed by their "objectivity." Husserl writes that the sciences must instead acknowledge their debt to theory (Husserl 1954/1970).

4. "One must grasp the totality of the child's becoming. One must reconstitute the dynamic development and not only enumerate a certain number of performances that the child either succeeds in or does not succeed in at a given moment. It is the same for Goldstein's aphasiacs: the automatic linguistic practice is preserved, but not the intelligent one. The aphasiacs do not demonstrate verbal destruction, but rather a fall to an inferior linguistic level. In pathology, one is initially concerned with symptoms that are defined by responses that the organism no longer gives to environmental stimuli and to the psychologist's questions. However, this does not give us the essence of the illness. One must reconstruct the symptomology by posing questions to the organism that are more precise than those of common sense. Truth only arises from the moment that one reaches the center of the personality" (Merleau-Ponty 1949–1952/1988: 483).

5. Merleau-Ponty extensively cites Margaret Mead's anthropological studies in his Sorbonne lectures. A good source for most of the studies and societies he references is Mead's *Sex and Temperament* (Mead 1935/1963).

6. "Once menstruation has begun, everything still remains to be done, that is their integration as an element of a whole. But this integration is not always, or even

often, completed (e.g., the abhorrence of menstruation in certain adult women). The girl who imagines that menstruation changes everything is very much deceived. Maturation will still have to establish a bond between the imaginary and the perceived, a bond between the fantasies about menstruation and the real facts" (Merleau-Ponty 1949–1952/1988: 504).

7. "We find this very idea in the psychology of form, an idea which is itself more a question than a response, gives us an unfinished solution. Thus, development is as little a destiny as it is an unconditioned freedom, for the individual always accomplishes a decisive act of development in a particular corporeal field. We find here once again Hegel's idea of 'surpassing while preserving.' The individual only moves beyond his or her first states if he or she agrees to retain them. Thus, we rejoin our general conceptions of the personal and interpersonal dynamic" (Merleau-Ponty 1949–1952/1988: 505–506).

References

Bigwood, Carol (1991). Renaturalizing the Body (with the Help of Merleau-Ponty). *Hypatia*, 6 (3), 54–73.

Bordo, Susan (1993). *Unbearable Weight*. Berkeley: University of California Press.

Husserl, Edmund (1970). *The Crisis of European Sciences and Transcendental Phenomenology*. Trans. David Carr. Evanston: Northwestern. (Original work published in 1954).

Laplanche, Jean (1989). *New Foundations for Psychoanalysis*. Trans. David Macy. Oxford: Blackwell.

Mead, Margaret (1963). *Sex and Temperament in Three Primitive Societies*. New York: Morrow Quill. (Original work published in 1935).

Merleau-Ponty, Maurice (1988). *Merleau-Ponty à la Sorbonne*. Paris: Cynara. (Original work presented 1949–1952).

——— (1995). *The Visible and the Invisible*. Trans. Alphonso Lingis. Evanston: Northwestern University Press. (Original work published in 1964).

——— (1996a). The Nature of Perception: Two Proposals. Trans. Forest W. Williams. In *Texts and Dialogues: On Philosophy, Politics, and Culture* (74–84). Hugh Silverman and James Barry, Jr. (Eds.) New Jersey: Humanities Press. (Original work presented in 1933).

——— (1996b). *Phenomenology of Perception*. Colin Smith (Trans.) London: Routledge. (Original work published in 1945).

Stoller, Silvia (2000). Reflections on Feminist Merleau-Ponty Skepticism. *Hypatia*, 15 (1), 175–182.

Sullivan, Shannon (1997). Domination and Dialogue in Merleau-Ponty's Phenomenology of Perception. *Hypatia*, 12 (1), 1–19.

Weiss, Gail (1999). *Body Images: Embodiment as Intercorporeality*. New York: Routledge.

Young, Iris (1998). Pregnant Embodiment. In D. Welton (Ed.), *Body and Flesh: A Philosophical Reader* (pp. 274–285). London: Blackwell. (Original work published in 1990).

——— (1990). *Throwing Like a Girl and Other Essays*. Bloomington: Indiana University Press.

PART II

Feminist Possibilities:
Reading Irigaray,
Reading Merleau-Ponty

CHAPTER 4

Phenomenology in the Feminine: Irigaray's Relationship to Merleau-Ponty

ANNEMIE HALSEMA

In an interview with Alice Jardine and Anne Menke, Luce Irigaray describes her first feminist philosophical book, *Speculum of the Other Woman*, as "a critique of the exclusive right of one sex to use, exchange, and represent the other" (Irigaray 1991: 103). In passing through the philosophical tradition, she unravels its aporia: the female sex. Her motivation for undertaking such an effort is that within a discourse exclusively masculine "the reality" of the feminine gender cannot be articulated, and being sexualized as feminine is a senseless, inappropriate, indecent utterance (Irigaray 1985: 148–149/1977: 145.).[1] In order to initiate change of the masculine discourse, she claims to begin to "elaborate a phenomenological description by a woman—Luce Irigaray, whose name is on the book—of the self-affection and self-representation of her body" (Irigaray 1991: 103). In other words, *Speculum of the Other Woman* is an effort to work out an account of the female sex that is no longer the object of male discourse, but the center of the process of creating a female subjectivity that experiences and defines itself.

For this aim, Irigaray means to give a phenomenological description of woman's body. Phenomenology here refers to describing women's lived experience, and has the political purpose of creating opportunities for women to develop subject positions of their own. Therefore, the masculine symbolic has to be opened up and reinterpreted. In other words, phenomenology enables Irigaray to criticize masculine discourse and to articulate what has hitherto remained unarticulated within it.

Starting from Irigaray's motivation for writing *Speculum of the Other Woman*, in this essay I suggest reading her philosophy as a phenomenology in the feminine.[2] Describing Irigaray's philosophy as phenomenological in the first place implies that it is continuous with the French postwar tradition of existential phenomenology, that is, with the work of Merleau-Ponty, Sartre, and Beauvoir.[3] Furthermore, it suggests a different reading of Irigaray's account of the body, which escapes the often proclaimed, but as much denied critique of essentialism.[4] Namely, a phenomenological account of the body is neither biological, nor essentialist; rather, the body is the starting point for having a (cultural) world and for relating to that world and to others. Finally, situating Irigaray's notion of embodiment in continuity with Merleau-Ponty's implies elaborating his phenomenology of the body explicitly toward a phenomenology that takes sexual difference into consideration. Therewith, I do not mean to say that Merleau-Ponty does not reflect on sexuality, which for him is related to embodiment,[5] nor that his thought is blind to sexual difference.[6] My aims are more limited, namely to show that Irigaray understands sexual difference starting from a phenomenological account of the body, and to reflect on the consequences.

Although Irigaray's work generally is not considered as phenomenological,[7] scholars such as Mortensen, Chanter, Vasseleu, and Heinämaa claim the key to understanding her work lies in her relationship to Heidegger, Levinas, Husserl and Merleau-Ponty.[8] I aim at continuing this line of thought by relating Irigaray's notion of the body to Merleau-Ponty's account of bodily intentionality.

The two texts in which Irigaray explicitly refers to Merleau-Ponty's works form my point of departure. In *An Ethics of Sexual Difference*, published in French in 1984, she rereads the chapter "The Intertwining—The Chiasm" from *The Visible and the Invisible*.[9] Her main critique is that Merleau-Ponty's analysis of the visible and the invisible remains solipsistic. Ten years later, in *To Be Two* (first appearance in Italian in 1994), she again reacts to Merleau-Ponty in a chapter on carnal love.[10] This time she cites passages from Merleau-Ponty's chapter on sexuality in *Phenomenology of Perception*. After criticizing Sartre, Levinas, and Merleau-Ponty, she here develops a phenomenology of the caress corresponding to her feminine desire.

The latter text is more openly critical than the former, which corresponds to the development of Irigaray's philosophy: whereas in her early works she concentrates on rewriting the philosophical tradition in a carefully mimetic manner, her writings of the 1990s are intended for a larger (and most often Italian) public, for which she phrases her theses more firmly. I will show that notwithstanding the differences between the two texts, in both of them Irigaray's main problem with Merleau-Ponty's work is its lack of intersubjectivity. In line with her intentions to combine critique with utopian alternatives,[11] in these texts Irigaray also works out an alternative phenomenology of sexual difference, in which the ethical relationship to the other is of central concern. Thereby, she aims at opening up and elaborating Merleau-Ponty's notion of the body toward an ethical understanding. In the next section, I will explicate Merleau-Ponty's notion of corporeal intentionality. After that, I will connect it to Irigaray's notion of sexual intentionality.

Corporeal Intentionality

The phenomenological notion of intentionality, that is, the way we perceive the world and others, is worked out by Merleau-Ponty in the *Phenomenology of Perception* as corporeal. Merleau-Ponty starts out from what Husserl described as the intention of phenomenology, namely to return to the "things themselves." He understands Husserl's directive as returning to the experience that precedes science, namely the basic experience of the world. Whereas the human sciences understand man as the object of biological, psychological, or sociological investigation, and reduce existence to a moment of the world, phenomenology seeks to assess the basic experience of the world. Science is only the second-order expression of this basic experience. Merleau-Ponty understands this experience as embodied consciousness, through which "from the outset a world forms itself round me and begins to exist for me," as he writes in the Preface of *Phenomenology of Perception* (Merleau-Ponty 1999: ix/1945: iii). Perception therefore cannot be understood as an act of consciousness in an idealist, i.e. Cartesian and Kantian, sense. Cartesian and Kantian analytical reflection in a paradoxical movement starts from our experience of the world, but understands the subject as a condition of possibility distinct from that experience. (Merleau-Ponty 1999 ix/1945:iii) Although the world is given for the Cartesian Cogito, it ceases to be part of our experience, and instead is *reconstructed*. Husserl has seen this well, yet perception for him remains an act of consciousness. Merleau-Ponty rather understands perception as "the background from which all acts stand out" and which is presupposed by them: it is prereflective and prescientific experience. It is the expression of a dialogue between the perceived world and the perceiver. Instead of being the initiator of the act of perception, the perceiver is already absorbed in his situation: he is *au monde*, in and to the world.

Être au monde implies at once belonging to the world (being part of the world), being somewhere in the world (having a position), and having a relation to it, being oriented toward it.[12] The body is the condition for it: "The body is the vehicle of being in the world, and having a body is, for a living creature, to be intervolved in a definite environment" (Merleau-Ponty 1999: 82/1945: 97). In other words, the body is the subject of perception. The body provides the horizon and perspectival point, which places us in the world. It is primarily *corps propre*, one's own body, living and phenomenal, that brings about experiences and is present to itself in these experiences. Merleau-Ponty writes: ". . . my body is not only an object among all other objects (. . .), but an object which is *sensible to* all the rest . . ." (Merleau-Ponty 1999: 236/1945: 273). The body, in short, is our general medium for having a world at all. (Merleau-Ponty 1999: 146/1945: 171).

This notion of the body has inspired feminist philosophers from Butler to Young, but is also severely criticized.[13] Elizabeth Grosz summarizes the feminist critique in questioning Merleau-Ponty's avoidance of sexual difference and specificity, and his generalizations regarding subjectivity, which tend to take men's experiences for human ones.[14] By understanding Irigaray's notion of the body in line with Merleau-Ponty's, in this essay I will take this discussion further. My first claim is that Irigaray sexualizes the phenomenological body. As said earlier, this does not imply that Merleau-Ponty would exclude sexuality, but rather that I understand Irigaray as explicitly working out his notion of the body toward sexual difference—even though she criticizes that notion. For this claim, first, the main similarities between Merleau-Ponty's and Irigaray's notion of the body will have to be shown. In this section, I will outline some of the main traits of Merleau-Ponty's notion of the body; in the next section I will show that Irigaray maintains them.

Merleau-Ponty in *Phenomenology of Perception* argues that the object status of the body alone, that is central in Cartesian thinking, does not do justice to the way we perceive. Our body is not simply a thing, but rather the origin of the perceived world: it causes things to exist under our hands and eyes. Therefore, he understands the body as the subject of perception. However, that does not exclude that it is an object as well. It is a thing that is surrounded by other things, that appears in space and time, and that can be seen and experienced. In addition, the body is my situation. That means that human existence is situated. To be a body implies to be tied to a certain world (Merleau-Ponty 1999: 148/1945: 173). Being tied to your situation, to what is given, however, does not mean that one cannot transcend his or her situation. Embodiment also is freedom, in the sense that we can take up our situation and transform it. Being a body thus does not imply *absolute* freedom, that is, the freedom of the existentialists that is ontological and has to be realized in transcending our facticity, but being a body for Merleau-Ponty implies *situated* freedom.

At all times, the body is not strictly a biological being, and neither is biology simply the basis of our embodiment, as it is often understood. Rather, the body signifies its environment and giving the environment a biological meaning is only one possible way of signifying the environment. Sometimes the body is restricted to actions necessary for the conservation of life, and accordingly, writes Merleau-Ponty, the body "posits around us a biological world" (Merleau-Ponty 1999: 146/1945: 171). At other times, the body transforms the mere biological actions into more figurative ones, which happens in motor habits such as dancing, for instance. Then new significance is given to these basic actions. At still other times, the body projects around itself a cultural world, namely when the meaning aimed at cannot be achieved by the body's natural means.

Merleau-Ponty understands biology as basic, because it concerns the literal needs of our body to conserve life, but at the same time fulfilling these needs incorporates us in a cultural world. When we create a biological world around us, we give a specific meaning to the world, namely as a resource to fulfill our needs. Yet, we are not simply biological beings that create a culture around us—thus separating biology from culture—but biology is a way of giving meaning to the world.

That leads to the following characteristic of Merleau-Ponty's notion of the body, namely that it leaves behind the dichotomy of nature and culture. He elucidates that neither in the psycho-physiological realm, nor in the realm of instinct is there a human nature finally and immutably given. Rather, the body signifies its environment, and therefore entails transcendence. It is potentiality, "I can" (Merleau-Ponty 1999: 137/1945: 160). Merleau-Ponty does not strictly divide the two domains, but claims, "it is impossible to superimpose on man a lower layer of behavior which one chooses to call 'natural,' followed by a manufactured cultural or spiritual world" (Merleau-Ponty 1999: 189/1945: 220–221). Human existence is at once natural and cultural: "everything is both manufactured and natural in man" (ibid.). Every word, every behavior at the same time owes something to man as purely biological being, and eludes the simplicity of that, because it transforms and (re)creates the environment.

In conclusion, the intentionality of the body implicates having a certain position in the visible world that surrounds us, being oriented toward that world, and constituting it. The body cannot be understood outside of culture and history: as the possibility for having a world, the body is at once the vehicle of being in the world, and intervolved in an environment (Merleau-Ponty 1999: 82/1945: 97).

Sexuate Intentionality

While Merleau-Ponty speaks of the body in a general sense, and reflects on what human embodiment implies, for Irigaray the body is not neutral, but sexuate. Discussing the body in general for her includes a masculine "neutral" way of speaking. Therefore, she most often speaks of sexual difference, instead of "the body" or "embodiment."[15]

In discussing sexual difference, she consequently couples nature and culture, leaving the dichotomy between nature and culture behind. Similar to Merleau-Ponty, who put aside this dichotomy in his reflection on the body because the body takes part of both at once, for Irigaray sexual difference includes both at once. In *Je, tu, nous*, for instance, she claims that the body is not a strictly natural entity. She describes sexual difference as situated at the junction of nature and culture, and objects to understanding sexual difference as a simple, extra-linguistic fact of nature, because it conditions language and is conditioned by it (Irigaray 1993b: 20/1990: 23).

Sexual difference conditions language in the sense that language is not gender neutral. Irigaray understands language as a product of sedimentation that conveys former languages' methods of social communication.[16] She does not consider linguistic structures to be universal in the brain of the speaking subject; rather, every era has its specific historic traits, of which sexual ideals are part. These have imposed their norms on the language we presently use. For the French language that includes among others that the masculine is dominant in syntax, and that the neuter or impersonal is expressed by the same pronoun as the masculine.

More important for our theme is that language conditions sexual difference. Irigaray's Lacanian background and her empirical linguistic research,[17] in which she analyzed speech utterances by men and women, convinced her of the connection between sex and the use of language. Men and women, she argues, use language in different ways. Particularly, while women privilege the relationships between two subjects, men tend to relate subject and object. This interweaving of sex and language implies that nature and culture, and the body as biological and cultural, cannot be perceived as distinct from each other. For neither Irigaray nor Merleau-Ponty, is the body strictly biological, or an "extralinguistic fact of nature," because it is always embedded in language, in culture.

Not only is the body not something strictly natural or something that exists outside of language, Irigaray also connects the body and consciousness. In *To Be Two* she speaks of "body-consciousness" (*corps-conscience*), in the context of a critique of a Sartrian notion of the body as simple natural facticity or factuality (Irigaray 2000: 33/1997: 62). In what follows, I will consider Sartre's notion of desire and compare Irigaray's comments with Merleau-Ponty's account of sexuality in *Phenomenology of Perception*. Merleau-Ponty in the chapter on sexuality also, in an implicit manner, reacts to Sartre. The comparison will enable us to envision the similarities as well as the differences between Irigaray's and Merleau-Ponty's account of the body.

For Sartre, in desire, the embodied consciousnesses that we are, decide to be factual. In desire, consciousness chooses to exist its facticity on another plane. Facticity is no longer fled, rather consciousness attempts to subordinate itself to its own contingency (Sartre 1966: 475/1943: 429). Desire is an individual "act" of being swallowed up in one's own body in addition to desiring the Other's body. "I make myself flesh *in the presence of the Other in order to appropriate the Other's flesh*," he writes (ibid.).

Irigaray in her interpretation of this passage stresses the activity of the lover toward the beloved, and does not pay much attention to the activity of the lover toward him/herself. She writes that for Sartre entering into a sexual relationship with the other includes "making" his consciousness descend into his body, and "paralyzing" his liberty (Irigaray 2000: 18/1997: 36–37). Desire aims at possession of the other, as a body with consciousness. She objects to the reduction of the other that is inherent in Sartre's account of desire, and to the principal conflict in the relationship between self and other. Yet, for Sartre desire must include that the self becomes flesh, otherwise the other *and* desire will escape me.

With respect to the body, the main problem for Irigaray is that even though Sartre acknowledges that the concrete relationship with the other is corporeal, there no longer is a bridge between the body and consciousness: the corporeal is split between a consciousness-gaze and a body-facticity (Irigaray 2000: 31/1997: 59). In contrast, for her, embodiment, and more specifically belonging to a gender, is not isolated from consciousness, but already involves consciousness. "In so far as I belong to a gender, my body (. . .) already involves a for-itself. It is not simple factuality or 'facticity,' but is already consciousness" (Irigaray 2000: 30/1997: 58). In other words, for Irigaray consciousness already inheres in embodiment, or more specifically, belonging to a gender. Being a body is not simply the facticity of *pour-soi*, as it is for Sartre, but is already consciousness.

In Merleau-Ponty's account of sexuality a similar argument is made. In the chapter on sexuality in *Phenomenology of Perception* he implicitly refers to Sartre (Merleau-Ponty 1962: 154–173/1945: 180–202). Sexuality for him is, as for Sartre, a way of relating to others. Moreover, both aim at a notion of sexuality in which it is not reduced to a psycho-physiological phenomenon. Yet, sexuality for Merleau-Ponty does not imply wanting to possess the other as pure transcendence and as body,[18] and reducing the other to his or her body, but rather signifying the other as sexually attractive. Sexuality is the constitution of a world: it arises from experiencing a situation as sexual. That means transcendence is inherent in sexual desire. In desiring someone we give him or her a sexual significance. Sexuality for Merleau-Ponty is a specific, always accessible dimension of relating to the other, which demands openness to the other, and does not inherently imply conflict with the other. Instead of bringing the consciousness of the other to his body and thereby keeping up a distinction between body and consciousness, Merleau-Ponty holds that embodiment in itself entails consciousness.

Embodiment entails consciousness in the sense that having a body includes signifying the world and others around us, as we have seen earlier. In the case of sexuality, giving meaning to others around us leads to perceiving the other as sexually attractive, and desiring him or her. It is precisely this notion of embodiment in which the body signifies our environment that associates Irigaray's notion of the body with Merleau-Ponty's. For both, body and consciousness do not coincide, but must be taken together. For both we are embodied beings, who, as body-subjects, give meaning to other beings and things in our environment.

Yet, in her reflection on carnal love, Irigaray does not agree with Merleau-Ponty's consideration of sexuality, but associates it with Sartre's. She says that his account of sexuality remains close to Sartre because he claims that in desiring another we aim at possessing him, as a body animated by consciousness (Irigaray 2000: 21/1997: 42). Indeed, for Merleau-Ponty, in sexuality our body becomes an object for the other, while remaining subject for the self. The body has a double structure, which results from being at once the subject of perception, that is, being able to perceive the world, and an object for others, insofar as my body is part of the world. On the basis of this subject-object structure of the body, Merleau-Ponty speaks of a dialectical structure in sexuality, which can be described as "the tending of an existence towards another existence which denies it, and yet without which it is not sustained" (Merleau-Ponty 1962: 168/1945: 195). Thus, it is not because of his closeness to Sartre—for whom the self-other relationship is a relationship of conflict—that Merleau-Ponty speaks of a dialectical structure in sexuality, but because of the double structure of the body.

By associating Merleau-Ponty's account of sexuality with Sartre's, Irigaray not only misunderstands Merleau-Ponty's notion of sexuality, by claiming that desire is about possession of the other, for we have seen that instead sexuality for Merleau-Ponty implies giving meaning to another. Also, she mistakes his notion of the body for one in which body and consciousness are separated, and in which consciousness animates the body, instead of seeing that for Merleau-Ponty embodiment in itself includes consciousness. And thirdly, she takes a larger distance from Merleau-Ponty than she should, for she, just like Merleau-Ponty, understands the body as at once subject and object. The difference between both thinkers is that Irigaray argues for the subject-object status of the body on the basis of gender: "in so far as I belong to a gender, my body already represents an objectivity for me" (Irigaray 2000: 21/1997: 42). Belonging to a gender realizes a dialectic between subjectivity and objectivity that escapes the dichotomy between them. Irigaray, rather, aims at a further complication of the dialectical structure Merleau-Ponty envisioned, than introducing an element that is completely absent in his thought. Also for Merleau-Ponty my body can be an object for me: in perception I can see and touch my own hand. Even though in *Phenomenology of Perception* with respect to sexuality he only works out the aspect of being object for the other, he does not ignore the objectivity of one's own body. Thus, Irigaray *elaborates* his phenomenological sketch of the body, more than she is able to criticize it.

Yet, in her account of embodiment as sexuate Irigaray more than Merleau-Ponty opens the path to intersubjectivity. Besides making it possible to think the relationship of the individual to his/her gender, gender as objectivity helps in perceiving the other as other. Along these lines, Irigaray draws the consequences of the double structure of the body and opens it up to an ethics.

Gender as Objectivity

For Irigaray the body represents an objectivity because it belongs to a *genre*.[19] In other words, there is a dialectical structure inherent in having a body itself. Dialectics is not reserved for the relationship to the other, but is already present in one's own embodiment, namely in the relationship of the individual to its genre.

In describing the aim of *Speculum of the Other Woman*, Irigaray specifies this dialectic. Her aim was "to construct an objectivity that facilitates a dialectic proper to the female subject, meaning specific relations between her nature and her culture, her same and her other, her singularity and the community, her interiority and her exteriority, etc. . . ." (Irigaray 1996: 62/1992: 106). Thus, dialectics pertains to the relationship between one's singularity, that is, one's particular history and genealogy,[20] and one's collective history, namely the history of one's genre. Also, it concerns the relationship between one's body, "nature" or "natural identity," and what Irigaray calls "a culture particular to this sex and this gender (*genre*)" (Irigaray 1996: 27/1992: 53). Culture here does not refer to human culture at large, but rather to development, growth. Thereby, it is of particular importance to be able to develop one's own individual relationship to one's genre and to the other genre (cf. "her same and her other"). Thus, Irigaray stresses the importance of *individual* development, in relationship to one's personal and collective history. A woman "should not comply with a model of identity imposed on her by anyone, neither her parents, her lover, her children, the State, religion or culture in general" (ibid.). The same goes for men. For both men and women a dialectical relationship to their genre should be established. Irigaray writes that what we need is "a dialectic of the relation of woman to herself and of man to himself, a double dialectics therefore, enabling a real, cultured and ethical relation between them" (Irigaray 1996: 39/1992: 72). This double dialectics entails that women and men should both for themselves develop "the accomplishment" of their gender.

The accomplishment of one's genre implies that having a sexuated identity is not something that is immediately given with the body or a simple natural fact, but that it involves development. Gender identity, for Irigaray, is a process of becoming, not of being or having. With regard to this point, her critique of Simone de Beauvoir—whose work is usually associated with *becoming*, instead of *being* a woman—is illuminating. Irigaray writes: "It's not as

Simone de Beauvoir said: one is not born, but rather becomes a woman (through culture), but rather: I am born a woman, but I must still become this woman that I am by nature" (Irigaray 1996: 107/1992: 168). For Irigaray, as for Beauvoir, gender identity entails a process of becoming: you have to become your gender, you are not your gender from the start. Having a sex is perhaps the necessary condition for, but is not in itself sufficient for having a gender identity. Yet, whereas Beauvoir—in an attempt to escape the situation of woman in her times—is strongly anti-naturalistic, Irigaray points to the fact that physiology should not be forgotten in becoming one's *genre*: "Of course, there is no question of [identity] being constructed in repudiation of one's physiology" (Irigaray 1996: 107/1992: 168). Instead, patriarchal culture should be opened up so that it allows women *and* men to develop identities in relationship to their sexuate bodies.

Thus, for Irigaray the body takes part in the construction of identity, yet identity is not given with the body. She writes: "no doubt female physiology is present but not identity, which remains to be constructed" (ibid.). In that sense "bodily women" have to become "cultural women," and Beauvoir and Irigaray are not so far apart as is often claimed.[21] Yet, gender identity is not *only* a construction for Irigaray. We just saw that one's physiology should not be forgotten. That means that the development of gender identity also entails elaborating who you already are. It is a process that involves not only the activity of the subject, but also passivity, or respect for the boundaries that embodiment includes. Belonging to a gender "is in part passivity, fidelity to the being I am, being given to me by nature and which I must endorse, respect and cultivate as one half of human identity" (Irigaray 1996: 107/1992: 167).

The development of a gender identity, in other words, starts from recognizing that we belong to a gender, which entails being part of something that is larger than oneself, being part of a community. Every individual has to accomplish that belonging in relation to her or his particular destiny (Irigaray 1996: 39/1992: 72). Irigaray in this respect also speaks of "accomplishing one's gender's perfection" (Irigaray 1996: 27/1992: 53). That is not an ideal that is similar for all women, but rather something that every woman (and every man) has to achieve by gathering her(him)self within her(him)self, and that every individual has to do for her- or himself. It is an individual task that everyone has to perform starting from her or his individual history and genealogy.

Returning to Merleau-Ponty's notion of the body, we can conclude that Irigaray understands the body as a subject that, in belonging to a gender, at once forms an objectivity. Thereby she complicates Merleau-Ponty's dialectics of subject-for-me object-for-the-other within sexuality. Irigaray explicates it as follows: "Belonging to a gender allows me to realize, in me, for me—and equally towards the other—a dialectic between subjectivity and objectivity which escapes the dichotomy between subject and object" (Irigaray 2000: 21/1997: 42). Gender as objectivity also bridges the Sartrian body-consciousness dichotomy. For the body is no longer a simple facticity, but contains a for-itself: it is "in-itself-for-itself," writes Irigaray (Irigaray 2000: 33/1997: 62). As such it represents a meaning for the other. Therefore, the body is not facticity but relationship with—"with me"—that is, my body relates to my subjectivity—"with my gender"—my body makes me belong to a gender—"with the other gender"—my body makes me have a meaning for the other gender (ibid.).

Thus, apart from relating one to one's own gender, gender as objectivity also brings on consequences for the relationship to the other gender. "Belonging to a gender represents a destination to the other more than it represents a biological destiny," writes Irigaray (ibid.). It is precisely this point, the relationship with the other that Irigaray misses in Merleau-Ponty's account of the body and sexuality. In this section we have seen that by means of belonging to a gender we relate to our bodies as objectivity. Thereby, Irigaray works out Merleau-Ponty's account of the double structure of the body, in which it is at once subject and object of perception. In the next section I will show in what respect gender as objectivity helps in perceiving the other as other.

A Phenomenological Ethics of Alterity

Irigaray claims that Merleau-Ponty's account of sexuality does not "favor the emergence of intersubjectivity." Rather, sexuality "maintains a duplicity in subjectivity itself in such a way that all of its actions, its sentiments, its sensations are ambiguous, murky, and incapable of being turned towards an other as other" (Irigaray 2000: 21/1997: 42). Instead of encountering the other, in Merleau-Ponty's account of sexuality, Irigaray argues, we only relate to ourselves. In short, Irigaray criticizes Merleau-Ponty not only for not escaping the subject-object dichotomy, but also for not understanding sexuality as intersubjective, as relationship to the other as other.

Also in the earlier text, "The Invisible of the Flesh," she criticized Merleau-Ponty for not considering intersubjectivity. There she investigates the notion of the flesh in *The Visible and the Invisible* that Merleau-Ponty brings into play for considering the intertwinement of subject and world, subject and other.[22] Trying to overcome the dichotomy of subject and object of perception, Merleau-Ponty in his latest text claims that they are reversible. Whereas he earlier thought the body as subject of perception and at the same time as part of the visible world, he now introduces the notion of the flesh as covering seer and seen, toucher and tangible. The flesh is the invisible other, a radical form of alterity that makes perception possible. Irigaray, in her commentary on

Merleau-Ponty's text, claims to support his call to recommence everything. Yet, for her recommencing implies bringing the maternal-feminine into language. As early as *Speculum of the Other Woman*—notably the third part on Plato's allegory of the cave—she calls upon us to relate to that forgotten, repressed origin. Merleau-Ponty's text reminds her of that origin, but she claims that he repeats the masculine gesture. Nostalgically, he appropriates it, instead of relating to it as his other (Irigaray 1993: 152–153/1984: 143–144).

Irigaray's main problem is Merleau-Ponty's alleged solipsism. She writes that in the world of the flesh, the subject and world collapse: I and world "form a closed economy." "Merleau-Ponty's seer remains in an incestuous prenatal situation with the whole," which is a mode of existence that she identifies with all men, at least in the West. Intersubjectivity, she maintains, is lacking in his account of the relationship I-world and I-other: "Although a pertinent analysis of the way I form a weave of sensations with the world, [Merleau-Ponty's] is one that excludes solitude even though its own systematization is solipsistic. This seer is never alone, he dwells unceasingly in his world. Eventually he finds some accomplices there, but he never meets others" (Irigaray 1993: 173/1984: 162). Irigaray misses an account of the place, of the alterity of the other. Thereby, as Cecilia Sjöholm argues, she does not give sufficient credit to the alterity that the flesh presents (Sjöholm 2000: 96). Apart from that, she also doesn't mention her reflections on the elements in *Elemental Passions* and *The Forgetting of Air*, that are very close to this notion of the flesh.[23] But let us concentrate on Irigaray's critique. Her aim is to break the solitude inherent in Merleau-Ponty's notion of the flesh. His remains a solipsistic ontology, she asserts, since he does not see the other "whose body's ontological status would differ from mine" (Irigaray 1993: 157/1984: 148). Merleau-Ponty's subject in a way never enters the world: "he never emerges from an osmosis that allows him to say to the other, 'Who art thou?,' but also 'Who am I?'" (Irigaray 1993: 183/1984: 170). Irigaray's critique is that alterity by Merleau-Ponty is not thought radically enough as alterity of the other. The maternal-feminine and the flesh can perhaps be associated, yet Merleau-Ponty's universe doesn't recognize real alterity, that is, the radical otherness of another being.

In the later text on Merleau-Ponty, in *To Be Two*, Irigaray expands upon this critique. She interprets perception as a means of acceding to the other, as a possible path of sensing the other, while at the same time the perceiver remains a subject (Irigaray 2000: 22/1997: 44). The objectivity of belonging to a gender helps to perceive the relationship to the other in this manner. It at once makes me aware of my own limitations, namely that I represent only half of mankind, hence, that I am not the whole.[24] Hence, it limits the self's narcissism. But this limitation also creates a space for the other to become.

The notion of the negative that Irigaray elaborates in *I Love To You* is illuminating in this respect. To develop this notion, Irigaray adds Hegelian dialectics. She claims in the Prologue to have discovered another meaning of the Hegelian negative, and considers this insight to be an important breakthrough for her work. She describes it as follows: "the negative can mean access to the other of sexual difference." It means "an acceptance of the limits of my gender and recognition of the irreducibility of the other" (Irigaray 1996: 13/1992: 32). The negative in sexual difference makes us aware of the limit imposed on us by our *genre*. This limitation is not a restriction, but for Irigaray is a constitutive or affirmative limit. It is the finitude discussed earlier in this essay, that we relate to in a passive manner, and that is vital for our identity.

Earlier in this essay, in describing Merleau-Ponty's notion of corporeal intentionality, I characterized the phenomenological account of the body as situated freedom. Being embodied entails being bound to one's situation, immanence, but also transcendence in the form of transformation of this situation. Irigaray's notion of the negative further elaborates this thought by inscribing finiteness in embodiment because of belonging to a gender. Sexual difference represents a negative within each individual: "Being sexuate implies a negative, a not being the other, a not being the whole, and a particular way of being: tied to the body and in relationship with the other" (Irigaray 2000: 34/1997: 63). The negative enables me to have an ethical relationship to the other of the other genre. Transcendence, in other words, does not only refer to signifying the world and others as it does for Merleau-Ponty, but also means relating to the other gender.

The notion of the negative also implies, apart from the fact that "you are not the whole, and I am not the whole," that we are not reducible to each other (Irigaray 1996: 103/1992: 161). We may not be substituted for one another. So the other is transcendent to me, and also transcendence reigns between us, that is, there is a resistance between us. The negative has an important function as the limit imposed on us by our gender, which should be recognized. Only by recognizing my own limits, can I meet the other in respect for his or her otherness, and recognize him or her as other. Recognizing this limit creates a space for the other, because he is no longer understood as the same, or destroyed. The negative creates an interval between them. Yet, apart from isolating one and the other, it is also the condition for the possibility of having a relationship with the other. For precisely the transcendence of the other makes him or her a mystery to me and enables an unending attraction between us.

Irigaray's negative in sexual difference is an ethical notion that at once enables development of the self and a respectful relationship to the other. On the basis of a phenomenological account of the body herewith she works out an ethics, in which finiteness and otherness are central categories. Her phenomenology of the caress in *To Be Two* illustrates very well the concern with embodied intersubjectivity.[25] She explicitly aims at describing the caress "corresponding to her female desire or will," and describes it as being awake to you, me, us (Irigaray 2000: 25/1997: 50). It is an awakening of the life of my body, that is most of the time inhibited by everyday activity. At the same time it is awakening to intersubjectivity, to touching the other and being touched by the other. Instead of Merleau-Ponty's ambiguity of the body in desire (subject for me and object for the other), and Sartre's making the other an object for me as desiring subject (or vice versa), Irigaray stresses the double intention of wanting to return to myself, in me, and wanting to be with the other, with you. The caress is a gift of conscience, of intention and also of parole addressed to the concrete presence of the other. She describes it as gesture-word, which returns the other to him- or herself, while I also return to myself.

Self-Limitation as Basis for Recognition of Otherness

My intention in writing this essay was to show that Irigaray's basic intuitions regarding the body are close to those of one of her predecessors in French postwar philosophy, Merleau-Ponty. Although Irigaray speaks of sexual difference rather than a neutral sense of embodiment or "the body," and notwithstanding her severe criticisms of Merleau-Ponty, which we have seen to be doubtful, the resemblances between her notion of the body and Merleau-Ponty's are striking. For both, embodiment entails consciousness. For both, the body is not a strictly biological being, but cultural, in the sense that we give meaning to our environment and understand our bodies by means of language. For both the body is at once subject and object.[26]

Yet, Irigaray elaborates Merleau-Ponty's notion of the neutral body toward a sexually differentiated one. Therewith, she does not take a distance from Merleau-Ponty, as she intends to, but further works out his notion of the body. By understanding the body as sexuate, she thinks intersubjectivity and escapes the solipsism inherent within Merleau-Ponty's thought. The phenomenology of sexual difference it results in is a phenomenology that reflects on being two, on relating to the other, in short: a phenomenology that is intersubjective.

Such a phenomenology of sexual difference cannot be charged with essentialism anymore. We have seen that a phenomenological account of the body is not essentialistic, because it does not consider the body as a fixed, a-historical, a-cultural ground for identity. We have also seen that it is Irigaray's specific intention for women (and men) to be able to develop their individual embodied identities. She doesn't opt for a universal femininity. In accordance with this conception of embodiment, in the last decade the main critique of Irigaray is no longer her supposed essentialism. The main critique her work faces now is that she privileges sexual differences over and above other differences, such as race, class, age, health.[27] What does that imply for the phenomenology of sexual difference she develops?

In itself sexual difference does not exclude other differences. For Irigaray sexual difference is the first we are confronted with in our lives. She thinks that respecting it can open the way to perceiving other differences: "... I think that it's because I'm able to situate *there* [in the difference between man and woman] the difference and the negative which I will never surmount . . . , that I'm able to respect the differences everywhere: differences between the other races, differences between the generations, and so on. Because I've placed a limit on my horizon, on my power" (Irigaray 1995: 110). Understood in this sense, the negative would apply to other differences as well, and would entail at once recognition of self-limitation on the basis of gender, skin color, age, physical health, and other embodied differences, *and* respect for the other as other.

In her latest works Irigaray seems sensitive to that idea. Even though she in earlier work considered sexual difference to be prior, and other differences secondary, recently she seems more open to considering diverse differences next to each other. In *I Love To You* she writes: "The problem of race is, in fact, a secondary problem—except from a geographical point of view?—which means that we cannot see the wood for the trees, and the same goes for other cultural diversities—religious, economic and political ones" (Irigaray 1996: 47/1992: 84–85). But in *Democracy Begins Between Two* Irigaray claims that sexual difference can be a model for respecting other differences. When man and woman as pair, living together, are able to respect each other, they perhaps could also respect other others.[28]

Applying the negative to other differences would imply developing not only a phenomenology of sexual difference in Irigarayan style, but phenomenologies of other embodied differences as well. It would mean a definite break with the neutral notion of the body in Merleau-Ponty's *Phenomenology of Perception*—but only with its neutrality and not with his conception of the body in itself as that what makes it that we have a position in the world and are oriented toward that world, and constitute a world around us. And, finally, it would signify a possibility for ethical accounts of the body. Ethics, in this respect, means first and foremost a call for self-limitation. Respect for otherness starts namely with acknowledging one's own finiteness. And there is nothing that makes us aware of that more pervasively than our embodiment.

Notes

I am grateful to Jenny Slatman, Veronica Vasterling, Agnès Vincenot, the editor of this volume, Gail Weiss, and an anonymous reviewer for their helpful suggestions and critical comments to earlier drafts of this paper.

1. References will be made to the English translation (before the dash), and to the French original (after the dash).

2. "Phenomenology in the feminine" is a refinement of Margaret Whitford's "philosophy in the feminine" (1991). Whitford in her introduction to Irigaray observes her ambiguity toward phenomenology. She writes that Irigaray is sympathetic to notions such as language, body, and ethics, which are elaborated particularly by Heidegger, Merleau-Ponty, and Levinas, but that she also points out the reproduction of the imperatives of the male body in their philosophies (1991: 151–152).

3. Although Irigaray's work is often perceived as breaking with Beauvoir's (see for instance Chanter 1995: 73–79)—especially because she aims at difference instead of equality—I understand Irigaray as also for a large part continuous with Beauvoir. Not only does she start from Beauvoir's Hegelian diagnosis of the situation of women, but both as well share a phenomenological view of the body as our way of being in the world (see Heinämaa 2003: xviii, and the relationship between Irigaray and Beauvoir described later in this essay).

4. See for this discussion: Fuss 1989; Schor 1989; Burke, Schor & Whitford 1994, part 1 of which contains several essays on Irigaray and essentialism; Chanter 1995. Alison Stone has given a new impulse to the discussion about Irigaray's essentialism, by claiming that in her late works she develops a radical form of realist essentialism that has the advantage of generating a powerful political theory (Stone 2003).

5. See 'The Body in Its Sexual Being' (Merleau-Ponty 1999: 154–173/1945: 180–202).

6. See for a very interesting feminist elaboration of Merleau-Ponty's philosophy of sexual being Silvia Stoller's dissertation (2006).

7. In contrast, Olkowski 2000 argues against the fact that Irigaray is most of the time seen as adhering to phenomenology, despite her critique of Merleau-Ponty. Olkowski aims at showing that Irigaray reveals the limits of phenomenology, rather than adhering to it. Notwithstanding her essay, mine starts from the assumption that Irigaray's closeness to phenomenology is not elaborated very well yet. In that respect my essay is closer to Sjöholm's—in the same issue of *Hypatia* as Olkowski—who argues that, even though Irigaray differs from Merleau-Ponty in important respects, she does share some basic intuitions concerning body, language, and phenomenal experience with him (2000: 93).

8. See Mortensen 1994, Chanter 1995, Vasseleu 1998, Heinämaa 2005.

9. L. Irigaray, "An Invisible of the Flesh," in: *An Ethics of Sexual Difference*. 1993, pp. 151–184. French original: "L'invisible de la chair," in: *L'éthique de la différence sexuelle*. 1984, pp. 143–171. See also on this text: Grosz 1994 and 1999, Kozel 1996, Ainley 1997.

10. L. Irigaray, chapter 2 and 3 in *To Be Two*, 2000. French version: *Être deux*. Paris: Grasset, 1997. Originally published in Italian: *Essere due*. Torino: Bollati Boringhieri, 1994. References will be made to the English translation and to the French version that is translated from the Italian by Luce Irigaray.

11. Irigaray refuses a strict division of the critical and utopian elements of her work. Instead, deconstruction and positive values should go hand in hand: "In order to criticize we need a horizon, a perspective from which we can criticize. A critique without an affirmative place from which it starts is a sensual reaction ..., a death drive, an impotence to construct, nihilism without a future" (Irigaray 1987: 153, my translation).

12. See Slatman 2003.

13. See Butler 1989, Young 1990. See also Stoller 2000 and 2006, who defends Merleau-Ponty against the accusation of ignoring differences.

14. See Grosz 1994, 1999.

15. Except for those places where she discusses how patriarchal language excludes the maternal body, and suggests that the body and language should be connected in understanding subjectivity. See for instance "Body Against Body: In Relation to the Mother"(1993a: 7–21/1987: 19–33), "The wedding between body and language" (2000: 17–29/1997: 35–55).

16. See "Women's Discourse and Men's Discourse" in *Je, tu, nous* (1993b: 29–36/1990: 35–44), and for this specific argument 1993b: 30/1990: 38. See also on language *I Love To You*, chapter 6 and 7 (1996: 69–95/1992: 117–150), and the volume edited by Irigaray, *Sexes et genres à travers les langues* (1990).

17. See for the results of Irigaray's researches among others 1996: 69–95/1992: 117–150.

18. That is how Sartre describes the ideal of desire: "to possess the Other's transcendence as pure transcendence and at the same time as *body*, to reduce the Other to simple facticity because he is then in the midst of my world but to bring it about that this facticity is a perpetual appresentation of his nihilating transcendence" (1966: 482/1943: 434).

19. The French *genre* is in this essay translated as gender, without thereby alluding to the sex/gender distinction. The French genre refers to grammatical gender, a style of discourse, or *genre humain* (humankind), and is broader than the sexual dichotomy. In her early works Irigaray often uses the word *sexe* (sex) instead of *genre* in order to avoid the traditional connotations associated with the latter (Irigaray 1993b: 31, footnote 3/1990: 38, footnote 2), but in her later works, starting with *Sexes and Genealogies*, she uses *genre* more often than *sexe*.

20. "This woman's singularity is in having a particular genealogy and history" Irigaray 1996: 39/1992: 72.

21. For instance by Schor 1989; Chanter 1995: 73–79.

22. Elizabeth Grosz summarizes Irigaray's objections in three points: 1. the dominance of vision in his writings submits them to a phallic economy in which the feminine figures as a lack or blind spot; 2. the concept of the flesh is implicitly coded in terms of the attributes of the feminine; 3. Merleau-Ponty disavows the debt that the flesh owes to maternity (1994: 104–107).

23. For instance in *The Forgetting of Air* air is the condition of possibility for perception, for light and dark, for voice, for presence and absence. Within the philosoph-

ical history "air would be the forgotten material mediation of the logos" (Irigaray 1999: 11/1983: 17). Air is the sensible transcendental condition, or the "physical ground" for all the oppositions that constitute the structure of metaphysics.

24. See Irigaray 1996: 103/1992: 161.

25. The phenomenology of the caress is elaborated in response to Levinas' "Phenomenology of Eros" in *Totality and Infinity*. Note that in *An Ethics of Sexual Difference* Irigaray also reinterprets this chapter, in "The Fecundity of the Caress" (1993: 185–217/1984: 173–199).

26. Intermediate in understanding the body as our place in the world for Irigaray is perhaps Simone de Beauvoir, who is acknowledged to adhere to Merleau-Ponty's body-concept. (See her description of the body as situation in *The Second Sex*, Beauvoir 1953.) That explains why Irigaray's work cannot simply be seen as opposing Beauvoir's, as she positions it herself (see the quote from *I Love To You* earlier in this text, note 3, and the first essay in *Je, tu, nous*, "A personal note: Equal or different?" 1993b: 9–14/1990: 9–15), she also continues Beauvoir's existential phenomenological sketch of women's situation in patriarchy.

27. Rosi Braidotti, for instance, writes that we "need more complexities both in terms of genders and across ethnicities, class and age" (2002: 15). See also Deutscher 2002 for the relationship between sexual difference and other differences, especially race and ethnicity, in Irigaray's later work.

28. See Irigaray 2001: 141. I must admit that in understanding sexual difference as *model* the priority of sexual difference over other differences is maintained. Such a priority over differences such as ethnicity and religion is hard to uphold in contemporary European multicultural societies, where the latter are more salient than sexual difference—even though sexual difference never loses its relevance. Besides developing phenomenologies of other embodied differences, what remains to be done are reflections upon the intertwinement of these phenomenologies.

References

Ainley, A. (1997). "The Invisible of the Flesh": Merleau-Ponty and Irigaray. *Journal of the British Society for Phenomenology* (1) 28: 20–29.

Beauvoir, Simone de (1953). *The Second Sex*. Trans. H. M. Parshley. Harmondsworth: Penguin.

Braidotti, R. (2002). *Metamorphoses. Towards a Materialist Theory of Becoming*. Oxford: Polity Press.

Burke, C., N. Schor, & M. Whitford (Eds.) (1994). *Engaging with Irigaray*. New York: Columbia University Press.

Butler, J. (1989). "Sexual Ideology and Phenomenological Description. A Feminist Critique of Merleau-Ponty's *Phenomenology of Perception*." In: *The Thinking Muse. Feminism and Modern French Philosophy*. Eds. J. Allen & I. M. Young. Bloomington & Indianapolis: Indiana University Press, 85–100.

────── (1990). *Gender Trouble. Feminism and the Subversion of Identity*. New York & London: Routledge.

Chanter, T. (1995). *Ethics of Eros. Irigaray's Rewriting of the Philosophers*. New York & London: Routledge.

Deutscher, P. (2002). *A Politics of Impossible Difference. The Later Work of Luce Irigaray*. Ithaca & London: Cornell University Press.

Fuss, D. (1989). "'Essentially Speaking': Luce Irigaray's Language of Essence." *Hypatia* (3) 3: 62–80.

Grosz, E. (1994). *Volatile Bodies. Toward a Corporeal Feminism*. Bloomington & Indianapolis: Indiana University Press.

────── (1999). "Merleau-Ponty and Irigaray in the Flesh." In *Merleau-Ponty, Interiority and Exteriority, Psychic Life and the World*. Eds. D. Olkowski & J. Morley. Albany: State University of New York Press, 145–166.

Halsema, A. (1998). *Dialectiek van de seksuele differentie. De filosofie van Luce Irigaray*. Amsterdam: Boom. (English title: *Dialectics of Sexual Difference. The Philosophy of Luce Irigaray*.)

Heinämaa, S. (1997). "What is a Woman? Butler and Beauvoir on the Foundations of the Sexual Difference." *Hypatia* (12) 1: 20–39.

────── (2003). *Toward a Phenomenology of Sexual Difference. Husserl, Merleau-Ponty, Beauvoir*. Lanham: Rowman& Littlefield.

────── (2005). "Verwunderung und sexuelle Differenz. Luce Irigarays phänomenologischer Cartesianismus." In *Feministische Phänomenologie und Hermeneutik*. Eds. S. Stoller, V. Vasterling & L. Fisher, Würzburg: Königshausen & Neumann, 192–207.

Irigaray, L. (1985a). *Speculum of the Other Woman*. Trans. G. C. Gill. Ithaca, New York: Cornell University Press. [*Speculum de l'autre femme*. Paris: Minuit, 1974]

────── (1985b). *This Sex Which is Not One*. Trans. C. Porter. New York: Cornell University Press. [*Ce sexe qui n'en est pas un*. Paris: Minuit, 1977].

────── (1987). *Luce Irigaray. Zur Geschlechterdifferenz Interviews und Vorträge*. Vienna: Wiener Frauenverlag.

────── (Ed.) (1990). *Sexes et genres à travers les langues*. Paris: Grasset.

────── (1991). Interview. In *Shifting Scenes. Interviews on Women, Writing, and Politics in Post-68 France*. Eds. A. A. Jardine & A. M. Menke, New York: Columbia University Press, 97–103.

────── (1992). *Elemental Passions*. Trans. J. Collie & J. Still. London: Athlone [*Passions élémentaires*. Paris: Minuit, 1982].

────── (1993). *An Ethics of Sexual Difference*. Trans. C. Burke & G. C. Gill. Ithaca, New York: Cornell University Press [*L'éthique de la différence sexuelle*. Paris: Minuit, 1984].

——— (1993a). *Sexes and Genealogies.* Trans. G. C. Gill. New York: Columbia University Press [*Sexes et parentés.* Paris: Minuit, 1987].

——— (1993b). *Je, tu, nous. Toward a Culture of Difference.* Trans. A. Martin. New York & London: Routledge [*Je, tu, nous. Pour une culture de la différence.* Paris: Grasset, 1990].

——— (1995). "Je—Luce Irigaray": A Meeting with Luce Irigaray, interview by Elizabeth Hirsch & Gary A. Olson. *Hypatia* (10), nr. 2, pp. 93–114.

——— (1996). *I Love To You. Sketch of a Possible Felicity in History.* Trans. A. Martin. New York & London: Routledge [*J'aime à toi. Esquisse d'un félicité dans l'histoire.* Paris: Grasset, 1992].

——— (1999). *The Forgetting of Air in Martin Heidegger.* Trans. M.-B. Mader. London: Athlone Press [*L'oubli de l'air chez Martin Heidegger.* Paris: Minuit, 1983].

——— (2000). *To Be Two.* Trans. M. M. Rhodes & M. F. Cocito-Monoc. London & New Brunswick: Athlone [*Être deux.* Paris: Grasset, 1997. Originally published in Italian: *Essere due.* Torino: Bollati Boringhieri, 1994].

——— (2001). *Democracy Begins Between Two.* Trans. K. Anderson. New York: Routledge.

——— (2002). *To Speak Is Never Neutral.* Trans. G. Schwab. London: Continuum [*Parler n'est jamais neutre.* Paris: Minuit, 1985].

Kozel, S. (1996). "The Diabolical Strategy of Mimesis: Luce Irigaray's Reading of Maurice Merleau-Ponty." *Hypatia* (11) 3: 114–129.

Merleau-Ponty, M. (1968). *The Visible and the Invisible.* Ed. C. Lefort, Trans. A. Lingis. Evanston: Northwestern University Press [*Le visible et l'invisible.* Ed. C. Lefort, Paris: Gallimard, 1964].

——— (1999). *The Phenomenology of Perception.* Trans. C. Smith. London & New York: Routledge [*Phénoménologie de la perception.* Paris: Gallimard, 1945].

Mortensen, E. (1994). *The Feminine and Nihilism. Luce Irigaray with Nietzsche and Heidegger.* Oslo, Kopenhagen: Scandinavian University Press.

Olkowski, D. (2000). "The End of Phenomenology: Bergson's Interval in Irigaray." *Hypatia* (15) 3: 73–91.

Sartre, J. P. (1966). *Being and Nothingness. An Essay on Phenomenological Ontology.* Trans. H. E. Barnes. New York: Washington Square Press [*L'être et le néant. Essai d'ontologie phénoménologique.* Paris: Gallimard, 1943].

Schor, N. (1994). "This Essentialism Which is Not One. Coming to Grips with Irigaray." In *Engaging With Irigaray*, Eds. C. Burke & N. Schor & M. Whitford, New York: Columbia University Press, 57–78.

Sjöholm, C. (2000). "Crossing Lovers: Luce Irigaray's *Elemental Passions.*" *Hypatia* (15) 3: 92–112.

Slatman, J. (2003). *L'expression au-delà de la représentation. Sur l'aisthêsis et l'esthétique chez Merleau-Ponty.* Leuven: Peeters.

Stoller, S. (2000). "Reflections on Feminist Merleau-Ponty Skepticism." *Hypatia* (15) 1: 175–182.

—— (2006). *Phänomenologie der Geschlechtlichkeit*. Unpublished dissertation, Nijmegen, The Netherlands.

Stone, A. (2003) "The Sex of Nature: A Reinterpretation of Irigaray's Metaphysics and Political Thought." *Hypatia* (18) 3: 60–84.

Vasseleu, C. (1998). *Textures of Light. Vision and Touch in Irigaray, Levinas and Merleau-Ponty*. London & New York: Routledge.

Weed, E. (1994). "A question of style." In *Engaging with Irigaray*. Eds. C. Burke, N. Schor, & M. Whitford. New York: Columbia University Press, 79–109.

Whitford, M. (1991). *Luce Irigaray. Philosophy in the Feminine*. London & New York: Routledge.

Young, I. M. (1990). *Throwing like a girl and other essays in feminist philosophy and social theory*. Bloomington & Indianapolis: Indiana University Press.

CHAPTER 5

The Language of the Lips, Merleau-Ponty and Irigaray: Toward a Culture of Difference

BRUCE YOUNG

> Therefore speak I to them in parables; because they seeing see not; and hearing they hear not, neither do they understand. And in them is fulfilled the prophecy of Esaias, which saith, By hearing ye shall hear, and shall not understand; and seeing ye shall see, and shall not perceive; for this people's heart is waxed gross, and their ears are dull of hearing, and their eyes they have closed; lest at any time they should see with their eyes, and should hear with their ears, and should understand with their heart. (Matt. 13: 13–15)

I use the term "subject-being" to designate not the self but a matrix wherein self is related to what is other than it and indeed is constituted in relation to this relation.[1] The self precipitates out within a matrix of relatedness to otherness: that form of relatedness to otherness wherein the self is constituted is what its subject-being is. There are different forms of relatedness to otherness, and these constitute different forms of subject-being, each of which opens up different possible ways of being a self.

In our culture subject-being has often been based on fear of otherness. This fearful subject fears to internalize fully and adequately all the ways in which other people, nature, and indeed our own selves resist identification with—fail to coincide with—what we can make "our own" or somehow render familiar to us; consequently, this subject in effect closes itself off from the reality of otherness. To take an example that should be familiar to philosophers, since Plato's day much epistemology has consisted in more or less ingenious attempts to "explain" knowledge by reducing the unfamiliar to the familiar; and in this respect, rationalism and empiricism just deploy different techniques to the same end. A subject that closes itself in this, or in more directly practical ways, dissimulates or misconstrues the transcendence of reality with respect to our power and knowledge; or tries to displace it into a beyond whence a supreme being is alleged to exercise total control and understanding on our behalf[2]; or acknowledges it only by construing it as a problem, threat, or barrier.

Merleau-Ponty construed otherness positively by construing it differently. He reconceptualized from the roots what otherness itself is, radically reforming it in a new ontological matrix. In the last phase of his work he began to articulate his ontology of noncoincidence more explicitly than before. Death cut him short. He left only sketches and a few posthumously published draft chapters for his planned book *Le Visible et l'invisible*.[3]

Because he did not live to complete that work, he did not fully elaborate a new account of intersubjectivity, although he did offer many sketches and hints. But at any rate, from everything he did complete we know noncoincidence to have been his point of departure for understanding otherness in general and intersubjectivity in particular.

What, then, is meant by "noncoincidence"? In the context of things and perceiving things, noncoincidence means (roughly speaking) that in that very differentiation from things perceived, which is effected by our perceiving them, we nevertheless inhere in the world of things and are things ourselves; and only so are we able to perceive things. In the context of intersubjectivity (so-called), it means that we belong, together with the other people from whom we are differentiated, to one common world of intercorporeal being; and this remarkable and quite specific—intercorporeal—commonality, far from undermining our mutual otherness, is its very source and support.

My use of the phrase "ontological matrix" is not mere jargon. Merleau-Ponty does not offer a new theory, a new ontology, within the traditional matrix, that is, within the network of basic presuppositions we have inherited from our cultural traditions about what otherness, sameness, subjecthood and so on are—presuppositions that precede all our theorizing about them, and so go a lot deeper than our usual conscious deliberations about such things, including the usual run of philosophical theories about them. Rather, as he stresses from the very first page of his last and tragically uncompleted work, he is out to question these root presuppositions themselves. What is new in him is, therefore, much more than yet another theory about "what is," or about whether allegedly different things are "really" different or "really" the same, or even about the "intertwining" of difference and sameness: after all, Plato himself stressed long ago that difference and sameness intertwined. Rather, Merleau-Ponty's vastly ambitious objective is to question and to alter our most basic inherited presuppositions about what difference, sameness and so on themselves are. The transition to a radically new ontological matrix is not effected just by setting out yet another theory about otherness (not even a "postmodern" one); it is, rather, a practical matter, a whole new way of relat-

The Language of the Lips, Merleau-Ponty and Irigaray 87

ing in practice to otherness, albeit one that carries with it and requires a new way of understanding (but also of perceiving and sensing) it.

All this needs much more discussion. Unfortunately, to get to grips with these far-reaching issues adequately needs a whole book—or many books. If Merleau-Ponty could not complete the job in the three hundred or so pages he left us of his last and still very incomplete work, it is hardly likely that any of us would be able to do it in thirty (or even three hundred) pages. I have tried to go a very little way in a book I am now completing: but meanwhile, it will be best to move on.

In the rest of this chapter I try to elucidate as best I can what is involved in Merleau-Ponty's project for a new ontological matrix via a critical discussion of the work of Lyotard and, more particularly, Irigaray.

In the course of living each of us discovers that the world does not coincide with us or our impulses and indeed that *we*—who after all are part of the world—do not coincide with ourselves or our impulses. Nobody can avoid this discovery but the culturally dominant response to it is one of refusal or evasion; so much so that it is hard to find words for it that do not make it look like a negative boundary of some kind—some barrier or threat to us and to whatever identities we might ever have as subject-beings. The descriptions we have ready to hand often do just that, because they are drawn from a repertoire whose limits are set by the negativistic framework which frames our culture. To discover apt words it is not enough to want to be radical, not even if one wants that *very* much. Consider this from Lyotard:[4]

> L'âme vient à l'existence sous la dépendance du sensible, violentée, humiliée.
>
> The soul comes into being subordinated to the sensorial: violated (fem.), degraded (fem.).

This registers noncoincidence but in a negativistic register. Lyotard here presents the soul as passive and the sensorial as active, thereby inverting the subordination of body to soul and of sensorial to intellectual more usual in the tradition. But he construes the soul's dependence negativistically, as something by which it is "degraded" (or "humiliated"). So he is offering a variant within the traditional matrix, not an alternative matrix. Moreover, the phallocentrism omnipresent in the tradition is reaffirmed in this inverted variant. It may be a merely grammatical fact that "soul" in French is feminine, but the primary meaning of the verb "violenter" is, according to the Collins-Robert French-English dictionary, "to assault sexually"; and Lyotard is unmistakably claiming that the mere fact of noncoincidence, more specifically the soul's dependence on sensoriality, somehow of itself constrains or "forces" it, that is, limits it negativistically.

Contrast Merleau-Ponty when he evokes noncoincidence[5]:

> Le corps nous unit directement aux choses par sa propre ontogénèse, en soudant l'une à l'autre les deux ébauches dont il est fait, ses deux lèvres: la masse sensible qu'il est et la masse du sensible dont il naît par ségrégation, et à laquelle, comme voyant, il reste ouvert.

> The human body unites us directly with things in its individual coming-to-be, as it joins together the lips of the two outlines which make it be: the sensorial mass it is with that sensorial mass from which it is born through segregation but to which, by seeing it, it remains open.

My translation is a free one, but at any rate the "lips" in this image evoke that opening from which we emerge in birth and so the feminine. By itself this would by no means distinguish it from phallocentrism. What defines phallocentrism is not that it never evokes the feminine but that it evokes it obsessively *as its own negative other*, supposed to "lack" what it "has"—and fears to lose. But Merleau-Ponty's image links these lips with a second opening. In our culture the adult subject (which corresponds to this second opening) is normally construed in relation to a pure activity wherein everything other than it is an object for it; so to rejoin the object this subject must either by "violating" it dominate and reintegrate it into itself or else allow itself to be "degraded" by submerging itself back into it. The "normal" adult subject, in this way, is a subject of loss, lived out both in repudiation of and nostalgia for an original unity as with the womb or with the earth, in short with the feminine or rather what is figured as such. The feminine gets linked with *everything by negating which this subject comes to be*, and then this subject in order to continue to be turns vampiric with respect to all of that: living women, living Nature, living otherness in general.

But Merleau-Ponty's image presents a second opening whereby adult subjects open themselves out to the world so that *it* may open up to them *without* their violating it *or* it degrading them. This images neither pure activity nor some equally pure passivity; and it avoids these alternatives because it images a reopening of the feminine within what is normally construed as a masculine domain or (what comes to the same) a neuter domain—neuter because within it the feminine has been neutralized. This implies, not the depositing of new material into the existing form of subject-being, but a reformation of it, which depends on *ceasing to construe noncoincidence negativistically* (ceasing to live it in refusal or evasion) so as to be set free to recognize it not as a threat to us but as something that, if we let it flower in us, will help us flower. This is why the image of a *double opening* (opening ourselves out to the world so it can open up to us) is appropriate. Now that, too, is a sexually

The Language of the Lips, Merleau-Ponty and Irigaray   89

loaded image. But its sexual coding is neither masculine (the subject "opens out" to the world); nor heterosexual (the world does not penetrate but "opens up" to a subject who opens out to it); nor is it phallocentric (what then "opens" within that subject who is now the world's partner and who may be male or female is a reopening of or to the feminine). And so this second opening symbolically opens up (the possibility of) a third opening: a different form of subject-being, beyond the alternation of pure activity and pure passivity or any combination between these equally deadly extremes. For if I (woman or man) not only relate *to the world* by opening out to it but also relate *myself* to that world by *locating myself in it*, then the world not only opens up to me but also opens up in me as I do in it. And that initiates a different form of subject-being, which among other things opens up a way beyond all presently dominant ways of relating to and living out sexuality.

Irigaray in a much-debated (and I think much misunderstood) passage makes use in her own way of the image of lips[6]:

> [A] woman "touches herself" all the time, and moreover no-one can forbid her to do so for her sex is composed of two lips which embrace continually. . . . The geography of her pleasure is far more diversified, more multiple in its differences, more complex, more subtle, than is usually imagined. . . . "She" is indefinitely other in herself. This no doubt is why she is called temperamental, incomprehensible, agitated, capricious . . . not to mention her language, in which "she" sets off in all directions leaving "him" unable to discern any coherent meaning. Contradictory words seem a little mad to the logic of reason, and cannot be heard by one who listens with ready-made grids, a ready-made code fixed in advance. For in her words too—when she dares to speak out—woman retouches herself ceaselessly. . . . One must listen with other ears so as to hear *an "other meaning" forever in the process of weaving itself, at the same time embracing words yet casting them off to avoid becoming fixed, immobilized in them.*

This text works at a number of levels that it weaves together in ways that are far from arbitrary. Obviously Irigaray's image evokes a woman's body; but not as defined by biology or anatomy—it is a woman's living experience of her lived body her image evokes. Now, just by evoking the body in this way, her image at once evokes at a second level woman's sexuality in *all* its dimensions (personal, cultural, spiritual). Third: her imagery, by bringing woman's sexuality into view the way it does, at once places it *and sexuality generally* in question, that is to say, makes us "wonder" about it; and by doing that the way it does brings into question wider issues about our relation as subjects to the world. More: in evoking what might be called "the language of the lips" in her concluding words the way she does, she not only gives those "with ears to hear" a commentary on how to hear her own words, she also gives body in these words to a whole different way of relating language to the body, words to the world, culture to nature, spirit to flesh—a different form of subject-being by exploring which women and men may perhaps find better ways of living sexuality and living life.

There is more to Irigaray's innovative use of language than this or that neologism, and much more than the failures or exaggerations that accompany a project as radical as hers. There is more to her innovations even than the fact that by means of them she enables herself to *parler femme*, to "speak (as a) woman," an achievement decreed impossible by hostile critics. In "speaking (as a) woman" in the ways she does, she gives a practical example of the new possibilities opened up by the new sort of ontological matrix Merleau-Ponty pioneered and from within which she speaks out in her own distinctive voice. For she "speaks out" from within a *different* and *unfamiliar* ontological matrix: the matrix of noncoincidence; and an understanding of this helps us better understand her work. It clarifies both the magnitude of her achievement and why she has been misread in ways which, otherwise, would be quite incredible.

Take for instance her words about woman's language in the passage just cited—on account of which she has been accused of portraying women as "irrational." Her point of departure is everyday experiences of a sort with which many of us are familiar, as when one speaker—often a man—demands of another—often a woman—to "say either yes or no," to "be precise," to "stick to the point" under circumstances where she feels that doing so obstructs what she wants to say although she is perhaps unsure of what that is or how to put it into words, at any rate words which he will understand. What is it she does when he accuses her of "wandering"? Often it is not that she is sheerly inarticulate, but that the forms of articulacy he is prepared to recognize do not permit her to articulate what she is trying to say. In particular: there are lots of questions that cannot be answered with a simple "yes or no," lots of points that one cannot "stick to" within the logic of either-yes-or-no, because they are too complex or multidimensional to be squeezed into that particular logic. This is why it is especially infuriating if he demands "clarity" of her: clarity is just what she is trying to achieve, but the sort of precision he wants to impose makes the clarity she seeks impossible. What she needs is a different form of articulacy, not poorer but richer than the only one he is willing to recognize. She, in her distinctive autoeroticism, already "touches herself all the time" without words being needed. But to *unfold* herself she *needs words* so as not just to "touch herself" but all the world. Yet words, though they enable her to "touch" all the world, risk making her "lose touch" with herself unless they open the world up to her *in such a way as to place her "in touch" with herself in it*. Such words determine a different "symbolic"—a different way of relating to the world via linguistic mediation—in which she may (Irigaray's image) "touch herself" in words that also "touch upon" the world, remaining "in touch" through these words *both* with herself *and* the world.

Now "touching oneself in touching the world" *cannot be done in standard propositional discourse*: the very form of the proposition prevents it. The subject (and its sex/gender) is symbolically neutralized in any proposition "he or she" enunciates: when I express propositions about myself I do not *express myself* but depict facts about myself. There is no point bemoaning this. It simply describes what propositions *are*: namely one way we do in fact use language, and which we could not do without. But neither Irigaray nor Merleau-Ponty require us to give up propositions. They do not reject the propositional but *contest its unilateral dominance or "imperialism."* In particular: they (like Wittgenstein) contest the prejudice that the propositional has primacy over all other ways of using language when it comes to articulating our relation as subjects to ourselves, each other and the world. Indeed they (like Wittgenstein) hold that the imperialism of propositional primacy impedes us when we try to articulate these things, and if taken far enough makes us inarticulate, or at the limit renders us altogether incapable of articulating them. Now, not only has the imperialism of propositional primacy long dominated our culture in one form or another, but an especially dogmatic form of it dominates today's academic culture. So, in contesting it Irigaray and Merleau-Ponty[7] contest all that.

Irigaray's claim can be put like this: the dominant forms of discourse under the imperialism of the propositional, just by claiming (and in a way achieving) "sexlessness," prevent women from *articulating* their own experience as the embodied beings they are—as women; and in depriving them of *this* articulacy make it impossible for them to *be* women with a subject-being of their own (one which enables them to give symbolic expression to instead of neutralizing their embodied being). To overcome this very specific sort of inarticulacy, Irigaray asks women not at all to give up reasoning but to reason differently—and better. Reasoning differently here means: reasoning in a different ontological matrix, a matrix of noncoincidence. Further: reasoning within this different matrix not only enables women to "speak (as) woman" but enables men to understand this different speaking if they too find the courage to enter this different matrix by opening themselves up in it. Perhaps they may even find themselves there: no longer as the "sex which is the only sex" but as the sex they only are. If I am a man I cannot "speak (as a) woman" for the simple reason that I am not one. But this does not prevent my understanding this different speaking; on the contrary, unless I recognize that I am not a woman it is not possible for me to understand her. For me to understand, for example, Irigaray's words about her experience of sexual joy is not for me to use them to conjure up in me that experience that is hers and that she so beautifully articulates, nor is it some vicarious reproduction in me of that. Rather it is to experience in her words another person, another experience, another sex and gender, which never will ever be mine. Understanding is not identification through some more or less forced fusion or coincidence: it consists in recognizing and internalizing into my own experience the other's nonidentity with me, thereby opening myself to her. And when I discover her as different to me, I can rediscover myself.[8] The "symbolic" within which it becomes possible to "speak (as a) woman" is not a semantics private to women, but a syntax that facilitates a dialogue of noncoincidence—that is, effective and articulate interaction between people who are different.

Within the dominant paradigm, to reason means to *detach oneself in thought* from one's contingent being so as to be able in this detachment to function as a mere particularization of reason-in-general, of reason in the abstract. But in the matrix of noncoincidence, reasoning is different. It is dialogical, but in a sense that differs from Habermas, because in a dialogue of noncoincidence each partner participates in flesh and blood and soul instead of as a detachable agent of reason aiming at achieving pure rational consensus in spite of our empirical differences. Rather, each participant in this dialogue participates as who and what she (he) is and is in process of becoming, and does not attempt in reasoning to detach herself from that but brings "that" with her into the dialogue and so reasons from and within her "situation." In short, she participates in dialogue as noncoincident with her dialogical partners and she (with them) remains noncoincident during as well as after the dialogue. To be sure, in entering into dialogue, each noncoincident partner accepts to dialogue with partners who differ from her and by so doing accepts to place herself in question. But placing oneself "in question" like this does not mean renouncing or abstracting from one's identity (who and what one is and is in process of becoming). It means *opening oneself to oneself by opening oneself in oneself to what is other than oneself*—recognizing thereby that not only is one noncoincident in relation to "the others" *but in relation to oneself as well.*[9] This is quite different from simply emoting by expressing oneself in an unmediated way as if one already "had" a preestablished fixed something there to express, a "true self," which remains unchanged in the process of being expressed or at most changes only by acquiring a true awareness of that essence of its own self that was there all the time but was previously hidden away. It is instead a question of expressing oneself by mediating oneself with others, renouncing thereby all illusions as to having some self-identity fixed in advance within oneself. So to open oneself like this means letting go of the fixed identities we are used to. But to lose these is not to lose one's real identity: it is to let go of one's illusions about one's real identity, illusions of fixity and certainty, which in a culture still unfree supply illusory substitutes for a real identity socially refused. Because I am real there is more to me than can be possessed in fixity, either practically or intellectually, whether by others or myself.

To "open oneself" in the sense I have tried to outline involves *recognizing the otherness of other people by internalizing in oneself the impossibility of internalizing the other*. This takes place via specifically and irreducibly intercorporeal interaction: we can perhaps pretend that our minds are fused, but not our bodies—unless we are raving.

When "she" in the Irigaray passage cited "dares to speak," her wandering words trail off into silence because "he" will not listen and so refuses the dialogue of noncoincidence. "With these ears"—that is within the traditional matrix—he *cannot* hear (Irigaray's Biblical allusion is seldom noticed). In order to listen he must learn to hear and see and feel and speak differently: within a matrix of noncoincidence. But this possibility is *open to him and everyone*. For however much our tradition has institutionalized refusal of it each and every one of us actually exists in noncoincidence: our illusions can never quite detach us from that.[10] All we need do is respond to what is there for us. The "language of the lips" can then start to *become a culture* in an *articulate dialogue of noncoincidence*.[11] And then "when our lips speak together," women to other women and to men, men to women and to other men, our world can start to be a different world.

Notes

1. Judith Butler remarks in similar vein: " 'The subject' is sometimes bandied about as if it were interchangeable with 'the person' or 'the individual' . . . [but] . . . no intelligible reference to individuals or their becoming can take place without a prior reference to their status as subjects" (*The Psychic Life of Power*: 10–11). Further: in Butler's view individuals achieve the status of subjects through processes of *assujetissement* (subjectivation) by which they get related in definite ways to others. "Subjectivation" suggests subordination but Butler argues that the possibility of subverting subordination is built into the process of achieving the status of subject.—In this chapter ways of relating to others that radicalize that possibility are explored.

2. In Luce Irigaray's *An Ethics of Sexual Difference* she writes: "As our tradition has it, this dimension is covered over, swallowed up, or relegated to the beyond" (71).

3. Maurice Merleau-Ponty, *Le Visible et l'invisible*. I cite this throughout my main text in the original French and give my own English translations. The standard English translation is by Alphonso Lingis: *The Visible and the Invisible* (Evanston: Northwestern UP, 1968).

4. Jean-François Lyotard, *Moralités postmodernes*, 205–206, my translation.

5. *Le Visible et l'invisible* p. 179: my translation. The standard translation runs: "The body unites us directly with things through its own ontogenesis, by welding to one another the two outlines of which it is made, its two laps [*sic*]: the sensible mass it is and the mass of the sensible wherein it is born by segregation and upon which, as

seer, it remains open" (136). "Laps" is an unfortunate typographical error: read "lips." This passage is mentioned by Irigaray when discussing Merleau-Ponty in *An Ethics of Sexual Difference*. In her often sharply critical account Irigaray does not allude to the points I discuss. Instead she makes her own use of the image of the lips in her own work; but the ways in which she does that can be clarified by recognizing that she, like Merleau-Ponty before her, works within a matrix of noncoincidence. It would be a miracle comparable to the immaculate conception if Merleau-Ponty's phenomenology of the body were free of male bias: he spoke and wrote as a man, and a man in the context of a time. But the point is that a matrix of noncoincidence enables *women* to speak and write *as women*; and Irigaray with others by doing that have *changed* the context. For the rest, some of Irigaray's sharper criticisms of Merleau-Ponty derive from her from time to time reading him within a traditional matrix; when that happens as occasionally it does she misreads him in ways remarkably similar to how others have misread her.

    6. Luce Irigaray, *This Sex which is not One*, 24–29. There is an earlier translation by Claudia Reeder in *New French Feminisms*, eds. Elaine Marks and Isabelle de Courtivron. I have combined the two translations, simply because there are bits in each of them I like.

    7. Wittgenstein rejected the traditional notion of philosophy as propositional as early as the *Tractatus*. In that enigmatic text the limits of the propositional are shown by subverting propositional imperialism from within (and from within *philosophy*). Logic (the principle of noncontradiction in particular) emerges in that work as resulting from minimal requirements for propositional representation. But its main point is that propositional representation is itself limited and that there are no "propositions of philosophy." It may be added that, while propositional imperialism has been and remains dominant in the Western philosophical tradition, there have always been counter-currents. Plato, in spite of Platonism, explicitly emphasized the limits of propositional knowledge, and contested the notion that philosophy is propositional. And while others, like Aristotle, Descartes, and Kant, sought to express their insights in special "metaphysical" or "synthetic a priori" propositions, these are according to their own account very peculiar "propositions" indeed. I will discuss these matters in detail in a forthcoming book.

    8. So much for the idea that Irigaray tries to create some sort of secret code capable of being understood by women only: no cruder misunderstanding of what it means to speak (as a) woman could be imagined. A curious misunderstanding besides, for Irigaray never tires of asking men to respond to her speaking. Certainly, speaking (as a) woman can be done only by women: but that is a different point. *Of course* men cannot speak (as) woman, that is why it matters to them as well as to women that they open themselves to understanding women's speaking. In so opening themselves, the possibility opens up for them to speak in their turn as the embodied beings they are: men. Irigaray points out time and again that precisely this possibility is blocked for men by the "erection" of their sex into a false universal by which they get trapped in, so to say, a fleshless body, a body functioning as the mere materialization of phallic power and which "stands" in permanence under the threat of castration (see *An Ethics of Sexual Difference*, 133). So this sort of opening to or of

the feminine, to the extent that it happens in a man, is something different from his getting "feminized," although I suppose it may look like that to men whose "masculinity" derives from nothing more substantial than their fear of women. It is also different from Deleuzean "becoming-woman" if only because the being which "opens," man or woman, is stubbornly and quite incurably embodied with its organs in its flesh.

9. Merleau-Ponty puts it like this in *Le Visible et l'invisible*, 159 (my translation): "Discussion is not exchange or confrontation of ideas: as if we produced them, showed them to others, looked at theirs, then went back to ours and corrected them. . . . We speak; at once others appear in relation to our words as roads which diverge from ours; we then remeasure the divergent road we ourselves are by theirs. Bold or shy, we each speak as whole beings, with our 'ideas' but also our inner ghosts and secret history which others uncover suddenly by putting them into the form of ideas. Life turns into ideas, which return into life and get caught up there in a whirlpool we enter tentatively, but then we with our words get swept along in the whirl of what we say and what is said to us, into a thought no longer ours alone. . . ." For the standard English translation see *The Visible and the Invisible*, 119. I think it is pretty clear that what we have here is a conception of what dialogue is which is significantly different from that in Habermas. For Habermas seems to proceed precisely as if he took "discussion" to be a process of "exchange or confrontation of ideas," wherein each of us "produced them, showed them to others, looked at theirs, then went back to ours and corrected them." In Habermas the different roads converge on consensus; in Merleau-Ponty they "diverge," without their being any requirement—transcendental or otherwise—that they should converge on consensus.

10. Judith Butler in effect recognizes this when she stresses (as she does in all her work) that we can never "live up to" what "normalization" processes would have us be.

11. See for example Luce Irigaray *I Love to You*.

References

Atkins, Beryl T., Duval, Alain, and Milne, Rosemary C. (1995). *French-English Dictionary*. Eds. Alain Duval and Vivian Marr. Glasgow and Paris: HarperCollins and Dictionnaire Le Robert.

Butler, Judith (1997). The Psychic Life of Power. Stanford: Stanford University Press.

Irigaray, Luce (1993). *An Ethics of Sexual Difference*. Trans. Carolyn Burke and Gillian C. Gill. London: Athlone.

——— (1996). *I Love to You*. Trans. Alison Martin. New York: Routledge.

——— (1985). *This Sex which is not One*. Trans. Catherine Porter with Carolyn Burke. Ithaca: Cornell University Press.

Lyotard., Jean-François (1993). *Moralités postmodernes*. Paris: Galilée.

Marks, E. and de Courtivron, I. (1981). "Irigaray" *New French Feminisms*. Trans. Claudia Reeder. New York: Schocken Books.

Merleau-Ponty, Maurice (1964). *Le Visible et l'invisible*. Paris: Gallimard.

——— (1968). *The Visible and the Invisible*. Trans. Alphonso Lingis. Evanston: Northwestern University Press.

Wittgenstein, Ludwig (1961). *Tractatus Logico-Philosophicus*. Trans. D. F. Pears and B. F. McGuinness. London: Routledge and Kegan Paul.

PART III

Literary Enactments:
Merleau-Ponty, Proust, and Stein

CHAPTER 6

Among the Hawthorns: Marcel Proust and Maurice Merleau-Ponty

PATRICIA M. LOCKE

Merleau-Ponty states that "no one has gone further than Proust in fixing the relations between the visible and the invisible, in describing an idea that is not the contrary of the sensible, that is its lining and its depth."[1] Merleau-Ponty argues that our experience of the natural world, like that of literature or music, has within it a logical coherence that only *is* as a corporeal idea, not as an inside reality of an outside appearance. To see how this prereflective knowing is demonstrated in *In Search of Lost Time*, let us look at the narrator's relation to hawthorn bushes. This motif, one among many references to flora, shows the young narrator's sensitivity to beauty. His vague appreciation of the natural world develops into sensitivity for art as a locus of truth.

Merleau-Ponty argues, "Perception as an encounter with natural things" is "as the archetype of the originating encounter, imitated and renewed in the encounter with the past, the imaginary, the idea" (1968: 158). Marcel Proust initially shows us a young, nameless narrator of unspecified age, open to the perception of a world not yet mediated by names. The middle volumes of his vast work play out the consequences of his originating encounter with the natural world, which affect his ability to love others and to become a writer. It is only in *Finding Time Again*, the last volume, that the narrator, now identified as Marcel, can restore his sensitivity to the world and begin therefore to write. Somehow the loss is a necessary prerequisite for time regained, reformed with the incorporation of the imaginary and of memory.

The first mention of hawthorns in *Swann's Way* is an old story of the elder M. Swann, often told by the narrator's grandfather. In order to distract him from the profound moment when his dead wife was being laid in her coffin, the tearful M. Swann is led out into his garden. At once, the old man has a sense that it is good to be alive surrounded by the sun, a little breeze and blooming hawthorn.

> Suddenly the memory of his dead wife came back to him and, no doubt feeling it would be too complicated to try to understand how he could have yielded to an impulse of happiness at such a time, he confined himself, in a habitual gesture of his whenever a difficult question came into his mind, to passing his hand over his forehead, wiping his eyes and the lenses of his lorgnon. Yet he could not be consoled for the death of his wife . . .[2]

Thus, from the outset, the perception of hawthorns is associated in the young narrator's eyes with the question of the appropriate response to death. Here the juxtaposition of the "impulse of happiness" and the pain of loss is woven into the creamy white blossoms and the sharp thorns. The felt sense of these natural textures and human emotions cannot be separated from each other, any more than perplexity is separable from the act of passing a hand across one's forehead.

The incident is raised to the level of family myth by the grandfather's retelling. His affection for his old friend of Combray extends into the next generation, to the young Swann. This M. Swann is the guest of Marcel's childhood who prevents his mother from giving him just one more goodnight kiss, evoking a primitive sense of loss in the young boy. Swann's difficult love story becomes the tale Marcel tells later, precisely because he feels it is entwined in his own.

Marcel relates his direct experience with hawthorns in this passage, which I quote at length:

> It was in the 'Month of Mary' that I remember beginning to be fond of hawthorns. Not only were they in the church, which was so holy but which we had the right to enter, they were put up on the altar itself, inseparable from the mysteries in whose celebrations they took part, their branches running out among the candles and holy vessels, attached horizontally to one another in a festive preparation and made even lovelier by the festoons of their foliage, on which were scattered in profusion as on a bridal train, little bunches of buds of a dazzling whiteness. But, though I dared not do more than steal a glance at them, I felt that the ceremonious preparations were alive and that it was nature herself who, by carving those indentations in the leaves, by adding the supreme ornament of those white buds, had made the decorations worthy of what was at once a popular festivity and a mystical celebration. Higher up, their corollas opened here and there with a careless grace, still holding so casually, like a last and vaporous adornment, the bouquets of stamens, delicate as gossamer, which clouded them entirely, that in following, in trying to mime deep inside myself the motion of their flowering, I imagined it as the quick and thoughtless movement of the head, with coquettish glance and contracted eyes, of a young girl in white, dreamy and alive. (2003a: 114)[3]

Here the narrator touches on the theme of nature's mysteries of beauty and sexual initiation, at which one can dare to steal only an oblique glance. The altar has been made vibrantly alive by the artistic arrangement of the hawthorn branches, thus transforming inanimate stone into a present place where everyone is welcome. The narrator is absorbed in a church setting in a way that is far from habitual. Instead, he weaves his own narrative of sacred mysteries. He attempts to trace out deep in his own body a gesture of flowering, as a plant, as a girl. He continues:

> When, before leaving the church, I kneeled in front of the altar, I suddenly smelled, as I stood up, a bittersweet scent of almonds escaping from the hawthorns, and then I noticed, on the flowers, little yellower places under which I imagined that scent must be hidden, as the taste of a frangipani must be hidden under the burned parts, or that of Mlle. Vinteuil's cheeks under their freckles. Despite the silence and stillness of the hawthorns, this intermittent scent was like the murmuring of an intense life with which the altar quivered like a country hedge visited by living antennae, of which I was reminded by the sight of certain stamens, almost russet red, that seemed to have preserved the springtime virulence, the irritant power, of insects now metamorphosed into flowers. (2003a: 116)

The young narrator kneels before nature, finding through direct sensual experience of texture and scent that the surface is what Merleau-Ponty calls depth in art. There is no idea separate from what appears, as a young girl's freckles rest intimately upon her cheeks. He experiences this intense connection to organic life in a church, drawing our attention to his desire for sexual ecstatic union. He imagines that the pain of sexuality, marked by stinging insects and thorns, can be transmuted into innocent, creamy white flowers like young girls.[4] He does not yet know that the lovely Mlle. Vinteuil is a lesbian with sadistic impulses. Later in the novel, young girls will be seen as a screen for male homosexual desires euphemistically described in terms of bees pollinating flowers.[5] But at this point in the narrator's life, his experiences are open and unexamined.

While walking through the countryside with his father and grandfather, the narrator comes across a profusion of blooming hawthorns. The living hedge is transformed into a series of chapels in the narrator's imagination, but he cannot achieve a mature understanding of what this means. The flower clusters now seem to him to have delicate tracery in the flamboyant style, a stony framing for "white flesh." Marcel's reversal of the naturalization of the church described above retains the sense of screening, with the sunlight filtered through the hawthorns "as if it had just passed through a stained-glass window" (2003a: 141).

> Then I came back to stand in front of the hawthorns as you do in front of those masterpieces which, you think, you will be able to see more clearly when you have stopped looking at them for a moment, but although I formed a screen for myself with my hands so that I would have only them before my eyes, the feeling they awakened in me remained obscure and vague, seeking in vain to detach itself, to come and adhere to their flowers. They did not help me to clarify it, and I could not ask other flowers to satisfy it. (2003a: 142)

Marcel displays an inchoate longing for a chiasmatic experience, where "every relation with being is *simultaneously* a taking and a being taken" as Merleau-Ponty states, "the hold is held, it is *inscribed* and inscribed in the same being that it takes hold of." Merleau-Ponty goes on to equate literature and philosophy in this working note, as they each acknowledge the chiasm and show this by words, on all sides of the visible.[6] Marcel does not yet have the language with which to describe his experience, but his sensitivity to the natural world will be a condition for becoming a writer. His instinctive gesture toward a screen will be thematized later in his life. The screen is a symbolic gesture toward the gap (*l'écart*) Merleau-Ponty insists upon, which permits connection without complete merging of self and other.

We return to this originating encounter. Next, his grandfather points out some pink hawthorn, "catholic and delicious," which infuses the narrator with rapture akin to seeing a painting of a subject only seen before in pencil sketch. He sees Swann's daughter Gilberte enshrined there.

> Suddenly I stopped, I could not move, as happens when something we see does not merely address our eyes, but requires a deeper kind of perception and possesses our entire being. A little girl with reddish-blond hair . . . was looking at us, lifting toward us a face scattered with pink freckles. (2003a: 143)

This deeper perception is grounded in the scent of flowers, sensitivity to their texture, and in the abrupt halt to walking. The little redhead, as delicate as a flower, and as prone to burn as a frangipani, looks at the narrator. Surrounded by a halo of visibility, the child holds latent in her look a whole future with Marcel, but he mistakes its meaning, caught up in the danger of being visible himself. His error sets off a series of delays, so Marcel becomes stranded in a not-yet stage of desire. The history of this exquisite retardation process is the several thousand paged *In Search of Lost Time*. The narrator will spend his life searching for the lost time, the time suspended in that moment when a look took possession of his whole being.

> I looked at her, at first with the sort of gaze that is not merely the messenger of the eyes, but a window at which all the senses lean out, anxious and petrified, a gaze that would like to touch the body it is looking at, capture it, take it away and the soul along with it; then, so afraid was I that at any second my grandfather and my father, noticing the girl, would send me off, telling me to run on a little ahead of them, with a second sort of gaze, one that was unconsciously supplicating, that tried to force her to pay attention to me, to know me! (2003a: 144)

The language of capture, anxiety, and force does not accompany Marcel's perception of the natural world. There is a significant difference in his gaze at the little girl, Gilberte, which causes all the senses to "lean out" of the window of his eyes. Marcel is ready to fall out, to fall in love, awakening to the possibility of being seen and seeing her.

At the same time, Marcel is torn, fearful that he might be caught in the act of desire by his father and grandfather, or rejected by the young girl. This paralyzing moment of anxiety accompanies risk for him. In the *Cogito* chapter of *Phenomenology of Perception*, Merleau-Ponty identifies a tacit *cogito* prior to the Cartesian one. This tacit *cogito*, a way of being present to oneself, ". . . knows itself only in those extreme situations in which it is under threat: for example in the dread of death or of another's gaze upon me."[7] This dread stems from a sense that the social world and the self are precariously given. One knows oneself as a fragile web of relationships in the moment of vulnerability. Marcel, however, rushes past this risky self-knowledge by attempting to control the responses of those around him.

Marcel's desire for full knowledge of the soul along with the body, like the desire for philosophical certainty, is destined to fail. It results in grasping for something that flows between the fingers. In volume five, *The Prisoner*, the narrator literally imprisons his lover Albertine, but his intense jealousy outlives his love. In that early walk with his father and grandfather, we see a simple glance toward a young girl framed by hawthorn, but like much of Proust, it is pregnant with the loss to come. In these two passages we also see the intertwined issues of the deep kind of perception that great art requires, and of the objectifying gaze of sexual conquest. It is not simple to separate these strands, because the desire to know goes hand in hand with the desire to be known. Each is accompanied with risk and vulnerability.

In *Phenomenology of Perception*, Merleau-Ponty indicates that the Hegelian dialectic of recognition in the master/slave episode does not apply to children, who believe they are already situated in an intersubjective world of peaceful coexistence (1962: 355). Proust brilliantly presents his namesake, Marcel, as a character who oscillates between childish openness to others, akin to his responsiveness to nature, and his more adult desires. This is especially evident in the confused evaluations Marcel gives of art at this undefined age between childhood and adulthood.

The most vivid example of the youthful narrator's relation to hawthorns (and to art) occurs as the family is about to leave Combray for Paris:

> [O]n the morning of our departure, after they had had my hair curled for a photograph, and carefully placed on my head a hat I had never worn before and dressed me in a quilted velvet coat, after looking for me everywhere, my mother found me in tears on the steep little path beside Tansonville, saying good-bye to the hawthorns, putting my arms around the prickly branches, and, like the princess in the tragedy burdened by vain ornaments, ungrateful to the importunate hand that with such care had gathered up my hair in curls across my brow, trampling underfoot my torn-out curl papers and my new hat. My mother was not at all moved by my tears, but she could not suppress a cry at the sight of my crushed hat and ruined coat. I did not hear it: "Oh, my poor little hawthorns," I said, weeping, "you're not the ones trying to make me unhappy, you aren't forcing me to leave. You've never hurt me! So I will always love you." And drying my tears, I promised them that when I was grown up I would not let my life be like the senseless lives of other men and that even in Paris, on spring days, instead of paying calls and listening to silly talk, I would go out into the countryside to see the first hawthorns. (2003a: 148)[8]

This passage incorporates a paraphrase of the queen's opening speech in Racine's play, *Phèdre*, which recalls the inevitable suffering that love brings. Phèdre suffers from the weight of the royal hair ornaments, and their attendant responsibilities. They stand between her desire for Hippolyte and her marriage to his father, Theseus. Her speech, as an overture to Racine's unfolding drama, points both to the vanity of presenting oneself formally adorned, and the despairing futility of incestuous love. Marcel's speech to the hawthorns accuses his mother, who has made him unhappy by her nightly separation from him. He vows in vain that he will always love his transposed first love, for hawthorns are more faithful than Mamma. They are also a more accessible substitution for Gilberte, who has snubbed him with "an indecent gesture."

The curled and elaborately dressed Marcel describes Phèdre as a princess (rather than a queen) and he withholds a wish. If Phèdre were an unmarried princess, her love for Hippolyte would not be taboo. If Mamma were not his mother, perhaps she wouldn't abandon him for his father. In his wish, she will never die. Because of the conflation of Phèdre and Mamma, Marcel does not realize that he too wants to *be* the princess, with a prince of his own to love him. The narrator returns many times to the theme of the play *Phèdre*, first to consider the relation of love and death, and second, to compare the display of formal acting (in the person of the actress Berma) versus unmediated experience. In any event, this poignant episode in which a young boy is found tearfully clinging to a hawthorn for dear life, with ripped and dirty clothing, solidifies the connection between the hawthorns and the frustration of sexual desire.

At this early stage of the narrative, Marcel remains in immediate contact with natural phenomena but already has enough book learning to demand the separation of text (Racine's play) from gesture (Berma's acting). Marcel only comes to appreciate the French formal style of acting when he is old enough to overcome the separation of word and gesture, to reject the artificial distinction between the visible and the invisible.

Truth in life as in art, Merleau-Ponty tells us, comes as a wound, piercing through habitual ways of seeing and thinking, through the sentimentality and convention of social life.[9] Marcel has to go through an education in love and loss before he can withstand truth's multiplicity. Looking back over his experiences near the end of the novel, he reflects:

> There had been a time when the fear of no longer being myself had horrified me, and similarly with each new love I felt (for Gilberte, for Albertine), because I could not bear the idea that one day the being who loved them would no longer exist, which seemed like a kind of death. But after so much repetition, this fear had by a natural process become transformed into a trustful equanimity.... For I understood that dying was not something new but quite the reverse, that since my childhood I had already died a number of times. (2003b: 347)

He comes to see that the transience of human life mirrors that of the natural world, much as hawthorns have a barren season. By the end of the novel, he can make use of these images of past losses as raw material for art. The temporal distance of the writer from the event is necessary for its transmutation into the truth *as* art. Marcel has to relinquish the gaze of capture to be absorbed in surface as depth.

Merleau-Ponty's discussion of three-dimensional depth in space (in *Phenomenology of Perception*) is expanded by his thoughts in the chiasm chapter of *The Visible and the Invisible*. Here he describes depth as "thickness of the flesh," which can be read as depth in time as well as space. He says, "... carnal being, as a being of depths, of several leaves or several faces, a being in latency, and a presentation of a certain absence, is a prototype of Being . . ." (1968: 139). These leaves, like those of other visible objects, gather together absent times and selves. They reflect one another, as do two mirrors facing each other. This echoing is somehow more real than the originary event, which itself gathers past and future. Through echoing activity engaging memory and imagination,

Marcel can acknowledge at last his inseparability from the world he has experienced. Merleau-Ponty insists that not only does the past remembered affect the present sense of self, but that there is an inverse relation from the present to a "dimensional present or *Welt* or Being, where the past is 'simultaneous' with the present in the narrow sense" (1968: 243–244). Episodes of involuntary memory confirm this dimensional present for Marcel, and by extension, for us.

Philosophers can look to art as a locus of truths, not to derive abstract ideas from literature, or to explain the world, but to reclaim a prereflective contact with the world. Merleau-Ponty asserts the "fundamental narcissism of all vision," noting that one discovers oneself existing as seen by the world as much as actively interpreting it. The philosopher may experience a loss of certainty as she too gives up the gaze of capture, or the need to assert conditions of possibility for experience. The world presents itself as shifting when the philosopher moves through it and is herself changing in both place and time. The mutuality of these presentations and multiple responses calls for phenomenological description and analysis. Flexibility and openness can be developed through sensitivity to the natural world and to art.

In "Metaphysics and the Novel," (1945) Merleau-Ponty claims:

> From now on the tasks of literature and philosophy can no longer be separated. When one is concerned with giving voice to the experience of the world and showing how consciousness escapes into the world, one can no longer credit oneself with attaining a perfect transparency of expression. Philosophical expression assumes the same ambiguities as literary expression, if the world is such that it cannot be expressed except in 'stories' and, as it were, pointed at.[10]

If philosophy becomes a "metaphysical literature," it implies that human life and action are too fluid to be constrained by the parameters of habitual categories. This approach to philosophy is in a sense amoral, since the ambiguities of human being do not stem from a "nature."

Merleau-Ponty stresses that personal experience of the world can be shared through art. Marcel's joyous reaction to episodes of involuntary memory results from his conclusion that he is a self that continues over time, able to enjoy once more the sensation of a madeleine dipped in tea long ago.[11] This experience is an impetus to writing, for Marcel's confirmation of a self, surviving and renewing itself through the many little deaths it undergoes, is one he can share with readers who inhabit a common world. In this way, loss is not in vain, and death is overcome by the *nunc stans*, the suspension of time in time.

The truth in art is necessarily screened and partial. It is a wounding that comes from life experiences, but it restores life in an aesthetic transfiguration.

Merleau-Ponty writes in a somewhat cryptic late working note that "the *true* hawthorns are the hawthorns of the past," referring to their original impression in a time that has become a mythical golden age for our narrator, a time before time (1968: 243). In the end, Marcel reflects on the goal of the writer, just before he will begin to write the overture to Combray saturated with the scent of hawthorn in bloom.

> What we call reality is a certain relationship between these sensations and the memories which surround us simultaneously . . . a unique relationship which the writer has to rediscover in order to bring its two different terms together permanently in his sentence. . . . Had not nature herself, from this point of view, set me on the way to art, wasn't she herself the beginning of art, she who made it possible for me, often after a long interval, to recognize the beauty of one thing only in another, noon at Combray only in the sound of its bells? (2003b, 197–198)

It is nature who carves hawthorn leaves like stone, and flowers like girls, making them participate with the sensitive eye in the recognition of depth in art. Through the motif of hawthorn, I have tried to show how nature gives itself to Marcel as artful, as a living church, as a symbol of life in death, and as an impetus to sexual awakening. This cluster of meanings can only be known as such through reflection, yet from a Merleau-Pontian perspective, the first task is to reclaim immediate perception, "liberated from the contingencies of time."

Notes

This essay is dedicated to Agnes Heller, Hannah Arendt Professor of Philosophy and Political Science at the New School for Social Research, in thanks for her integrity as a philosopher and her sensitivity towards Proust.

1. Merleau-Ponty, Maurice. *The Visible and the Invisible*, ed. Claude Lefort, trans. Alphonso Lingis. Evanston: Northwestern University Press (1968), 149.

2. Proust, Marcel (2003a), 15. Proust's continuous novel was originally published in eight parts between 1913 and 1927. The Penguin Classics edition, with multiple translators, is based upon Marcel Proust (1987–1989) *À la recherche du temps perdu*, ed. Jean-Yves Tadié. Paris: Pléiade, Gallimard.

3. The hawthorn (*Crataegus oxyacantha*) is a small tree of the rose family. It was used in ancient Athens to adorn attendants to brides, who carried large bouquets of hawthorn as a symbol of hope. Hymen's altar (and the nuptial chamber) was lighted by hawthorn wood torches. In Rome, hawthorn became associated with warding off sorcery, and its leaves were put in babies' cradles. Earnest and Johanna Lehner (1990), 59.

More recently in twentieth-century Ireland, Anne O'Byrne reports that white hawthorn (also called may or in French *l'aubépine*) is considered unlucky. She and her siblings were admonished for gathering the flowers to decorate home May altars to Mary. The impulse to decorate altars with the branches apparently persists! She further reports that hawthorns are sometimes fairy trees. "In Kilmore, a village near Wexford, there are two hawthorns that have come to be cross trees, which means that every time a funeral passes on the way to the graveyard, a wooden cross is put at the foot of one of these trees, so that there is now a pile of crosses stacked there." As wishing trees, hawthorns are seen laden with small objects tied to the branches as petitions to Mary or local saints. Pieces of ribbon, children's toys, holy pictures and rosary beads dangle from hawthorns in Donegal near holy wells. Personal communication, June 11, 2002, Dr. Anne E. O'Byrne, Philosophy Department, State University of New York at Stony Brook, Stony Brook, New York.

4. Proust, Marcel (2004a), 471: "The men and youths, the old or middle-aged women, in whose company we think we take pleasure, we conceive of as shallow beings, existing on a flat and insubstantial surface, because our only awareness of them is that of unaided visual perception; but when our eye ventures in the direction of a young girl it is as though it acts on behalf of all our other senses: they seek out her various properties, the smell of her, the feel of her, the taste of her, which they enjoy without the collaboration of the hands or the lips; and because of desire's artful abilities in transposition, and its excellent spirit of synthesis, these senses can draw from the color of cheeks or breasts the sensations . . . of forbidden contact, and can rifle girls' sweet succulence, as they do in a rose garden when plundering the fragrances of the flowers, or in a vineyard when gloating with greedy eyes upon the grapes." By volume six, the narrator is able to begin to see others in three dimensions.

5. One such episode concludes with the narrator as voyeur and self-styled "moral botanist" commenting ". . . there were various kinds of conjunction, certain of which, by their multiplicity, their barely perceptible instantaneity, and especially the absence of contact between the two agents, were even more reminiscent of those flowers which in a garden are fertilized by the pollen from a neighboring flower that they never touch." Marcel Proust (2004c), 29–30.

6. Refer to the sense of chiasm, as in Merleau-Ponty (1968), working note, 11/60, 266.

7. Merleau-Ponty, Maurice (1962), 404.

8. This promise is in sharp contrast to the first afternoon of spring the young adult Marcel later spends in the back room of a Parisian restaurant, drinking champagne with a prostitute and her paramour, in "hours of boredom" and intoxication. Proust, Marcel (2004b), 164.

9. The narrator describes a figurative wound in Proust (2004b, 113) as follows:

> I felt so great a pang of longing for Mme. de Guermantes that it took my breath away: it was as if part of my breast had been cut out by a skilled anatomist and replaced by an equal part of immaterial suffering, by an equivalent degree of nostalgia and love. And, however neat the surgeon's stitches

are, life is rather painful when longing for another person is substituted for the intestines; ... and then how utterly unsettling it is to be obliged to *think* with part of the body!"

Merleau-Ponty dwells on the difficulty of thinking with a part of one's body particularly in the case of Schneider in *Phenomenology of Perception*.

10. Merleau-Ponty, Maurice (1964), 28.

11. Proust, Marcel (2003b), 179–180.

References

Lehner, Earnest and Johanna Lehner (1990). *Folklore and Symbolism of Flowers, Plants and Trees*. New York: Tudor Publishing.

Merleau-Ponty, Maurice (1962). *Phenomenology of Perception*, trans. Colin Smith. New York: Routledge.

——— (1964). "Metaphysics and the Novel," in *Sense and Nonsense*. Trans. Hubert L. Dreyfus and Patricia Allen Dreyfus. Evanston: Northwestern University Press, 26–40.

——— (1968). *The Visible and the Invisible*, ed. Claude Lefort, trans. Alphonso Lingis. Evanston: Northwestern University Press.

Proust, Marcel (1987–1989). *À la recherche du temps perdu*, ed. Jean-Yves Tadié. Paris: Pléiade, Gallimard.

——— (2003a). *In Search of Lost Time*. Vol. 1, *Swann's Way*, general ed. Christopher Prendergast, trans. Lydia Davis. New York: Penguin Classics.

——— (2004a). *In Search of Lost Time*. Vol. 2, *In the Shadow of Young Girls in Flower*, general ed. Christopher Prendergast, trans. James Grieve. New York: Penguin Classics.

——— (2004b). *In Search of Lost Time*. Vol. 3, *The Guermantes Way*, general ed. Christopher Prendergast, trans. Mark Treharne. New York: Penguin Classics.

——— (2004c). *In Search of Lost Time*. Vol. 4, *Sodom and Gomorrah*, general ed. Christopher Prendergast, trans. John Sturrock. New York: Penguin Classics.

——— (2003b). *In Search of Lost Time*. Vol. 6, *Finding Time Again*, general ed. Christopher Prendergast, trans. Ian Patterson. London: Penguin Classics.

CHAPTER 7

"Mixing the Outside with the Inside": Interior Geographies and Domestic Horizons in Gertrude Stein

JUSTINE DYMOND

> Outside and inside are both intimate—they are always ready to be reversed, to exchange their hostility. If there exists a border-line surface between such an inside and outside, this surface is painful on both sides.
>
> —Gaston Bachelard, *Poetics of Space*

In *The Geographical History of America*, Stein asks, "If there was no geography no geographical history would there be any human mind not as it is but would there would there be any human mind" (376). Stein frequently expostulated on the connections between geography and interiority in seemingly reductive terms,[1] but here she suggests in broader, philosophical terms that *consciousness* exists because of place and space. Stein implies here what seems very un-Steinian, that the "human mind" is specific to its historical moment and geography, and thus she anticipates the grounding of subjectivity in its horizon as theorized by Merleau-Ponty.

Important to my analysis here is the constitutive role of space for understanding the presentation and performance of gendered subjectivity within and with*out* Stein's writing. The reciprocal dynamic of intersubjectivity—the interior shaped by an exterior horizon, and vice versa—means that the gendered and racial politics of geography, such as migration, dislocation, and domestic spatiality, deserve attention as one reads Stein's exploration of gendered embodiment. Edward W. Soja warns, "We must be insistently aware of how space can be made to hide consequences from us, how relations of power and discipline are inscribed into the apparently innocent spatiality of social life, how human geographies become filled with politics and ideology" (*Postmodern Geographies* 6). Soja defines "spatiality" as "a triple dialectic of space, time, and social being" (12). Early twentieth-century writers, influenced by the art, philosophy, and science of their time, were interested in the spatial dimensions of perception and subjectivity. For example, in Virginia Woolf's *To the Lighthouse*, the "nature of reality" shifts as the narrative perspective shifts, not only when a new subject beholds objects. Objects in space also create the subject's horizon of perception. But more importantly, as Merleau-Ponty explored in his last book, *The Visible and the Invisible*, the horizon of objects constitutes the subject through a "fleshly intercorporeity." While Merleau-Ponty's philosophy emerges from a post-WWII sensibility, he does not situate his thinking in a specific political or historical context. But if we consider "intercorporeity" alongside "spatiality," then intersubjectivity cannot be considered outside of particular historical and geographical conditions.

Many modernist writers wrestled with the historically racial and spatial dimensions of gendered subjectivity. Specifically in Stein's work, the treatment of the characters' intersubjectivity arises from a phenomenological nexus of racialized, gendered, and classed embodiment, a nexus in transformation from the sentimental subject to a modern subject. Stein famously proclaimed her story "Melanctha"—steeped in blatant racial stereotyping—to be "the first definite step away from the nineteenth century and into the twentieth century in literature" (*The Autobiography of Alice B. Toklas*: 54). Two of Stein's books, *Three Lives* (1909) and *Tender Buttons* (1914), do indeed resist the narrative logic of the nineteenth-century heterosexual marriage plot and rearrange our "natural" relationship to language through self-conscious linguistic play. Stein's break with psychological realism explores othered subjectivities through stylistics that often satirize the sentimental structures housing compulsory heterosexuality. In this way, she reconstitutes the relationship between space and sexuality and the borders between the self's interior and exterior. In *Tender Buttons*, Stein pushes the boundaries of her earlier stylistics to the point of nonsense-making, interrogating the very linguistic foundations of interiority. In remapping the narrative and linguistic structures that shape and reinforce interiority, she purposefully disorients the reader who refuses to "wander" from conventional desires. However, while Stein sheds the deterministic view she skirted in *The Geographical History of America*, Stein's narrative wanderings are contained and returned to their beginnings by racial determinism. Her early works, such as "Melanctha," are problematic in their more explicit racism, but *Tender Buttons* and other later works also include racialized language in their effort to collapse the distinction between exteriority and interiority.

As this essay will show, Stein's attempts to shake up binary linguistic systems and rearrange the syntactical structures that constitute a subject's interiority nonetheless accomplish "mixing the outside with the inside" (*Autobiography*: 156). And in this mixing, Stein writes against the generic and gendered dynamics of sentimental geographies, revealing the narrative logic of sentimental romance even while re-encoding racialized embodiment as spatially deterministic. Ultimately, this inability to "wander" from a deterministic perception of racial subjectivity raises questions about the seeming break with nineteenth-century literary traditions professed by Stein herself and other modernists. But Stein's "experiments" also reveal that "painful surface" in Bachelard's terms, or the *chiasm*, in Merleau-Ponty's terms, where self and other, interior and exterior, are not complete unto themselves.

Interior Geographies

In *Three Lives* and *Tender Buttons*, Stein creates a topography of the interior geographies of her characters. In her early collection of stories, *Three Lives*, these interior geographies are noteworthy for their seeming *lack* of conventional psychological interiority.[2] The title character of "The Gentle Lena," the last story in *Three Lives*, submits without any seeming resistance to the gendered norms that actively groom her for marriage and child-bearing. The "patient, gentle, sweet and german" Lena remains extraordinarily passive even though "Lena did not care much to get married" (249) and her aunt, Mrs. Haydon, arranges for her to marry Herman Kreder. Paradoxically, it is in the narrative's hyperattention to Lena's passivity (and her ethnicity) that the story's overdetermined logic turns itself inside out.

The narrator embeds Lena's passivity into the very syntax of the prose. Thus, instead of expressing Lena's emigration from Germany to the United States in active tense, the narrator tells us, "Lena *had been brought* from Germany to Bridgepoint by a cousin and had been in the same place there for four years" (240; my emphasis). In Germany, Lena is "disturbed" by the "roughness" around her but even so "Lena did not really know that she did not like it" (245). Even her response to the prospect of marriage is one of indifference—"did not care much"—rather than active aversion. Her groom-to-be feels much more active disdain for marriage: "Herman Kreder knew more what it meant to be married and he did not like it very well. He did not like to see girls and he did not want to have to have one always near him" (251). Indeed, "[h]e liked to go out with other men, but he never wanted that there should be any women with them" (252). On the day he and Lena are to get married, Herman disappears and when his father finds him in New York at his sister's house, it takes his father several days to convince Herman to return to Bridgepoint to be married. The narrator says, "Herman's married sister liked her brother Herman, and she did not want him not to like to be with women" (260). It is difficult to miss Herman's preference for men, but the pressure of heterosexual normativity overwhelms Herman's resistance and he and Lena eventually marry.

The only moments of Lena's own autonomous desires come in brief but recurrent glimpses of an inarticulated interiority. But their repetition makes their significance clear. While she sits in the park supervising her employer's children, "The other girls, of course, did tease her, but then that only made a gentle stir within her" (241). When Herman doesn't show up for the wedding, Lena cries on the streetcar going home. The conductor approaches her as if to comfort her but his attentions are somewhat menacing—"She moved away from the man into the corner" (254). By contrast, when other passengers board the car, a "nice lady went and sat beside her and Lena liked it" (255). Lena's preference for girls and women causes no more than "a gentle stir within her," but it is nonetheless this hint of same-sex desire that makes the hegemonic drive toward heterosexual marriage a tragedy for Lena. Notably, when Lena is no longer at "home," when she is in the park with "the other quicker girls" who "always teased her" or when she rides the streetcar after the failed wedding, Lena experiences desires for other women, however subtle and muted. But frozen in her passive state, Lena's stirrings occur only by circumstance in these exterior, transient spaces away from domestic interiors.

With no thought to openly resist marriage, pregnancy, verbal abuse from Herman's mother, or the other cultural pressures that shape Lena's embodiment of the heterosexual, domestic ideal, she submits to her prescripted life. By the end of the story, the repression of any desires that transgress this gender discipline is so great that even in death, Lena remains passive and her baby overshadows her, as we can see in the narrator's syntactical diminution of her death: "When the baby was come out at last, it was like its mother lifeless" (270). The irony here is that Lena's barely noticed death is the logical outcome of her passivity in life. Herman gets what he wants, since "He never had a woman any more to be all the time around him" (270). The only person who misses Lena is the "good german cook who had always scolded Lena, and had always to the last day tried to help her" (270).

By the end of "The Gentle Lena," the common characteristics of a sentimental heroine—gentleness, goodness, sweetness, in a word, submissiveness—have only to be bested by the ultimate submission to death. The evacuation of any agency on Lena's part contributes to Stein's deconstruction of the marriage plot, which achieves through its plodding, repetitive, circular construction a kind of monstrous resonance by the end. In the last sentence, "Herman Kreder was very well content now and he always lived very regular and peaceful, and with every day just like the next one, always alone now with his three good, gentle children" (271). Those attributes, "good, gentle," and their association with innocence, purity, and German-ness, are in this last sentence endowed with a sinister quality, a defamiliarization so thorough that it is difficult not to hear the hard, death-like edge of "gentle" after reading "The Gentle Lena."

In the overdetermined narrative logic of "The Gentle Lena," Lena's tragedy has a farcical tone and the distortion of the sentimental marriage plot depends upon geographical distances, but also on the distance Stein creates between reader and Lena. What sympathy we have quickly evolves into pity as Lena's doom is dictated not only by culturally defined sex roles, but also by the repetitive, predatory nature of the story's prose.[3] Lena's near lack of interiority in the narration, and hence her further objectification by the story, signals Stein's significant break with realism.

Stein's experimental exploration of spatiality in subject formation, and her offensive foregrounding of the racial politics of narrative, happen in a different way in "Melanctha," also found in *Three Lives*, where the story relies heavily on interiorization to answer its central question:

> Why did the subtle, intelligent, attractive, half white girl Melanctha Herbert love and do for and demean herself in service to this coarse, decent, sullen, ordinary, black childish Rose, and why was this unmoral, promiscuous, shiftless Rose married, and that's not so common either, to a good man of the negroes, while Melanctha with her white blood and attraction and her desire for a right position had not yet been married. (125)

Several critics have hailed "Melanctha" for its portrayal of same-sex desire[4] and point to Melanctha's relationship with Rose Johnson and later Jane Harden, and the failed romance with Jefferson Campbell, as evidence. Indeed, sentences such as "It was not from the men that Melanctha learned her wisdom. It was always Jane Harden herself who was making Melanctha begin to understand" (139) and "She [Jane] loved Melanctha hard and made Melanctha feel it very deeply" (140) leave little room for doubt that Melanctha's "wisdom" is rooted in same-sex sexual relationships. Though Melanctha pursues relationships with Jeff Campbell and the betting man Jem Richards, who gives her an engagement ring, she never marries. If there is a tragic love story it is in the heartbreak caused by Rose Johnson's rejection of Melanctha: "Melanctha never again saw Rose Johnson, and it was hard to Melanctha never any more to see her. Rose Johnson had worked in to be the deepest of all Melanctha's emotions" (238).

Throughout the novella, Melanctha's sexual desires are repeatedly described as "wandering" or "straying" and are associated with specific places: "From the time that Melanctha was twelve until she was sixteen she wandered, always seeking but never more than very dimly seeing wisdom" (133). Interestingly, Melanctha's mother, 'Mis' Herbert, also has a tendency to "wander": "'Mis' Herbert has always been a little wandering and mysterious and uncertain in her ways" (128), and yet Melanctha tries to keep her wanderings secret from her mother and father. Her wanderings frequently take her into male territory[5]—construction sites, rail yards: "Often she was alone, sometimes she was with a fellow seeker, and she *strayed* and stood, sometimes by railroad yards, sometimes on the docks or around new buildings where many men were working" (132; my emphasis). In the early pages of the story at least, she seems naïve and flirtatious and "always made herself escape." Once she meets Jane Harden, "Melanctha Herbert soon always wandered with her" (138).

In a sense, the narrative also wanders but it does so within boundaries circumscribed by the marriage of Rose Johnson and the birth of her child that soon after dies. One could argue that the narrative classically begins *in medias res*, opening with Rose's problematic delivery, which occurs in terms of chronology later in time than most of the narrative. Thus, the story circles back and by the end almost verbatim repeats its opening descriptions of Melanctha helping Rose through labor: "Melanctha did everything that any woman could, she tended Rose, and she was patient, submissive, soothing and untiring, while the sullen, childish, cowardly, black Rosie grumbled, and fussed, and howled, and made herself to be an abomination and like a simple beast" (228). Thus Rose's "marriage plot" contains Melanctha's wandering desires, reinscribing Melanctha's "marriage plots" even as they never reach the closure of the conventional sentimental romance.

Melanctha's enclosure within Rose Johnson's "marriage plot" maps onto the narrator's foregrounded racial enclosures, as the descriptions heavy handedly render Rose Johnson in graphically racist terms and imply that Melanctha's liminal position as a mulatta contributes to her unresolved yearnings. Indeed, the narrator defines Rose's domesticity in disturbing racial terms: "The baby though it was healthy after it was born did not live long. Rose Johnson was careless and negligent and selfish and when Melanctha had to leave for a few days the baby died. Rose Johnson had liked her baby well enough and perhaps she just forgot it for a while, anyway the child was dead and Rose and Sam were very sorry, but then these things came so often in the negro world in Bridgepoint that they neither of them thought about it very long" (230–231). Thus, while "Melanctha" does indeed "wander" from the conventions of the sentimental marriage plot, this deformation of the sentimental provokes the surfacing of graphically racist language, which reinscribes the borders between an implied white culture and an inferior "negro world" devoid of proper sentimental motherhood. Stein thus suggests that peeling back the sentimental plot exposes its racialized underpinning, which effectively still *pins* Melanctha and modernist experimentation down.

One might further argue that the text's expression of "queerness" depends upon the narration's racial architecture—Melanctha's (and Stein's) sexual "otherness" tempered by the text's familiar othering of African American subjects. *Tender Buttons* in its more experimental approach to portraying a queer domesticity, on the surface at least, seems to avoid the racial explosiveness of *Three Lives*. Indeed, *Tender Buttons* creates more profound disorientation for the reader unwilling to "wander" from conventional narrative structures. And yet, while *Tender Buttons* explores the interior landscape of othered subjectivity, Stein continues to deploy racially encoded language to test the boundaries of her modernist break with the nineteenth century.

Domestic Horizons: "Mixing the Outside with the Inside" in Tender Buttons

Much Stein scholarship has focused on her experiments in detaching the signifier from the signified in language "to reformulate relations between words outside the laws of grammar" (Smedman 570). In "'Cousin to Cooning': Relation, Difference, and Racialized Language in Stein's Nonrepresentational Texts," Lorna J. Smedman writes, "Stein's early nonrepresentational texts work with the materiality of the world, self-consciously playing with the aspects of language such as aural puns (including mistranslations from other languages to English and transsyllabification), rhyme, morphemes, visual format, and punctuation" (573). Psychoanalytic feminist critics have celebrated Stein's texts as *écriture féminine*, demonstrating the power of her writing to subvert phallogocentrism. But, as I have argued, Stein's subversion overtly depends upon, and indeed results in, the violent reinscription of racializing language. Smedman argues that "[r]acialized signifiers, which foregrounded the issue of difference by embodying America's brutal racist history, posed the greatest challenge to Stein's project" (570). Here, I will extend the discussion of Stein's experiments with nonrepresentational language to show that her linguistic experiments more profoundly deform sentimental form and have important phenomenological implications. And yet even as *Tender Buttons* profoundly reshapes the linguistic frame of space and sexuality, Stein is unable to deconstruct linguistic racial coding in the same way. Thus, while Stein collapses gendered embodiment and domestic space, *Tender Buttons* is still haunted by the racialized signifiers that define interior spaces.

Merleau-Ponty writes that "just as my body sees only because it is a part of the visible in which it opens forth, the sense upon which the arrangement of the sounds opens reflects back upon that arrangement . . . if my words have a meaning, it is not *because* they present the systematic organization the linguist will disclose, it is because that organization, like the look, refers back to itself: the operative Word is the obscure region whence comes the instituted light, as the muted reflection of the body upon itself is what we call natural light" (*The Visible and the Invisible*: 153–154; emphasis in original). Here, Merleau-Ponty argues, as Stein does, that words have meaning because they signify the whole system, or horizon, of signs in which they operate as meaningful sounds. He associates this reflection in language with the body's emplacement in a horizon. Just as the body is both sentient and sensible, that is, sensing the world and sensed in the world, language is a material object—to be heard and seen, to be touched by the lips, teeth, and tongue—in the horizon of things it names.

It is that very doubleness of being, the sentient and sensible body, that forms the subject that perceives itself as an interior subjectivity though it arises from its relationship to other bodies and things. Merleau-Ponty writes that "at the same time we are separated from [what we perceive] by all the thickness of the look and of the body; it is that this distance is not the contrary of this proximity, it is deeply consonant with it, it is synonymous with it. It is that the thickness of flesh between the seer and the thing is constitutive for the thing of its visibility as for the seer of his corporeity; it is not an obstacle between them, it is their means of communication" (*The Visible and the Invisible*: 135). How then does the "thickness" of the seer and the thing seen, that opacity that allows both to be seen, illuminate Stein's verbal pyrotechnics?

Stein's language in *Tender Buttons* invites us on a tour of her interiority, the interior space of her domestic life and her self, at the same time that it creates a barrier to our knowing that interiority. Stein's text is like the "thickness" of the body and the look that we perceive and that we are separated from by its opacity. Our will to make sense of her textual body draws us to its language, but for some readers that textual body remains an opaque stone, which appears to contain no interiority. The text thereby turns on its head the notion of *which* subjectivities are *in the know*. However, if the reader is willing to allow "the arrangement of sounds" to reflect "back upon that arrangement," thereby exposing the structure of sense-making, Stein's text provokes a radical intercorporeality where Bachelard's "border-line surface" between exteriority and interiority dissolves, blurring not only the outside and inside of a text but also the boundaries between where the textual body ends and the reader's "incarnate mind" begins. For the text's interior exists only so far as the reader is willing to play with the text otherly than she has with other texts whose meaning depends upon the conventional mimetic function of signifier and signified. By unmooring the word from its signified and thereby allowing sound, rhythm, and syntax to both disrupt and proliferate meanings, Stein rearranges our outsides. This unhinging of our usual relationship to language and therefore to the world of its representation, forces us to confront the body's role in thought-making: the conventional mimetic function of language depends on the body's orientation to the world *outside* it. Stein's text becomes a reshaped outside, which orients our inside, but that outside only takes shape through the "incarnate mind." Furthermore, if we can challenge the *naturalness* of mimesis in language, we can also challenge the *naturalness* of representation that produces what Bachelard calls the "painful" "border-line surface" between dichotomous pairings: inside/outside and subject/object.

In *The Autobiography of Alice B. Toklas*, Stein explains in third person her intentions in writing *Tender Buttons*:

> They were the beginning, as Gertrude Stein would say, of mixing the outside with the inside. Hitherto she had been concerned with seriousness and the inside of things, in these studies she began to describe the inside as seen from the outside. (156)

With this declaration of intention, Stein announces an undertaking of ontological proportions. To project the inside onto the outside, as for example in *Three Lives*, reflects a still lingering concern with psychological realism. But to *mix* "the outside with the inside" or to see the inside "from the outside" suggests a project that questions the distinction between an inside and an outside, and therefore Stein makes a decisive break with psychological realism and its sentimental dream of transparency.

In an initial reading, *Tender Buttons* appeared to me like mere nonsense, a flat landscape of words where no distinguishable voice existed. In a subsequent reading, I detected small hills in that landscape, patterns of recurring words—center, cover, red, dirty, copper, shudders—that suggested containment and obfuscation. Upon further readings, the speaker's voice began to take more shape: I could hear Stein (or Stein's persona in the text) inviting the reader inside the house of her text and introducing the reader to the "Objects," "Food," and "Rooms" of her private domestic sphere, the home where she and Toklas lived and loved together. But this voice continues to remain mischievous, coy, flirtatiously revealing and hiding, always "there [but] behind the door." As has been widely examined by critics, Stein's language play was on one level a code for lesbian sexuality. We can easily understand then that for Stein to introduce us to the domestic sphere where she sat center stage writing and collecting art, is also to unveil, though in a somewhat obscured manner, her sexuality. Stein's sexuality is therefore contained in and represented by an interior space whose walls and rooms obscure the "otherness" of Stein's lifestyle. Her language in *Tender Buttons* produces yet another level of representation and simultaneous obfuscation of sexuality. The reader inclined to read otherly will perceive, as Joseph A. Boone describes in "Queer Sites in Modernisms: Harlem/The Left Bank/Greenwich Village," the "textual descriptions that—like the coded gay body—simultaneously flaunt and conceal 'meaning' in a masquerade of allusion and self-referentiality" (250).

Concealing meaning suggests that *Tender Buttons* is a text organized around an absent center, lesbian sexuality encoded in language but never explicitly revealed. In addition, there is no explicit perspective to orient the text since there are no characters in the conventional sense. Marguerite S.

Murphy points out, "The first-person pronoun rarely appears, giving the prose a superficial impersonality" (389). When the first-person does appear, it is brief: "I hope she has her cow" (25); "I spy" (52). In a curious absenting of perspective, the narrative voice of the section titled "Rooms" never identifies itself, lending the voice a disembodied quality, even though the speaker does suggest action and a history through, respectively, passive construction and past tense, as in this passage: "To begin the placing there is no wagon. There is no change lighter. *It was done*. And then the spreading, that *was not accomplishing* that needed standing and yet the time was not so difficult as they were not all in place" (63; emphasis mine). There are no other traditional signals of a narrating consciousness, except, of course, for the consciousness implied in the selection of language. However, the author does introduce us to rooms where she is always "there behind the door" but never revealed to us except indirectly through the language of her outside, that is, the objects in her house. The central reason for entering these rooms and these pages, to find Stein *in* them, is then frustrated. She knows this and so orders us to "Act so that there is no use in a centre" (63). Yet the text itself shows some anxiety over this lack of a center, by occasionally re-announcing its absence ("it is not very likely that there is a centre" [68]). The speaker's return to this problem of the center suggests an interesting paradox: Perhaps the text's center is its declaration that it has no center.

By bringing attention to "the miserable centre," Stein performs a sleight of hand, creating a text that continually points to what is absent. Stein's text circles around a *particular* absent body made present through the text's encoded language: the sexual other. But unlike other texts in which homosexuality is represented by silences or gaps in the narration, *Tender Buttons* transforms the signifieds represented by signifiers and encodes lesbian sexuality into things—red roses, hats, a feather, shudders, etc. Stein thus inverts the usual mimetic function of language to represent lesbian sexuality. However, it is not simply that Stein substitutes signifiers as a way of coding sexuality; *Tender Buttons* enacts a much more complicated rearrangement of the conventional relationship between words and their signifieds.

When the "author of all that ... in there behind the door" gives us a tour of "Rooms," pointing out "A little lingering lion and a Chinese chair, all the handsome cheese which is stone, all of it and a choice, a choice of a blotter" (64), we quickly become disoriented if we continue to read with the assumption that words are transparently representational. As soon as we think we have grasped an image that makes sense, the next word undercuts our sense of security in that perception. What were once familiar words and objects become foreign ones combined with other unexpected but familiar words and objects. To illustrate further this disorienting effect of ordinary objects, let us look at the section headed "A Shawl":

Mixing the Outside with the Inside 121

> A shawl is a hat and hurt and a red ballon [sic] and an under coat and a sizer a sizer of talks.
> A shawl is a wedding, a piece of wax a little build. A shawl.
> Pick a ticket, pick it in strange steps and with hollows. There is hollow hollow belt, a belt is a shawl.
> A plate that has a little bobble, all of them, any so.
> Please a round it is ticket.
> It was a mistake to state that a laugh and a lip and a laid climb and a depot and a cultivator and little choosing is a point it. (27–28)

In the first sentence, the combination of nouns upsets the conventional sense of association and category. In some instances, a shawl may be worn like a hat, and therefore resembles one, but if we settle into that logical association, we are quickly discomfitted by "hurt." Perhaps we shift our associative category to sounds: hat and hurt; but then again "red ballon" muddles that attempt at sense-making. Skipping down to the last sentence of this section, we can see that Stein further confuses the sense-making of syntactical order. By beginning the sentence with "It was a mistake to state that," she creates an expectation of meaning from a phrase that grounds us in its familiarity (though its passive construction erases a subject *who* states). However, what follows frustrates any meaning established in that first phrase: "a laugh and a lip and a laid climb." Perhaps we take some consolation from the alliteration and the way a voice does indeed climb in pitch when these words are spoken, but then, how do we make sense of the remainder of the sentence, which seems to deviate entirely from the syntactical construction at its opening? We don't, unless we have been patient enough to listen to our disoriented interaction with Stein's words. In this way, we may notice that familiar objects and words depend upon an ordering, that is, an arrangement in a system of positions, for their sense-making. Words take on meaning in relationship to one another, that is, by virtue of their syntactical positions in a sentence. When those positions are disrupted within a sentence, as in "This which is not why there is a voice is the remains of an offering," that disruption exposes each word's dependence on the other words and its difference from them to have any meaning. As Stein writes in the opening of "Objects," "All this and not ordinary, not unordered in not resembling. The difference is spreading" (9). Meaning in language arises from words "not resembling" each other and from their ordered syntactical positions, not from their assumed signifieds.

But Stein goes even further than the word itself when she interrogates difference as an organizing principle of language; she examines this concept at the level of the phoneme. In the following passage, Stein interrogates the why of difference and sameness in words that all share a phoneme (*er*): "Why is there a circular diminisher, why is there a bather, why is there no scraper, why is there a dinner, why is there a bell ringer, why is there a duster, why is there a section of a similar resemblance, why is there that scissor" (70). If this passage is read as a list of objects or things—bather, scraper, dinner, etc.—we see one meaning: a catalog of things in the room, which the narrator both asks us to see and whose existence she asks us to question: what are the purposes of these things? But if we read the passage aloud, we can see another possibility for meaning: why do all these words share the phoneme *er* and yet do not necessarily share the same sense? Sometimes *er* signals an agent, the *one* who bathes, the *one* who dusts, but that does not hold for *dinner* and *scissor*. Stein asks us to consider the rich yet arbitrary arrangement of sounds that form words, revealing that meaning rests on an arbitrary foundation, "the centre having spelling" (73). As containers, the signifiers slip and slide around their signifieds.

Stein denaturalizes our relationship to language. In *Tender Buttons*, Stein's seeming nonsense reveals the linguistic structures that provide the sense-making of heteronormative spaces. Stein's domestic interiors thus appear to be nonsense to readers anchored by the "oneness"—the conventional marriage—of signifier and signified. To find sense, however fleeting, in *Tender Buttons* requires a fundamental rearrangement of the reader's sexual subjectivity as grounded in language. In this way, *Tender Buttons* is perhaps a precursor (flirtatious foreplay?) to Stein's book-length poem *Lifting Belly*, which even more intensely invites the reader's interaction with the text to expose the lesbian desire and sexuality central to the poem.

In a paradoxical sense, *Lifting Belly* has a more playful surface than does *Tender Buttons*, which allows for easier access to its interiority. But, as with *Tender Buttons*, meaning in *Lifting Belly* depends upon the interaction between the reader's body and the materiality of language.[6] In deceptively simple language and syntax, particularly compared to *Tender Buttons*, the words are arranged on the page in short, declarative bursts that look like lists of dialogue moving in a linear manner down the page. However, unless the reader indulges in play with Stein's text, she may soon be frustrated; if she insists on a one-to-one correspondence between language and meaning here, the poem will quickly appear meaningless. Take this passage, for instance:

> Say did you see that the wind was from the east.
> It usually is from the South.
> We like rain.
> Sneeze. This is the way to say it.
> You meant a pressure.
> Indeed yes.
> All the time there is a chance to see me. I don't
> wish it to be said so.

> The skirt.
> And water.
> You mean ocean water.
> Not exactly an ocean a sea.
> A success.
> Was it a success.
> Lifting belly is all there. (7)

In this passage, meaning does not necessarily build from line to line; rather, meaning happens recursively, returning upon itself sometimes and sometimes opening out to another word aurally, as in "Not exactly an ocean a sea./A success." The movement reminds me more of the advance and retreat of waves, a repetition in sound or rhythm that may never end. Its origin may be in "the east" or "the South," "a pressure" like a "[s]neeze," moving in multiple directions, revealing that "[l]ifting belly is *all* there."

A reader unwilling to unmoor language from its mimetic function will be left high and dry of meaning in the following passage from *Lifting Belly*:

> I say lifting belly and then I say lifting belly and Caesars. I say lifting belly gently and Caesars gently. I say lifting belly again and Caesars again. I say lifting belly and I say Caesars and I say lifting belly Caesars and cow come out. I say lifting belly and Caesars and cow come out. (33)

Here, Stein gives the reader a hint: the repetition of "I say" explicitly suggests speaking aloud the words on the page. The sounds of the language spoken aloud (Caesars/seizures) provide more meaning than do the letters arranged on the page. The lowing of a cow implies moaning, but in order to make that connection, reading has to encompass more than seeing words on the page. Though it is a commonplace that in poetry sound underscores meaning, in *Lifting Belly* there are places where sound *is* meaning.

In *Tender Buttons* and *Lifting Belly*, the possibilities for making meaning are in the hands of the reader, and therefore the meaning is never fixed in a single, authoritative voice but, rather, is open to an unlimited range of meanings produced by an infinite variety of voices. It is in the reader's pleasurable (and possibly painful?) struggle to make sense out of Stein's attempt to create non-sense that any meaning emerges. Of course, the necessity of the reader's engagement with the words on the page in order to produce meaning from those words is true for any text, but *Tender Buttons* depends primarily on the reader's own emplacement, embodied subjectivity, and the reader's body's enactment—the movement of eyes across the page, returning to a previous sentence, skipping ahead to the next section, perceiving the section titles together, etc.; the mouth's forming of words; the ears' hearing the sounds of words that exist only in that hearing, not on the page—to create multiple possibilities of meaning.

However, I certainly do not propose that simply relinquishing one's assumptions about the *naturalness* of the signifier and signified immediately makes Stein's text comprehensible, and in that way, containable. Rather, that perceptual and ontological shift allows for the possibility of meaning, but in *Tender Buttons*, and particularly in *Lifting Belly*, meaning is rarely fixed or containable. Thus, even the reader who reads *otherly* must struggle with slippery meanings—each seeming grasp of a meaning loosens as a potential meaning proliferates other meanings, such as my own early encounters with *Tender Buttons* illustrate.

It is in this continual potential for meaning created by the reader's interaction with the text that *Tender Buttons* performs what Merleau-Ponty calls the "fundamental phenomenon of reversibility." What Stein does is to place the "incarnate mind" in the materiality of objects, including the materiality of language, but not only to show the outside ("Objects," "Food," and "Rooms") that constitutes her inside (her writing, her ideas, her sexuality). She also demonstrates how the outside—*Tender Buttons*—creates the inside of the reader and, thereby, shows how the fluidity of subjectivity arises from the *chiasm* of the subject's uncompleted reversibility to itself. In a sense then, we are always reaching over the *chiasm* between ourselves and Stein's text, to create the "paradox of expression."

However, the absence in the center is arguably recuperated by racialized language, recommitting to the sense-making—to the narrative-making and world-making—of racial difference. As noted previously, "Melanctha," and other early works, express a more explicit racism, but *Tender Buttons* also includes racialized language in its attempt to collapse the border between exteriority and interiority. For example, in the "Food" section of *Tender Buttons*, Stein writes, "[N]eedless are niggers and a sample sample set of old eaten butterflies with spoons" (55). Smedman argues that Stein's experiments with separating signifiers from signifieds fail when she employs racialized language: "Stein exuberantly played with loaded signifiers—'wife,' 'wedding,' 'Caesar,' and, most famously, 'rose'—shaking them so hard that they were emptied of their gendered, historical denotations and connotations, available for her own particular significations. She attempted the same thing with racialized signifiers such as 'nigger' or 'coon,' but these terms did not have the elasticity of 'wife' or 'rose'" (575). In Smedman's view, Stein ultimately cannot unload racial signifiers of their signifieds, partly because in such words "the materiality of the word is suddenly grounded in the materiality of the body" (578) and because of "the power such frozen linguistic formulations have over American speech—and thought" (580). In this reading, Stein's word play encounters limits when language is so embedded in the materiality of the body that language replicates the very violence it signifies by fragmenting the image of the body into racialized parts. Racialized language then reinscribes the difference on which binary systems rest—white/black, male/female, outside/inside—in its resistance to nonsense.

In her essay on Stein and race, Laura Doyle proposes that Stein did not wield such racialized language innocently. Though Doyle does not analyze *Tender Buttons* directly, she argues that Stein "makes use of whites' racialized sexual stereotypes of blacks and mulattas to realize" her deformation of "the tradition of sentimental fiction in English" ("The Flat, the Round, and Gertrude Stein": 265). If the reader is unable to see anything but nonsense in her texts except when encountering the starkly meaningful language of race, does Stein then perpetuate, rather than undermine, the static comprehensibility of the racialized other and lesbian sexuality? Does Stein reinscribe the normalization of heterosexuality and whiteness?

This danger exposes, at least partially, the structure that enables other texts to create mimetic sense. In other words, the risk of unintelligibility in Stein's texts suggests that the sense-making of mimetic language, and therefore of thought, depends upon another ordered arrangement, that of the gendered and heterosexual economy of desire, and that the gendered and heterosexual economy of desire depends upon an ordered, racialized *linguistic* arrangement. Can language then be separated from the world, the cultural and historical specificity in which language arises, and yet reorient our historically and culturally emplaced subjectivities?

Stein's texts remain problematic, then, in their attempt to decontextualize language (even as they recontextualize language in relation to the reader's embodied subjectivity). This "problem" arises particularly as Stein tries to decontextualize the signs of the racialized other, in which is inscribed the painful surface, as Bachelard writes, on both sides of the inside/outside dichotomy. Words that resist such unmooring and collapsing of interiority and exteriority perform another "fundamental phenomenon of reversibility" since they reify the constitutive power of language to construct subjectivity as an inside created by an *othered* outside. Stein does attempt to reposition the "border-line surface" of the other by relieving language of the weight of history, but ultimately the attempt to unload that weight itself reflects the overdetermined meaning of racial signifiers. Stein's narrators and her formal experimentation cannot fully undo the racially embedded meanings of modernity's racializing legacy.

Stein's failure to shake language's exteriority and our interiorities fully of history and geography returns us to Merleau-Ponty's "thickness" of the flesh. In disorienting the reader's interiority through the reader's embodiment of her linguistic play, Stein presents us with a textual fleshiness. This fleshiness reminds us of the other's sentient presence at the same time that it requires our sentience to create meaning. That meaning—in its myriad possibilities—may echo back from a canyon of familiar objects in the landscape: the gendered, racialized, heteronormative structures of nineteenth-century sentimental and literary traditions that Stein and other modernists wrote in and against. But in those echoes, our interiorities are chiasmic, opening up across a space of difference, and revealing the strangeness of our own embodiment.

Notes

1. Stein biographer James R. Mellow reports, "Meeting someone for the first time, she [Stein] had a disconcerting habit of fixing her eyes sharply on the visitor and asking a barrage of questions: Where was he from? How old was he? What did he do? What was his parentage? In later years, to the dismay of friends, she had refined the technique to the simple, 'What is your blood?'" (15). When Picasso married the Russian ballet dancer Olga Koklova, Stein disapproved; she thought it "was a mistake and later evolved the queer [sic] theory that it was due to the superficial attraction of a similar orientalism in both nationalities. 'Scratch a Russian and you find a Tartar. Scratch a Spaniard and you find a Saracen,' she maintained" (Mellow 243).

2. This lack is particularly ironic given that before Stein became a serious writer she studied medicine and psychology and, while pursuing her literary career, she became an enthusiast of the sociologist Otto Weininger. See Maria Damon, "Writing, Social Science, and Ethnicity in Gertrude Stein and Certain Others." *Modernism, Inc.: Body, Memory, Capital* (Eds. Jani Scandura and Michael Thurston. New York: New York University Press, 2001). Also, James R. Mellow, *Charmed Circle: Gertrude Stein & Company* (New York: Praeger Publishers, 1974), 120–121.

3. Mellow writes, "In her own work, Gertrude claimed, she had achieved the 'destruction of associational emotion in poetry and prose.' She had arrived at the knowledge that 'beauty, music, decoration, the result of emotion should never be the cause, even events should not be the cause of emotion nor should they be the material of poetry and prose.... They should consist of an exact reproduction of either an outer or an inner reality'" (311).

4. See, for example, Charles Caramello, *Henry James, Gertrude Stein, and the Biographical Act* (Chapel Hill: University of North Carolina Press, 1996).

5. For a fuller analysis of the male spaces in Stein, see Jeanne Tara Hart's *Tender Horizons: The American Landscape of Austin and Stein* (Dissertation, University of Maryland, College Park, 1996).

6. In *Queer Poetics: Five Modernist Women Writers*, Mary Galvin's chapter on Stein also examines how Stein's language play necessarily presumed a reader who reads "otherly." Galvin writes, "We cannot stand outside the poem [*Lifting Belly*] in judgment of its 'meaning' or its structure; we must participate in the construction of its 'meaning' or else it remains meaningless" (48). However, Galvin does not examine the politics of race or spatiality in her essay.

References

Bachelard, Gaston (1964). *A Poetics of Space*. New York: The Orion Press.

Boone, Joseph A. (1996). "Queer Sites in Modernism: Harlem/The Left Bank/Greenwich Village." *The Geography of Identity*. Ed. Patricia Yaeger. Ann Arbor: University of Michigan Press.

Caramello, Charles (1996). *Henry James, Gertrude Stein, and the Biographical Act*. Chapel Hill: University of North Carolina Press.

Damon, Maria (2001). "Writing, Social Science, and Ethnicity in Gertrude Stein and Certain Others." *Modernism, Inc.* Eds. Jani Scandura and Michael Thurston. New York: New York University Press.

Doyle, Laura (2000). "The Flat, the Round, and Gertrude Stein: Race and the Shape of Modern(ist) History." *Modernism/Modernity*. 7.2: 249–271.

Galvin, Mary (1999). *Queer Poetics: Five Modernist Women Writers*. Westport, CT: Praeger Publishers.

Mellow, James R. (1974). *Charmed Circle: Gertrude Stein & Company*. New York: Praeger Publishers.

Merleau-Ponty, Maurice (1968). *The Visible and the Invisible*. Evanston: Northwestern University Press.

Murphy, Marguerite S. (1991). "'Familiar Strangers': The Household Words of Gertrude Stein's *Tender Buttons*." *Contemporary Literature* 32: 383–402.

Smedman, Lorna J. (1996). "'Cousin to Cooning': Relation, Difference, and Racialized Language in Stein's Nonrepresentational Texts." *Modern Fiction Studies* 42.3: 569–588.

Soja, Edward (1989). *Postmodern Geographies: The Reassertion of Space in Critical Social Theory*. New York: Verso.

Stein, Gertrude (1909/1998). *Three Lives*. New York: The Library of America.

—— (1914/1991). *Tender Buttons*. Los Angeles: Sun & Moon Press.

—— (1933). *The Autobiography of Alice B. Toklas*. New York: Random House.

—— (1936/1998). *The Geographical History of America*. New York: The Library of America.

—— (1953/1995). *Lifting Belly*. Tallahassee: The Naiad Press.

Woolf, Virginia *To the Lighthouse*. 1981 (1927). New York: Harcourt Brace & Company.

PART IV

Ethical Challenges:
Recognition, Reciprocity,
Violence, and Care

CHAPTER 8

Beyond Recognition: Merleau-Ponty and an Ethics of Vision

KELLY OLIVER

> The idea we have of the world would be overturned if we could succeed in seeing the intervals between things (for example, the space between the trees on the boulevard) as *objects*, and inversely, if we saw the things themselves—the trees—as the ground. Merleau-Ponty ("Film and the New Psychology" 1945: 48)

Sartre's paranoid notion of the look, exemplified by his famous peeping Tom caught in the act of looking through a keyhole, can be read as a contemporary reenactment of Hegel's lord and bondsman's struggle for self-consciousness through recognition. For Hegel, the struggle for recognition also begins with a look. It is the sight of the other self-conscious body mimicking one's actions that makes one want to kill it: "Each *sees* the *other* do the same as it does; each does itself what it demands of the other, and therefore also does what it does only in so far as the other does the same" (*Phenomenology of Spirit*, 1977: 112, my emphasis). For Sartre, however, the primary experience that brings me to myself is the experience of shame that results from being caught in the act by another person (*Being and Nothingness*, 1956: 386). Like Hegel's theory of the onset of self-consciousness through the master-slave relationship, Sartre's theory is premised on the claim that even in concrete relations each person is attempting to enslave the other: "while I seek to enslave the Other, the Other seeks to enslave me. . . . Conflict is the original meaning of being-for-others" (1956: 475). I am imprisoned by the look of the other, yet through the look of the other I am aware of myself as a subject. The look of the Other turns me back on myself so that I can see the way in which I always escape myself; I see my possibilities. When I see myself as an object for the Other and realize that who I am is constituted in that look, the look of the Other confronts me with the nothingness at the core of my being; and at the same time I refuse to be reduced to that look. So begins the Sartrian struggle with the Other, which supports Sartre's character Garcin's conclusion in *No Exit* that "there's no need for red-hot pokers. Hell is other people" (Sartre 1976: 47).

This alienating look, this evil eye, is also at work in psychoanalytic conceptions of self-consciousness and sexual difference. For Sigmund Freud the sight of the supposedly "castrated sex" of women initiates all of the rage, jealousy, and murderous impulses of the oedipal situation: "Probably no male human being is spared the terrifying shock of threatened castration at the *sight* of the female genitals (*Three Essays on the Theory of Sexuality* [1905], 1962: 216, my emphasis); "They [females] notice the penis of a brother or playmate, strikingly *visible* and of large proportions, at once recognize it as the superior counterpart of their own small and inconspicuous organ, and from that time forward fall a victim to envy for the penis" (*Some Psychological Consequences of the Anatomical Distinction Between the Sexes* [1925], 1972b: 187, my emphasis). For Freud, the castration threat and penis envy that both initiate and resolve the oedipal situation revolve around looking at the other sex.

With Jacques Lacan, the evil eye becomes the essence of the gaze. Lacan wildly suggests that the eye of the gaze is "the eye filled with voracity, the evil eye" (*The four fundamental concepts of psychoanalysis* 1981: 115). This is not an individual evil eye controlled by its bearer. Rather, it is a universal evil eye that for Lacan comes to define the eye in relation to the gaze. In this paranoid universe the subject "operates by remote control" in response to the evil eye of the gaze. Fundamental to the power of the evil eye is the power to separate, which is what causes the subject's alienation, condemnation, and even damnation: "It is striking, when one thinks of the universality of the function of the evil eye, that there is no trace anywhere of a good eye, of an eye that blesses. What can this mean, except that the eye carries with it the fatal function of being in itself endowed—if you will allow me to play on several registers at once—with a power to separate" (1981: 115). From beginning to end, the subject is separated from the object of his desire. And, for Lacan, this separation is connected to vision. The *sight* of the other incites aggression because sight only serves to remind us of the abyss separating us from others. Lacan's early account of the mirror stage is a prime example of the way that sight incites antagonism toward others. For Lacan the alienating function of the I as it is misrecognized in the mirror releases aggressivity in relation to any other (*Ecrits*, 1977: 6). In the mirror stage, it is the gap between the recognition of my own limitations and my misrecognition of the ideal other as myself that inaugurates the antagonism between self and others in the struggle for recognition.

From Hegel's master-slave struggle to Freud's account of castration and envy, from Sartre's accusing look of the other to Lacan's evil eye of the gaze, vision creates a sense of lack or alienation. It seems that what we see when we recognize ourselves in or against the other is the empty void between us that alienates us not only from others but also from ourselves; and we spend the rest of our lives in the futile and violent attempt to fill that gap. We imagine that by getting rid of the other we can close the space between us and overcome alienation.

Philosophers such as Emmanuel Levinas and Luce Irigaray have challenged this emphasis on vision in the history of philosophy, specifically with regard to recognition. The problem, however, is not with vision *per se*, but with the particular notion of vision presupposed in theories of recognition or misrecognition. In these theories, what makes all intersubjective relationships struggles or hostile encounters is not their emphasis on vision, but the presupposition that space is empty and that vision both traverses and fails to traverse that empty space. What we cannot see on this notion of vision are the elements that connect us to others and the world. Yet, these are the elements that make vision possible, light, air, matter, that fill the space between us. What we do not recognize makes recognition possible. We need not discount vision; rather, we can follow Merleau-Ponty's reformulation of vision and what it means to see in order to develop an alternative notion of subjectivity based on ethical responseability.

Contra Sartre, Merleau-Ponty rejects the view that "the other can enter into the universe of the seer only by assault, as a pain and a catastrophe" (1968: 78). The other is not my negation or destruction because "there is an intersection of my universe with that of another" (1968: 80). Merleau-Ponty insists that radical alterity requires neither that we are in conflict with others nor that we are forever cut off from others. He argues that I am not fixed by the accusing gaze of the other. In *The Visible and the Invisible*, he says "that one knows the other not only in what he suffers from him, but more generally as a witness ... because he is not a pure gaze upon pure being any more than I am.... For the other to be truly other, it does not suffice and it is not necessary that he be a scourge, the continued threat of an absolute reversal of pro and con, a judge himself elevated above all contestation, without place, without relativities, faceless like an obsession, and capable of crushing me with a glance into the dust of my world " (1968: 80, 82).

For Merleau-Ponty, the body itself mediates the relationship between subject and object, self and other. The body is both subject and object "because a sort of dehiscence opens my body in two, and because between my body looked at and my body looking, my body touched and my body touching, there is overlapping encroachment, so that we must say that the things pass into us as well as we into the things" (1968: 123). The thickness of flesh and permeability of skin makes "intercorporiety" possible (1968: 141). Unlike Levinas who leaves Sartre behind by rejecting any philosophy of subjectivity, Merleau-Ponty rethinks subjectivity through the body. Both the thickness of the flesh and the permeability of the skin make communication with the world and others possible (1968: 135). The thickness of the flesh guarantees relations, while the skin ensures that we can distinguish our experience from another's. Yet, since the flesh and skin are not objects, but synergetic, we are never cut off from others. The skin is a boundary, but a permeable boundary.

Flesh makes communication possible because it is the "reversible." By reversible, Merleau-Ponty means that we are both sensing and sensible, both subject and object. By virtue of our flesh, we can sense and be sensed by others and by ourselves. The reversibility of the tangible opens up an "intercorporeal being," which extends further than any one individual and founds the "transitivity from one body to another" (1968: 143). Merleau-Ponty goes so far as to suggest that I can almost experience something of the other's embodiment. In *The Visible and the Invisible*, he gives the example of the difference between hearing my own voice and hearing the voice of another. I have a different relation to my own voice because it emanates from my body and I am affected by the vibrations of my body as I speak. "But if I am close enough to the other who speaks to hear his breath and feel his effervescence and his fatigue, I almost witness, in him as in myself, the awesome birth of vociferation" (1968: 144). At this point, Merleau-Ponty suggests the radical notion that I can feel the other's pain. There can be an exchange of synergy between bodies and if I am close enough to another person, I can experience the movements of her body in the same way that I experience the movements of my own. More than this, I can feel her effervescence and fatigue.

For Merleau-Ponty, it is precisely because of the boundaries and the connections between skin and flesh, which is our difference and the distance between us, that relationships and communication take place. He says that "this distance is not the contrary of this proximity, it is deeply consonant with it, it is synonymous with it. It is that the thickness of the flesh between the seer and the thing is constitutive for the thing of its visibility as for the seer of his corporeity; it is not an obstacle between them, it is their means of communication" (1968: 135). Distance is not alienating or threatening. It does not forever separate me from the world and from others. Rather, for Merleau-Ponty distance is enabling and vision is precisely how: "Vision alone makes us learn that beings that are different, "exterior," foreign to one another, are yet absolutely together are "simultaneity" (1964: 187). Unlike Lacan's gaze that either cuts us off from the world and others or fixes us in a triangle of unfulfillable desire, Merleau-Ponty imagines vision as a means of connection and communion. Rather than the alienation and conflict at the heart of either Sartre or Lacan's notions of the gaze, with Merleau-Ponty we find wonder at the gap between us, the distance that enables us to relate to each other.

Merleau-Ponty does not accept the Cartesian conception of space that privileges the perspective of some God's-eye view on my seeing. He insists that "space is no longer what it was in the *Dioptric*, a network of relations between objects such as would be seen by a witness to my vision or by a geometer looking over it and reconstructing it from the outside" (1964: 178). This sentiment suggests that Merleau-Ponty's conception of space and vision stands opposed not only to Descartes' *Dioptric* but also to Lacan's triangle of desire that defines the gaze in terms of a third party by whom we are seen in our relationship. Merleau-Ponty, it seems, should accept neither Lacan's characterization of vision as a deluded self-centered enterprise of the autonomous subject, nor his notion of the anonymous gaze as more accurate to our relationships, or their ultimate impossibility.

While for Lacan the anonymity of vision makes it alienating, for Merleau-Ponty the anonymity of vision makes relationships possible without subjects dominating their objects. In *The Visible and the Invisible*, he says that "there is here no problem of the alter ego because it is not *I* who sees, not *he* who sees, because an anonymous visibility inhabits both of us, a vision in general, in virtue of that primordial property that belongs to the flesh, being here and now, of radiating everywhere and forever, being an individual, of being also a dimension and a universal" (1968: 142). For Merleau-Ponty vision is not the product of an autonomous self-centered subject; and although it may be anonymous, vision is not inhuman. He argues against the "inhuman gaze" (1962: 361). Humanity is the reversibility of flesh, an openness to the world, the eye's welcome to the world. Humanity is the intertwining of being and meaning, what he calls the intertwining of visible and invisible. While Lacan insists that meaning and being are caught in an exclusive either/or relationship, Merleau-Ponty suggests that we live in both. He says "Meaning is invisible, but the invisible is not the contradictory of the visible: the visible itself has an invisible inner framework, and the in-visible is the secret counterpart of the visible" (1968: 215).

One fundamental reason why Merleau-Ponty can imagine vision bringing us together is that he has a conception of vision and of space that is different from the theorists of recognition and lack. For him, vision is part of a system of sensation and space is filled with the flesh of the world. He describes palpitations of the eyes as analogous to tactile palpitations in what he calls a *vision-touch system*. "Vision is a palpation with the look" (1968: 134) and the world is visible because it is tactile. Vision is dependent upon tactility and the necessary connection, even reversibility, between the body and the visible world. For Merleau-Ponty the corporeality of the visible world is the connective tissue that nourishes and sustains the possibility of seeing. In *The Visible and the Invisible*, he describes vision in terms of thickness, corpuscles, tissues, grains, waves, channels, circuits, currents, embryos, and pregnancy, the very corporeality out of which sensation, thought, and language are born.

In addition to describing vision as part of a vision-touch system, he insists that the separation of the senses is misguided because all of the senses are interconnected in one body, each sense is really a complex of sensations that fundamentally implicates the others, and sensation operates in the reversible world of sensible and sentient, which folds the senses back onto themselves in a way that produces new levels of sensation and consciousness. The senses translate each other and work together to form perception. In this way, vision never works merely through the eyes. It is always the result of a coordinated effort between all senses. More than this, the so-called mind's eye or mental image supposedly connected to visual images is also the result of a coordination of the senses. The mirror, then, is not the threshold of the visual world, as Lacan maintains. Rather, the mirror image is perceived through a complex network of sensations working together, developed in coordination with the most proximal sense, touch.[1]

Merleau-Ponty's vision-touch system as part of what he calls a "corporeal schema" or system ("The Child's Relation with Others," 1960: 117) resonates with psychologist J. J. Gibson's theory of perceptual systems. Discussing Gibson and Merleau-Ponty together will help refine a theory of vision in the context of its environment and will help develop a notion of our relation to the environment more generally. Gibson has developed what he calls *ecological optics* in order to explain how vision works as a perceptual system (1950, 1961, 1966).[2] He argues that there are not just five senses but various perceptual systems. He rejects the notion of a sense or sense organs in favor of his notion of perceptual systems, which are the result of cooperative efforts between parts of the body and the body as a whole. Every perceptual system operates through the whole body along with a set of organs and not just one sense organ such as the eyes or ears.

In the words of Merleau-Ponty, our corporeal perceptual system "is first and foremost a system whose different introceptive and extroceptive aspects express each other reciprocally, including even the roughest of relations with surrounding space and its principal directions. The consciousness I have of my body is not the consciousness of an isolated mass; it is a *postural schema*. It is the perception of my body's position in relation to the vertical, the horizontal, and certain other axes of important coordinates of its environment. In addition, the different sensory domains (sight, touch, and the sense of movement in the joints) which are involved in the perception of my body do not present themselves to me as so many absolutely distinct regions" (1960: 117; cf. 1945: 50). Rather, for Merleau-Ponty and for Gibson the senses form a totality.

The basic perceptual system upon which all others depend is the orientation to gravity. Merleau-Ponty points out that "the operation of a postural schema—that is, a global consciousness of my body's position in space, with the corrective reflexes that impose themselves at each moment, the global consciousness of the spatiality of my body—all this is necessary for perception (Wallon). In fact the effort at equilibrium continually accompanies all our perceptions except when we are lying on our back" (1960: 122). Gibson explains that the hairs in the inner ear operate as a sense organ receptive to gravitational pull. All living beings respond to gravity. When awake and upright, animals are constantly negotiating the force of gravity in order to maintain their posture and position (Gibson, 1966: 51).

Whereas Merleau-Ponty tries to revise traditional notions of vision by associating vision with touch, Gibson develops his ecology of optics in which vision is part of a system of perception. Influenced by Gestalt psychology, both Merleau-Ponty and Gibson attend to the environment in which perception takes place. While Merleau-Ponty associates vision with touch in order to make it a more proximal sense, Gibson points out that touch is not as proximal as it seems since more often than not only hairs protruding from the skin touch other objects. Gibson says that "the tactual system is not, then, strictly a 'proximity sense' as traditionally assumed, for the appendages of the skin protrude into the environment" (1966: 100). If vision can be proximal and touch is not as proximal as it seems, then distinctions between the senses begin to break down.

For Merleau-Ponty, as part of the vision-touch system, vision is proximal in that it is possible because our flesh touches the flesh of the world. It is possible because the world also has flesh. Vision touches the world and people in it not in order to fix it or them in the gaze. Rather, as Merleau-Ponty says in "Eye and Mind," vision is movement, more like a caress than a grip, more like a motion picture than a photograph (see 1964: 162). And, space is thick with the flesh of the world. Merleau-Ponty criticizes Descartes' conception of space as "having no true thickness" (1964: 174). Space is not made up of Cartesian points separated by infinite gaps between them in some geometrical arrangement. Rather, space is full of light and motion that cannot be located in any one point. There are no gaps between us and the world since we touch it with our eyes, working as they do in coordination with all of sensation. As Merleau-Ponty says, "it is more accurate to say that I see according to it, or with it, than that I *see it*" (1964: 164). "[T]he world is all around me, not in front of me.... I live in it from the inside; I am immersed in it" (1964: 178). I do not see the world; I see according to it, with it. So too, I do not see other people in the world; I see with them.

For Merleau-Ponty, we are connected to, and part of, our environment, not in a mechanical way but rather as a dynamic receptivity or responsiveness "as if there were an a priori of the organism, privileged conducts and laws of internal equilibrium which predisposed the organism to certain relations with its milieu" (1962: 4). This milieu, or what Merleau-Ponty also calls the setting, *l'entourage*, of perception has everything to do with what is perceived (1946:

14). Merleau-Ponty's focus on environment and setting in his phenomenology of vision again resonates with Gibson's ecological optics. Gibson argues that perceptual systems are attentive to the information in the environment. Information is available in various forms of energy—electrical energy, chemical energy, thermal energy, mechanical energy, photic energy, magnetic energy, etc. The body is receptive to these various types of energy. Gibson claims that evolution has made different plants and animals more or less sensitive or receptive to different kinds and frequencies of energy. He points out that different species have different types of eyes and therefore have different types of sight. When thinking about the nature of vision, it might be provocative to remember that only animals with two eyes on the front of their heads focus on objects in front of them. Moreover, what is seen is not only determined by the type and placement of eyes, but also the movement of eyes and the body as a whole. Movements of the body attend to the information available in energy. Gibson claims that "these adjustments constitute modes of attention, and they are senses only as the man in the street uses the term, not as the psychologist does. They serve to explore the information available in sound, mechanical contact, chemical contact, and light" (1966: 58). Energy, then is the medium through which we perceive the world.

The density and temperature of the medium also determine what kind and how much information we can gather from our environment. Most basically, the density and temperature of the medium determines how we move through our environment. We move more quickly and easily through air than through water. We don't move through solids. As Gibson points out, other animals move through water or fly through the air: "the bodies of animals, their behavior, and their organs for receiving stimulation depend profoundly on elements in the Greek sense—on whether they live *in* the water or *on* the land, or fly in the air" (1966: 8). Gibson maintains that the air or atmosphere is a medium through which we perceive the world: "The atmosphere, then, is a medium. A medium permits more or less unhindered movements of animals and displacements of objects. Fundamentally, I suggest, this is what is meant by 'space'" (1966: 14). Space, or what Gibson calls "airspace," is a medium. It is not empty but full of various forms of energy, vibrations, particles, and waves. On Gibson's analysis space is the medium through which information is available to perceptual systems. Airspace enables and facilitates the movement of information that connects us to our environment.

Irigaray concludes her *Elemental Passions* with an ode to the density of air: "I opened my eyes and saw the cloud. And saw that nothing was perceptible unless I was held at a distance from it by an almost palpable density. And that I saw it and did not see it. *Seeing it all the better for remembering the density of air remaining in between.* But this resistance of air being revealed, I felt something akin to the possibility of a different discovery of myself" (1992:

105, my emphasis). Space is not empty because it is filled with the density of air. And, the density of air connects and separates everything on earth. Remembering air and the density of air reminds me that I am both connected to and different from those around me. Remembering what cannot be seen, the density of air, allows me to better see what cannot be seen, the difference and communion between myself and others. Seeing what is different from me and what is between me and difference opens the possibility of a different discovery of myself.

Throughout *Forgetting of Air in Martin Heidegger*, Irigaray suggests that the philosopher has forgotten air and thereby forgotten that he is nourished and supported by air (1999). By forgetting air, the philosopher imagines that he is thrown into an empty abyss, where he confronts only nothingness. The abyss, she reminds us, is not empty; it is full of air. And air is not nothing. Applying her analysis to Sartre and Lacan, we could say that the alienating gap or separation inherent in vision or the look or the gaze is the product of what Irigaray calls the oblivion of air (1999).

Light, along with air, enables seeing. Gibson says that "terrestrial airspaces are 'filled' with light; they contain a flux of interlocking reflected rays in all directions at all points. This dense reverberating network of rays is an important but neglected fact of optics, to which we will refer in elaborating what may be called *ecological* optics" (1966: 12). His notion of ecological optics is "neither mentalistic nor physicalistic, but treats light as a means by which things are seen" (1966: 222). He maintains that "the environment consists of *opportunities* for perception, for *available* information, of *potential* stimuli. Not all opportunities are grasped, not all information is registered, not all stimuli excite receptors. But what the environment affords an individual in the way of discrimination is enormous. . . . The animate environment affords even more than the physical environment does since animals have more characteristics than things and are more changeable" (1966: 23). By *information* Gibson does not mean something registered by the intellect; rather, information is registered by the body (cf. 1966: 2–3). Gibson develops his ecology of perception to counteract theories of perception that attribute it to either the physical world itself or the mind of man. Perception originates neither in the world nor in the subject; rather perception is a relationship between the two. Gibson considers the environment in which we see, ecological optics. Sight is the result of a relationship with, and responsiveness to, our environment.

We are constantly responding to different types of energy in our environment—mechanical, chemical, heat, photic. This energy is registered by the human body in different ways. We are more or less aware of the processes of our response to energy in our environment. We feel hot or cold in response to heat or thermal energy and radiation. We see daylight or darkness in response to light or photic energy. We smell and taste in response to chemical energy.

We hear in response to mechanical energies. But we are less aware of other energies that affect us constantly. For example, we aren't conscious of our body's response to the forces of gravity even though it takes constant effort to remain upright and stable in relation to the earth. Only recently with attention to seasonal depression have we become aware of the effects of sunlight and light energy on our moods. When we consider the energy that surrounds, sustains, and connects us to the world and other people, the phrase "the forces of nature" takes on a new meaning.

Turning away from Gibson's discussion of information and back to Merleau-Ponty's phenomenology, we could say that space enables and facilitates communication and communion. Rather than function as an obstacle, an empty abyss between us, space is full of the energy of life that connects us to the environment that sustains us. Moreover, space, and the energies that move through it, connect us to each other. The space between us facilitates rather than prevents relationships. For Merleau-Ponty, the distance necessary for vision is not alienating but enabling because of the interconnection between the senses and the elements that make vision possible. We are not separated from ourselves, others, and the world by an abyss. If vision is part of a sensory system that includes what we take to be more proximal senses like touch, taste, or smell, vision becomes a sort of touching, a palpitation with the eyes. Vision itself becomes a proximal sense. If the eyes are flesh—porous membranes—and not solid mirrors or windows or Lacanian bowls, then vision like the other senses necessitates a type of interpolation of elements that cannot be imagined as an impassable abyss or alienating gap (cf. Lacan 1981: 94). If various interconnected elements—air, light, waves, particles, nerves, tissues—interacting makes vision possible, then distance is never empty space, an unbridgeable gap, or an abyssal void. Rather, the distance between us is the connective tissues of earthly elements. Stephen Melville nicely describes the trajectory of Merleau-Ponty's philosophy of vision when he says: "Vision is the place where our continuity with the world conceals itself, the place where we mistake our contact for distance, imagining that seeing is a substitute for, rather than a mode of, touching—and it is this anesthesia, this senselessness, at the heart of transparency that demands our acknowledgment and pushes our dealings with the visual beyond recognition" (1996: 109).

Beyond recognition is the kinship between my body and the earth, which is full of energies that sustain me. Merleau-Ponty describes this kinship in his lecture "Husserl at the Limits of Phenomenology":

> For the Copernican, the world contains only bodies (*Körper*). Through meditation we must again learn of a mode of being whose conception we have lost, the being of the 'ground' (Boden), and that of the earth first of all—the earth where we live, that which is this side of rest and movement, being the

ground from which all rest and all movement are separated, which is not only made out of Körper, being the 'source' from which they are drawn through division, which has no 'place' being that which surrounds all place, which lifts all particular beings out of nothingness, as Noah's Ark preserved the living creatures from the Flood. There is a kinship between the being of the earth and that of my body (Leib). . . . This kinship extends to others, who appear to me as other bodies, to animals whom I understand as variants of my embodiment, and finally even to terrestrial bodies since I introduce them into the society of living bodies . . . (1970: 121)

This kinship between our bodies and the earth and other beings suggests a fundamental ethical relationship to the world. If all of our perception and awareness is a response to the forces of nature, a response to the movement of energies in our environment, then the ability to respond becomes responsibility. Our perception of our bodies is dependent upon forces in the environment. More than this, our conception of our bodies and of ourselves is a response to the movement of energy in our environment, most particularly social energy generated in our relationships with other people. Our kinship to the earth and other beings is based in our ability, even necessity, to respond to the environment. A subject who "refuses to support this bond absolves itself from its most fundamental obligation—its obligation to its founding possibility."[3]

The ethical imperative implicit in the fact that all of our perceptions, and ultimately all of our conceptions, are responses to the world and others becomes more apparent when we turn from a discussion of physical energy to a discussion of social or psychic energy that enable communication and communion. Just as heat energy, chemical energy, mechanical energy, and photic energy sustain life, social energy, and psychic or affective energy, also surround us, connect us, and move through us to sustain us. All relationships and all of human experiences are the result of the flow and circulation of social and psychic energy. When one's setting or entourage becomes literally friends, family, and attendants, then the relation between percepts and concepts becomes complicated. Merleau-Ponty insists on the primacy of perception, which is a practical activity of the body, but he also maintains that the interaction between bodies is formative in perception. In his analysis of the child's relation to others, he concludes that primary relationships profoundly modify perception (1960: 100), and that "'intelligence' is only another name designating an original type of relation with others" (1960: 140). These passing remarks suggest that both percepts and concepts are the result of relationships with others.

Moreover, if, as Merleau-Ponty maintains, the psyche is not a state of Consciousness accessible only to myself but rather it is a relation to the world and to others (1960: 116–118), then we must imagine that affects are dynamic effects of this relationship. Not only are precepts and concepts the result of embodied relationships, but also psychic or social energy moves between bodies. In radical if fleeting passages, Merleau-Ponty suggests that the transitivity between people can be more than a mere projection of one's own feelings or attitudes onto another, but rather a migration of feeling or affect itself: for example, in *The Visible and the Invisible*, as noted earlier, he says that "if I am close enough to the other who speaks to hear his breath and feel his effervescence and his fatigue, I almost witness, in him as in myself, the awesome birth of vociferation" (1968: 144); or in that same text, he speaks of a synergy between bodies; consider when in "The Child's Relations with Others" he says that "there is initially a state of pre-communication, wherein the other's intentions somehow play across my body while my intentions play across his" (1960: 119); or, when in that same text he says that "it is the simple fact that I live in the facial expressions of the other, as I feel him living in mine" (1960: 146).

In his work on child development, Merleau-Ponty concludes that imitating facial expressions is a milestone in development since the infant must translate the visual image of another's expression into its own motor language in order to reproduce the expression of the adult, for example a smile. The work of psychologists Nicholas Meltzoff and Keith Moore, however, has shown that even *newborn* infants can imitate the facial and manual gestures of adults (1977, 1983). Their studies show that imitation of facial and manual gestures by infants is the result of an inherent coordination between visual systems and motor systems that preexists any conditioning or demand for recognition (1977, 1983). They hypothesize that "this imitation is mediated by a representational system that allows infants to unite within one common framework their own body transformations and those of others. According to this view, both visual and motor transformations of the body can be represented in common form and directly compared. Infants could thereby relate proprioceptive motor information about their own unseen body movements to their representation of the visually perceived model and create the match required . . . the proclivity to represent actions intermodally is the starting point of infant psychological development, not an end point reached after many months of postnatal development" (1983: 708).

Meltzoff and Moore show that sensory, perceptual, and motor systems are linked from birth. Specifically, visual systems work in conjunction with motor and proprioceptive systems such that imitation is not the result of some sort of recognition but rather it is the result of coordinated sensory systems. This conclusion suggests that infants are responsive to their environment from birth and that sociosomatic interpersonal interaction is innate rather than acquired through any Lacanian mirror stage recognition. Primitive social interactions such as imitation are the result of complex sensory-perceptual systems that are inherently responsive. Shaun Gallagher and Meltzoff conclude that "recent studies of newborn imitation suggest that an experiential connection between self and others exists right from birth" that there "is already an experience of pre-verbal communication in the language of gesture and action" (1996: 212, 227). This research suggests an exchange of social and psychic energy between adult and infant. We can interpret the imitation of facial and manual gestures between adults and infants as what psychologist Daniel Stern calls *affective attunement*, which suggests the circulation of affective energy between adult and infant (Stern, 1985).[4] Our relations to other people, like our relations to the environment, are constituted by the circulation and exchange of energy. We are connected to the world through the circulation of energy that enables our perception, thought, language, and life itself. Indeed, we are conduits for energy of various sorts. Affective energy circulates between and among us. It is never contained. We are constantly negotiating affective energy transfers. Like other forms of energy, affective energy is invisible but has a powerful effect.

In his discussion of religious life, Emile Durkheim identifies social energy as a sort of "electricity" generated when people are gathered together (1995: 217). The experience of social electricity should be familiar to anyone who has attended a rock concert, a powerful religious service, a political rally, or even an aerobics class. The sum of collective energy is greater than its individual parts. This is why group experiences can be so powerful. This is also why we can feel energized by being part of a group. So too, we can feel energized, or drained of energy, by interpersonal relations. Durkheim's analysis of religious experience suggests that social energy operates as or like physical energy. He says "the heat or electricity that any object has received from outside can be transmitted to the surrounding milieu, and the mind readily accepts the possibility of that transmission. If religious forces are generally conceived of as external to the beings in which they reside, then there is no surprise in the extreme ease with which religious forces radiate and diffuse" (1995: 326–327). Durkheim also proposes "the radiation of mental energy" (1995: 210). Just as our bodies radiate heat and electromagnetic energies, our psyches radiate affective energy. Just as thermal energy from our bodies can warm the bodies of others, affective energy from our psyches can affect the psyches of others. In important ways, the psyche is a material biological phenomenon, a biosocial phenomenon.[5] Or, as Merleau-Ponty postulates, the psyche is itself a relation to the world and others.

The idea that our environment is filled with dynamic energy opens up an alternative to the idea that we exist as separate self-contained units. If the dynamic energy that surrounds us touches us, permeates us, affects us, nourishes us, then we are neither self-contained nor separated. Rather, we are profoundly dependent upon our environment and other people for the energy that sustains us. Far from being alienated from the world or others, we are intimately and continually connected, and responding, to them. We are by virtue of our response to the biosocial energy that surrounds us. Biosocial energy operates, is sustained, and expands, through responsive energy loops. And, we are energized in our relationships with others. Vision is another form of the circulation of energy that involves not only photic energy or light but also psychic energy or affect. We see in and through this circulation of biosocial energy. Moreover, the circulation of dynamic energy guarantees that we are connected to our environment and other people.

If space is not empty, and if vision connects us rather than separates us, if vision is indeed a proximal sense like touch, then visual recognition is neither the assimilation of all difference into sameness nor the alienation, exclusion or abjection of all difference. Rather, since vision connects us to the world and other people, then we can imagine an alternative to recognition and an alternative form of recognition, which give rise to alternative conceptions of subjectivity and of ethical responsibility.

Vision, and all sensation and perception, and even all intellection and reflection, is possible only by virtue of our ability to respond to our environment: the earth and other people. This responsibility is the very ground for the possibility of our experience. Thus, we have an ethical obligation to this founding possibility, a responsibility to the ability to respond. Insofar as subjectivity itself is possible only by virtue of the ability to respond, we are indebted to our environment for the ways in which it enables response. Our responsibility to our founding possibility obligates us to take responsibility for our responses. Perhaps this is why in *The Primacy of Perception* Merleau-Ponty says that "it is the very demand of rationality which imposes on us the need to act in such a way that our actions cannot be considered by others as an act of aggression but, on the contrary, as generously meeting the other in the very particularity of a given situation. . . . Just as the perception of a things opens me up to being by realizing the paradoxical synthesis of an infinity of perceptual aspects, in the same way the perception of the other founds morality by . . . placing my perspectives and my incommunicable solitude in the visual field of another and of all the others" (1946: 26). We have an obligation not only to respond, but also to respond in a way that opens up rather than closes off the possibility of response by others. This is what I take Levinas to mean when he says that we are responsible for the other's responsibility, that we always have one more responsibility, one more response to give. We are responsible for the other's ability to respond. To serve subjectivity, and thereby humanity, we must be vigilant in our attempts to continually open and reopen the possibility of response. So too, we have a responsibility to open ourselves to the responses that constitute us as subjects.

Of course, the world is full of irresponsible responses, hostile responses, or merely negligent responses that close down relationships. And, even with the best of intentions there is miscommunication and misunderstanding. Just as an optical or auditory illusion can be the result of the body's inability to register and respond to photic or mechanical energy, miscommunication can be the result of the inability to register and respond to social or affective energy. Gibson maintains that we can refine our perception by attending to particular energies and their effects. For example, the wine connoisseur can train her palate to taste and differentiate between subtle chemical differences. The art critic can train her eye to distinguish between subtle differences in light. The musician can train her ear to distinguish between differences in sound wavelengths. So too, we can train ourselves to be attuned to subtle differences in affective energies in relationships. In fact, it seems that just as some people are better able to distinguish between differences in chemical, photic, or mechanical energies, some people are better able to distinguish between psychic energies. In order to cope in the social world, we learn to respond to psychic energy even if, like other forms of energy, we aren't consciously aware of it.

We need to become consciously aware of affective energy not only in order to continue to try to understand ourselves and enable a process of interpretation that opens up rather than closes off the possibility of relationship, but also because we have an ethical obligation to do so. The possibility of subjectivity is founded on responsiveness to physical and social energy. These forces are what connect us to the world and other people. Whereas our dependence upon other forms of energy may bring with them ethical obligations to the earth and atmosphere, social energies bring with them special obligations to humanity, which may include other animal species. The radical notion that we are responsible for our responses and their ability to open responses from others and the environment resonates with Sartre's suggestion that we are responsible even for our emotions and Levinas's insistence that we are responsible even for the other's responsibility.

To invoke Sartre and Levinas together on the issue of responsibility might raise a few eye-brows and more than a few questions. For there seems to be a fundamental tension between the world of Sartrian responsibility in which subjects struggle against the other's objectification of them in order to assert their freedom as transcendent self-consciousness or beings for themselves, and the world of Levinasian responsibility in which subjects are held hostage by their indebtedness to the encounter with the infinite through the face-to-face relationship with the other that engenders their own transcendent self-consciousness. For Sartre, transcendence comes against the accusing and objectifying other while for Levinas transcendence comes through the encounter with the other upon whom I am completely dependent. For Sartre, subjectivity is a struggle for independence that is inherently antagonistic; for Levinas subjectivity is an acknowledgement of a fundamental and primordial dependence that should give way to generosity.

Merleau-Ponty may be hinting at this tension between independence and dependence, between hostility and generosity, between guilt and indebtedness, between the finite objectifiying look of the other and the infinite face-to-face encounter, when in "Metaphysics and the Novel" in the context of discussing Simone de Beauvoir's novel *L'Invitée*, he says "I am not this particular person or face, this finite being: I am a pure witness, placeless and ageless, equal in power to the world's infinity" but "if another person exists, if he too is a consciousness, then I must consent to be for him only a finite object, determinate, *visible* at a certain place in the world" (1948: 29). Because I am visible, therefore I am finite, but because I am a witness, therefore I am infinite. Like Beauvoir with her ethics of ambiguity, Merleau-Ponty seems to be struggling to formulate a theory of subjectivity and ethics that neither leaves us in the Sartrian position of killing off the other in order to exist or the Levinasian position that sometimes seems to suggest sacrificing the self for the sake of the other. In his reading of Beauvoir's novel, Merleau-Ponty concludes that "love does exist. Communication exists . . ." (1948: 40).

As both seer and seen, the reversibility of the flesh reveals not only the paradox of perception but also the paradox of ethics. For Merleau-Ponty, the seer and the seen inhabit the same world and flesh and coporeality; they are part of each other's entourage: "As soon as I see, it is necessary that the vision (as is so well indicated by the double meaning of the word) be doubled with a complementary vision or with another vision" (1968: 134). On the one hand, vision has the sense of literally seeing something in front of you; and on the other hand, vision has the sense of understanding something you don't literally see—as in "I see what you're getting at"—or vision has the sense of having a vision, as in a vision of the future or a vision of God. This double vision does not hinder communication or initiate aggression, but on the contrary it enables communication and communion.

Already suggested in Merleau-Ponty's invocation of the double meaning of vision is the double meaning of witness. Although he doesn't develop the concept, Merleau-Ponty frequently uses the verb witness (témoigner) to describe our relation to the world, particularly when he stresses the activity of the object and the passivity of the subject in perception. Even in the phrase that I just quoted "I am a pure witness . . . equal in power to the world's infinity" there is a tension between the sense of *witness* as a passive observer in the world and the sense of *witness* as actively giving testimony of the world; this is the difference between witnessing the power of the world and witnessing to or testifying to the power of the world.

Witnessing means both testifying to something that you have seen with your own eyes, something that you recognize, and testifying to something that you cannot see, something beyond recognition. On the one hand there is the juridical sense of witnessing to what you know from experience as an eyewitness, and on the other hand there is the religious sense of witnessing to what you believe through blind faith. Both of these senses of witnessing come together in the ethical-political sense of witnessing to the unspeakable horrors of the Holocaust, and other situations of torture, abuse, and oppression, which not only involves testifying to the events observed, the historical facts, but also to the experience of those events and facts that is beyond intellectual comprehension. Those events, which reside in the visible, the historical facts that call for an eye-witness, inhabit the finite world of beings in the world; the world in which human beings become subjects through their interactions, particularly through other people's images of them, or something like Sartre's look of the other that defines what I will call one's subject position. On the other hand, that which is beyond the visible world, and remains invisible to the historical facts, is the experience of subjectivity itself, the experience of the witnessing relationship that engenders one's sense of agency and humanity. This experience is the encounter with infinity in relationships, through which we become subjects, something like Levinas's face-to-face. What I am calling subjectivity is possible by virtue of the structure of witnessing.

The structure of witnessing is produced and sustained by dialogic interaction with other people. It is the structure of addressability and responsibility inherent in subjectivity. In order to think, talk, act as an agent, this witnessing structure must be in place. Having a sense of oneself as a subject and an agent requires that the structure of witnessing as the possibility of address and response has been set up in dialogic relations with others. The possibility of address and response, the structure of witnessing itself, enables what psychoanalyst Dori Laub calls the "inner witness" (1992: xx). Through relationships with other people we develop a sense of an inner witness, to whom we address our lives. Without this inner witness, we lose the ability to make sense of our lives, to articulate our experience, and to act as agents in the world. We make sense of our experience and our own agency by telling our experiences to others; even if we don't literally describe our experiences to another person, we give them meaning by thinking them to ourselves as we might tell them to another. According to Laub, who, as a survivor himself, works with other Holocaust survivors, the Holocaust and other situations of extreme torture or oppression undermine or destroy the inner witness necessary for subjectivity and agency. On the other hand, responsible address and response can restore the inner witness and thereby the structure of witnessing, or subjectivity itself.

We could say that the inner witness operates as a negotiating voice between subject positions and subjectivity. If one's subject position is the finite socio-historical position in which one finds oneself, and one's subjectivity is the structure of witnessing as infinite responsibility, then the inner witness is where subject position and subjectivity meet. The inner witness is a necessary part of the structure of subjectivity as responsibility itself and it is constitutive of one's subject position. On the one hand, if the inner witness is an incorporation of dialogic relations with others, of external witnesses, then its ability to create an enabling and empowering subject position is determined by the socio-historical context of the dialogic relations with others. On the other hand, since subjectivity is itself the structure and process of witnessing, the place and function of the inner witness are also necessary to give the subject a sense of itself as an agent.

Subject positions and subjectivity are constituted through the possibility of witnessing in the double sense of eye-witness to the visible world and witnessing to what is beyond visual or intellectual recognition. The tension inherent in witnessing is the tension between subject positions, which are historically determined, and subjectivity, which is an infinite responsibility. Subject positions, although mobile, are constituted in our social interactions and our positions within our culture and context; our opportunities and self-conceptions are very much influenced by social position and other people's opinions of us—Sartre's look of the other. Subject positions are determined by history and circumstance. As Merleau-Ponty says "history is other people" (1946: 25). Subject positions are our relations to the finite world of human history and relations—what we might call politics. Subjectivity, on the other hand, is experienced as the sense of agency and response-ability that are constituted in the infinite encounter with otherness, which is fundamentally ethical. And, although subjectivity is logically prior to any possible subject position, in our experience, they are always profoundly interconnected.

In talking about the subject and subjectivity we must consider subject position. The subject and subjectivity are inherently political. One's social position and history profoundly influence one's very sense of oneself as an active agent in the world. Yet, the contradictions and inconsistencies in historical and social circumstances guarantee that we are never completely determined by our subject position. It is possible to develop a sense of agency in spite of, or in resistance to, an oppressive social situation. In addition, the open structure of witnessing at the heart of subjectivity insures that establishing and reestablishing a positive inner witness is always possible. Moreover, the infinite responsibility constitutive of subjectivity makes it inherently ethical. We have an obligation to our founding possibility, the ability to respond. We have a responsibility to our environment, including the earth and its inhabitants.

Merleau-Ponty's insistence on embodied subjectivity suggests the connection between finite subject position and infinite responsibility when he says that "... the body is ... the place where the spirit takes on a certain physical and historical situation" ("An Unpublished Text" in *The Primacy of Percep-*

tion, 1962: 5). In what I hope is a response to the work of Merleau-Ponty that opens it onto its own most promising engagements with otherness, and in the spirit of his double-vision, we see that subjectivity itself is necessarily both political and ethical.

Notes

1. Cynthia Willett makes a very persuasive case that the mirror stage recognition is the result of a touch, along with the mother-infant song and dance (1995).

2. I would like to thank Edward Casey for recommending Gibson's work to me.

3. These are the words used by Eva Kittay to describe the ethical obligation inherent in relations of dependency. Eva Kittay, "Welfare, Dependency, And a Public Ethic of Care," in *Social Justice*, 25: 1, issue 71, spring 1998, 131.

4. For a discussion of Stern and the notion of affective attunement see my *Family Values* (1997); see also Cynthia Willett's *Maternal Ethics* (1995).

5. For more developed analysis of the psyche as a biosocial phenomenon, see my *Family Values: Subjects Between Nature and Culture* (1997). See my discussion of the psyche as biosocial in the work of Julia Kristeva in the introduction to *The Portable Kristeva* (1998). See also Teresa Brennan's "Social Pressure" (1997).

References

Brennan, Teresa (1992). *The Interpretation of the Flesh*. London: Routledge.

——— (1993). *History After Lacan*. New York: Routledge.

——— and Martin Jay. Eds. (1996). *Vision in Context*. New York: Routledge.

——— (1997). "Social Pressure." In *American Imago*. Vol. 54, No. 3, 257–288.

Descartes, René (1965). *Discourse on Method, Optics, Geometry, and Meteorology*. Trans. P. J. Olscamp. Indianapolis: University of Indiana Press.

——— (1989). *The Meditations Concerning First Philosophy*. In *Philosophical Essays*. Trans. Laurence LaFleur. New York: Macmillan.

Durkheim, Emile (1995). *The Elementary Forms of Religious Life*. Trans. Karen Fields. New York: The Free Press.

Freud, Sigmund (1950). *The Perception of the Visual World*. Boston: Houghton Mifflin.

——— (1962). "Three Essays on the Theory of Sexuality (1905)." Trans. James Strachey. New York: Basic Books.

——— (1972a). "The Passing of the Oedipus-Complex (1924)" in *Sexuality and the Psychology of Love*. Trans. Joan Riviere. New York: Collier Books.

——— (1972b). "Some Psychological Consequences of the Anatomical Distinction Between the Sexes (1925)" in *Sexuality and the Psychology of Love*. Trans. Joan Riviere. New York: Collier Books.

Gibson, J. J. (1961). "Ecological Optics." In *Vision Research*, 1, 253–262.

——— (1966). *The Senses Considered as Perceptual Systems*. Boston: Houghton Mifflin.

Hegel, G. W. F. (1977). *Phenomenology of Spirit*. Trans. A. V. Miller. Oxford: Clarendon Press.

Irigaray, Luce (1992). *Elemental Passions*. Trans. J. Collie and J. Still. New York: Routledge.

——— (1993). *An Ethics of Sexual Difference*. Trans. C. Burke and G. Gill. Ithaca: Cornell University Press.

——— (1996). *i love to you*. Trans. A. Martin. New York: Routledge.

——— (1997). *Être Deux*. Paris: Grasset.

——— (1999). *Forgetting of Air in Martin Heidegger*. Trans. Mary Beth Mader. Austin: University of Texas Press.

Jay, Martin (1994). *Downcast Eyes: The Denigration of Vision in Twentieth-Century French Thought*. Berkeley: University of California Press.

Kittay, Eva (1998). "Welfare, Dependency, And a Public Ethic of Care." In *Social Justice*, 25: 1, issue 71, spring 1998.

Lacan, Jacques (1977). *Ecrits*. Trans. Alan Sheridan. New York: Norton.

——— (1981). *The four fundamental concepts of psychoanalysis*. Trans. Alan Sheridan. New York: Norton.

——— (1988). "Seminar on 'The Purloined Letter.'" Trans. J. Mehlman. In *The Purloined Poe*. Ed. J. Muller and W. Richardson. Baltimore: Johns Hopkins Press.

Laub Dori & Shoshana Felman (1992). *Testimony: Crises of Witnessing in Literature, Psychoanalysis, and History*. New York: Routledge.

Levinas, Emmanuel (1969). *Totality and Infinity*. Trans. Alphonso Lingis. Pittsburgh: Duquesne University Press.

——— (1987). *Time and the Other*. Trans. Richard Cohen. Pittsburgh: Duquesne University Press.

——— (1989). *The Levinas Reader*. Ed. Seán Hand. Cambridge, MA: Blackwell Publishers.

——— (1991). *Otherwise Than Being*. Trans. Alphonso Lingis. Boston: Nijoff.

——— (1993). *Collected Philosophical Papers*. Trans. Alphonso Lingis. Boston: Kluwer Academic Publishers.

——— (1996). *Emmanuel Levinas Basic Philosophical Writings*. Ed. A. Peperzak, S. Critchley, and R. Bernasconi. Bloomington: Indiana University Press.

Melville Stephen (1996). "Division of the Gaze, or, Remarks on the Color and Tenor of Contemporary 'Theory.'" In Brennan and Jay Ed. *Vision in Context*. New York: Routledge, 101–116.

Merleau-Ponty, Maurice (1962). *Phenomenology of Perception*. Trans. Colin Smith. London.

——— (1964a). *The Primacy of Perception*. Ed. James Edie. Evanston: Northwestern University Press, 1964. "An Unpublished Text" 1962. Trans. Arleen Dallery. "The Primacy of Perception and Its Philosophical Consequences" 1946. Trans. James Edie. "The Child's Relations with Others" 1960. Trans. William Cobb. "Eye and Mind" 1961. Trans. Carleton Dallery.

——— (1964b). *Sense and Non-Sense* (1948). Trans. Hubert L. Dreyfus and Patricia A. Dreyfus. Evanston: Northwestern University Press.

——— (1968). *The Visible and the Invisible*. Trans. Alphonso Lingis. Evanston: Northwestern University Press.

——— (1970). "Husserl at the Limits of Phenomenology" & "Nature and Logos: The Human Body," In *Themes from the Lectures at the Collège de France 1952–1960*. Trans. John O'Neill, Evanston: Northwestern University Press.

——— (1973). "Dialogue and the Perception of the Other" (1969). In *The Prose of the World*. Trans. John O'Neill. Ed. Claude Lefort. Evanston: Northwestern University Press.

——— (1993). "The Experience of Others (1951–2)" Trans. Fred Evans and Hugh Silverman & "Phenomenology and Psychoanalysis: Preface to Hesnard's *L'Oeuvre de Freud*" Trans. Alden Fisher, In *Merleau-Ponty & Psychology*. Ed. Keith Hoeller. Atlantic Highlands: Humanities Press.

Oliver, Kelly (1995). *Womanizing Nietzsche: Philosophy's Relation to "the Feminine."* New York: Routledge.

——— (1997). *Family Values, Subjects Between Nature and Culture*. New York: Routledge.

——— (1998). *Subjectivity Without Subjects*. Rowman & Littlefield

——— (2001). *Witnessing: Beyond Recognition*. Minneapolis: University of Minnesota.

Sartre, Jean-Paul (1956). *Being and Nothingness*. Trans. Hazel Barnes. New York: Washington Square Books.

——— (1976). *No Exit*. Trans. Stuart Gilbert. New York: Alfred Knoff.

Vasseleu, Cathryn (1998). *Textures of Light: Vision and Touch in Irigaray, Levinas and Merleau-Ponty*. London: Routledge.

Willett, Cynthia (1995). *Maternal Ethics and Other Slave Moralities*. New York: Routledge.

CHAPTER 9

Ethical Reciprocity at the Interstices of Communion and Disruption

SALLY FISCHER

The question of the possibility of the foundation of an ethics and its connection to embodied alterity has been a topic of debate and the subject of critique in Continental and feminist philosophies for many years now. Traditionally, to have an ethics was to have beforehand an answer to the question of our relation to the other, which presupposes the question of who we are as ethical agents. Traditional attempts to answer this question in terms of our human nature (which leaves us with the question: we, who?) or a supposed foundation in disembodied reason have been deconstructed from both mainstream Continental and feminist perspectives. Merleau-Ponty, however, has been able to deconstruct the notion of the human being as a transhistorical metaphysical constant, and has opened up an understanding of the body-subject that leaves room for different bodies, or different bodily styles of existence, variously inscribed. At the same time, he offers a phenomenological analysis of the common fundamental structures of embodied existence, which are always and already co-extensive with our interpersonal relations. His phenomenology of embodied intersubjectivity, I believe, can serve as a fruitful ground from which to build an ethics of interpersonal relations. While Merleau-Ponty himself never wrote an ethics, he did remark in a discussion with a colleague, that "It was never my intention to posit the other except as an ethical subject" (Merleau-Ponty 1964a: 30).

In this chapter, I will critically examine Merleau-Ponty's understanding of the epistemological relation between embodied subjects for its ethical implications, including those implications that directly bear upon a feminist ethics of embodied existence.[1] To this end, it will be necessary to understand his notion of intercorporeality in light of the decentering and disruption, which is found at the very heart of the communion of embodied subjects. I hope to show that his account of embodied intercorporeality, slightly *reformulated*, offers a better way to understand his notions of reversibility and reciprocity inherent in our prereflective existence. While some have recognized the fecundity of his account of reversibility and reciprocity for a more positive account of interpersonal relations in terms of dialogical relations, it is first of all necessary that these notions not be predicated on a carnal generality based upon a single style of embodied existence. While Merleau-Ponty was never explicitly concerned with embodied difference in terms of gender/sex/race relations, it is possible to show that his interpretation of bodily intentionality can incorporate bodies variously inscribed and those who inhabit different styles of being in the world. Second, it is necessary to take care not to ignore the inherent dangers in assuming a too facile interpretation of our primordial communion with others. Deconstructivist and feminist philosophies have clearly recognized the dangers of totalizing notions of community. Finally, then, at the end of this paper, I will outline a Merleau-Pontian response to the false dichotomy of a too facile understanding of community on the one hand, or the abandonment of the ideals of community by positing a "dwelling-together of strangers" on the other hand. It is the disruption within the heart of intersubjectivity that allows for the possibility of ethical communion and reciprocity, of a hermeneutical dialogical relation, which, I argue, has the potential to maintain an openness to the other and to limit relations of domination.

In order to limit the scope of this essay, I will refer primarily to Merleau-Ponty's earlier work in the *Phenomenology of Perception*. However, I think it will be clear that much of his account here regarding intersubjective relations in terms of an intercorporeality is taken up, albeit with a different focus, in his later ontology of the flesh. While I think that there are indeed some aspects of Merleau-Ponty's *phenomenological* notion of alterity that have been rightly criticized, I hope to show that there is a possible reading of reciprocity in the *Phenomenology* that is open to difference. Furthermore, I find that his notion of the hermeneutical body-subject so clearly portrayed in the *Phenomenology* is crucial to the dialogical ethics implicit in his position, and I shall begin with a brief description of this hermeneutical embodied subjectivity.

A Few Words About the Hermeneutical Subject

Much of our existence is spent in a prereflective intercorporeal intertwining with the world and with others. To perceive an object is to *inhabit* it, and the objects form a system, a world in which I dwell as a certain style of existence, a perspective I incorporate and project toward that world. In the temporal structure of the lived body, there is a hermeneutics at play, whereby I can take up my sedimented past and to some degree project a set of expectations toward my present situation, in light of that situation or task before me or that which I imagine. On a prereflective level, by means of a bodily intentionality, we are capable of a certain creativity, of bending the sedimented style of the habit-body in order to incorporate a new behavior, or in order to accomplish some new task. In our dialogue with the world and others, as Merleau-Ponty notes, there is a bodily projection or intentional arc that aims to achieve a kind of global equilibrium in light of one's given situation and one's task at hand. But in Merleau-Ponty's notion of subjectivity, our prereflective, prepersonal life is only one moment/stage/level of our existence. He clearly maintains a hermeneutical dialectical account of subjectivity in terms of our capacity to prereflectively express our sedimentations in language, culture, our own past experiences, etc., and to express ourselves in terms of reflective consciousness as well. There is an ambiguous dialectic operative between these two moments or stages of consciousness. Much of the text of the *Phenomenology of Perception* describes our embodied existence in terms of the general structures of behavior, namely, motility, bodily gesture, sexuality, and speech. But our personal existence can in turn become sedimented in these general structures of behavior. Reflective consciousness is never bifurcated from its prereflective corporeal grounding in the lived body, but is never wholly at one with it either. The bottom line is that there is no natural or static concept of the human—no essential nature, other than our capacity to express our sedimentations through these fundamental structures of embodied being in the world.

Communion

Merleau-Ponty's phenomenological critique of transcendental idealism on the one hand, and empirical realism in the form of mechanistic physiology on the other hand, insists that we must rethink perception, "not as a constitution of the true object, but as our inherence in things" (Merleau-Ponty 1962: 350–351). Bodily existence is the condition of possibility of a genuine presence in the world; it establishes our first consonances with the world and others. "The very first of all cultural objects, and the one by which all the rest exist, is the body of the other person as the vehicle of a form of behavior" (Merleau-Ponty 1962: 348). Merleau-Ponty writes about a "living thought" (1962: 128), which doesn't consist in a representational schema, but rather "understands" a situation in terms of having an *internal* relation: prereflective intentional threads interwoven with others and the world. Thus perception of another must be recast not in terms of a constituting consciousness, but as the subject of a pattern of behavior, which brings with it an intelligibility because it arises out of a shared being-in-the-world. A gesture, for example, is "understood" when we have *incorporated* it into our world. He claims that the expressive face "can carry an existence, as my own existence is carried by my body," (Merleau-Ponty 1962: 351), and "it is as if the other person's intention inhabited my body and mine his" (1962: 185).

While in his later work he abandons the Cartesian language of "subject/object" to speak about our fundamental inherence in the "flesh," in the *Phenomenology* Merleau-Ponty struggles with an adequate description of this internal relation that eludes the grasp of Cartesian thought. Nevertheless, perhaps we can find a phenomenological precursor to his ontology of the flesh, when he claims that this internal relation "causes others to appear as the completion of a *system*" (Merleau-Ponty 1962: 352). This system, founded upon intercorporeality, is grounded in my prereflective existence as a prepersonal, anonymous subject. From this carnal generality, we are always already outside of ourselves, outrun by the world and others. From this carnal generality, there is a slippage of our perspectives into one another and we can find communication between our different perspectives in a shared world.

Prereflective existence is thus lived as a global equilibrium, and perhaps there is even a kind of proto-ethics to be found in this interconnectedness. Merleau-Ponty calls perception itself "a sort of dialogue" (1962: 320) where the body, in its power of lived expression, is the "medium of communication" (1962: 181). We dwell in the world and with others in a prethetic and affective dialogical reciprocity from the start, which precludes any absolute solipsism.[2] He says that "my body and the other's are a whole, two sides of one and the same phenomenon, and the anonymous existence of which my body is the ever-renewed trace henceforth inhabits both bodies simultaneously" (Merleau-Ponty 1962: 354). But according to Merleau-Ponty, this trace of another who is already a part of me is not yet a *personal* other, is not an other in all of her irreducible particularities. One feels a kind of global responsibility to the other *before* the other is thetically constituted as an "I." The body's capacity of response in terms of attaining a global equilibrium in a given situation, the bodily responsibility to the other that one feels pre-reflectively in this protomorality, is toward the prepersonal *anonymous* other.

A difficulty, to be sure, hovers over this aspect of Merleau-Ponty's account of embodied subjectivity: Namely, the fact that by describing this bodily felt communion between general, or anonymous subjects, he writes as if there were only one kind of body or bodily style, and not many (when biological differences are considered in terms of class, race, and gender). Moreover, as Shannon Sullivan and Judith Butler have recognized, he does not address the possibility that these differences, too, inhere in *depth*, in language and culture. Indeed, the subject described throughout the *Phenomenology* is set along the lines of a historically masculine body-subject. Both Iris Young and Judith Butler, in earlier works, have offered critiques of Merleau-Ponty's phenomenology for this very problem, especially the chapters on the spatiality of the lived body and on sexuality, respectively. Young shows that Merleau-Ponty's description can be read as taking as normative a masculine style of appropriating lived space, and that the traditional western style of feminine bodily comportment, viewed in light of this norm, can be defined as an "inhibited intentionality" and an "ambiguous transcendence" (Young 1989: 58). Merleau-Ponty uses the centripetal existence of a brain-damaged, WWI veteran called Schneider to reveal to us the normal, centrifugal intentionality of the lived body by which we can take up our situation and in terms of an intentional arc, project toward the world our aims at hand. Just as Schneider's relation to the world is seen as pathological because his existence is confined to a world simply given, the description of a feminine style of comportment that Young brings to light also initially *appears* as quasi-pathological because of its inhibited intentionality, for example, by not appropriating maximum bodily space in order to perform a task; or in the case of sports, of waiting for the ball to come to her instead of reaching out toward the ball, not projecting her body in "unbroken directedness upon the world in action" (Young 1989: 59). Young is clear that this centripetal existence that characterizes the inhibited intentionality of traditional feminine comportment is a historical/cultural manifestation, but what we are left to ask is whether this is a kind of *pathology* at all, whether it is comparable to the pathology that Schneider manifests, for example. If this is the case, and I don't think that it is, then it would seem that Merleau-Ponty's understanding of normative bodily intentionality is so tied to the traditionally masculine style of inhabiting the world that the notion of prereflective bodily existence reduces all the different styles to this one, or else categorizes them as privative or pathological.

If we interpret Merleau-Ponty's *specific* examples in the *Phenomenology* as the norm, then indeed we might say that he is guilty, as Butler claims in her earlier work, (Butler 1989) of naturalizing his own historical situation of gender relations by taking the traditionally masculine, heterosexual experience as paradigmatic of normal bodily intentionality. Both of the analyses by Young and Butler do a good job of pointing out the problem of describing the notion of embodied intentionality in terms of the historically masculine body. Because of this problem, a reformulation of Merleau-Ponty's notion of the body is necessary in order to include different styles of comportment, speech, and sexuality. However, there is nothing within his larger phenomenology that would preclude such a reformulation. I claim that we can have a Merleau-Pontian account of prereflective intersubjectivity that includes difference: different styles of behavior, gesture, speech, and sexuality. The problem is not that he is essentializing the body, for he is very clear that there is no simply "natural" human being.[3] There is, for Merleau-Ponty, no one normative or essential style of taking up the world as long as we have the capacity of transcending the givens of our situation (which Schneider lacks). In his chapter on speech, for example, he says, "it is no more natural, and no less conventional, to shout out in anger or to kiss in love, than to call a table 'a table.' . . . Everything is both manufactured and natural in human beings" (Merleau-Ponty 1962: 189). Thus, as Beth Preston correctly claims regarding Young's essay "Throwing Like a Girl," the feminine style of bodily comportment is neither privative of the norm (read, historically masculine style) nor positive as a norm itself. We need not define different styles of taking up one's situation to be privative as long as the subject can take up her situation in terms of an intentional arc; the "how" of this intentional arc is sedimented in language, culture, and history. Preston, for example, compares the lace-maker with the softball player—both will have very different modes of incorporating space, but both styles can be consonant with their aims (Preston 1996: 172). The sexed and gendered body need not present a problem at this point in his philosophy. Since the intentional arc is still there, it is, like any other lived body, simply trying to maintain a kind of global equilibrium in between what we aim at and what is given (Merleau-Ponty 1962: 144).

The upshot of this is that because we are hermeneutical subjects who exist within an ambiguous dialectic between our prereflective and reflective moments or stages, any notion of "co-naturality" gets historicized, and the so-called anonymous generality of prereflective and pre-egological subjects, since they are embodied and dwell in a historical lifeworld, is the generality of bodies marked by sex, gender, race, etc. In other words, there is no generality as such. Thus, a reformulation of Merleau-Pontian prereflective intercorporeality requires that we rid it of the notion of a thoroughgoing *generality*, but not necessarily of a prereflective intercorporeality, for as long as there is some aspect of a shared *world*, we will see that there can also be a shared being in the world through the dialogical aspect of embodied existence.

The problem, then, comes *not* in his apparent naturalizing of one style of human behavior—for according to his own philosophy, a description of our embodied existence is open to various bodily styles of taking up the world. The real problem comes in the relation *between* these styles, in terms of the way his descriptive account of reciprocity may play out when we look at this in-between. As I mentioned above, our intercorporeality is described in terms of reversibility and reciprocity. He states that reciprocity at the level of the lived body is a necessary condition for there to be another, for there to be an alter Ego at all (Merleau-Ponty 1962: 357). But at times, Merleau-Ponty seems to shift from description to prescription in his claims about our dialogical relations with others. While there is never a complete reversibility, communication is fundamental, always already there in some fashion, and, it seems, a good—alienation, the objectifying look of the stranger is felt as unbearable only because it takes the place of possible communication (Merleau-Ponty 1962: 361). Embodied communion is the primordial ground of our co-existence. But perhaps, once we expand our understanding of prereflective intercorporeality to include the different styles of bodily existence, this primordial communion in terms of its *reciprocity* will not be such a facile given, or rather, may not *necessarily* be a "good."

The crux of the matter depends upon how we think the term reciprocity. If it is simply to maintain between two sides or poles of intercorporeality a kind of exchange that facilitates a global equilibrium with one another in the shared world, then it is possible that this might be something along the lines of Aristotle's notion of *isos*, or an equality in terms of a so-called fair equilibrium. This kind of reciprocity in terms of an interdependence can take place between unequals, such as the way Aristotle describes friendship between the superior husband to the subordinate wife (Aristotle 1984: 1831). We can imagine how this dynamic equilibrium might play out in Merleau-Pontian terms in a lived dialogue through gestural body language, for example. At the prereflective stage, there is an internal relation between my body and the other's, where the other's gestures have for me a kind of intelligibility by which I can respond in gesture from inside this dialogical intertwining. Because at this level, neither of us perceives the other thetically, neither is posited, nor technically subordinated to the status of an object. This intercorporeality is before, or beneath any objectification, yet there can be a subordination that takes place within the dynamic of gestures, comportment, sexuality, speech even at this prereflective level.[4]

However, Merleau-Ponty often seems to have a more genuine form of reciprocity in mind when he describes our intercorporeality. Namely, one where there is in place a certain primordial openness or receptivity to the other, in which a space is freed up for another's perspective, and where the face and gestures of another have the power to provoke in me a felt response. Closing oneself off to the other's perspective in terms of the call of the other's bodily language or expressivity, then, is a derivative form of this responsible inbetween. But certain bodies have historically been inscribed with the status of less than human subjectivity. Because of this lived dialectic between the two moments of reflective and prereflective existence, this status has been sedimented culturally and historically in our prereflective existence, and lived in the prereflective lifeworld.

For example, in the 1990s a woman in Kenya attempted to bring to court the first case of spousal abuse, which was not yet actionable,[5] partly because this kind of lived dynamic between husband and wife is a common cultural style of bodily intentionality in terms of gesture and response. One would like to think that the kind of dynamic in this system of self/other prereflective dialogue is a negative instance of the way "the other person's intention inhabits my body and mine his" (Merleau-Ponty 1962: 185). In the example of a prereflective lived dominance of one over the other, there is no openness, availability, or sensuous listening of the dominating partner to the other's intentions, gestures, speech. We cannot then assume that there simply and already exists as a proto-ethical ground this more genuinely reciprocal interpretation of intercorporeality. We must then view the stronger notion, this more *genuine* form of dialogical intercorporeality as only a *partial* ground, and also as a goal.

Disruption

While Merleau-Ponty doesn't explicitly discuss the dominance of the lived body in terms of gender or race relations, what he does say about our decentered and ambiguous relation to ourselves may mitigate this important difficulty in what is otherwise a fecund notion of intersubjectivity. I think that we can find in his notion of *decentered* embodied subjectivity that is played out from *within* our communion an interpretation of the epistemological/ethical relation in which neither reduces the Other to the Same at a thetic level, nor understands the dynamic interplay between lived bodies as a closed circle, dynamic, or dialogue. Because I am already from the start decentered from my self, and because from within the dialogical relation with the other I am disrupted, lifted out of the closure of my perspective by the other, there is no solipsistic, immanent, or interiorized "I." I am always already inside the dialogue and outside of myself, and this decentering and disruption helps keep the dialogical, hermeneutical circle open.

In *Signs*, Merleau-Ponty reminds us that while we are woven into the same fabric as the world and as others, "things are only half open before us, unveiled and hidden" in their "inexhaustible richness" (1964b: 167). We see a similar account in the *Phenomenology*. I live as a style in the plenum of the world and in this I recognize my finitude, that mine is only one of many possible perspectives (Merleau-Ponty 1962: 364). On the one hand, I do not first perceive the other by a total grasp, by reducing the other to the objective gaze of the interiorized "I." Our primordial grasp of the other, as we have seen, arises laterally, through the styles of behavior and through the style of the shared world. I do not at first perceive the other by reducing what is Other to the Same. There is an irreducibility about the other that creates ruptures in our intercorporeality, so my relationship is at once one both of distance and of openness. He says, "solitude and communication cannot be the two horns of a dilemma, but two 'moments' of one phenomenon" (Merleau-Ponty 1962: 359). An ethical reading of Merleau-Ponty's notion of intersubjectivity thus walks an important fine line between maintaining a dialogical reciprocity with the other and allowing for a certain degree of irreducible otherness, and these two sides are intertwined in their ethical role.[6]

We can see this within his understanding of language, which sets up an especially important kind of dialogue. Language, including gesture, provides both an exposure, an opening of myself to the other, and a decentering of my own embodied consciousness He writes:

> There is one particular cultural object which is destined to play a crucial role in the perception of other people: namely, language. In the experience of dialogue, there is constituted between the other person and myself a common ground; my thought and his are interwoven into a single fabric, my words and those of my interlocutor are called forth by the state of the discussion, and they are inserted into a shared operation of which neither of us is the creator. We have here a dual being; where the other is for me no longer a bit of behavior in my transcendental field nor I his; we are collaborators for each other in consummate reciprocity. Our perspectives merge into each other, and we co-exist through a common world. In the present dialogue, I am freed from myself, for the other person's thoughts are certainly his; they are not of my making. . . . And indeed, the objection which my interlocutor raises to what I say draws from me thoughts which I had no idea I possessed, so that at the same time I lend him my thoughts, he makes me think too. (Merleau-Ponty 1962: 354)

I am not only intimately connected with the other, together woven into a shared world, a shared language, but I am also decentered, disrupted from my own perspective from within this dialogue. Furthermore, because I am a hermeneutical subject, I am not completely bound to this shared language, nor enclosed in my own perspective. Moreover, I can be surprised, disoriented, disrupted and pulled out of my perspective through the words or gestures of the other.

However, I cannot be disrupted from my own perspective unless I am already to some extent in communion with the other, unless I have one foot already inside the dialogical circle. But this is not a problem, since I can never wholly extricate myself out of the intersubjective milieu, nor out of my sedimentation in the institutions of language, culture, etc. He says that, "I can only fly from being into being" (Merleau-Ponty 1962: 360). Yet, interconnectedness in a shared world and in a shared language is not *essentially* co-existence in a symbolic world defined along historically "masculine" parameters; instead the claim is that there is some overlapping of shared perspectives, that is, a way to get inside the dialogue in the first place. The type of communion offered in Merleau-Ponty's account is one always already imbued with disruption, where the subject is always simultaneously co-extensive with others in a shared cultural world *and* decentered from herself and her perspective. Because he offers a hermeneutical account of the self, we have the capacity to bend the spaces between the words and their silences in order to stretch language into some fresh meaning, and this can, in turn, become sedimented back into the lifeworld.

We have seen that the experience of the lived body makes possible a special kind of dialogical relation between persons: a communicative relation that has the potential to mutually make room for each other's perspective. Without an intersubjective world, and without the possibility of this more genuine reciprocity, "My awareness of constructing an objective truth would never provide me with anything more than an objective truth for me, and my greatest attempt at impartiality would never enable me to prevail over my subjectivity" (Merleau-Ponty 1962: 355).[7] We could never be capable of reflective attempts at impartiality if we could never get to *other* perspectives in the first place. On the one hand, Merleau-Ponty never denies the truth of individual existence. Even in the reciprocity of communion, there is no fusion of horizons: "The grief and anger of another have never quite the same significance for him as they have for me" and "our situations cannot be imposed on each other" (Merleau-Ponty 1962: 356). On the other hand, there can be a commitment to co-existence, which "must be experienced on both sides" (Merleau-Ponty 1962: 357), and this requires me to accord a place for perspectives other than my own. I am tempted to interpret his phenomenological description quasi-prescriptively when he says, "I enter a pact with the other, having resolved to live in an interworld in which I accord as much place to others as to myself" (Merleau-Ponty 1962: 357). Clearly this expresses a potentially ethical attitude. Yet it is certainly no guarantee, since he also recognizes that "it would be hypocritical to pretend that I seek the welfare of another *as if it were mine*" (Merleau-Ponty 1962: 357). Indeed, if I sought the other's welfare as if it were my own, I would be incapable of understanding it as *another* perspective. The goal then is not a *fusion* of perspectives, not an attempt to try to live another's experiences, since this would simply consist in reducing his or her perspective to my own. Instead, entering a pact in which I accord a place to another must mean (1) attempting to understand the other's welfare *as* his or her own, and (2) constructing the "objective truth"[8] together regarding what *our* welfare might mean. But this kind of co-existence requires establishing a relation of corecognition, replacing the "unbearable gaze" with possible communication.

Thus we must view this prereflective interworld as both our primordial ground, *and*, as a goal through which to achieve a more genuine reciprocity. So the hermeneutical *moral* process, then, aims to achieve a reciprocity of intercorporeality open to difference, and not based on dominance. Rather than a habitual dynamic of domination, we would seek to clear a space for the unique meaning exhibited in the other's style of being in the world. At a thetic level this is easier to see. We might engage in a continuous and reflective effort to keep open the flow of perspectives, and on a social level try to break up or deconstruct monological power clusters, oppressive systems. This is what some have called a kind of "terrible vigilance" (Levin 1998: 351) or a "cautious humility" (Caputo 1988: 260). But because we are beings who exist in an ambiguous dialectic between our reflective and prereflective levels of existence, we need to understand this terrible vigilance also in Merleau-Ponty's terms of a kind of lived ethical pact, where it must become *sedimented* deeply into our lifeworld that we accord as much place to others as to ourselves. To do this is to dwell at the interstices of communion and disruption.

Concluding Remarks

Lastly, I would like to relate the above interpretation of the ethical implications in Merleau-Ponty's phenomenology to an interesting notion of interpersonal ethical relations proposed by Iris Young in her article, "The Ideal of Community and the Politics of Difference" (Young 1990). In that essay, Young claims that it is impossible to reduce differences to a commonness and to provide a unified dialogical relationship without a "remainder," that is, without excluding some elements and without distinguishing what is essential from what is inessential. Following thinkers like Derrida, Young argues that the traditional ideal of community exhibits a similar "logic of identity" that is found in trying to define the person as a self-identical unity, the Cartesian subject, for example, with its immediate presence to self and unity of self-consciousness. She finds that both liberalism and communitarian ethics, for example, deny difference and privilege instead a kind of relation that subsumes the other. Liberal individualism does this by positing the self as a kind of Cartesian self-sufficient unity, and communitarianism by positing fusion as an ideal, where persons' ends, intentions, vocabulary, and practices somehow become identical. Both approaches presuppose the transparency of subjects to one another.

Her solution to this problem, in contemporary urban society, is to maintain the goal of the nonoppressive city by a kind of "being-together of strangers," whose differences are irreducible. Yet, while she advocates interpersonal relationships that are defined by "an openness to an unassimilated otherness," she offers no suggestion as to how that might be compatible with her goal of maintaining the nonoppressive *city*. Here, I think, *city* (or any form of social aggregation) must be read as some kind of cohesive, but nontotalizing *unity*. Doesn't the goal of trying to work together toward nonoppressive social relations imply some kind of building-together through dialogue, and not simply a being-together? Doesn't it imply the construction of shared, or perhaps new intentions or projects?

I would like to suggest that the "ethics of difference" that Young offers is, taken by itself, more problematic than the use of it as an important facet of a hermeneutical dialogical ethics. Instead, an ethics that is founded on Merleau-Ponty's notion of decentered embodied intersubjectivity must be one that includes an "ethics of difference" as an ongoing check, a way to keep open a hermeneutic dialogue and to remain wary of falling into solipsism or into a dynamic of domination. But this does not require that we replace the notion of dialogical relation and its open-ended telos of emancipatory communion.[9] We have seen that some level of dialogical communion is *necessary* in order for me to be open to the other's perspective at all. If I have no dialogical relation with the other, then neither can I appreciate difference, nor can I be disrupted from my own perspective. It is possible, moreover, that such a dialogical ethics can cross certain sex/race/class/cultural and gender differences with which embodied existence presents us by means of an open-ended hermeneutical process and *goal* of community.

On the other hand, Young's suggestion of an "ethics of difference" is fruitful in that it can be viewed as a necessary facet of the open-ended goal of a dialogical hermeneutics toward a nontotalizing, nonmarginalizing community. It is a necessary tool in order to keep the dialogical circle open, in order not to be lured into the dangers inherent in the ideal of "consensus," which, in its desire for comm(unity), denies those other styles of taking up the world.

This facet of an ethics, too, follows from a Merleau-Pontian notion of embodied intersubjectivity. Merleau-Ponty avoids the problem contained in the Cartesian notion of subjectivity to which Young refers. That is, he avoids an "essential identity" of the subject by defining the embodied subject as always decentered from herself, and also decentered through her dialogue with the other. If, in the face of such a disruption by the other, we do not try to overrun the other by imposing our own intentions, it is possible that we can both maintain this openness or clearing—*and* try to build together with the other new meaning, new values. It is the combination of these two sides that leads to an ethical dimension more fruitful than the solution of the difference approach alone. Because we have one foot already inside the dialogue in terms of our shared sedimentation in language and in the lifeworld, it is possible to reinterpret our own understanding in light of the other's. We begin from the protoethical soil of partial carnal reciprocity, yet this soil simultaneously holds out to us a more prescriptive dimension precisely because carnal reciprocity is imperfect. But this prescriptive dimension doesn't mean anything unless one maintains that persons can change, construct new meanings and values together, and develop new lived attitudes. To enter into an ethical pact with the other requires that we keep the dialogical circle open to the disruptions of our own perspective by the other, and at the same time, aim to facilitate a nontotalizing dialogical communion in which we can dwell in our everyday sensuous existence.

Notes

1. An earlier version of this paper was presented to the Annual Merleau-Ponty Circle Conference, held in Washington DC, September 13, 2000. I am very grateful for the many contributions to the dialogue on this topic from members of the Circle.

2. For example, when he discusses my perceptual relation to the blue sky, he says "I must find the attitude which will provide it with the means of becoming determinate... I must find the reply to a question which is obscurely expressed. And yet I only do so when I am invited by it" (Merleau-Ponty 1962: 214).

3. See Nancy Holland (2000). "In a Differerent Ch[I]asm" in *Rereading Merleau-Ponty*, edited by Lawence Haas and Dorothea Olowski. New York: Humanity Books, 315–335. Holland offers an interesting discussion of the masculine bias in the *Phenomenology* alongside her own critique of Butler's early work. Moreover, she argues that in Merleau-Ponty's later work, the relation between lived experience and language is "far from the 'masculinist' attempt to get a grasp on things..." (327), but rather is a chiasmic relation not dissimilar from the way I describe the relation between prereflective and reflective experience in the hermeneutical subject we find in his earlier philosophy. Holland states that "[t]he fact that the body is a 'lived meaning' even in Merleau-Ponty's earlier work already entails that it is lived through the meaning given it, not merely by the life of which it is a part, but also by the cultural and linguistic context in which that life unfolds" (328).

4. Maurice Hamington develops an account of an embodied care ethic from Merleau-Ponty and Jane Addams. See Hamington, Maurice (2004). *Embodied Care: Jane Addams, Maurice Merleau-Ponty, and Feminist Ethics*. Chicago: University of Illinios Press. Hamington lucidly demonstrates the intertwining of theoretical knowledge (e.g., law) and praxis in our embodied habits and claims that "what 'counts' as knowledge should include what the body knows and exhibits through habits" (39). Following thinkers such as Gail Weiss, who has argued that approaches to morality must include the role of the body as an intercorporeality, Hamington uses Merleau-Ponty's epistemology to develop an ethics of care that does not sever embodied and cognitive knowledge. Weiss, Gail (1999). *Body Images: Embodiment as Intercorporeality*. New York: Routledge.

5. This unsuccessful attempt at taking legal action preceded a domestic violence and family protection bill, which was introduced in parliament in 2001. The bill was aimed to protect women from violent partners, and to allow spouses and children to seek compensation for medical bills and counseling. The bill was not passed. Future drafts of the bill have since been rejected, although women in parliament continue to push for it to be passed.

6. See Sonia Kruks (2006). "Merleau-Ponty and the Problem of Difference in Feminism" in *Feminist Interpretations of Merleau-Ponty*, edited by Dorothea Olkowski and Gail Weiss. University Park, Pennsylvania: The Pennsylvania University Press. In her article, Kruks recognizes that intercorporeality does not guarantee harmonious intersubjectivity, and can in fact be the locus of conflict and domination. Kruks suggests that beginning with the notion of the prepersonal 'One' may "help us to grasp significant

aspects of human existence that span such distinctions as race, class, and gender..." (35). She argues that the prepersonal body allows us a prethetic recognition of the other's pain or pleasure insofar as they share similar perception, motility, and spatiality of the human body. However, this does not prevent one from suppressing this recognition: "We can indeed both 'deny' and 'sustain' one another" (39). Kruks suggests that it is the shared elements of our embodiment that may foster a more ethical intercorporeality that 'sustains" rather than "denies" the other. She presents a useful example of using a recognition of shared embodiment for strengthening some of the potentially converging goals of diverse groups working toward feminist causes (42–44). Yet, at the same time, this brings to light the more difficult task of cultivating a sustaining and supporting affective disposition between men and women in cultures with high levels of domestic violence and less equality in the public sphere. It is easier to suppress our embodied recognition of the other where there is less of a shared interworld, in this case, between the sexes. Kruks offers an insightful analysis of the central role of embodiment in cultivating the affective disposition necessary to forge a common ground, but perhaps it is Hamington's notion of the "caring imagination" (see ft.4 above) that may give us a clue as to how the "gap of denial" in the interworld between sexes, races, etc., may be connected or healed. Again, the goal is not sameness, but rather toward a more responsible, ethical relation between our differences. Hamington states: "Embodied care requires imagination to overcome the limitations of physical existence. As individual human beings with discrete bodies, we are separated from one another by time, space, and socially constructed differences. Even our closest intimates do not share the same body. We use imagination to traverse those distances and make caring possible. As Merleau-Ponty indicated, my body may apprehend another's habits or movements to reveal that the other is an embodied subject and object just like myself, but knowing how another might feel or think or how best to proceed in a given situation requires applying imagination to the information given in perception. There is an imaginative dimension to caring." Hamington, Maurice (2004). *Embodied Care: Jane Addams, Maurice Merleau-Ponty, and Feminist Ethics*. Chicago: University of Illinios Press, 64–65. Moreover, Hamington is clear that the caring imaginiation is not solely an intellectual power, but rather "[w]e cannot dissociate the creative capacity of the mind from the body's ability to radiate beyond itself" (74).

    7. Here Merleau-Ponty is using "for me" in a sense that is pejorative (for Merleau-Ponty), that is, in the sense of a constituting consciousness.

    8. It should be clear that this is an intersubjective, historical endeavor.

    9. Here I am not implying any Habermasian overtones. I use "emancipatory" in the sense of a disruption of one's own perspective in terms of the ongoing goal of a "genuine" dialogical reciprocity. Communion, as I have said, is meant to represent the deep sense of "being-with" invoked in Merleau-Ponty's notion of co-existence.

References

Aristotle (1984), *Nichomachean Ethics*, Book VIII.7. Jonathon Barnes, ed. Princeton: Princeton University Press, 1831.

Butler, Judith (1989). "Sexual Ideology and Phenomenological Description" in *The Thinking Muse: Feminism and Modern French Philosophy*. Ed. Jeffner Allen and Iris Young. Bloomington: Indiana University Press, 85–100.

Caputo, John (1988). *Radical Hermeneutics*. Bloomington: Indiana University Press, 260.

Hamington, Maurice (2004). *Embodied Care: Jane Addams, Maurice Merleau-Ponty, and Feminist Ethics*. Chicago: University of Illinois Press.

Holland, Nancy (2000). "In a Differerent Ch[I]asm" in *Rereading Merleau-Ponty*, ed. Lawrence Haas and Dorothea Olkowski. New York: Humanity Books, 315–335.

Kruks, Sonia (2006). "Merleau-Ponty and the Problem of Difference in Feminism" in *Feminist Interpretations of Maurice Merleau-Ponty*. Ed. Dorothea Olkowski and Gail Weiss. University Park: Pennsylvania State University Press, 25–47.

Levin, David Michael (1998). "Tracework: Myself and Others in the Moral Phenomenology of Merleau-Ponty and Levinas" in *International Journal of Philosophical Studies* vol. 6 (3), 351.

Merleau-Ponty, Maurice (1962). *Phenomenology of Perception*. Trans. Colin Smith. New York: Routledge Press. Originally published as *Phenomenologie de la perception*. Paris: Gallimard, 1945.

——— (1964a). *The Primacy of Perception*. Trans. William Cobb. Evanston: Northwestern University Press. Originally published as *Les relations avec autrui chez l'enfant*. Paris: Centre de Documentation Universitaire, 1960.

——— (1964b). *Signs*. Trans. Richard C. McCleary. Evanston: Northwestern University Press. Originally published as *Signes*. Paris: Librairie Gallimard, 1960.

Preston, Beth (1996). "Merleau-Ponty and Feminine Embodied Existence" in *Man and World* 29, 172.

Sullivan, Shannon (1997). "Domination and Dialogue in Merleau-Ponty's *Phenomenology of Perception*" in *Hypatia*, vol. 12, no.1, winter, 1–19.

Young, Iris (1989). "Throwing Like a Girl" in *The Thinking Muse: Feminism and Modern French Philosophy*. Ed. Jeffner Allen and Iris Young. Bloomington: Indiana University Press, 51–70.

——— "The Ideal of Community and the Politics of Difference" in *Feminism/Postmodernism*. New York: Routledge, 300–323.

CHAPTER 10

Merleau-Ponty, Reciprocity, and the Reversibility of Perspectives

GREG JOHNSON

I would like to begin with two hypotheses. First, the condition for the possibility of an *ethic* of reciprocity where we *choose* to respond to the other in a way that recognizes them as worthy of being-in-relation, this condition that is the very possibility of ethics, politics, and justice itself, is *reversibility*. Second, Maurice Merleau-Ponty provides an understanding of reversibility that provides one of the best frameworks for approaching this question. More specifically, it is Merleau-Ponty who offers a way of understanding reversibility as that which simultaneously binds us to one another, something important both to ethics and politics, and that which liberates ethics and politics from an old-style metaphysics of sameness and an ontology of full presence.

The very notion of reversibility is a concern of many thinkers in general and feminist thinkers in particular. Seyla Benhabib and Iris Young have engaged the possibility of reversibility and its limits in a sustained fashion. They illustrate how reversibility raises important questions about intersubjectivity in general and the interrelation of incarnate subjects in particular. They further show that reversibility lends itself to a feminist questioning of age-old problems in philosophy: otherness/sameness; identity and difference, and, that reversibility is more than a metaphysical or ontological category. Reversibility, as they convincingly show, is thoroughly ethical and political. In this chapter, I take up the interpretations of reversibility offered by Young and Benhabib and offer a Merleau-Pontian account of reversibility to this discussion. In doing so, one of my aims is to remain faithful to Merleau-Ponty's own philosophical commitments yet equally sympathetic to feminist concerns that emerge in the light of Benhabib and Young. Merleau-Ponty's contribution to this question of reversibility is significant for the following reasons.

First, Merleau-Ponty contributes to an understanding between the "I" and the "we" where the former is not lost or subsumed into the latter. Second, the element of reversibility as that which binds us yet keeps us apart is, I will suggest in the final part of this essay, the condition for an *ethic* of reciprocity, which is of particular importance to Young's proposal. Yet, as we will see, reciprocity *becomes* possible in a Merleau-Pontian framework only insofar as we respond to the condition that enables us to "think from the others'" position, which means responding in a manner that illuminates this condition of reversibility. Conversely, the choice of nonreciprocity, a choice that often deems the other unworthy of being-in-ethical-relation, is a choice that deadens this condition of reversibility. What is needed, then, is an understanding of this condition of reversibility that does not *a priori* guarantee an ethic of reciprocity, but which, with an awareness of this condition, makes it possible. My claim is that Merleau-Ponty provides us with such an understanding of reversibility.

To set the stage I offer an illustration that raises the specter of reversibility and its importance for moral reasoning and transformative politics. I then turn to the discussion between Benhabib and Young where I show how the issue of reversibility is of particular importance to their projects. Following this I offer my Merleau-Pontian account and show how his understanding of reversibility allows us to engage the other in a way that neither does violence to them (Young's concern), nor leads to solipsism, which hinders the possibility of critique (Benhabib's concern). Finally, I conclude by showing how Merleau-Ponty's idea of reversibility is essential for understanding *how* an ethic of reciprocity might be possible. Here I elaborate more the claim in my initial hypothesis, namely, that the condition for the possibility of an ethical response of reciprocity presupposes a notion of reversibility. Let me now turn to my initial example that raises the issue of reversibility.

Arendt and the Political Relevance of Reversibility

In *Eichmann in Jerusalem*, Hannah Arendt suggests that Adolf Eichmann succumbed to the Nazi plan to exterminate six million Jews because he lacked the ability, in her words, "to think from the standpoint of somebody else" (Arendt 1963: 49).[1] In short, he was unable to reverse perspectives with those whose death he willingly commissioned. Had he been able to do this, she implies, Eichmann could have understood the suffering he caused and would have taken measures to halt these senseless acts. He would have, in other words, reciprocated, which could (or should) have altered his course of action. In contrast Arendt tells us about Anton Schmidt who was able to place himself in the position of innocent Jews being murdered, that is to say think from the position of the other, recognize their extreme suffering, and risk his life saving them (for which he was eventually executed). Arendt's point is forcefully made: the reversibility of perspectives is essential both to moral reasoning and transformative politics.

As an historical point of reference, Arendt's interest in the reversibility of perspectives results from her reading of Kant's *Critique of Judgment*, from which she gets the notion of practicing "enlarged thinking."[2] For Arendt enlarged thinking is the ability to think in a representative manner that Anton Schmidt practices. Her gloss on Kant's remark is summarized in two important places, which reveal more clearly her view of reversibility. The first, which appears in her *Lectures on Kant's Political Philosophy*, is more general in scope. She writes:

> [A]n "enlarged mentality" is the condition *sine qua non* of right judgment; one's community sense makes it possible to enlarge one's mentality. Negatively speaking, this means that one is able to abstract from private conditions and circumstances, which, as far as judgment is concerned, limit and inhibit its exercise. . . . Communicability obviously depends on the enlarged mentality; one can communicate only if one is able to think from the other person's standpoint; otherwise one will never meet him, never speak in such a way that he understands. By communicating one's feelings, one's pleasures and disinterested delights, one tells one's *choices* and one chooses one's company. . . . (Arendt 1982: 73–74)

The second passage provides a more thorough account of what enlarged thinking means in reference to the faculty of judgment.

> The power of judgment rests on a potential agreement with others, and the thinking process which is active in judging something is not, like the thought process of pure reasoning, a dialogue between me and myself, but finds itself always and primarily, even if I am quite alone in making up my mind, in an anticipated communication with others with whom I must finally come to some agreement. From this potential agreement judgment derives its specific validity. This means, on the one hand, that such judgment must liberate itself from the 'subjective private conditions,' that is, from the idiosyncrasies which naturally determine the outlook of each individual in his privacy and are legitimate as long as they are only privately held opinions but which are not fit to enter the market place, and lack all validity in the pubic realm. And this enlarged way of thinking, which as judgment knows how to transcend its individual limitations, cannot function in strict isolation or solitude; it needs the presence of others 'in whose place' it must think, whose perspective it must take into consideration, and without whom it never has the opportunity to operate at all. (Arendt 1961: 220–221)

These passages contain much that would require detailed interpretation. However, for my purposes I will highlight four important points. First, enlarged thinking suggests that those with whom we interact affect our opinions and ideas. Our judgments and thinking have an indispensable communicative dimension that precludes us from making judgments in an isolated fashion. An enlarged mentality is not simply a private activity but a public matter in that one's private interests always affect and are affected by others. Second, while enlarged thinking does mean thinking from the standpoint of the other it does not mean that we lose our identity or co-opt the identity of another under our own identity. Enlarged thought here is to be understood as an *attempt* to understand the position of the other in undistorted ways. Third, because we are always affected by others in our judgments, and these others remain wholly other by virtue of their transcendence to us, certain spaces must be created where the perspectives of the other can be articulated and adopted in order to insure a noncoercive and nonco-optive politics of enlarged mentality. Fourth, enlarged thinking is a quintessential political activity because it is a mode of thinking that empowers us to deal with the other in his or her particularity and still enables us to make claims to communal validity. Thus, it is no surprise that for Arendt enlarged thinking is "the mode of thinking that is essential for politics—the debate, opinion formation, persuasion, and augmentation that are characteristic of action" (Bernstein 1983: 217–218).[3] This Arendtian background sets the stage for the resurgence of this concept in contemporary political philosophy. In the following section I recount a recent debate where enlarged thought, and its connection to reversibility, is central. I offer this debate because it enables us to see how a Merleau-Pontian account of reversibility might contribute to this question.

The Resurgence of Reversibility

In recent years, feminist political philosophers have taken up the issue of reversibility and engaged its viability. First, following Arendt, Seyla Benhabib reconsiders reversibility within her own proposal of communicative ethics and argues for a version of the Arendtian notion of enlarged thinking.[4] Reciprocity and reversibility are understood better in the context of two of her more general claims. Second, Benhabib asserts, we cannot assume all people reason in the same fashion. This "generalized" view of the self is both inattentive to the "concrete" selves that participate in the reasoning process and is incapable of individuating among selves. Second, to the extent that we can speak of solidarity we must do so in a way that does not completely fuse differing parties. Rather, each party is taken on her or his own terms as capable of seeing something different. From each location, therefore, we are able, through dialogue, to generate connections that yield new possibilities for knowledge. Enlarged thinking, she concludes, is "a capacity for presenting to oneself the perspectivality of the world, of taking cognizance of the many points of view through which a matter must be seen and evaluated. This capacity is not empathy, in that it does not mean to 'feel with others,' but signifies instead a cognitive ability to "think with others'" (Benhabib 1996b: 191).

According to Benhabib, however, enlarged thought is distinct from either a formalistic understanding of the Kantian categorical imperative, on the one hand, or simply cultivating empathy, on the other hand. Put differently, the Kantian universal formula, "Act only according to that maxim whereby you can at the same time will that it should become a universal law," becomes, "Act in such a way that the maxim of your actions takes into account the perspective of everyone else in such a way that you would be in a position to 'woo their consent'" (Benhabib 1992: 136). In her reformulation of Kant's universal formula of the Categorical Imperative as that which is able to "woo the consent" of others, Benhabib elaborates more specifically how enlarged thinking functions.

> For Kant this [distinguishing empathy from enlarged thinking] was not an issue since he assumed that, thinking for one, a pure rational being could think for all. If we reject Kantian a priorism, and his assumption that as moral selves we are all somehow identical; if, in other words, we distinguish a universalist morality of principles from Kant's doctrine of a priori rationality, then I want to suggest we must think of such enlarged thought as a condition of actual or simulated dialogue. To "think from the perspective of everyone else" is to know "how to listen" to what the other is saying, or when the voices of others are absent, to imagine to oneself a conversation with the other as my dialogue partner. (Benhabib 1992: 137)

The point worth emphasizing here is that the universalistic emphasis drawn from Kant is not dismissed but instead modified so that it is dependent on the multiple contexts out of which moral judgments are made. To think from the standpoint of everyone else requires the application of contextual moral and political judgment. To be sure, we do not cease in trying to convince the other of the merits of our own position. After all, we try to "woo the consent" of the other but in a way that does not perform a violence to their singularly unique position. One way we accomplish this is by paying attention to what Benhabib calls "general interest." Pursuing a general interest does not mean we necessarily aspire to complete unanimity. Instead, general interest allows us to argue from our situation for ideas to which all *could* consent, not *must* consent. General interest, then, is a regulative ideal that governs our dialogical interactions and as such it emphasizes the willingness to seek reasonable agreement with the other, yet with full awareness that consent may not be achieved. The important distinction, then, is between "consensus" and "reaching an agreement," which is arguably the one point, as we will see in Young's criticism, on which Benhabib is most often misunderstood.

Benhabib rejects a notion of general interest that has as its goal the uncovering and dis-covering of rational criteria available to all. Moreover, the goal is not one in which fundamental particularities, often the locus of much disagreement, are constrained either beforehand or in the dialogical process so that consensus is procured.[5] Such a conception of general interest would be a byproduct of viewing the other solely as a generalized other. Rather, the concept of general interest opposes fixed and context-independent principles of universalizability. Furthermore, to speak of general interest does not mean that we treat dissenting voices as mere anomalies to the larger more dominant theories. General interest, linked with the practice of enlarged thinking, means that we can be aware of and entertain the multiplicity of *all* voices including the disenfranchised, and that these voices do not have to agree upon a number of premises *before* genuine dialogue takes place.[6] As Benhabib stresses, "Above all these decisions should not exclude the voice of those whose 'interests' may not be formulable in the accepted language of public discourse, but whose very presence in public life may force the boundaries between private needs and public claims, individual misfortunes and collectively representable grievances" (Benhabib 1992: 96–97). In the end, general interest and enlarged thought function together so that we can at once remain sensitive to differences and still engage in social critique with the hope of "wooing" those whose vision for the world differs from ours.

A Critique of Reversibility: Iris Marion Young

Benhabib's interest in enlarged thinking has not gone without criticism. Iris Young, more than any other political philosopher, has criticized Benhabib on several points mentioned above. Young's critique against Benhabib runs as follows. First, Young believes that Benhabib's reliance on the notion of enlarged thought runs the risk of "closing off differentiation among subjects that Benhabib wants to keep open" (Young 1994: 167). Understood in this way the notion of enlarged thinking, according to Young, presupposes mirror sameness or most problematically the interchangeable nature of subjects. It is, in other words, a symmetrical view of subjects where "I project onto them a perspective that complements my own" (Young 1994: 168–169). Instead of seeing ourselves mirrored in others, Young argues for interaction based on asymmetrical reciprocity, which means encountering otherness in a way that does not reduce their otherness to sameness. To be sure, we possess similarities, but similarities that do not require or result in ontological sameness. To the degree that we engage in enlarged thinking, we do so with full awareness that the other is always beyond our hermeneutical desires to make the unfamiliar "other" a familiar "same" (cf. Young 1996: 127f).

Young's second criticism of Benhabib is that Benhabib reduces reciprocal recognition to the ontological concept of reversibility, which Young contends is not only problematic for the reasons above, but because such a move cannot be accomplished even if it is desirable. Here the target of criticism is with the notion of shared experiences that, once again, attempts to govern the act of practicing enlarged thinking. Talk of reversibility, on Benhabib's model, assumes the equally legitimate nature of all perspectives, but for Young this is not the case where structured social injustices exist (like racism, for example). When members of privileged groups "imaginatively try to represent to themselves the perspective of members of oppressed groups, too often those representations carry projections and fantasies through which the privileged reinforce a complementary image of themselves (Young 1994: 171). Instead of aiding the communicative process, reversibility impedes dialogical communication. Imagining or thinking you know how another person feels can be detrimental to a dialogical encounter because if you have represented the other position to yourself then there is a good chance, on Young's reading, that one will try to make the other's unfamiliarity familiar, and in doing so become blinded to the ways these perspectives conflict with the very misunderstandings about them that, ironically, one seeks to address by imaginatively representing them.

Young's final criticism of Benhabib is that a symmetrical understanding of reciprocity, the kind attributed to Benhabib's proposal, does not allow for the important embodied components of greeting, rhetoric, and storytelling, which Young claims are essential for understanding reciprocity as asymmetrical. These components, inspired by Young's own reading of Arendt, are vital because they not only recognize the situatedness of the interlocutors, they also reflect the necessary elements that shape public and dialogical communication.

Over against her criticism of Benhabib, Young's alternative includes the following. First, like Benhabib, Young proposes an "egalitarian reciprocity," which depends more on differences than unity. As she says, "Understanding another social location can here mean that there has been successful expression of experience and perspective, so that other social positions learn, and part of what they understand is that there remains more behind that experience and perspective that transcends their own subjectivity" (Young 1996: 128). Second, the reversibility of perspectives is denounced while reciprocality, as asymmetrical, is retained. That is, we engage each other from specific locations and in privileging these locations in our interactive encounters we acknowledge, vis-à-vis the need for recognition, that these perspectives prevent, or at least should do so, any reversing of perspectives where asymmetry finally gives way to symmetry. In the end, Young believes her alternative of asymmetrical reciprocity leaves open the notion that things about the other will not be understood, which opens more the possibility that we will listen to specific claims, interests and expressions of those with whom we seek dialogue (cf. Young 1994: 172).[7]

Benhabib's response to Young is essentially an elaboration of her earlier thoughts with new emphases. First, Benhabib reemphasizes the importance of embodiedness. I say reemphasizes because in her book *Situating the Self* she argues for an embodied and embedded understanding of communicative ethics and criticizes disembodied and disembedded understandings as "illusions of a self transparent and self-grounding reason, the illusion of a disembedded and disembodied subject, and the illusion of having found an Archimedean standpoint, situated beyond historical and cultural contingency." And, she is quick to assert, "They have long ceased to convince. . . . [L]et me state here my own adieu to these ideals" (Benhabib 1992: 4). To be sure, Benhabib does not go as far as Young in privileging lived bodily experiences in guiding deliberative processes because the embodied components of greeting, storytelling, and rhetoric, although important for informal communication do not provide the basis for public democracy (cf. Benhabib 1996a: 83). Second, Benhabib points out, and correctly I think, that Young mischaracterizes her position as one arguing solely for symmetrical reciprocity instead of asymmetrical reciprocity. Benhabib reminds Young that she never uses this language. In fact, Benhabib reemphasizes her own distinction between "formal" and "complementary" reciprocity, the former suggesting a more symmetrical relationship while the latter an asymmetrical one. Third, and what is more strongly stated in recent discussions, Benhabib claims that Young's position runs the risk of falling prey either to a form of "extreme nominalism" or "essentializing group identities." Instead of nominalism or group essentialism, Benhabib believes that taking seriously the reversibility of perspectives, via enlarged thinking, creates the possibility of transforming our already preconceived notions of certain issues. Arguing more forcefully, she concludes, "Precisely because reversibility of perspectives is possible, social learning around issues like sexism, racism, and ethnic discrimination is possible. Moral change and political transformation can only take place through learning to take the standpoint of the other into account" (Benhabib 1994: 188; 189).

Before turning to my Merleau-Pontian account of reversibility, let me offer a brief summary of the discussion thus far. This debate between Benhabib and Young reveals clearly the stakes in this dilemma. On the one hand we need a view of reversibility that does not assume the transparency of selves, which does not perpetuate the tyranny of sameness (Young's concern and her subsequent proposal to avoid this). On the other hand, we need a view of reversibility that does not lead to solipsism or nominalism, a view that can cause potential paralysis, which will hinder our efforts at transformative politics (Benhabib's concern and proposal to avoid this). With these salient features of this debate in place, I now want to pursue my claim that Merleau-Ponty's understanding of reversibility helps us to negotiate this dilemma. After all, Merleau-Ponty was as concerned about reversing perspectives as Arendt and Benhabib. Like them, he believed that to fail in this regard meant to open the door for what he called "corruption." Writing in opposition to the colonization of Indochina in 1947, Merleau-Ponty states that "It is in a precise sense scandalous that a Christian should show himself so incapable of getting outside himself and his 'ideas,' and should refuse to see himself even for an instant through the eyes of others" (Merleau-Ponty 1964: 324). Let me now turn to my Merleau-Pontian account.

Reconsidering Reversibility: Merleau-Ponty

Defining reversibility might seem to be an easy task. It both is and is not. It is seemingly an easy task because in many respects reversibility suggests a simple inversion of something similar. But insofar as it is more than a simple inversion of the same, reversibility is complicated. Thus, to get at a richer understanding let's consider the following components that can deepen our understanding of reversibility. Let me begin with some general remarks.

First, reversibility, that "ultimate truth" for Merleau-Ponty, evokes the idea of mutuality but not of complete and perfect mutuality (Merleau-Ponty 1968: 155). True, it is that which implies an interconnectedness of me with others where the other can refer to both the human and extra-human. Second, reversibility participates in what could be called the movement of transcendence, which is to say that the Other "transcends me, for example, in such regional sameness as species likeness, communal likeness, addresses to me, or likenesses of occurrences" (Scott 1997: 36). Because of this movement of transcendence summoned by reversibility, shared human experience, to the degree of either complete and fixed unity or unanimous consensus among us before agreement is possible, is problematized. What this movement of transcendence suggests, then, is that reversibility also means *withdrawal*. That is to say, the other is in a reversible stance from us in a sense of withdrawal insofar as we can never completely, exhaustively or transparently know the position of the other. And here is the understanding I believe to be lost when we bypass reversibility too quickly for reciprocity. As Merleau-Ponty writes, "I can count on what I see, which is in close correspondence with what the other sees ... and yet at the same time *I never rejoin the other's lived experience*" (1968: 10). We never rejoin the other's lived experience because it always transcends us to the point that it withdraws itself from us. This point is worth pursuing.

Reversibility for Merleau-Ponty is located within the framework of what he calls "flesh." It has its roots, however, in the *Phenomenology of Perception* where he writes that my body "perceives the body of another, and discovers in that other body a miraculous prolongation of my own intentions, a familiar way of dealing with the world" (Merleau-Ponty 1962: 354). Such a remark foreshadows what Merleau-Ponty says throughout *The Visible and the Invisible* such as, for example, his claim that "My body is made of the same flesh as the world (it is a perceived), and moreover this flesh of my body is shared by the world, the world *reflects* it, encroaches upon it and it encroaches upon the world" (1968: 248).

Merleau-Ponty is clear that flesh is *not* to be understood as analogous to the flesh of our body. Even though the flesh of the world is not "*self-sensing* as is my flesh, . . . I call it flesh nonetheless . . . in order to say that it is a *pregnancy* of possibles. . . . It is by the flesh of the world that in the last analysis one can understand the lived body (*corps propre*)"—(1968: 250). So, even though flesh is not modeled on our flesh, our flesh, nevertheless, participates in and influences universal flesh. That is, flesh is universal in the sense that it cannot be exhausted or subjugated to our experiences of it as an object. This is why Merleau-Ponty can say that "my body is made of the same flesh as the world (it is a perceived), and moreover this flesh of my body is shared by the world, the world *reflects* it, encroaches upon it and it encroaches upon the world . . . , they are in a relation of transgression or of overlapping" (1968: 248–249).

What is suggested by the use of the word flesh as opposed to body is the idea that there is a pre-ontological dimension to embodiment; that is, a dimension that is prethematic and that in a preschematic way illuminates an ideal political community. David Michael Levin helpfully remarks that flesh articulates, however ambiguously, a new "historical project for the ontological truth of our incarnation as human beings" (Levin 1985: 67). That is to say, flesh prepares or orients us in a primordial way that, in Levin's words, makes us ready for "the mutual recognitions in a primordial sociality and [makes us] ready for the mutual recognitions and reciprocities constitutive of a more mature social world, a moral and political community" (Levin 1990: 42). As we see, flesh is linked to and derived from an examination of the body but is not to be understood *as* the flesh of our body (cf. 1968: 136–137). Or, more correctly, our bodies are not flesh yet our bodies participate in universal flesh, which means that our bodies are present to flesh insofar as they are, at a certain level, similar "stuff." Without this commonality, something Young tends to overlook, nothing would be there. Flesh, then, signifies commonality in which our bodies participate. Thus, flesh possesses both a corporeal and an incorporeal significance, which Merleau-Ponty describes in the following way.

> [F]lesh is not matter, in the sense of corpuscles of being which would add up or continue on one another to form beings.... The flesh is not matter, is not mind, is not substance. To designate it we should need the old term "element," in the sense it was used to speak of water, air, earth, and fire, that is, in the sense of a *general thing*, midway between the spatio-temporal individual and the idea, a sort of incarnate principle that brings a style of being wherever there is a fragment of being. (1968: 139)

Said differently, flesh is that which "extends further than the things I touch and see at present." Flesh is "there" and announces how we not only exist in a social world but how this social world also dwells in us via our participation in universal flesh (1968: 143). In this regard, we could say that flesh has a texture, but a texture understood as intertwinement or reversibility; a reversibility always imminent and never realized in fact.[8]

Let me put this discussion more directly in terms of reversibility. Through our participation in and through flesh, we are linked to others in a way that cannot reduce them to our own hermeneutical frameworks, that is, make them as unfamiliar threats familiar extensions of ourselves. Moreover, our participation in universal flesh means that we do not act in isolation because, as bodies (in the *Phenomenology of Perception*) and bodies-as-flesh (in *The Visible and the Invisible*), we are intercorporeally linked with each other, which means that our actions, movements, or visions concerning society "touch" others as much as theirs "touch" us. Let me elaborate.

First, flesh, like embodiment in the *Phenomenology of Perception*, is a phenomenological concept but not a biological one, which means that, among other things, it resists being reduced to a category whereby we explain our relationship to it in terms of causality. As a phenomenological concept, flesh pays attention to and resonates with the body of lived experience (cf. Levin 1985: 330). Second, flesh illuminates our common intercorporeality so that we can think both identity and difference. In this regard, flesh is nothing other than a label for that most basic problem running throughout the history of philosophy: "the problem of sameness and otherness, of identity and difference, of the One and the same" (Madison 1990: 29). Put in more political terms, flesh orders our thinking about society—that is, how it might be, or could be—more in terms of becoming rather than actuality. Thus, flesh is not some kind of telic principle that constitutes or even regulates our experience of it. To the contrary, flesh as a "wild being" or "general thing" problematizes any once-and-for-all positing of transhistorical, dis-embodied visions of our life together and instead, presents our coexistence together as that which organically unfolds in the manner of life itself, first in lived bodily experience and now in universal flesh. Third, flesh is universal insofar as it gestures more fully toward that dimension which ontologically, or better pre-ontologically, orients us and enables us to act in harmony—not a harmony in which otherness is reduced to sameness, but harmony where the Other always transcends us; a transcendence characterized as alterity. It is a harmony that illuminates the possibility of something rather than nothing. In a word, flesh is that "stuff" that keeps us together and at the same time keeps us apart. It is in this regard that flesh can be thought of as a nonorderly order by which I mean the following.

On the one hand, flesh is a "being in latency" (1968: 136), a "sort of incarnate principle" (1968: 139) that is "not contingency, or chaos, but a texture that returns to itself and conforms to itself" (1968: 146). It is a texture that generates intercorporeity. On the other hand, flesh is a "wild being" and has "no name in traditional philosophy to designate it" (1968: 139), which means that it cannot be reduced to some kind of eidetic principle that keeps Otherness always in the cross-hairs of sameness. There is an order to flesh but an order that does not express rigid control and mastery over Otherness. Instead, it is an order that illuminates a primordial energy that empowers us to act in an intertwining manner whereby we find ourselves living in the facial expressions of the other (and he or she in mine). Flesh is that which reveals reversibility because flesh is, in Merleau-Pontian terms, another way of thinking about "the system of 'me-and-other'" (Merleau-Ponty 1964b: 146).

Above I said that as participants in universal flesh we "touch" each other with our actions, movements, and ideas. I say this because the understanding of reversibility I am suggesting here, following Merleau-Ponty, is an asymmetrical understanding that is best understood on the model of one hand touching the other (1968: 39). For example, it is not the same whenever I touch myself as when another touches me. To be sure, these two experiences of touching are not dissimilar; neither do they coincide. As reversible there is similarity between these experiences but not sameness: Similarity within asymmetry. Further, it indicates the inability of one hand to completely coincide with the other. This means that the reversibility of flesh is not about complete self-transparency between subjects, for this would mean falling into what Merleau-Ponty calls the thesis of "coincidence." And because Merleau-Ponty affirms a thesis of "non-coincidence," there is always a distance between me and the other that cannot in the end be overcome by virtue of our singular locations. This means that, first, we can never know completely what the other feels because we are not they and they are not we, just as my one hand touching the other can never know completely what the other hand feels. Second, because Merleau-Ponty's reversibility is hermeneutically informed he is aware that in interpreting the other we can never understand his or her intentions in a transparent fashion, much in the same way, we can never exhaust the interpretation of a text. There is always a distance between the other and me. This does not mean, to be sure, that we cannot enter into the world of the Other, an insight not lost on either Arendt or Merleau-Ponty. Rather, it means, in a positive manner, that in our efforts to know the Other in his or her singularity there will be, to invoke an idea from Paul Ricoeur, a "surplus of meaning," which is to say that the Other as transcendent always escapes our attempts to represent them transparently, and this surplus of meaning insures that the interpretive process remains alive (cf. Ricoeur 1976). This is what I take Merleau-Ponty to mean when he says that we borrow from the other, take from or encroach upon the other, and intersect with the other in a way that is chiasmic. Once again, touch is the model where things "touch me as I touch them and touch myself: flesh of the world—distinct from my flesh: the double inscription outside and inside. The inside receives without flesh: not a "psychic state," but intra-corporeal, reverse of the outside that my body shows to the things" (1968: 261).

Understood in this light, to speak of reversing perspectives is to signify our intercorporeality, modeled on touching, as that which makes possible the illumination of the presocial and pro-moral quality of flesh and body-as-flesh. It speaks of an intercorporeality defined by intertwining and reversibility, one modeled on a primordial understanding of the body-as-flesh. This is why, as the condition for seeing and being seen, touching and being touched, hearing and being heard, the reversibility of flesh motivates us to illuminate more fully the outlines that already socially attune us to a concealed ideal of intercorporeal subjects (cf. 1968: 148 and Levin 1988: 333).

We can conclude from the above discussion that, first, as a medium, flesh locates us within a particular framework. Second, the reversibility of flesh as the "flesh of the world" is "a *pregnancy* of possibles," which means that flesh at least indicates the potentiality to intertwine our becoming together, what Merleau-Ponty refers to as intercorporeity. Insofar as we participate in flesh we apprehend, albeit briefly, the ideal community of intercorporeal beings (1968: 250). It is for these reasons that I believe that the reversibility of flesh, while not receiving extensive delineation in Merleau-Ponty's political writings, is, nevertheless, shot through with political overtones. Consider, for example, a comment he makes in *Humanism and Terror*. He says, "To understand and judge a society, one has to penetrate its basic structure to the human bond upon which it is built; this undoubtedly depends upon legal relations, but also upon forms of labor, ways of loving, living, and dying" (Merleau-Ponty 1969: xiv). That which is prior to the legal relations and orients our relationships characterized by love, life, and dying are other ways of thinking about our participation in universal flesh. There is, in short, reversibility here: "each the other side of the other" (1968: 263). So, flesh, we might say in this respect, is a "surface" in that it allows for diverse values and commitments. Thus, borrowing a thought from Charles Scott, flesh can be thought of as

> the space of 'the' people in the sense that the multiplicity, divergence, and struggle of individuals is maximized rather than a unity of the principles and values

that regulate people and make them appear as 'one.' By acting and thinking in reference to such space one is able to engage practices and discourses, not in the name of 'higher' values but by focusing attention 'on the realities that have gone unnoticed' and by showing 'what is intolerable and what it is in an intolerable situation that makes it truly intolerable.'" (Scott 1997: 184)

In the end, Merleau-Ponty enables us to confront constructively the problems of radical individual nominalism or detrimental group essentialism, one a concern of Young, the other a potential implication of her rejection of reversibility. The element of reversibility, developed within the framework of Merleau-Pontian universal flesh, speaks clearly to the fact that we are inhabited by and inhabit a common world. I say "common" here to indicate the politics of "touch," or what we might call a "politics of communion." As an adventure in communion, illuminated by the reversibility of flesh, our intertwinement is a dialectical coinhabiting whereby we always struggle to resist the extremes of the implications of any discussion of reversibility: On the one hand, individual solipsism, which precludes any reversibility, and, on the other hand, group essentialism that eradicates otherness. The latter concern is that of Young and one to which Merleau-Ponty responds. As he himself knew, we can *never* in a transparent manner subsume the other under the same because "our situations cannot be superimposed on each other" (1962: 356). This is why he could conclude the following.

> If, moreover, we undertake the same project in common, this common project is not one single project, it does not appear in the selfsame light to both of us, we are not both equally enthusiastic about it, or at any rate not in quite the same way, simply because Paul is Paul and I am myself. Although his consciousness and mine, working through our respective situations, may contrive to produce a common situation in which they can communicate, it is nevertheless from the subjectivity of each of us that each one projects this "one and only" world. (1962: 356)

If we retrieve a view of reversibility like that of Merleau-Ponty, then where does this leave us with reciprocity in general and Young's "asymmetrical reciprocity" in particular? In the remainder of this chapter, I want to take up this question and begin thinking through this relationship from the Merleau-Pontian understanding offered above.

Conclusion: Reversibility and/or Reciprocity

Let me begin this final section by indicating how I understand reciprocity.[9] To reciprocate is first to recognize you as worthy of a response. Reciprocity, then, is a *decision*. In a moment of indecision I decide to recognize you as someone with whom I am intertwined and with whom I could relate through my response to you. Thus, to reciprocate is to reflect this intertwinement through my response toward you that is an ethic, a way of comporting myself toward you in the response. Reciprocity is *not* that which makes my decision to reciprocate possible. It is the response to you that illuminates an always-already condition of being-with-you, which is the condition of reversibility as flesh as outlined above. Reciprocity, therefore, requires, or better presupposes reversibility. To say that reciprocity is a response that reflects this condition of reversibility is to say, further, that reciprocity is a *particular kind* of response to reversibility.

Reciprocity, then, illuminates this condition of reversibility in a way that reflects our being-together toward a future. Reciprocity, as that which takes seriously the otherness of those we encounter, is, for lack of a better word, a positive response to this condition of reversibility. It is a response that, upon realizing the reversible stance we find ourselves in, can make us alter our course of action. Reciprocity is that which Anton Schmidt employed in the service of saving Jews from Hitler's death camps, but one made possible because of the condition he found himself in with Jews being murdered, a condition of reversibility.

The point I am emphasizing here is that our choice to reciprocate is possible only because I find myself in a condition by which I can reverse perspectives with you, a condition for our being-together. While this may be a contestable point, I remain convinced, following Merleau-Ponty, that reversibility, however, is *not* yet an ethical stance. It is, rather, the condition for my ethical (non)response. Neither is it a cognitive capacity that we all share that, with proper activation, enables us to respond accordingly. And here we see how a phenomenologically grounded account of reversibility differs from Benhabib's Habermasian communicative account. Reversibility is not something I *do*; neither is it a procedural apparatus that *ensures* we will respond ethically. Rather, reversibility is the condition for the possibility *of* the doing, it is the condition for the possibility *of* the procedure, which in this case is the choice of reciprocity. And this condition, as I have been developing it from Merleau-Ponty, is *both* the condition for being-together *and* being-apart, which is to say it is a condition that can either be illuminated or deadened. The condition of reversibility, then, is the condition for the response in general and the ethical response in particular.

I can, on the one hand, respond in a way that reveals this condition as a condition for our flourishing. On the other hand, I can, through my choice not to reciprocate, conceal this condition, which is the condition that keeps us apart. And the reality is that we do not always act in ways that illuminate reversibility whereby reciprocity is possible. As Eichmann illustrates, I may respond in a way that deadens this condition and decide you are unworthy of recognition and worthy of death. We could, for instance, argue that Eichmann did not possess the *capacity* to reverse perspectives, as does Arendt and Benhabib following her. In not "thinking from the standpoint of the other" Eichmann was deficient in some way, perhaps cognitively or imaginatively. This explanation, a viable one I think, still nevertheless makes reversibility something we *do*, namely, imaginatively leap to the others' position so that we "see" their suffering and respond in a way that does not kill them. It further makes the choice of reversing, through an imaginative leap to the other, a potentially violent move where we *make* the other who is unfamiliar familiar. In this case, then, Young's criticisms are correct.

On the other hand, if reversibility is the condition for the possibility of Eichmann's decision either to reciprocate or not, Eichmann, on my Merleau-Pontian reading, is *still* in a condition of reversibility with those whose death he commissioned. His response is one that refuses this condition, rejects its possibility for being-together and as a result refuses the condition of reversibility. We could further speculate that Eichmann did in fact recognize the place of the other, put himself in their shoes, so to speak, and *still* decide to kill them. His response, in this case, would be one that does not extend reciprocity but rather refuses it *based on* the condition that he, as Nazi, finds himself in with Jews who are other, and whom he decides are not worthy of the title "human." His *decision* to carry out the killings is a choice *not* to reciprocate but a choice that is still possible because of the condition of reversibility, in this case a reversible stance he refuses to illuminate and instead deaden. In the end, the way we comport ourselves toward the other, whether in ways that help us flourish, or ways that violate us, is possible because of the condition of reversibility. This, as I have argued above, is one of the principal insights of Merleau-Ponty's notion of reversibility and how it might be extended to the question of reciprocity.

To conclude, what I have tried to show in this essay is that Merleau-Ponty's notion of reversibility as flesh is one that resonates with Benhabib and Young in two ways. First, it is the condition for a being together, which is a condition for ethical relation itself. This means that reversibility functions in a critical manner, something with which feminist philosophers like Benhabib are rightfully concerned. Second, his account helps us to understand that the condition we find ourselves in enables us to choose or respond to each other in ways that are asymmetrically reciprocal, even if and when those ways might inflict violence. The point here is that both are choices made possible by the condition of reversibility, and both responses are equally possible. This condition of reversibility, from a Merleau-Pontian perspective, is one that does not assume a completely mutual understanding but recognizes the other in a way that can understand their sufferings so that in our response we can choose to recognize this otherness and not eradicate it (something feminist philosophers have shown convincingly). I have argued that a Merleau-Pontian view of reversibility, while similar to Arendt and Benhabib, is unique and provides an understanding of reversibility that addresses Young's concerns and enables us to rethink the relationship between reversibility and reciprocity, which, in the end, enables us to begin again a reconsideration of the larger relationship between ontology and ethics.

Notes

1. What I offer below is only one suggestion for understanding the contemporary interest in this notion. There are no doubt other stories.

2. The passage in reference is §40 of Kant's *Critique of Judgment* (1987) where Kant says: "[Let us compare with the *sensus communis*] the common human understanding, even though the latter is not being included here as a part of the critique of taste. The following maxims may serve to elucidate its principles: (1) to think for oneself; (2) to think from the standpoint of everyone else; and (3) to think always consistently." It should be noted that my intent here is not to argue either for this reading of Kant or to assess Arendt's interpretation of it. Rather, I am concerned only with showing Arendt's interest in this concept of enlarged thought and how it has resurfaced in recent political exchanges.

3. See also Bernstein's helpful chapter "Judging—The Actor and the Spectator," in Bernstein (1986).

4. Arendt as both influence and dialogue partner is present in Benhabib's early work, *Critique, Norm, and Utopia* (1986), given its fullest consideration in *Situating the Self* (1992), and is still an interest, albeit of less focus, in her contribution in *Democracy and Difference* (1996).

5. Benhabib's example here is Bruce Ackerman who proposes engaging in "conversational restraint," which he describes in the following way.

> When you and I learn that we disagree about one or another dimension of the moral truth, we should not search for some common value that will trump this disagreement; nor should we try to translate our moral disagreement into some putatively neutral framework; nor should we seek to transcend our disagreement by talking about how some hypothetical creature would resolve it. *We should simply say nothing at all about this disagreement* and try to solve our problem by invoking premises that we do agree upon. In restraining ourselves in this way, we need not lose the chance to talk to one another about our deepest, moral disagreements in countless other, more private, contexts. Having constrained the conversation in this way, we may instead use dialogue for pragmatically productive purposes: to identify normative premises all political participants find reasonable (or, at least, not unreasonable). (Ackerman 1989: 16–17. Emphasis added). As quoted in Benhabib (1992: 96–97)

6. For a different account on this matter see John Rawls's (1971) notion of the "original position."

7. Young's fuller account of asymmetrical reciprocity can be found in her article "Asymmetrical Reciprocity (1997a), which is reprinted in Young (1997b).

8. I have not mentioned the specific connection with Merleau-Ponty's discussion of "chiasm." Since the discussion of the relationship between chiasm and reversibility would be altogether different, I have chosen not to pursue it here.

9. I have developed this argument more carefully in my essay "On the Importance of Reversibility in Deliberative Democracy," *Social Philosophy Today*, vol. 19, 2004. Other Merleau-Ponty scholars have noted the distinction between reciprocity and reversibility. I am thinking specifically of David Michal Levin, whose work I mention above, and Gary Madison, (1999). I am indebted to their work.

References

Ackerman, Bruce (1989). "Why Dialogue?" *Journal of Philosophy* 86, 5–22.

Arendt, Hannah (1961). *Between Past and Future: Six Exercises in Political Thought*. New York: Meridian Press.

——— (1963). *Eichmann in Jerusalem: A Report on the Banality of Evil*. New York: Penguin, 1963.

——— (1982). *Lectures on Kant's Political Philosophy*. Ed., Ronald Beiner. Chicago: University of Chicago Press.

Benhabib, Seyla (1986). *Critique, Norm, and Utopia: A Study of the Foundations of Critical Theory*. New York: Columbia University Press.

——— (1992). *Situating the Self: Gender, Community and Postmodernism in Contemporary Ethics*. New York: Routledge Press.

——— (1994). "In Defense of Universalism—Yet Again! A Response to Critics of Situating the Self." *New German Critique*, no. 62, spring–summer, 173–189.

——— (1996a). "Toward a Deliberative Model of Democratic Legitimacy," in *Democracy and Difference: Contesting the Boundaries of the Political*. New Jersey: Princeton University Press, 67–94.

——— (1996b). *The Reluctant Modernism of Hannah Arendt*. Thousand Oaks, London, New Delhi: Sage Publications.

Bernstein, Richard J. (1983). *Beyond Objectivism and Relativism: Science, Hermeneutics, and Praxis*. Philadelphia: University of Pennsylvania Press.

——— (1986). *Philosophical Profiles*. Philadelphia: University of Pennsylvania Press.

Kant, Immanuel (1987). *Critique of Judgment*. Trans. Werner Pluhar. Indianapolis: Hackett.

Levin, David Michael (1985). *The Body's Recollection of Being*. London: Routledge, Kegan & Paul.

―――― (1988). *The Opening of Vision: Nihilism and the Postmodern Situation.* London: Routledge, Kegan & Paul.

―――― (1990). "Justice in the Flesh," in *Ontology and Alterity in Merleau-Ponty.* Ed. Galen A. Johnson and Michael B. Smith. Evanston: Northwestern University Press, 35–44.

Madison, Gary (1990). "Flesh as Otherness," in *Ontology and Alterity in Merleau-Ponty.* Editors. Galen A. Johnson and Michael B. Smith. Evanston: Northwestern University Press, 27–34.

―――― (1999). "The Ethics and Politics of Flesh," in *The Ethics of Postmodernity: Current Trends in Continental Thought.* Evanston: Northwestern University Press, 174–190.

Merleau-Ponty, Maurice (1962). *Phenomenology of Perception.* Trans. Colin Smith. London: Routledge and Kegan Paul.

―――― (1964a). *Signs.* Trans. Richard McCleary. Evanston: Northwestern University Press.

―――― (1964b). Maurice Merleau-Ponty, *The Primacy of Perception.* Trans. William Cobb. Ed. James Edie. Evanston: Northwestern University Press.

―――― (1968). *The Visible and the Invisible.* Trans. Alphonso Lingis. Ed. Claude Lefort. Evanston: Northwestern University Press.

―――― (1969). *Humanism and Terror.* Trans. John O'Neill. Boston: Beacon Press.

Rawls, John (1971). *A Theory of Justice.* Cambridge: Harvard University Press.

Ricoeur, Paul (1976). *Interpretation Theory: Discourse and the Surplus of Meaning.* Fort Worth: Texas Christian University Press.

Scott, Charles (1997). *On the Advantages and Disadvantages of Ethics and Politics.* Bloomington: Indiana University Press.

Young, Iris Marion Young (1990). *Justice and the Politics of Difference.* Princeton: Princeton University Press.

―――― (1994). "Comments on Seyla Benhabib's, *Situating the Self.*" *New German Critique.* No. 62, Spring–Summer, 165–172.

―――― (1996). "Communication and the Other: Beyond Deliberative Democracy," in Benhabib (1996a), 120–135.

―――― (1997a). *Intersecting Voices: Dilemmas of Gender, Political Philosophy and Policy.* Princeton: Princeton University Press.

―――― (1997b). "Asymmetrical Reciprocity: On Moral Respect, Wonder, and Enlarged Thought," *Constellations: An International Journal of Critical and Democratic Theory,* Vol. 3, No. 3, 340–363.

CHAPTER 11

Entering the Place We Already Live: A Phenomenology of Female Voice

JANICE McLANE

> Language most shews a man: Speak, that I may see thee.
> —Ben Jonson *Timber, or Discoveries Made upon Men and Matter*, para. 121

Despite all efforts to the contrary, women's voices do emerge from the silence that patriarchies demand. This reclamation is remarkable, given the degree to which women are discouraged from or even forbidden expression. The present essay is one phenomenology (among many possible) of such expressive renewals. In it, I will initially sketch the Merleau-Pontian connections between openness, the 'I can' (a sense of confidence in our own bodily potentialities), and language. I will then discuss the silencing of women in terms of the 'I can' and intersubjectivity, finishing with comments on how women resist such patriarchal oppression. This last point naturally presses toward the question of what concretely constitutes the best path(s) to the recovery of female voice. Such a discussion would, however, require another essay—or book—unto itself. For that reason, at the end of this work I will limit myself to general comments.

The essay is titled "Entering the Place We Already Live" for two reasons. First, it is a basic tenet of Merleau-Ponty that we live and speak as embodied beings. As women regenerate censored voices, then, what we claim is a more profound grasp *of* our lived and speaking bodies. Second, it is also true that as bodily, women's experience can never be entirely absent or silenced. No matter how injured or incomplete, some authentic personal voice must exist as long as we live. Thus greater self-articulation is always a possibility for human beings, since the chance for it ends only with our death.

That any person's experience can never be entirely repressed also implies that women communicate in and even through silence. Merleau-Ponty touches on this when considering a "hysterical" young woman who literally cannot speak. Although speech is physically possible for her:

the move towards the future, towards the living present or towards the past, the power of learning, of maturing, of entering into communication with others, have become, as it were, arrested in a bodily symptom, existence is tied up and body has become "the place where life hides away." (1962: 164)

The passage makes clear that this young woman expresses her unconscious constriction of the power to act via her silence. Yet such hiding is to a greater or lesser extent part of all women's lives. Patriarchies, while not completely annihilating, by definition enjoin women to keep our experience at a stifling and alienating distance. Thus for all women, as for this "hysteric," the body is simultaneously accessible and "the place where life hides away."

Openness, the "I Can," and Language

To expand this consideration of expression and voice, I will now refer to Merleau-Ponty's theory of meaning. For Merleau-Ponty, all meaning is an instance of an embodied Gestalt: the perception of a figure against a ground (1962: 186). As he says in *The Visible and the Invisible*, "There is no other meaning than carnal, figure and ground—Meaning = their [figure's and ground's] dislocation, their gravitation'" (265). Human expression thus appears through human embodiment; most directly, through gesture. Our gestures—broadly taken to include posture, movement in general, language, and ultimately even thought—create nesting systems of figure against ground (1962: 146, 184). Human gesture might be called a lived divergence (écart), an evolving difference between my body and objects, my body and other persons, my body and the world.

Gesture is also part of what Merleau-Ponty calls the "I can": the body's basic motor intentionality (1962: 137). Instances of the "I can" include gesture, perception, thought, memory, and language. Merleau-Ponty describes all instances of the "I can" as "rays of the world." A "ray of the world" is not a synthesizing activity as is Kant's transcendental unity of apperception. Any such underlying synthesis of experience would imply the world and our experience of it are a closed system, a view quite foreign to Merleau-Ponty (1962: 38–39). The human body and the "I can" are rather *openness* upon the world, to other people, and to our own lives (1962: 426, 1964: 118, 138). For Merleau-Ponty, each of us casts ourselves into perceiving, speaking, and moving as a fisherwoman casts her line into waters both familiar and unknown.

This openness upon the world is both an individual and an intersubjective experience. For while remaining distinct, all human beings also share and are part of the corporeal common world. Just as the "hiatus between my right hand touched and my right hand touching, between my voice heard and uttered ... is not an ontological void, a non-being: it is spanned by the total being of my body, and by that of the world" (1962: 141–142, 147–148), so the hiatus between one person and another is spanned by the total being of our common situation, our common embodiment, and the common world. Action arises only in and through this sharedness or intersubjectivity of the world. We *are* our bodies in action; we are our bodies insofar as we are part of the shared carnal world. Thus meaning and intersubjectivity are intimately linked: each is an aspect of embodiment, and each is an aspect of the other.

Because the shared world and our individual selves are aspects of one another, meaning is always expressive of the speaker as a specific person *and* as the generalities—family, religion, country—to which she belongs. Personal identity simultaneously embodies both the individual and the communal, and the "slippage" between the two. That is, at one moment we bring to the foreground the immediate specificity of our lives, the next, we emphasize the ways that we are typical of our generation, neighborhood, economic class; a third moment, we ponder how the two conflict and harmonize. Thus identity is never fixed, but instead resides in the variegated nexus of embodied meaning that is our lives.

Nevertheless, human beings embody and commit ourselves more deeply to some meanings rather than others. These commitments are the way we comport ourselves in the world and to others, or, phrased differently, how we are open to the world. The freedom of our actions indeed resides in the fact that through them, we commit ourselves to some particular meaning. But making such commitments requires power—the power to speak, to perceive, to act.[1] "Our commitments sustain our power," says Merleau-Ponty (1962: 453–456). Power, freedom, and commitment are therefore all aspects of one another, and exist in the embodied ambiguity of human identity.

If it is then in both specific and shared existence that identity resides, then expression or voice must be similarly ambiguous. Self-expression must be the individual's specific voice as well as her expression of being part of a general group of human beings. But there are generalities and generalities. Some generalities make human life possible—I am a human being, I am a daughter, I am a writer. Oppressive systems, however, function by as fully as possible enforcing generalities and shared identities that embody power and privilege for one social group by dominating others. An obvious historical example is the definition of "race" as a set of physical characteristics (whiteness, blackness, redness, yellowness) associated with supposed ontological/biological states of superiority and inferiority, civilization and savagery, humanness and subhumanity. Similarly for women, living in a world that denigrates femaleness, voice will always be partly a struggle to discern how expression in both its individual and group aspects is supported or undermined, and persistence in speaking despite oppressive constraints. Given the complexity of human identity and expression, then, we cannot expect female voices to be uniform, whether in their development, their sabotage, or their reclamation.

Silence as the Origin of Meaning

These considerations lead us to a final Merleau-Pontian theme: silence and Being. In its most basic sense, our abandonment to openness is also what Merleau-Ponty calls our "contact with Being" (1968: 125). This contact is both immediate and nonarticulated. Were it mediated and articulated, openness to the world would require a synthesizing self; that is, a mediator and articulator underlying such contact. But phenomena are not controlled or created by us; they are the "thing[s] simply perceived" (1968: 263). Thus our plunge into the world is precisely that—a plunge that we make, but never fully control.

However, the nonarticulation of our contact with Being is also the *source* of articulation, and thus the source of language. What Merleau-Ponty says of the philosopher is true of all persons:

> His entire "work" is this absurd effort. He wrote in order to state his contact with Being; he did not state it, and could not state it, since it is silence. . . . But, because he has experienced within himself the need to speak, the birth of speech bubbling up at the bottom of his mute experience, the philosopher knows better than anyone that what is lived is lived-spoken, that, born at this depth, language is not a mask over Being, but—if one knows how to grasp it in all its roots and all its foliation—the most valuable witness to Being, that it does not interrupt an immediation that would be perfect without it, that the vision itself, the thought itself, are, as has been said, "structured as a language," are *articulation* before the letter, apparition of something where there was nothing or something else. (1968: 125–126)

This helps us understand why Merleau-Ponty declares that:

> the intention to speak can reside only in an open experience. It makes its appearance like the boiling point of a liquid, when, in the density of being, volumes of empty space are built up and move outwards. (1962: 196)

Our connection with Being is thus both unmediated connection *and* articulation. The articulation of language, like our connection with Being, is another plunge into the world, one that itself is not known until it is expressed, and thus comes alive.

These insights immediately raise a question: what is the difference between the silence of Being, and the silencing of women and of all oppressed groups? Addressing this question must, however, be deferred until after oppressive silencing is itself examined.

Silence and Voice

I move now to a consideration of the silencing of women by patriarchies. Much has been written about this subject, and I do not intend to recapitulate prior analyses. However, I will note that internal and external silencing are equally powerful, and that without the internal regulation of dominated peoples, external oppression would also wither. That women cannot voice our experience is not only because of the outside forces arrayed against us. It is also because, like Merleau-Ponty's "hysterical" young woman, women have become committed to distancing our lives from ourselves.

Such distancing from self occurs, says Merleau-Ponty, when:

> our memories and our body, instead of presenting themselves to us in singular and determined conscious acts, are enveloped in generality. Through this generality we still 'have them,' but just enough to hold them at a distance from us. We discover in this way that sensory messages or memories are expressly grasped and recognized by us only insofar as they adhere generally to that area of our body and our life to which they are relevant. Such adherence or rejection places the subject in a definite situation and sets bounds, as far as he is concerned, to the immediately available mental field, as the acquisition or loss of a sense organ presents to or removes from his direct grasp an object in the physical field. (1962: 162)

Women are encouraged not to acquire contact with our own activity and experience, but to lose it by distancing ourselves from any aspect that may threaten the preeminence of men. This covers a very wide range of life, indeed. The "generality" in which women envelop ourselves, on the other hand, has its own character. It is the female body insofar as it *does not* threaten men: constrained, male-oriented, desexualized or over-sexualized in specific ways, obedient, laboring (but laboring invisibly), and silenced or speaking only in a tightly scripted voice.

Another way to consider the generalities in which women blur our experience is to see them as modifications of gesture. As we have seen, any modification of gesture is by definition a transformation of meaning. However, "feminine" gestures are by and large a bodily system that chokes a person's "plunge into the world." It is not that this existential plunge is stopped entirely. Instead, the plunge is pulled back short the moment it is begun. In this way the immediacy of the moment often becomes for women bodily and existential stutter.

> Until the barrel-organ stopped playing Constantia stayed before the Buddha, wondering, but not as usual, not vaguely. This time her wonder was like longing. . . . There had been . . . running out, bringing things home in bags, getting things on approval, discussing them with Jug, and taking them back to get more things on approval, and arranging father's trays and trying not to annoy father. But it all seemed to have happened in a kind of tunnel. It wasn't real. It was only when she came out of the tunnel into the moonlight or by the sea or into a thunderstorm that she really felt herself. What did it mean? What was it she was always wanting? What did it all lead to? Now? Now?
>
> She turned away from the Buddha with one of her vague gestures. She went over to where Josephine was standing. She wanted to say something to Josephine, something frightfully important, about—about the future and what . . .
>
> "Don't you think perhaps—" she began.
>
> But Josephine interrupted her. "I was wondering if now—" she murmured. They stopped; they waited for each other.
>
> "Go on, Con," said Josephine.
>
> "No, no, Jug; after you," said Constantia.
>
> "No, say what you were going to say. You began," said Josephine.
>
> "I . . . I'd rather hear what you were going to say first," said Constantia.
>
> "Don't be absurd, Con."
>
> "Really, Jug."
>
> "Connie!"
>
> "Oh, *Jug*!"
>
> A pause. Then Constantia said faintly, "I can't say what I was going to say, Jug, because I've forgotten what it was . . . that I was going to say."
>
> Josephine was silent for a moment. She stared at a big cloud where the sun had been. Then she replied shortly, "I've forgotten too." (1922: 113–115)

This "stutter" is of course the result of external oppression, but it is also habitualized by women: our own experience, direct thought, desire, or action are often replaced by a generalized blankness, the very emptiness of which signifies that we have "broken . . . the circuit of all actions relating to" specific parts of our lives (1962: 162).

This "breaking of a circuit" is what Iris Young describes in her germinal essay "Throwing Like a Girl" as "inhibited intentionality" and "discontinuous unity." As Young puts it:

> Feminine bodily existence ... simultaneously reaches toward a projected end with an "I can" and withholds its full bodily commitment to that end in a self-imposed "I cannot." (1990: 148–149)

Importantly, however, Young states that the "I cannot" of inhibited intentionality is *self-imposed*. How can we understand this? How can the "I can," which is how we hold the world before us become the stuttering "I cannot"? The answer is that it doesn't—that is, the "I can" does not disappear. What rather happens is that the "I cannot" becomes part of what *I can do*. In feminine existence, the "I cannot" is incorporated into the "I can" as motility and intentionality. In feminized "rays upon the world," what "I can" do is hold myself so that "I cannot" do what I originally could and did intend to do. Thus the feminized gesture is revealed as an inability to act. The style of the "I can" that is "I cannot" need not be conscious; in fact, it usually isn't. "I cannot" is rather a way in which I experience broad swathes of my experience, as an opening upon the world, which is simultaneously a closure suffused with the blankness of impotence.

In terms of language, the broken circuit means that just as there is throwing like a girl, so there is talking like a girl: quietly, sweetly, politely, without strong language or strong opinions, or, most extremely, remaining silent. The fact that many women do not speak quietly is not a sufficient counter-example to disprove this, for it is precisely on the grounds that they are too loud or strident that such women are criticized and attacked. Women instead are both culturally assigned and commit ourselves to actual silence and debased speech: to confusion, chattering, platitudes and niceness, depressive silence, self-attack, or attack of others—especially those like ourselves or in other oppressed groups. All these are contacts with the world and with other persons, but they are linguistic gestures full of epicycles, reverses, convolutions, stops, stutterings, and inhibitions.

Thus for women, language, which in its direct form:

> counts as an arm, as action, as offense and as seduction because it brings to the surface all the deep-rooted relations of the lived experience wherein it takes form, and which is the language of life and of action but also that of literature and poetry.... (1962: 126)

—*that* language is denied us insofar as we are plagued either by external force or an internal straitjacket of patriarchalized femininity.

It is important to recall, however, that Merleau-Ponty also calls silence part of Being and of the immediacy of the world. We can differentiate the silence of our contact with Being from the silence of oppression by calling the latter an *enforced* lack of articulation. The silence of oppression is not Merleau-Ponty's "great mute land which we never leave" (1962: 126), but the alienation of a human core from the lived body's simultaneous silence and articulation in the lived moment. Whether this disintegration into generality comes from others or the self, women lose by it the only possible route both to self-knowledge and genuine communication: the direct living of our lives, and discovery of them as they are lived.

In fact, we might say that patriarchalized femininity denies women the silence of Being. The nature of feminine labor, the constraints of "feminine" and "modest" gestures, oppressive forms of intersubjectivity, can pry women from or clutter the time needed for attentiveness to our lives. An extended quotation from the Russian writer Anna Tsetsaeyva in Tillie Olsen's powerful book *Silences* eloquently attests to this phenomenon.

> To tell you the truth, I've been driven so hard by life that I feel nothing. Through these years (1917–1927) it was not my mind that grew numb, but my soul. An astonishing observation: it is precisely for feeling that one needs time, and not for thought. Thought is a flash of lightning, feeling is a ray from the most distant of stars. Feeling requires leisure; it cannot survive under fear. A basic example: rolling 1 1/2 kilos of small fishes in flour, I am able to think, but as for feeling—no. The smell is in the way. The smell is in the way, my sticky hands are in the way, the squirting oil in the way, *the fish* are in the way, each one individually and the entire 1 1/2 kilos as a whole. Feeling is apparently more demanding than thought. It requires all or nothing. There is nothing I can give to my own [feeling]: no time, no quiet, no solitude. I am always in the presence of others, from 7 in the morning till 10 at night, and by 10 at night I am so exhausted—what feeling can there be? Feeling requires *strength*. *No*, I simply sit down to mend and darn things: Mur's, S.'s, Alya's, my own. 11 o'clock. 12 o'clock. 1 o'clock. S. arrives by the last [subway] train, a brief chat, and off to bed, which means lying in bed with a book until 2 or 2:30. The books are good, but I could have written even better ones, if only.... (1978: 145)

Thus not only articulation, but even perception of our own experience becomes difficult for women. Perception, too, is an "I can," the possibilities of which are intricately woven with those of language and the threat of which must be blunted inside patriarchy. The threat of perception is not only that women who perceive clearly might also act clearly and in their own interests. It is also that, as Merleau-Ponty says, perception is itself an act of violence, of aggression (1962: 126).

Given the receptivity of perception, this statement may seem paradoxical. But like water, which is yielding yet embodies storms and tides, the scouring away of rock and earth, drowning and death, so is perception receptive, while its very elusiveness embodies the lack of final control one person has over another. Perception is a power to affirm or negate human existence in the fact that, and the way that, we perceive human beings; as such, it is always an aggression. Patriarchies very much dislike having such power in the hands of women, lest it be turned negatively toward men; patriarchies therefore undermine the confidence women have in our own perceptions. I am not claiming by this that language and its action, perception and its violence, cease to exist for women entirely. Rather, they are hidden from men and from women ourselves in the generalities of approved femininity, whatever form that may take in a particular era and culture.

The "I Can" and the "I Cannot"

At this point we must explore more deeply how the "I can" incorporates into itself the "I cannot." This incorporation occurs in the context of intersubjectivity, as do all human actions and meanings. Intersubjectivity implies a world shared through the reversibility of perceiving and being perceived, recognizing and being recognized. But although Merleau-Ponty speaks of such sharing as anonymous and general (1962: 142), perception and recognition are also singular and particular.

Inside patriarchies, women are recognized primarily as enhancers or reflectors of male power. To the extent that a man is consciously or unconsciously committed to male domination, women either are not perceived, or their actions are interpreted as referring only to men. As Marilyn Frye puts it, "It is as though women are assumed to be robots hooked up to the senses of men—not using senses of our own, not authoring perception, not having and generating a point of view" (1983: 166).

A personal example might be helpful at this point. I've always loved to bake. Once when I was ten or twelve, in the kitchen with my mother baking cookies, one of my uncles came in and said, "Jannie, that's great. You're going to make someone a good wife someday." This was not a bad man, and he meant to praise me. But though his words did recognize my actions, and me, they did so in a particular way. My love of baking became a qualification to serve some hypothetical future male, rather than something I liked to do and was good at. I was furious, but remained silent. After all, this was my uncle, I was a child, and he was "being nice."

In that moment, my uncle could not even conceive that I would do something other than to prepare myself to serve a man. My mother could not, did not want to, or did not feel it possible to correct him—that is, she could not assist me in regaining the autonomy he denied. And, importantly, I also learned that at that moment my uncle was *not present for me* as a full human subject—he was present only as an unperceptive, intrusive force.

This last is important, because it illustrates a theoretical point I am trying to unpack—namely, that if women lose the power to express our lives, if in some sense we cannot speak, it is not only because we are not recognized as speaking, acting subjects. It is also because, under oppression, *there is no one to whom to speak*, and there is no one to speak to because men have absented themselves from women by not seeing women as speaking subjects. Thus, curiously, just as women cease to be full human subjects for men, so men cease to be full human subjects for women. Intersubjectivity becomes a system of false recognition in which women are seen only as generalities that are *less* than human, while men are seen as generalities that are *more* than human. As Virginia Woolf famously put it, "Women have served all these centuries as looking-glasses possessing the magic and delicious power of reflecting the figure of man at twice its natural size" (1929: 53). Of course to be a mirror is to be not-human—but then, so is being twice the size of an actual person. One is the state of being an object; the other, the state of being a monstrosity.

Thus the debased, mutilated intersubjectivity, which constitutes oppression is a truncated reversibility that, like the "I cannot" in the "I can," is impregnated with its own repression. On the female (oppressed) side, this truncated reversibility occurs as a woman attempts to hold the whole tension of intersubjectivity within herself. That is, lacking genuine intersubjective recognition from the outside, a woman creates a new *internal* reversibility or community, inside which her intentions are completed. Externally, however, her actions remain incomplete so that she may fit into the oppressive system presented to her. Inside this new level of reversibility, any initial direct intention is stopped and redirected toward the woman herself. That is, the woman casts herself forth, but this intention is fragmented and dissolved, only to be reassembled as arm, action, and offense toward the woman herself, appearing as a self-policing internal voice proclaiming the woman is bad, not nice, not good enough, stupid, selfish, etc., etc. The initial impulse is thus in some sense maintained, yet transformed into a distance from herself, from other persons, and the world.

As Judy Grahn writes in her poem "Descent to the Roses of the Family":

> No one has ever robbed me
> and many, yes many have robbed me,
> but no one has ever robbed me
> as this has robbed me
> my own recurrent paralysis
> the grip of the blue haze
> its clutch at my heart
> the dying feeling, the not caring
> the days on end of it

> the weeks, the years left out of themselves
> the blue gauze shield
> over my heart. (1987: ?)

If a woman does feel permitted to be directly and outwardly aggressive, it will usually take place only toward those like her or socially weaker than herself. Altogether, this means that a woman inside patriarchy tends to see neither herself not others as truly human, but as parts of a lopsided system of victim-victimizer, in which women can play the role of victimizer, but more often are assigned and take on the role of victim.

Feminized actions are thus often presented by women (and by men) as being in fact *passivities*—that is, I didn't do it, it just happened, I'm just bad and defective, someone else made me do it—or, if a woman's actions are recognized as good, they are attributed to someone or something else—luck, a man, duty, God, and so on. Likewise if a woman speaks, her words are often either ignored or presented as someone else's; she perceives, but her views may be presented as acceptances of what others perceive. A new self-regulation is habitualized, so that her voice never disappears, but reappears in other forms.

The Recovery of Voice: Silence and Silence

If what I have just argued is true, then a woman reclaiming her voice must both retrain herself to directly express her intentions, and reestablish an embodied community in which she and others can speak directly without being destroyed. I am not offering here a political or personal blueprint for each woman to do this. Women experience voice and voicelessness, power and powerlessness, in many ways. Fundamentalist religions, for example, tend to cast women as tremendously strong, but always ultimately subservient to men—a fact that could also be stated as, fundamentalist women are cast as subservient to men, yet ultimately also see themselves and are seen as tremendously strong. Working- and middle-class "supermoms" can determine many things in their own lives, yet find their voices constricted by exhaustion, economic disadvantage, and responsibility—which also means that though burdened by exhaustion, economic disadvantages, and responsibilities, working- and middle-class supermoms can determine many things in their lives. To shift generations, many young women take pleasure in greater opportunity, activity, and education than their mothers and grandmothers ever could, yet grow to understand a woman's "true" voice only as that conforming to a highly (hetero)sexualized, "perfect"-bodied, up-to-the-minute copy of music videos, television, magazines, and movies—which of course can be expressed by saying many young women are constrained by media and peers to speak in highly determined, often self-destructive ways, yet still use their increased opportunity, activity, and education to build a life of their own. Scores of cultural/historical changes can be rung on this simultaneous "I can" and "I cannot" of female voice, and how each woman should pursue a freer "I can" and diminish a subjugated "I cannot," cannot be adequately addressed here.

Nevertheless, the previous analysis emphasizes the degree to which the reclamation of voice is never purely an individual endeavor. That is, while such reclamation must be undertaken by women as individuals, it must also be undertaken by women insofar as they live themselves *as women*, that is, as members of a general group in relation to other general groups: significantly, to men. While this statement is a feminist truism, its significance is often forgotten in debates about what constitutes "true" feminist action or "real" feminism, what it is to be "really" a woman, really a member of a particular race or class or religion, really to possess a vocation or avocation. There can be no final and absolute boundaries among any of our identities; nevertheless, these identities are specific and real. To reclaim a voice thus requires continual attention and awareness to the ambiguities of our lives, not least in their day-to-day, embodied relation to others.

Finally, I wish to focus on the nature of silence. For if oppression is an enforced lack of articulation, while our contact with Being is the silence of living in the "great mute land which we never leave," then at one level what women must do to reclaim our voices is rediscover—silence.

In *The Visible and the Invisible*, Merleau-Ponty says that silence is a "fecund negative instituted by the flesh . . . the negative . . . is the doubled-up, the two leaves of my body, the inside and the outside articulated in one another" (1962: 263). The silence of oppression stops our voices short, turning them upon ourselves in a violent "I cannot" and seeks to deny the reciprocity of intersubjectivity. But to return to the silence of Being, the silence from which language arises, is to enter more fully into reversibility, the doubled nature of a self connected to others. It is in the acceptance of such contact with Being, extraordinary or mundane, that our voices emerge, for it is our living of the moment's immediacy that escapes articulation, yet is articulation itself.

Thus for women to reclaim our voices, we must repossess our lived bodies as fully as possible. Iris Young wrote of throwing like a girl as the "I cannot" of the feminine lived body. Yet to regain our voices, perhaps it *is* necessary to throw like a girl. That is, we must throw ourselves into the world more as a small girl does: with abandon, with desire, with elation and sadness and perception. This is no permanent possession, no once-for-all grasping of our lives and their meaning. For as Merleau-Ponty says,

Whether it is a question of another's body or my own, I have no means of knowing the human body other than that of living it, which means taking up on my own account the drama which is being played out in it, and losing myself in it. (1968: 198)

Note

1. Apart from other persons and the world we share with them, there is no freedom, since, as Merleau-Ponty points out, even "proudly willed solitude ... is a certain mode of the *Mit-Sein*" (1962: 454).

References

Frye, Marilyn (1983). *The Politics of Reality: Essays in Feminist Theory*. Trumansburg, NY: Crossing Press.

Grahn, Judy (1987). *The Queen of Swords*. Boston: Beacon Press.

Mansfield, Katherine (1922). "The Daughters of the Late Colonel," in *The Garden Party and Other Stories*. New York: Alfred A. Knopf.

Merleau-Ponty, Maurice (1962). *Phenomenology of Perception*. Trans. Colin Smith. London: Routledge & Kegan Paul.

——— (1968). *The Visible and the Invisible*. Trans. Alphonso Lingis. Ed. Claude Lefort. Evanston: Northwestern University Press.

Olsen, Tillie (1978). *Silences*. New York: Delacorte Press/Seymour Lawrence.

Woolf, Virginia (1929). *A Room of One's Own*. London: L. and V. Woolf.

Young, Iris Marion (1990). *Throwing Like a Girl and Other Essays in Feminist Philosophy and Social Theory*. Bloomington: Indiana University Press.

CHAPTER 12

Resources for Feminist Care Ethics in Merleau-Ponty's Phenomenology of the Body

MAURICE HAMINGTON

> What is interesting is not an expedient to solve the "problem of the other"—it is a transformation of it.
>
> —Maurice Merleau-Ponty

On April 20, 1999, Columbine High School in Littleton, Colorado became part of the national vocabulary for all the wrong reasons.[1] One of the millions of people who watched the news reports of the shooting rampage was 15-year-old Rashad Williams of San Francisco, California. Williams, a high-school track athlete, learned that one of the wounded students was a fellow runner, Lance Kirklin, who had been shot in the legs, face, and chest requiring numerous surgeries and an extensive convalescence. Although he had not met Kirklin, Williams decided to act. He collected sponsorships for running in the Bay-to-Breakers 7.5–mile race in San Francisco. Williams ultimately collected more than $40,000 in pledges to help defer a portion of Kirklin's enormous medical expenses. What moral theory best explains Williams's action? Traditional approaches might offer duty, consequences, or virtue as the ethical impetus. Although those elements may have been present, none is entirely satisfactory.[2] Perhaps Williams's extraordinary willingness to act on behalf of another is at least partially explained by something more foundational than a moral theory: an embodied ethic of care.[3] I suggest that such actions reflect an embodied approach to morality explicated by the philosophy of Maurice Merleau-Ponty. In interviews, Williams's statements indicated a physical empathy with Kirklin:

> "I just think of the hurt, mental and physical."
> "I thought it could have been me, so I just put the shoe on the other foot."
> "What if I would never be able to walk again?" (National Public Radio, "Morning Edition," April 21, 2000)

203

Kirklin is white and lives in a suburban community. Williams is African American and lives in an urban community, and yet Williams transcended distance and social circumstance to care enough to act on behalf of a fellow human being in pain. His moral imagination had the embodied resources to allow him to make meaningful reciprocal connections that prompted his actions. In Merleau-Ponty's words, "the factual presence of other bodies could not produce thought or the idea if its seed were not in my own body" (Merleau-Ponty 1968: 145). Merleau-Ponty describes a corporeal-based reciprocity that I believe has important implications for morality, particularly that of care ethics.

The development of an ethic of care is one of the most significant innovations in moral philosophy during the latter part of the twentieth century. Care ethics galvanized research and writing by feminists in a number of disciplines around the notion that rules and consequences do not exhaust the content of morality. Care is a relational approach to ethics that emphasizes personal connection, context, and affective responses. Since the 1980s when the term "care ethics" was first coined, numerous books and articles have clarified and extended this nascent moral trajectory. Although feminist philosophers have led this charge, there has been an ironic lack of attention paid to the embodied aspect of care ethics. The irony lies in the widespread feminist critique of disembodied modernist moral theory and the extensive work that feminists have offered in returning attention to the body in other areas such as epistemology and sociology.

In this chapter, I claim that Merleau-Ponty's phenomenology of the body offers significant resources for understanding the corporeal dimension of care and is therefore worthy of further exploration by theorists interested in the embodied aspect of morality. A notion of *embodied care*, which combines Merleau-Ponty's phenomenology of the body and the work of feminist care ethicists, revolves around three interrelated claims: (1) Knowledge is necessary, but not sufficient, for caring; (2) What "counts" for knowledge should include what the body knows;[4] (3) Merleau-Ponty's corporeal-centered epistemology can be extrapolated to reveal the embodied basis of care. This chapter is concerned with the third claim. Specifically, I will suggest that Merleau-Ponty's development of the notions of perception, foreground-background focus phenomena, habit, and the flesh can enrich an embodied morality of care through a richer understanding of the body's epistemological participation in caring.

I will begin with a brief discussion of how feminist care ethics has been understood. This will be followed by a delineation of essential ideas from Merleau-Ponty's work that facilitates a more robust understanding of care. Ultimately, I contend that through Merleau-Ponty's work, an ethic of care should not be viewed as an alternative ethical theory but as a foundational aspect of human morality that is central to ethical theorizing.

Feminist Care Ethics

A groundswell of feminist scholarship led to the realization that care should be given greater attention in moral philosophy. The catalyst for focusing attention on care was the 1982 publication of Carol Gilligan's *In A Different Voice: Psychological Theory and Women's Development*. In an often-repeated story, Gilligan observed an overlooked alternative moral "voice" while working with acclaimed Harvard psychologist Lawrence Kohlberg who had devised a structure for measuring moral development along a six-stage hierarchy.[5] Early applications of Kohlberg's instrument indicated that females were scoring lower on his hierarchical scale. Gilligan viewed the results as indicative of a problem with the instrument and its underlying moral theory rather than a moral deficiency of women. She identified care as an unattended aspect of morality.

The major distinctions between Kohlberg and Gilligan's approach to morality center upon concepts of connection, particularity, and emotion.[6] For Kohlberg, morality is absorbed in adjudication: what constitutes right action and principles of moral assessment. For Gilligan, care reframes moral concerns on the connections between people and the relationships established. While Kohlberg (through Kant and Rawls) assumes that individual moral agents are autonomous and thus freely enter into relationships that elicit duties, Gilligan views individuals as entangled in a web of dynamic relationships, not all of which are freely chosen. Care ethics posits humans as interconnected and ethics as an expression of sustaining these connections. Accordingly, human relations are concrete and therefore particular. While Kohlberg stressed universal principles, Gilligan argues that moral action requires knowledge of particular others and their circumstances, not a universalized case. For Gilligan, care does not provide the "right" action for all people at all times, but the appropriate action given the circumstances. Human interconnection implies more than autonomous rational agents making detached moral decisions as valorized by Kohlberg's work. Although Kant avoids the emotive, Gilligan's approach embraces feelings as a moral capacity that facilitates an ethical response by creating connection and motivating action. This particularization of care ethics to individual others opens the door to the integration of Merleau-Ponty's phenomenology of the body. Instead of abstract principles, specific embodied others are valued.

Following Gilligan, feminist scholars Susan Hekman, Virginia Held, Rita Manning, Nel Noddings, Sara Ruddick, Joan Tronto and others have contributed significant elaborations and extensions of care ethics.[7] Today, no discussion of ethics from a feminist perspective is complete without some mention of care. Feminist care ethicists have employed divergent methodologies, assumptions, and conclusions, but ultimately they share a concern for connection and particularity over universality and abstraction. Although emotive and affective responses have been stressed, little specific treatment of the embodied dimension of care has been developed. Many feminists have clearly rejected the disembodied, abstract understanding of modern moral theory, yet few have explored how care actuates in the experience of lived "fleshy" bodies. Feminist philosophers such as Annette Baier, Claudia Card, Marilyn Friedman, and Virginia Held have gestured toward an embodied ethic in an attempt to overcome Cartesian mind/body dualism, but have not developed a comprehensive treatment of corporeal care.[8] As Gail Weiss laments, "I am worried that the body has been left out of the picture altogether" (Weiss 1999: 140).[9] Merleau-Ponty's philosophy offers significant epistemological and operative insight into corporeal behavior and experience that can contribute to feminist analyses of care.

Merleau-Ponty's Corporeal-Centered Epistemology

Merleau-Ponty never developed a comprehensive moral schema, however, his corporeal-centered epistemology has important implications for ethical theory. If indeed, "the body is our general medium for having a world," as Merleau-Ponty indicates, then the body must necessarily be our medium for having morality as well (Merleau-Ponty 1962: 146). A corporeal-centered epistemology is incompatible with the abstract notion of ethics based in universal principles and truths that has held sway through much of the Western philosophical tradition. Merleau-Ponty describes the body as radically contingent: "The things—here, there, now, then—are no longer in themselves in their own place, in their own time; they exist only at the end of those rays of spatiality and of temporality emitted in the secrecy of my flesh" (Merleau-Ponty, 1968: 114). The body and the world are caught up with one another. This intermingling is indicative of the boundary-breaking alternative epistemology Merleau-Ponty provides that animates the relationality found in care ethics.

The following sections will explore four elements of Merleau-Ponty's corporeal-centered epistemology—bodily perception, habit, focus phenomena, and the reciprocity of the flesh.

Perception

Merleau-Ponty claims that embodied knowledge begins with the centrality of perception. "All knowledge takes its place within the horizons opened up by perception" (Merleau-Ponty 1964: 3–4). Accordingly, David Abram describes

Merleau-Ponty's understanding of perception as the "silent conversation" that our body has with the world around it (Abram 1996: 52). Abram's use of the term "conversation" reflects the interconnectedness that Merleau-Ponty finds in perception. "Perception is not a science of the world, it is not even an act, a deliberate taking up of a position, it is the background from which all acts stand out, and is presupposed by them" (Merleau-Ponty 1962: x–xi). Rather than discrete sets of knowledge, Merleau-Ponty finds human perceptions hopelessly interconnected: "Whenever I try to understand myself the whole fabric of the perceptible world comes too, and with it come the others who are caught in it" (Merleau-Ponty 1964: 15). A corporeal-centered epistemology as drawn from Merleau-Ponty's work transgresses traditionally understood boundaries.

Merleau-Ponty views perception as an integration of mind and body; subjectivity is physical. The world cannot be perceived separate from the contribution of the body/subject.[10]

> The theory of the body schema is, implicitly, a theory of perception. We have relearned to feel our body; we have found underneath the objective and detached knowledge of the body that other knowledge which we have of it in virtue of it always being with us and of the fact that we are our body. In the same way we shall need to reawaken our experience of the world as it appears to us in so far as we are in the world through our body, and in so far as we perceive the world through our body. But by thus remaking contact with the body and with the world, we shall also rediscover ourself, since, perceiving as we do with our body, the body is a natural self and, as it were, the subject of perception. (Merleau-Ponty 1964a: 203)

Here, Merleau-Ponty summarizes his corporeal epistemology and the central role of bodily perception. Attending to the body is a process connected to understanding the world. Given his commitment to a phenomenological approach, Merleau-Ponty makes few prescriptive statements. However, in the above passage, Merleau-Ponty finds a connection between attending to the body and self-discovery, which suggests that heeding embodied knowledge is a choice. If we choose to attend to our body, we can "reconnect" with the world.

Noddings claims that relation is ontologically basic to human existence (Noddings 1984: 4). Gilligan found in the different voice of care "the tie between relationship and responsibility, and the origins of aggression in the failure of connection" (Gilligan 1993: 173). Merleau-Ponty posits a theory of perception that is inherently sensitive to interconnectedness because perception cannot be separated from the body or the world. Accordingly, a perceptive whole is created that includes explicitly articulated knowledge as well as tacit corporeal understanding. Our bodies' participation in providing that unarticulated "other knowledge" creates attachments or webs of unattended understanding. When confronted with an other, my body will garner much more information than I am conscious of regarding expressions, mannerisms, gestures, smells, sounds, and yet I will know the other by some perceptive whole. Our perceptions are rich and complex providing an enormous amount of information, which make it possible for us to care.

Extrapolating Merleau-Ponty's analysis, when presented with moral dilemmas, a plethora of perceptions come into play, which, by contrast, makes formulaic representations of ethics absurdly reductionist. The entanglements of humanity are simply too great to be entirely accounted for in traditional justice approaches to morality. Embodied care attends to some of that complexity, such as in human perception, but there is a trade off because a degree of ambiguity follows corporeal existence, as Merleau-Ponty repeatedly acknowledges. The injunction not to steal is exceedingly clear in its simplicity, but the human capacity to perceive the subtleties of relational dynamics is a murky, albeit potentially robust and fruitful, avenue of moral concern.

Habit

Merleau-Ponty integrates bodily motility and habit into perception. "The phenomenon of habit is just what prompts us to revise our notion of 'understand' and our notion of body. To understand the harmony between what we aim at and what is given, between the intention and the performance—and the body is our anchorage in a world" (Merleau-Ponty 1962: 144). One way that bodies provide a means for being-in-the-world is through movement. A habit is the capturing of a movement by the body and giving it meaning through its interaction with the world. Merleau-Ponty describes something more than the repetition of behavior commonly associated with the definition of habit. He claims that, "it is the body that 'catches' and 'comprehends' movement. The acquisition of a habit is indeed the grasping of a significance, but it is the motor grasping of a motor significance" (Merleau-Ponty 1962: 143). This habitual knowledge in the body remains unthematized unless we make the effort to attend to it.

Do our bodies also know habitual activities of care? Of course. There are arms that know how to comfort, hands that know how to share joy, and faces that know how to express rapt attention. These are learned behaviors that exhibit care. They are our many habits of care often performed without much reflection, however, attending to them reveals a rich notion of moral knowledge. If my young daughter hurts herself and cries, I comfort her by hugging her body. This is not a habit in the sense of a repeated motion like typing, but my body has captured the subtle movements necessary to communicate care.[11] My arms do not squeeze her forcefully as if I were holding a fifty-pound sack of potatoes. My arms do not jostle her as if this were "roughhousing." My arms gently caress in a manner that reflects the concern and affection appropriate for the moment. I move into her personal space and apply just the right amount of pressure with my hands and arms to pull her close to my chest. The hug may only last seconds, and few words may pass between us, but important knowledge is transferred. We will not consciously attend to all of the subtleties of the physical movement. I do not announce, "I am putting my arm around you now for the purposes of comfort." My thoughts are all focused on the event that has occurred and the task of comforting my daughter. My tone of voice will reflect my concern. In addition to the care communicated, I have also modeled a habit that her body catches in the unarticulated conversation of our bodies. If she is exposed to this model of caring repeatedly, it is more likely that she will employ this habit of care when confronted with similar circumstances.

Figure-Background Phenomenon

Merleau-Ponty posits that being in the world constitutes a discrimination of perceived physical phenomena and our context within it. "I understand the world because there are for me things near and far, foregrounds and horizons, and because in this way it forms a picture and acquires significance before me, and this finally is because I am situated in it and it understands me" (Merleau-Ponty 1962: 408). The body can be both figure and background. As Merleau-Ponty observes, the body "effaces" at the moment of perception thus allowing our consciousness to attend to immediate activities oblivious to the finer motor tasks and background actions required (Merleau-Ponty 1968: 9). He describes this thematization as the figure-background structure of perception or perceptual focus (Merleau-Ponty 1962: 13). The perceptual disappearance of the sense organ is significant to Merleau-Ponty because it instantiates the subjectivity of the body.

> In so far as it sees or touches the world, my body can therefore be neither seen nor touched. What prevents its ever being an object, ever being 'completely constituted' is that by which there are objects. It is neither tangible nor visible in so far as it is that which sees and touches. The body therefore is not one more among external objects . . . (Merleau-Ponty 1962: 92)

When I watch fireworks in the sky I am not thinking about how my eyes are operating but I am caught up in the experience of the event. My body works in the background in order to place perception at the foreground, as if "it were built around perception that draws through it" (ibid.). This perceptual focus opens up the world to the body. It makes externality possible and therefore our knowledge of the world possible.

The body's recessive quality, its ability to focus consciousness on perceiving the world, is not the same as a passive role. Our body is in constant motion and operation to allow us to maintain perceptual focus. These operations of the body that allow us to be in the world also fuel the "other directedness" that is an integral part of care. Noddings describes "engrossment" as an intense preoccupation with the other that comes with caring: "I receive the other into myself, and I see and feel with the other. I become a duality" (Noddings 1984: 30). For Noddings it is essential that engrossment take place in order for caring to occur. "At bottom, all caring involves engrossment. The engrossment need not be intense nor need it be pervasive in the life of the one-caring, but it must occur" (Noddings 1984: 17). Merleau-Ponty's distinction between figure-background interactions provides a useful way of framing Noddings's understanding of engrossment. To be engrossed one must be outwardly focused, not attending to the minutia of personal bodily operations. The body has the spectacular ability to place itself in the background and put the other in the foreground.[12] It is not that the body does not continue its perceptual dance with the environment, but attention is focused outward making it possible to care for an "other."

The same phenomena that Merleau-Ponty describes as the body being built around perceptual focus also establish the body as built around care. Without the foreground-background distinction, the ability to care would be imperiled by the bombardment of sense data vying for my attention or concern. Fortunately, this is not the case. When another person enters the room, they immediately stand out as more than just another object in my sphere of perception. They are indeed an object (they are not me), but I also perceive them as sharing the subjectivity that I have (they are like me). The perceived other body is a person who I can possibly care about. Their embodiment makes them stand out in my perceptual sphere as the possible subject for a complex relationship that may include care, as opposed to the chair in the room for which I cannot have a rich relationship or a deep sense of care. The focus phenomenon facilitates many different types of actions, but it is important for care because it allows for the attending to other embodied individuals as objects/subjects.

Thus far, I have only addressed care in regard to activities in the foreground. However, embodied care can also be part of the background of perceptual focus. In a caring relationship my body collects a variety of sensory information including visual, tactile, and olfactory data much of which I may not even be aware of. My mind/body will fill in missing data about the other. For example, a synchronicity is developed between bodies that spend a great deal of time with one another. Familiar bodies require less of the explicit communication of language as each body "reads" the other's nonverbal communication with increasing nuance. A facial expression or gesture that is ambiguous to a stranger communicates a specific understanding between intimates. The perceptual foreground of the other in a caring relationship transfers knowledge to the perceptual background of the silent dance that occurs between the bodies involved. The foreground perceptual focus of a parent and child may be on a bedtime story being read but the background interaction of bodies hugging one another tacitly communicates love, tenderness, and security. As Weiss indicates, "to raise a child . . . is not a matter of 'shaping the mind' but rather, arises out of an embodied exchange . . ." (Weiss 1999: 160).

The foreground-background phenomenon contributes to Merleau-Ponty's corporeal-centered epistemology by demonstrating how the human body can focus attention and thus learns about the particularity of other embodied beings. It also suggests how the body can nurture a caring relationship through the unspoken background caring phenomena occurring between bodies. The perceptual focus phenomenon is another example of how the human body is built around the possibility of caring.

The Flesh

Another resource for care ethics found in Merleau-Ponty's work is the slippery notion of the flesh that overcomes the boundaries of individualistic epistemology in the Western philosophical tradition. "One must see or feel in some way in order to think, . . . every thought known to us occurs to a flesh" (Merleau-Ponty 1968: 146). The flesh is much more than skin. In Merleau-Ponty's words, "The flesh is not matter . . . it is not fact or sum of facts 'material' or 'spiritual' . . . the flesh is in this sense an 'element' of Being" (139). The flesh is our entrée into the life-world. Part of that life-world is other embodied persons. Through the flesh, the corporeality of humanity is interconnected and intertwined:

> . . . there is finally a propagation of these exchanges [touching] to all the bodies of the same type and of the same style which I see and touch—and this by virtue of the fundamental fission or segregation of the sentient and the sensible which, laterally, makes the organs of my body communicate and founds transitivity from one body to another. (Merleau-Ponty 1968: 143)

On this account, experience is understood as open ended both temporally and laterally across other bodies. An experience of mine is integrated with previous experiences giving rise to structures and patterns that are further blended with the experience of others in the ongoing emergence of intersubjective meaning.

The flesh constitutes subject and object in an ambiguous relationship enabled by human embodiment as experienced, for example, when one of my hands touches the other. My hand can experience both being touched and touching, but this experience is not temporally unified in that I do not perceive touch and touching in the same instance. According to Merleau-Ponty, "it is a reversibility always imminent and never realized in fact" (Merleau-Ponty 1968: 139). This reversibility creates reciprocity or "weaving relations between bodies" (144). However, the flesh also constitutes subject and object in the void between the touching and the touched, between subjective and objective experience. The flesh spans or bridges these experiences to provide us with holistic meaning. "My flesh and that of the world therefore involve clear zones, clearings, about which pivot their opaque zones" (148).

Every sensory experience I have from birth contributes to my knowledge of my body both tacit and explicit. I learn to interact and move through my environment adapting as I go. However, the flesh as Merleau-Ponty describes it, allows for continuity over time, space, and individual bodies. Merleau-Ponty explains, "my body is made of the same flesh as the world (as it is perceived) and moreover this flesh of my body is shared by the world" (Merleau-Ponty 1968: 248). Because I share a corporeal existence with other beings, there is a continuity of sensory perception and understanding. This continuity is not a perfect colonization of others' experiences, or as Merleau-Ponty describes it, "not yet incorporeal," but an extrapolation that is much more than abstraction. It is an "intercorporeal" understanding (143). The experience of the other becomes a "generalized I" of unrealized potential in all of my own experiences (Merleau-Ponty 1973: 138). The flesh is a powerful nexus between what it is to be other and what it is to be me. In the words of David Abram, "Humans are tuned for relationship. The eyes, the skin, the tongue, ears, and nostrils—all are gates where our body receives the nourishment of otherness" (Abram 1996: ix).

What Merleau-Ponty has described in the reversibility and intertwining of the life-world through the flesh can be extrapolated to provide a basis for corporeal understanding of care. Because of the ambiguity of subject and object in my body's experience of its perceptual world, I am able to perceive and reflect upon my own body. It may slip into invisibility when I become outwardly focused upon sensory experience, but awareness of my own body always resurfaces. The body's reversibility not only allows it to open the world to me but also allows me to view my body as an object in that world.

> There is a circle of the touched and the touching, the touched takes hold of the touching; there is a circle of the visible and the seeing, the seeing is not without visible existence; there is even an inscription of the touching in the visible, of the seeing in the tangible—and the converse. (Merleau-Ponty 1968: 143)

When confronted with other bodies as objects in the world, the reversibility of the flesh allows for an ambiguous, limited, understanding of the other body. That other body that I perceive is also subject and object. I recognize its form (a body) and movement and immediately I have a level of shared knowledge that is both tacit and explicit. When confronted with another body, even if it is a foreign body attired and socially constructed very different from my own, there is still a fundamental connection and understanding in the flesh that Merleau-Ponty refers to as the "propagation" of bodily experiences. If a knife accidentally cuts that other body, I do not have to ask whether pain was felt. Through the continuity of the flesh, my body knows that pain comes with such a violation because of my own aggregate experiences. An affective or felt response precedes any reflective consideration of the circumstances as I engage in instinctive bodily reactions such as a wince, or gasp, or movement. Corporeal knowledge creates the potential of sympathetic perception that makes care possible.

In Merleau-Ponty's notion of the reversibility of the flesh, my body is both subject and object for me, both active and observed, the toucher and the touched; my disposition toward my body is not neutral. Under most circumstances, I do not place my body in harm's way.[13] I do not routinely allow my body to burn itself or cut itself except by accident. I care for my body. Although I make many errors of judgment or give in to excesses from time to time, I generally make decisions for my body's benefit, and my body directs me toward acts that allow it to thrive and flourish. The ambiguous continuity of the flesh extrapolates my positive affective relationship with my body to other "bodied" people. I not only recognize that others will have analogous regard for the well being of their bodies that I do, but I also extend those feelings to other bodies. Merleau-Ponty's life ended before he could fully develop his radical theory of intersubjectivity; nevertheless, this notion of embodied care appears consistent with his robust notion of our interconnectedness. He claimed that others "are not fictions with which I might people my desert—offspring of my spirit and forever unactualized possibilities—but my twins or flesh of my flesh" (Merleau-Ponty 1964a: 15).

Merleau-Ponty's notion of the flesh continues to be a source of philosophical speculation and it has intriguing possibilities for positing the radical interconnectedness of the world. The relational knowledge inherent in such a connection of intercorporeality provides another avenue by which the potential for care may be found.

A comprehensive study of Merleau-Ponty's insight into embodiment and intersubjectivity could fill volumes. What we have suggested is that four central elements of his analysis—perception, habit, the figure-background phenomenon, and the flesh—provide a robust understanding of how our bodies are capable of learning the requisite knowledge for the possibility of caring.

The Body: Cared For/Caring

In acknowledging the unarticulated aspect of embodied knowledge, Michael Polanyi has aptly claimed, "We can know more than we can tell" (Polanyi 1967: 4). Merleau-Ponty's notion of the reversibility of the flesh as both subject and object, touched and touching points to what we cannot tell. This reversibility also applies to the experience of embodied care. The earliest experiences of human bodies (ideally) are that of being cared for: being fed, burped, hugged, etc. While caring-for is most pervasive with infants and children, throughout our lives the experience of another's care for us is often entangled with corporeal interaction such as a touch or a hug. We "learn" what it is to care for others by how we are cared for. As with other aspects of our embodied epistemology, some of what we know about caring can be articulated while other aspects of caring remain a tacit knowledge of the body.

For example, when I teach my daughter to ride a bike, the knowledge necessary is largely contained in the body. The requisite balance, momentum, and coordination needed to ride a bicycle can only be learned through practice and the acquisition of habits. Once the body "learns" to ride a bike that knowledge is not easily lost. While bike riding makes for an interesting case study for applying Merleau-Ponty's understanding of embodied knowledge, and is consistent with many of the examples he offers, of more significance for the purposes of this inquiry is the subtle interaction between my body and my daughter's body as she learns to ride. As she takes her first few pedals, I stand in close proximity ready to catch her if she falls (there are no training wheels). I go so far as to place my hand on her back to facilitate catching her, but it also lets her know that I am there. My voice is reassuring yet determined. Our conscious attention is on the task at hand: learning to ride a bike. However, there is a subtext of the dance between my body and my daughter's that goes largely unnoticed. She wobbles and reaches for me and I grab her. She falls and cries. I hold her, comfort her, and inspect the scrape. My daughter explicitly learns how to ride a bike but implicitly she learns how to care as well. Her body captures the motions and knowledge necessary for bike riding at the same time it seizes the tactile and auditory cues for caring knowledge. Because there is a reversibility to care, what my daughter learns from me contributes to her embodied resources for caring for others.[14] While learning to ride a bicycle has little moral significance, knowing how to convey care to others is of paramount importance in human interaction.

Polanyi, in a trajectory consistent with Merleau-Ponty's work, claims that the tacit knowledge of the body comes about through active participation or what he refers to as "indwelling" (Polanyi 1967: 17). Care, empathy, and compassion can be described at length but there remains an element of understanding that is only available through direct embodied experience. Simultaneously, Rita Manning claims that praxis is an essential part of care ethics: "We cannot develop and sustain the ability to care unless we do some active caring" (Manning 1992: 69). The relational aspect of care requires some degree of physical presence and involvement: being cared for and caring for others.

Embodied Knowledge: The Starting Point for Empathy

If Merleau-Ponty is correct about the knowledge our body provides us with, then the body is also the basis for a key component of care: empathy. To be empathetic is to engage our imaginations to understand someone else's feelings, actions, or situation. However, we are incapable of empathizing in a vacuum. I cannot empathize with those I have no knowledge of. For example, if there is life on another planet, I have no feelings for that life because I have no knowledge of it. Yet, humans have an enormous capacity to empathize. We can have feelings for strangers when they are suddenly hurt or we can shed tears for fictional characters in movies. The common denominator capable of overcoming physical and social distance is our embodiment. If I see a stranger trip and fall, I can empathize with them, perhaps even act on their behalf because I know something of this experience myself. Through the intermingling of the flesh I have a glimmer of what the stranger experiences. I too have a body and have experienced gravity and the weight of my body hitting a surface unexpectedly. I may never have articulated this experience but my body knows of it. I know how I would care for my body in this situation and I have the opportunity to care for someone else's. Care is always a choice but the human connection through the body is there. I have the corporeal resources to give flight to my imagination of what the other might feel. Empathy is a crucial link between what the body knows, what can be imagined, and care. Caring without empathy is perhaps only imaginable as a type of superficial or professional care and even then, prolonged interaction between embodied beings has the potential to elicit creeping empathy. Merleau-Ponty may not have intended to create moral theory, but his understanding of embodiment and the intertwining of the flesh provide the basis for empathy and a foundation for care.

To know something of another's experience and empathize is not to *own* that experience. There is the warranted concern among postcolonial theorists, feminists, and others that the potential for claiming ownership and therefore misrepresenting someone else's position is a problematic perspective that may reflect asymmetrical power relations. For example, Maria C. Lugones and Elizabeth V. Spelman express a concern that the voices of women of color are lost or distorted when white women and women of color develop theory together. The authors identify the dichotomy of the "outsider" and "insider" to describe the theorizer's subject position: ". . . only when genuine and reciprocal dialogue takes place between 'outsider' and 'insiders' can we trust the outsider's account" (Lugones and Spelman 1995: 501). History is replete with examples of those who claim to "know" what others feel and therefore act in their best interest. As philosopher Sullivan points out, our bodies can, and often do, err in interpreting the actions of other bodies (Sullivan 2001: 71–73). Sullivan reads Merleau-Ponty's phenomenology of the body as too ambiguous: not taking enough of people's culturally inscribed differences into account. According to her critique, by eliding social differences, Merleau-Ponty is making too much of the potential for communication and common ground. Sullivan's point is well taken; however, this is where I believe Merleau-Ponty's comfort with ambiguity is helpful. The continuity of the flesh must be understood as tenuous and partial. It is perilously presumptuous to believe that one can fully know how another person feels or perceives. Nevertheless, the body is what humans share and the grounding for common understanding. Sullivan ultimately rejects Merleau-Ponty's notion of embodiment as anonymous because she sees it as complicit in a traditional patriarchal view of interchangeable subjectivity that ignores difference including that of gender. Since my project is to extrapolate Merleau-Ponty's phenomenology into the particularity of care ethics, I believe that his insights can be appropriated without suffering the pitfalls of the universal body Sullivan is concerned about. The empathetic understanding that I am extrapolating from Merleau-Ponty's corporeal epistemology is always partial, always incomplete, should always reflect a certain humility given its ambiguities, and yet it exists.

Weiss argues that morality cannot be reduced to an intellectual endeavor. Although feminist care ethics has successfully offered alternatives to rationalist approaches to morality, Weiss claims that, "the body's role in calling us to respond ethically to one another has continued to be egregiously neglected" (Weiss 1999: 161). Merleau-Ponty's work can be an important vehicle for the kind of analysis Weiss desires because he calls for philosophers to reacquaint themselves with the body. It has been my contention in this article that Merleau-Ponty's philosophy of the body provides an epistemological foundation for an embodied notion of care. He demonstrates the crucial role embodiment plays in structuring knowledge and deriving existential meaning. Merleau-Ponty describes the bond "between the flesh and the idea, between the visible and the interior armature which it manifests and which it conceals" (Merleau-Ponty 1968: 149). There is a presumption of knowledge in care ethics, for we cannot care for that for which we have no knowledge. Merleau-Ponty expands the definition of knowledge beyond explicit rational considerations of the mind to implicit knowledge grounded in the body. The elaboration of an embodied epistemology is a significant step in developing a comprehensive understanding of embodied care. The body is not merely a vessel for sensory input because it participates in perception and meaning making as part of the flesh of the world.

Notes

1. I would like to acknowledge the helpful comments of Gail Weiss as well as those of the participants in the 2000 Merleau-Ponty Circle.

2. While one may argue that we have a *duty* to help others, few would contend that we have a moral obligation to help a stranger to the extent that Williams did. The positive *consequences* outweigh the negative of Williams's actions but was this action the optimal choice to generate maximum happiness? Certainly, Williams acted *virtuously* but his responses don't use the language of virtue.

3. For a full explanation of what I have labeled "embodied care" please see Maurice Hamington, *Embodied Care: Jane Addams, Maurice Merleau-Ponty and Feminist Ethics* (Urbana: University of Illinois Press, 2004).

4. While I cannot fully elaborate claims (1) and (2) here, a brief explanation might be useful. The first claim, that knowledge is a prerequisite, but not a sufficient condition of care, is an acknowledgment of the epistemological aspect of relationality. It is very difficult to care for that which I do not know. The greater the knowledge of another, the greater the possibility of care, but this is not a matter of correspondence. Care is always a choice, and we may choose not to care, or care little, for those we know well. The second claim, that embodied knowledge should be given greater value, is a critique of pervasive Cartesian mind/body dualisms that disparage the role of the body in knowledge creation and ethics. I suggest that the body "knows" how to care or has the potential to know how to care, as we shall see as we explore Merleau-Ponty's phenomenology of the body.

5. Lawrence Kohlberg, "Stage and Sequence: The Cognitive Developmental Approach to Socialization," in *Handbook of Socialization Theory and Research.* Ed. D. A. Goslin. (Chicago: Rand McNally, 1969).

6. See Lawrence Blum, "Gilligan and Kohlberg: Implications for Moral Theory," in *An Ethic of Care: Feminist and Interdisciplinary Perspectives.* Ed. Mary Jeanne Larrabee (New York: Routledge, 1993), 50–53.

7. Maurice Hamington and Dorothy C. Miller, eds. *Socializing Care* (Langham, MD: Rowman and Littlefield, 2006); Susan J. Hekman. *Moral Voices, Moral Selves: Carol Gilligan and Feminist Moral Theory* (University Park, PA: Pennsylvania State University Press, 1995); Virginia Held. *The Ethics of Care: Personal, Political, and Global* (Oxford: Oxford University Press, 2006); Rita Manning. *Speaking From the Heart: A Feminist Perspective on Ethics* (Lanham, MD: Rowman and Littlefield, 1992); Nel Noddings. *Caring: A Feminine Approach to Ethics and Moral Education* (Berkeley: University of California Press, 1984); *Starting at Home: Caring and Social Policy* (Berkeley: University of California Press, 2002); Sara Ruddick. *Maternal Thinking: Toward a Pol-*

itics of Peace (Boston: Beacon Press, 1995); Joan Tronto. *Moral Boundaries: A Political Argument for an Ethic of Care.* (New York: Routledge, 1993).

8. Annette Baier. "Hume, the Women's Moral Theorist?" In *Women and Moral Theory.* Eds. Eva Kittay and Diana Meyers (Lanham, MD: Rowman and Littlefield, 1987), 37–55; Claudia Card, ed. *Feminist Ethics* (Lawrence, KS: University Press of Kansas, 1991); Marilyn Friedman. *What Are Friends For?* (New York: Cornell University Press, 1993); Virginia Held. *Feminist Morality: Transforming Culture, Society, and Politics* (Chicago: University of Chicago Press, 1993).

9. Gail Weiss's chapter on "Bodily Imperatives" is a notable exception to the lack of feminist work on the body's role in morality.

10. For a helpful discussion of Merleau-Ponty's gestalt approach to perception, see Adrian Michael Mirvish, "Merleau-Ponty and the Nature of Philosophy." *Philosophy and Phenomenological Research* 43 (June 1983): 449–476.

11. In this case, I am using a tactile example, but habits of care need not all involve touch. For example, I can care for someone by listening attentively to what they have to say. My body has habits surrounding listening that can demonstrate care without ever touching the speaker. Eye contact, posture, facial expressions, and stillness participate in care-centered listening. These bodily behaviors can communicate a real interest, or engrossment, in what the speaker has to say.

12. Drew Leder describes the conscious focus on the activity rather than the involved body parts as the disappearance or recession of the sense organ from the perceptual field it discloses. Given Leder's notion of disappearance, engrossment appears to be an extension of the manner in which our bodies thematize the world. Drew Leder, *The Absent Body* (University of Chicago Press, 1990), 14.

13. I acknowledge that there are many people who engage in self-harming behavior that can result from a number of conditions including depression, suicidal ideation, and cultural ideology. In these cases there are powerful emotional, psychological, or sociological forces at play that over ride the body's tendency for self-preservation.

14. Polanyi contends that there is so much that we cannot tell that, "the transmission of knowledge from one generation to the other must be predominately tacit." In describing the phenomenal structure of tacit knowing, Polanyi refers to attending from a proximal term, or object, to a distal term. We invest meaning in the distal term through bodily "subception" or the tacit acquisition of knowledge through transposition of bodily experiences into perception (Polanyi: 61).

References

Abram, David (1996). *The Spell of the Sensuous: Perception and Language in a More-Than-Human World.* New York: Vintage Books.

Baier, Annette (1987). "Hume, the Women's Moral Theorist?" In *Women and Moral Theory.* eds. Eva Kittay and Diana Meyers. Lanham, MD: Rowman and Littlefield, 37–55.

Blum, Lawrence (1993). "Gilligan and Kohlberg: Implications for Moral Theory," in *An Ethic of Care: Feminist and Interdisciplinary Perspectives*. Ed. Mary Jeanne Larrabee. New York: Routledge, 49–68.

Card, Claudia, ed. (1991). *Feminist Ethics*. Lawrence: University Press of Kansas.

Friedman, Marilyn (1993). *What Are Friends For?* New York: Cornell University Press.

Gilligan, Carol (1993). *In a Different Voice: Psychological Theory and Women's Development*. Cambridge: Harvard University Press.

Hamington, Maurice (2004). *Embodied Care: Jane Addams, Maurice Merleau-Ponty and Feminist Ethics*. Urbana: University of Illinois Press.

Hamington, Maurice, and Dorothy C. Miller, eds. (2006). *Socializing Care: Feminist Ethics and Public Issues*. Lanham: Rowman and Littlefield.

Hekman. Susan J. (1995). *Moral Voices, Moral Selves: Carol Gilligan and Feminist Moral Theory*. University Park: Pennsylvania State University Press.

Held, Virginia (1993). *Feminist Morality: Transforming Culture, Society, and Politics*. Chicago: University of Chicago Press,.

—— (2006). *The Ethics of Care: Personal, Political, and Global*. Oxford: Oxford University Press.

Kohlberg, Lawrence (1969). "Stage and Sequence: The Cognitive Developmental Approach to Socialization," in *Handbook of Socialization Theory and Research*. Ed. D. A. Goslin. Chicago: Rand McNally.

Leder, Drew (1990). *The Absent Body*. Chicago: University of Chicago Press.

Lugones, Maria C., and Elizabeth V. Spelman (1995). "Have We Got a Theory for You! Feminist Theory, Cultural Imperialism and the Demand for 'Woman's Voice,'" in *Feminism and Philosophy: Essential Readings in Theory, Reinterpretation and Application*. Eds. Nancy Tuana and Rosemarie Tong. Boulder: Westview Press, 494–507.

Manning, Rita (1992). *Speaking From the Heart: A Feminist Perspective on Ethics*. Lanham, MD: Rowman and Littlefield.

Merleau-Ponty, Maurice (1962). *Phenomenology of Perception*. Trans. Colin Smith. London: Routledge.

—— (1964a). *Signs*. Evanston, IL: Northwestern University Press.

—— (1964b). *Primacy of Perception*. Trans. James M. Edie. Evanston: Northwestern University Press.

—— (1968). *The Visible and the Invisible*. Ed. Claude Lefort. Trans. Alphonso Lingis. Evanston: Northwestern University Press.

—— (1973). *The Prose of the World*. Ed. Claude Lefort. Trans. John O'Neill. Evanston: Northwestern University Press.

Mirvish, Adrian Michael (1983). "Merleau-Ponty and the Nature of Philosophy." *Philosophy and Phenomenological Research* 43 (June): 449–476.

National Public Radio (2000). "Morning Edition." April 21.

Noddings, Nel (1984). *Caring: A Feminine Approach to Ethics and Moral Education*. Berkeley: University of California Press.

——— (2002). *Starting at Home: Caring and Social Policy*. Berkeley: University of California Press.

Polanyi, Michael (1967). *The Tacit Dimension*. New York: Anchor Books.

Ruddick, Sara (1995). *Maternal Thinking: Toward a Politics of Peace*. Boston: Beacon Press.

Sullivan, Shannon (2001). *Living Across and Through Skins: Transactional Bodies, Pragmatism and Feminism*. Bloomingtion: Indiana University Press.

Tronto, Joan (1993). *Moral Boundaries: A Political Argument for an Ethic of Care*. New York: Routledge.

Weiss, Gail (1999). *Body Images: Embodiment as Intercorporeality*. New York: Routledge.

PART V

Sedimented Meanings:
Conservation and Transformation

CHAPTER 13

Can an Old Dog Learn New Tricks? Habitual Horizons in James, Bourdieu, and Merleau-Ponty

GAIL WEISS

> Habit! that skilful but slow-moving arranger who begins by letting our minds suffer for weeks on end in temporary quarters, but whom our minds are none the less only too happy to discover at last, for without it, reduced to their own devices, they would be powerless to make any room seem habitable.
> —Marcel Proust, *Remembrance of Things Past*

In this quotation from *Swann's Way*, Marcel Proust identifies habit as a phenomenon that operates independently from the mind, one that the mind itself is dependent on in order to "make any room seem habitable." By marking the connection between habit and habitability, Proust draws our attention to how habit enables us to *inhabit* our world, or, more precisely, how habit enables an unfamiliar space to be transformed into a familiar environment. In his portrayal of habit as a "skilful arranger," Proust offers us an image of habit as an active agency that goes about its business without our express knowledge or consent but that nonetheless plays an indispensable role in our everyday life.

This depiction of habit stresses its positive aspects, its ability to make us feel at home in our world, but Proust also hints at the challenges habit poses to the mind because of the latter's dependence upon it. For if the mind needs to draw upon habit to construct a familiar life-world, and if habit, that "slow-moving arranger," performs its function in its own time, this poses a challenge to the modern philosophers' view of the mind as a self-sufficient entity and suggests that habit has its own temporality, its own rhythms, and its own significances that invisibly leave their traces on all aspects of our psychic life.

Ultimately, Proust himself is quite ambivalent about habit throughout the seven books that constitute *Remembrance of Things Past*. Continually personifying habit as in the quote with which I began, both his narrator and the main character, Marcel, often decry its negative influence on our lives. In a parenthetical comment toward the end of book seven, "Time Regained," Marcel laments the power of habit, "which cuts off from things we have witnessed a number of times the root of profound impression and of thought which gives them their real meaning" (Proust Volume III: 775). Here habit seems to be at odds with meaning, dulling rather than enhancing the significance of mundane experience. In the course of his magnus opus, Proust seems to seesaw back and forth between these two views of habit.[1] On the one hand, he suggests that habit provides us with a sense of familiarity and security that is essential for daily life, and, on the other hand, he just as frequently portrays habit as stultifying, as condemning us to mindless repetition and reinforcing social conventions that long ago lost their utility. How are we to reconcile these two conflicting views of habit? Can habit keep "an old dog from learning new tricks?" or is habit precisely what provides a necessary foundation for new meanings to emerge? Proust's texts raise these questions again and again and leave us to ponder their answers.

Over the years, habit has been ambivalently depicted not only in literature by authors such as Proust, but also in philosophy and psychology. These depictions range from a purely negative view of habit as the bane of our existence, condemning us to repeating the past without learning anything from it, to accounts that describe habit as a class-based phenomenon, varying not only from one social class to another, but also from one culture to another, and finally, to more positive understandings of habit as a source of comfort, as expressive of an ethics, and as a creative bodily experience that makes innovation possible. Nowhere are these various portrayals more intermingled than in the following passage from the chapter on habit in William James's *The Principles of Psychology* (Volume 1). "Habit" he declares:

> Is thus the enormous fly-wheel of society, its most precious conservative agent. It alone is what keeps us all within the bounds of ordinance, and saves the children of fortune from the envious uprisings of the poor. It alone prevents the hardest and most repulsive walks of life from being deserted by those brought up to tread therein. It keeps the fisherman and the deck-hand at sea through the winter; it holds the miner in his darkness, and nails the countryman to his log-cabin and his lonely farm through all the months of snow; it protects us from invasion by the natives of the desert and the frozen zone. It dooms us all to fight out the battle of life upon the lines of our nurture or our early choice, and to make the best of a pursuit that disagrees, because there is no other for which we are fitted, and it is too late to begin again. It keeps different social strata from mixing. Already at the age of twenty-five you see the professional mannerism settling down on the young commercial traveler, on the young doctor, on the young minister, on the

young counsellor-at-law. You see the little lines of cleavage running through the character, the tricks of thought, the prejudices, the ways of the 'shop,' in a word, from which the man can by-and-by no more escape than his coat-sleeve can suddenly fall into a new set of folds.

And, he dramatically (ominously?) concludes, "On the whole, it is best he should not escape. It is well for the world that in most of us, by the age of thirty, the character has set like plaster, and will never soften again" (James, 1950: 121). "Better for whom?" we may well ask. Indeed, James's attention to the relationship between habit and class in the above passage is striking not only because he notes the crucial, yet largely invisible role habit plays in the maintenance of mutually exclusive social classes but also for the classist assumptions he makes about the desirability of those very structures. Moreover, James does not restrict his comments to the ways in which habit ties an individual to a particular class; he also suggests that habit ineluctably forms an individual's character, and that this has important ethical implications. Specifically, he claims that:

> The hell to be endured hereafter, of which theology tells, is no worse than the hell we make for ourselves in this world by habitually fashioning our characters in the wrong way. Could the young but realize how soon they will become mere walking bundles of habits, they would give more heed to their conduct while in the plastic state. We are spinning our own fates, good or evil, and never to be undone. Every smallest stroke of virtue or of vice leaves its never so little scar. (James 1950: 127)

In order to address the rich implications of these provocative passages, we must first discuss James's view of the physiology of habit. According to James, habit is a material phenomenon that is manifested as a set of concatenated nerve discharges that forms a "reflex path." We might compare such a system to a row of upright dominoes. Once the first domino is knocked over, the rest follow one after the other, and, apart from any outside interference with the trajectory, the movement once begun, will lead to a predictable (or habitual) conclusion resulting in the toppling over (firing off) of all the dominoes (nerve-centers). On his account, each of our habits has its own nerve path, and, through repetition over time, the path becomes more and more fixed and less subject to change (or interference). Anticipating later behaviorists' accounts of the mind as initially a tabula rasa, James argues that our organisms begin their development in a "plastic" state, open to any number of possibilities. Over time, as certain actions become repeated in a characteristic sequence, such as getting out of bed, going into the bathroom, showering, brushing one's teeth, then reentering the bedroom to dress, specific neural pathways are formed that correspond to these sequences. As these routines become both internally and externally ingrained, one finds oneself performing the entire sequence without being consciously aware that one is doing so. Maurice Merleau-Ponty calls this "bodily intentionality" a process whereby the body functions in a purposeful, directed fashion without requiring our explicit attention. If our routine is interrupted in media res, a conscious adjustment is often needed to resume the activity, since the ordinary pathway has been disrupted, and must be "jump-started" as it were, by artificial (that is, conscious) means. While most adults can succeed in returning to their previous activity in the face of such disturbances, those who cannot help us to see how vital this skill is to daily life.[2]

Schneider, the disabled World War I veteran described by Merleau-Ponty and early-twentieth-century Gestalt psychologists, represents an extreme case of lack of plasticity, insofar as his brain injuries rendered him incapable of altering his mundane routines in any way, or in resuming them if they were interrupted. His only choice was to begin all over again with the first movement in the sequence in order to bring the action to completion. Merleau-Ponty claims that what Schneider has lost is an "intentional arc," an embodied awareness of how diverse aspects of one's experience are interconnected. This intentional arc, Merleau-Ponty suggests, provides us with an affective sensibility that enables the integration of quite dissimilar experiences into a synthetic whole. Schneider, unlike the "normal subject,"

> can no longer put himself into a sexual situation any more than generally he occupies an affective or ideological one. Faces are for him neither attractive nor repulsive, and people appear to him in one light or another only in so far as he has direct dealings with them, and according to the attitude they adopt towards him, and the attention and solicitude which they bestow upon him. Sun and rain are neither gay nor sad; his humour is determined by elementary organic functions only, and the world is emotionally neutral. (Merleau-Ponty 1962: 157)

The intentional arc, as Merleau-Ponty describes it, subtends our specific intentional acts and can endow a set of diverse experiences with an affective unity that gives them a more generalized meaning.[3] Habit itself plays a vital role in linking together a series of actions that, on the surface, may seem to have very little in common with one another except insofar as they become associated with a more generalized project as in the case of the various activities associated with a morning routine. And, while the morning routine example helps us to understand the mechanisms at work in the formation of our physical habits, James's emphasis on character in the quotes cited earlier makes it clear that our habits extend to much more than such mundane matters as which side of our teeth we begin brushing first. According to James, our choices of novels to read, places to travel, courses to take, relationships to pursue, are also all either a product of or at least strongly influenced by habit. Indeed, an individual's entire character, James asserts, is constituted through the integrated functioning of his or her respective habits; on his account, then, we are truly "creatures of habit" and whether this constitutes an indictment or a compliment depends upon the specific nature of the habits that the individual has cultivated over time.

Given the increasing resistance of our habits to change, morally speaking it becomes crucial on James's account that we form "good habits" that will function automatically as our "second nature." At the same time, we must move early on to nip potentially bad habits in the bud before they can literally take root in the form of a hardened pathway in our central nervous system. Rather than view the automatism that characterizes oft-repeated actions as a nonmoral phenomenon precisely because it seems to bypass our conscious awareness, James seems to be offering us a very anti-Kantian picture of morality, one that requires volition merely as a preliminary step destined to give way to nonvolitional, moral behavior.[4] With the distinction between good habits and bad habits, moreover, and James's invocation of the physiological basis for all of our habits, it is clear that he understands the moral universe to be coincident with the Husserlian life-world, that is, there is no separable moral domain that would provide a basis for distinguishing from the outset between moral and nonmoral actions. Indeed, James's moral judgment on those individuals who are unable to form decisive habits of even the most mundane sort, is abundantly clear in the following passage:

> There is no more miserable human being than one in whom nothing is habitual but indecision, and for whom the lighting of every cigar, the drinking of every cup, the time of rising and going to bed every day, and the beginning of every bit of work, are subjects of express volitional deliberation. (James 1950: 122)

One of the most fascinating aspects of James's discussion of habit, is the complex relationship he traces between the plasticity of the central nervous system, a plasticity that makes the construction of new habits or the alterations of old ones possible, and the fixity that he simultaneously attributes to our characters, and to the social classes themselves. When he emphasizes plasticity, it would seem that we have the unlimited potential to develop new habits or revise old ones; on the other hand, when he stresses the fixity of our individual likes, dislikes, and habitual routines, we seem as far as possible from possessing the freedom and transcendence of the Sartrian for-itself and more and more like Skinnerian automatons doomed to respond to a given stimulus with a preprogrammed set of responses. James seems to resolve the tension between plasticity and fixity by suggesting that we begin our lives in the plastic state, and over time, as specific neural pathways are established and reinforced, we lose the initial plasticity and become more set in our ways. It might seem as if James would lament this loss of flexibility, but, as the earlier quotes demonstrate, he does not. Rather, in passages that echo Plato's famous statements about the importance of raising youth properly in *The Republic*, James argues that good habits lead to good character and so we should seek to form good habits before we are enslaved to bad ones.

Ultimately, James exhorts us to increase the domains of our everyday life that are governed by fixed, habitual responses, not because he thinks that good habits are an end in themselves, but in order to "free" consciousness to take up more intellectual pursuits such as psychological introspection or other forms of philosophical contemplation. So, just when it seems as if the mind is no more than a bundle of habits, James suggests that these habits actually serve to free the mind to do its "own proper work" (James 1950: 122).

While there is much in the Jamesian account of habit that merits further attention, I have focused in rather broad strokes on the main features of his analysis in order to set the stage for a discussion of the ambivalence that surrounds the phenomenon of habit in more recent authors. Specifically, I would like to address in detail two quite different descriptions of habit that have been proposed by Bourdieu and Merleau-Ponty in order to see how they are both indebted to, and markedly depart from, the Jamesian model. One of the virtues of James's description of habit, as I see it, is his emphasis upon the indispensable role habit plays in our daily life, shaping our characters as it shapes the materiality of our world. A negative aspect of his description, on the other hand, is that while James views habit as responsible for establishing our moral characters, his plasticity/fixity model also makes it difficult to see how significant individual and social change can ever really occur.

By turning to Bourdieu's account of habit, or, more precisely, a phenomenon he refers to as the habitus, we can throw into relief the close relationships that exist between our own habits and the habits of others; at the same time, the problem of whether and how we are determined by our largely class-prescribed habits also becomes more pressing. Merleau-Ponty takes the bodily dimensions of habit as his point of departure. Paradoxically, I will argue, his emphasis on the body is precisely what enables us to see how individual and cultural innovation can occur within the context of the habitual horizons that we appeal to to make sense of our lives. Through a critical exploration of these diverse accounts of habit, moreover, including their masculinist assumptions, we can arrive at a deeper understanding of the possibilities habit offers for extending as well as diminishing our grasp upon the world.

Bourdieu is well aware of the challenges that habit poses to the traditional freedom/determinism antinomy. If one argues that we are responsible for the habits we initially develop, as James suggests, one can uphold a sense of human freedom, but, to the extent that our habits function in a largely unconscious manner and are primary determinants of our character, any freedom we might first possess seems to be greatly diminished over time. With his notion of the habitus, Bourdieu attempts to account for both the freedom and the determinism that are revealed in our habitual responses to one another and to the world that we share.

Bourdieu describes the habitus as a system of acquired dispositions that we internalize in early childhood. These dispositions are first and foremost tied to our social class, and are transmitted through the primary agents of socialization, one's family, one's peers, and the educational system. According to Bourdieu, there is no aspect of our daily life that is immune to the influence of the habitus. The foods we enjoy, the art we appreciate, the leisure activities we pursue, our professional aspirations, our political views, and our relations with others, are all directly attributable to the specific habitus we have grown up with, whether or not we recognize this to be the case. Indeed, Bourdieu maintains that,

> This infinite yet strictly limited generative capacity is difficult to understand only so long as one remains locked in the usual antinomies—which the concept of the *habitus* aims to transcend—of determinism and freedom, conditioning and creativity, consciousness and the unconscious, or the individual and society. Because the *habitus* is an infinite capacity for generating products—thoughts, perceptions, expressions and actions—whose limits are set by the historically and socially situated conditions of its production, the conditioned and conditional freedom it provides is as remote from creation of unpredictable novelty as it is from simple mechanical reproduction of the original conditioning. (Bourdieu 1990: 55)

The habitus is infinite to the extent that it is continually expanding in response to new situations; it is at the same time limited to expressing the specific conditions of existence that define a given class in its past, present, and foreseeable future. Of course, the actual situation may turn out quite differently than we anticipate, and the disjunction between the expectations we have formed on the basis of our habitus and the actual situations we find ourselves confronting is precisely what defines the habitus as a generative structure, that is, a structure that is capable of what Bourdieu calls, "regulated improvisation" or the ability to alter existing schemes to fit new experiences.

Thus, the habitus, as Bourdieu describes it, is not an optional framework that we occasionally appeal to in our daily existence; rather, it provides the basis for making distinctions and arriving at value judgments about the world of our concern. As Bourdieu observes:

> The *habitus* is a spontaneity without consciousness or will, opposed as much to the mechanical necessity of things without history in mechanistic theories as it is to the reflexive freedom of subjects 'without inertia' in rationalist theories. (Bourdieu 1990: 56)

Bourdieu often refers to the habitus as a structuring structure: it consists of a set of structural dispositions that emerge out of our existence that in turn give structure to our existence. There is no such thing as pure perception on this account, that is, perception unaffected by the habitus in which we have been raised. "The 'eye,'" Bourdieu asserts, "is a product of history reproduced by education" (Bourdieu 1984: 3).

More specifically, the habitus provides us with an internalized system of classificatory schemes through which we interpret new situations by relating them to similar situations we have experienced in the past. This evolving set of structures arising out of, and materialized in, distinctive cultural practices is governed, Bourdieu states, by its own "logic of practice." This improvisational, open-ended logic emerges from and is in turn applied to the concrete situations we encounter. While it lacks the coherence and systematicity of a formal logic that seeks to represent those practices in accordance with the law of noncontradiction, it has the advantage of being better able to capture both the synchronic and the diachronic dimensions of our lived experiences.

For Bourdieu, our habits are themselves a function of our class habitus. There are even habitual ways of rebelling against the habitus, efforts he sees as doomed to failure. Objectification of the habitus that governs one's practices is, perhaps, one possibility of obtaining some reflective distance from that habitus; however, he argues that objectification is itself a cultural practice whose theoretical distancing cannot remove us from the habitus once and for all. In his words: "There is no way out of the game of culture; and one's only chance of objectifying the true nature of the game is to objectify as fully as possible the very operations which one is obliged to use in order to achieve that objectification" (Bourdieu 1984: 12). In his early work, *Outline of a Theory of Practice*, Bourdieu explains why this is so:

> If agents are possessed by their habitus more than they possess it, this is because it acts within them as the organizing principle of their actions, and because this *modus operandi* in forming all thought and action (including thought of action) reveals itself only in the *opus operatum*. (Bourdieu 1977: 18)

Although in this particular passage, the habitus seems to be all-encompassing, determining us through and through, Bourdieu's Foucaultian emphasis on the generative dimensions of the habitus is crucial to understanding how the habitus itself can develop and change over time. As a dynamic rather than static structure, it does not continually present us with ready-made solutions or fixed ways of viewing a given problem. Indeed, as the September 11, 2001, tragedy in the United States has shown us, unexpected events can suddenly occur that were not anticipated from within a given habitus, events that nonetheless have the power to radically affect and even transform the habitus itself. The failure of ready-made responses in the face of the large-scale devastation and loss of life that took place in both New York City and Washington DC on the morning of September 11th, was immediately apparent even to the politicians from whom responses were demanded. Rather than seeing this failure as an impetus for the formation of a new habitus, most public figures, starting with President George W. Bush, invoked a prior habitus, calling for the end of the current "age of cynicism" and a return to patriotism and unconditional respect for, and loyalty to, the nation. And, as civil liberties that Americans have long taken for granted are being revoked on a daily basis in the name of the current "war on terrorism," it has become readily apparent that profound changes in the habitus, even when they are propelled by external events that demand immediate responses, are not always for the better.

Although the September 11th example reveals how events themselves can outstrip the capacity of a given habitus to formulate an adequate response to them, an over-hasty, passionate embrace of a previous, more conservative habitus should caution us against seeing the breakdown of one habitus as necessarily progressive. In fact, rapid U.S. movement toward a less-tolerant society in which innocent people of Middle Eastern origin face public suspicion as well as the risk of being detained as potential terrorists, makes it abundantly clear why the shift from one habitus to another (which I believe is happening in the United States at present) may make political resistance more rather than less difficult.

Sudden upheavals in the habitus undoubtedly challenge our ability to maintain habitual routines. These routines themselves, no matter how mundane, themselves come to take on new meaning when the very possibility of continuing to pursue them is suddenly in question. In the *New York Times* daily biographical profiles of the victims who died on September 11th that were published in the two years following the plane crashes, what surviving family members invoke again and again are the daily habits of their lost loved ones. Whether it is a penchant for working in the garden, walking a dog, swimming in the ocean, listening to music, playing and/or coaching sports, cooking meals for family, driving in the country, working to renovate a house, calling home twice every day, cheering on a beloved team, or encouraging friends when they are down, the victims come to life for the strangers who read about them *through* the repetitive activities that they pursued day after day. Many of the surviving family members pledged to carry on their loved one's commitment to these habitual activities to the best of their ability to honor the memory of who that person was and what that person valued in life. In such cases, these habits themselves take on a higher purpose and remind us that it is precisely in the mundane, intersubjective dimensions of existence that the habitus is most profoundly experienced.[5] Reading about these strangers, I find myself incredibly moved by the descriptions of the simple things in life that they treasured and enjoyed. Some of the pleasures, such as the joy of seeing one's children grow up each day, I also share, and yet, throughout my reading of the profiles, I never lose sight of the fact that this is about their experience, their lives, and not my own. In fact, it is often the descriptions of the personalities and activities I most disidentify with that I find most compelling.

Bourdieu's Marxist emphasis on how our social class defines the particular habitus we internalize, makes it clear how he would account for the emotional power of these short biographical sketches. I resonate to the habitual activities of the victims and their attachment to them, he might well argue, because I myself have enjoyed the same or similar activities and because the majority of the victims and I are from the same social class. However, it is difficult to see why, on this account, I would feel an equally strong (if not even stronger) emotional response to the descriptions of the victims who occupied a different habitus, for instance those people who were recent immigrants to this country occupying blue-collar jobs and trying to make enough money to send to family members back in their home countries. The only way Bourdieu could make sense of this is by appealing to the habitus within which I am immersed and by claiming that it prescribes the type of response I should have to others who do not share my habitus and whose situation is worse off than my own.

Due to the all-encompassing role Bourdieu attributes to the habitus in an individual's life, it is difficult to see what room is left for individual expression that is not reducible to being an expression of our class habitus. This is because Bourdieu, like Marx, presupposes a tremendous degree of commonality in the experiences of different individuals who are members of the same social class. In *The Logic of Practice*, for instance, he maintains that:

> The practices of members of the same group or, in a differentiated society, the same class, are always more and better harmonized than the agents know or wish, because, as Leibniz again says, 'following only (his) own laws,' each 'nonetheless agrees with the other.' The habitus is precisely this immanent law, *lex insita*, inscribed in bodies by *identical histories*, which is the precondition not only for the co-ordination of practices but also for practices of co-ordination. The corrections and adjustments the agents themselves consciously carry out presuppose mastery of a common code. . . . (Bourdieu 1990: 59, my emphasis)

If we understand this common code on the order of a Wittgensteinian language game, an evolving, yet pervasive language game that encompasses all of our social practices, the claim that individuals ascribe similar meanings to specific cultural practices because they share a common habitus is quite compelling. What I find problematic, however, is Bourdieu's assertion that this common code is "inscribed in bodies by identical histories," for what two bodies can truly be said to possess identical histories? The supposition of identical histories not only fails to do justice to the specificity of each individual's bodily experiences, but it also leaves out of account the contingencies that give an idiosyncratic flavor to each of our social experiences as well.

Bourdieu binds the individual even more tightly to his or her habitus moreover, when he defines a person's style as "never more than a deviation in relation to the style of a period or class . . ." (Bourdieu 1990: 60). Even the notions of intentionality and subjective experience become a function of the habitus that, in an important sense, produces them insofar as "The fact of collective practice takes the place of intention and can have the effect of producing a subjective experience and a sense of institution" (Bourdieu 1990: 258).

The virtue of this subsumption of individual experience and individual history into the social dispositions that comprise the habitus is that the problem of "the Other," which haunts both phenomenology and existentialism never arises; our experience is communal from the outset, and this also establishes the ground for objective apprehension of that experience because intersubjective verification is always possible. On the other hand, when Bourdieu posits that members of the same social class possess the same habitus that has been inscribed in their bodies by their identical histories, one begins to wonder if the price for a more satisfactory account of the intersubjective foundations for our experience than he claims phenomenology has hitherto provided, is far too high.

While Bourdieu's account of the habitus might appear to be much more open-ended than the Jamesian view of our habits and character as hardening like plaster by the time we are thirty, both men, it would seem, have difficulty explaining how radical change or spontaneous innovation can really occur either on an individual or on a societal level.[6] Merleau-Ponty's understanding of the habit body as "dilating our being in the world," that is, as expanding rather than limiting our possibilities, offers, I would argue, a way of accounting for the creative aspects of habit that cannot be done justice to by either James or Bourdieu. However, James's and Bourdieu's respective understandings of social class as the omnipresent horizon out of which our tastes, aptitudes, and habitual proclivities emerge, has the potential to deepen Merleau-Ponty's own discussion of the habit body in crucial ways.

Although Bourdieu continually refers to the primary role the body plays in the materialization of the social practices that contribute to, and are interpreted within, a given habitus, and though he often expresses the primacy of bodily experience in Merleau-Pontian terms, he fails to distinguish, as Merleau-Ponty does, the idiosyncratic ways in which individual bodies and individual gestures express a unique or personal relationship to the world. For Bourdieu, the body is first and foremost the site where the natural and the social are inextricably intertwined in an ongoing process whereby the natural is socialized and the social is naturalized. The basic schemes that differentiate human bodies from nonhuman bodies (e.g., up/down orientation) and male bodies from female bodies (e.g., genitalia and the social domination of one sex by the other), are, he acknowledges, foundational to the development of the habitus and help to bridge the divide between one social group's habitus and that of another. However, the specific properties, aptitudes, habits, and desires that are unique to a given body and that directly affect its mode of engagement with the world, can only be understood as functions of an individual's social class and are not seen as meaningful by Bourdieu unless they shed light on the latter.

Such a view, I am suggesting, seems patently inadequate in accounting for the power of the brief descriptions of the lives of the victims of September 11, 2001. For, while they certainly reveal the profound influence of a given habitus in each individual's life, reinforcing the pervasiveness of that habitus in the process, they also highlight that particular individual's unique way of *inhabiting* that habitus, of making it her or his own.

Moreover, James's ethical preoccupation with the notion of an individual's character (even if it is destined to become fixed like stone) seems to be quite misplaced if character is itself merely a "deviation from a social norm." The descriptions of variations among individual experiences and specific habitus that phenomenology could potentially offer, Bourdieu rejects from the outset, because he views phenomenology as a subjectivist philosophy ignorant of the social conditions that have enabled the "taken for granted" world to appear as such. Notwithstanding this indictment, I would like to argue for the usefulness of phenomenology for Bourdieu's project, a project that I believe is seriously flawed unless it can avoid the reduction of the individual to his or her social class. This collapse of the person into his or her social class has the unfortunate effect not only of making the individual subject disappear but also of making social class appear to be much more monolithic and stable an entity than it ever actually is. Challenging the hegemonic functioning of a particular class identification, I believe, is an important first step to challenging the hegemonic functioning of "character" on an individual level, as posited by James. Rather than turning our attention to idiosyncratic experiences or idiosyncratic ways of responding to them as a means of combating the ubiquity of the habitus and/or a fixed character, I would like to turn now to Merleau-Ponty's description of the habit body because I believe it offers us a way of affirming both the individual and the communal aspects of our experience without separating them from one another or collapsing them into a single phenomenon.

Bourdieu often critiques phenomenology for limiting itself to describing that which can be rendered an intentional object of consciousness. He sees the Husserlian emphasis on the noetic/noematic relationship as inescapably subjectivist, and as trapping us within a domain of intentionality that forces us to deny the meaningfulness of nonintentional aspects of our experience. The habitus, Bourdieu insists, is just such a nonintentional phenomenon that is unwilled and almost never an explicit object of intentional awareness. Indeed, it is precisely the pervasiveness and improvisational character of the habitus for Bourdieu, that makes it resistant to being grasped intentionally. However, consciousness for Husserl is itself a similarly elusive phenomenon; it is the basis for all of our experience without being reducible to one or more of those experiences. And, I would argue, the body plays just such a role for Merleau-Ponty who describes a bodily intentionality that arises out of bodily movement but does not require our explicit awareness. Nor does the bodily intentionality we exhibit mark the limit of our bodily possibilities.

Like Bourdieu and James, Merleau-Ponty affirms that our habitual activities unfold without our explicitly attending to them: "When I run my eyes over the text set before me, there do not occur perceptions which stir up representations, but patterns are formed as I look, and these are endowed with a typical or familiar physiognomy" (Merleau-Ponty 1962: 144). The immediacy with which we grasp these typical "patterns" belies any appeal to the specific project of an intentional consciousness; rather, this activity is accomplished by what Merleau-Ponty calls, the "body-subject." It is not consciousness, Merleau-Ponty observes, but "the body which 'understands' in the cultivation of habit" (Merleau-Ponty 1962: 144). Our habitual responses to the world of our concern, he suggests, rather than restricting the meaning and range of our experiences, actually expand them. "Habit," Merleau-Ponty asserts, "expresses our power of dilating our being in the world, or changing our existence by appropriating fresh instruments" (Merleau-Ponty 1962: 143). In contrast to this depiction of habit as a dilation of our being in the world, a view which requires further exploration, Gilles Deleuze identifies habit as a contraction, or more accurately, as a series of contractions that draw "something new from repetition—namely difference (in the first instance understood as generality)" (Deleuze 1994: 73). Habit, Deleuze maintains, "concerns not only the sensory-motor habits that we have (psychologically), but also, before these, the primary habits that we are; the thousands of passive syntheses of which we are organically composed" (Deleuze 1994: 74).

Despite the striking contrast in the imagery they use to describe habit (a dilation of our being in the world for Merleau-Ponty, and a contraction for

Deleuze), both Merleau-Ponty and Deleuze portray habit not as antithetical to innovation but as precisely what enables us to engage the world in new and different ways. While Deleuze is much more comfortable with the Bourdieusian disappearance of the individual subject, he accomplishes this much differently than does Bourdieu. If the Bourdieusian subject is a particular materialization of a specific habitus, the Deleuzian subject dissolves altogether into its molecularity, the "thousands of passive syntheses of which we are organically composed." The Merleau-Pontian subject, however, while expanded by his or her acquisition of new bodily habits, at the same time is never reducible to them. Each of these habits offers, for Merleau-Ponty, a different way of inscribing ourselves in the world and of inscribing the world in our body. In his words: "To get used to a hat, a car or a stick is to be transplanted into them, or conversely, to incorporate them into the bulk of our own body" (Merleau-Ponty 1962: 143). Rather than a self-sufficient consciousness or even a self-contained body, Merleau-Ponty offers us a view of the body as an open system of dynamic exchanges with the world, exchanges that, in their habituality, ground the body ever more firmly within the world, and, in the process, offer us new ways of engaging and transforming it. If a cane can become an extension of our arm, if a car can become a motor extension of our entire body, and if the typist's familarity with the keys, represents "knowledge in the hands" rather than a conscious acquisition of a particular skill, then we can see the acquisition of habits as a primary means of establishing the relationality of the body-subject, that is, its process of defining itself through the reversible relationships it sustains with its world.

In response to the concerns I raised earlier about the loss of individuality and resistance that attends Bourdieu's understanding of the habitus, Merleau-Ponty's emphasis on the singularity of each and every body-subject makes it clear that each will find his or her own habitual ways of negotiating and thereby extending the parameters of his or her world. The specific bodily knowledge exhibited in the blind man's use of his cane or the typist's familiarity with the keys, cannot be adequately grasped through their class affiliations though this latter may help us to understand why he uses a cane rather than another visual prosthesis or why she is a secretary rather than a corporate executive. For Merleau-Ponty, the development of habitual ways of being in the world is precisely what shows us that: "my body must be apprehended not only in an experience which is itself instantaneous, peculiar to itself and complete in itself, but also in some general aspects in the light of an impersonal being" (Merleau-Ponty 1962: 82). As a specificity that possesses through its habits the power of generality, the body, according to Merleau-Ponty, "is my basic habit, the one which conditions all the others, and by means of which they are mutually comprehensible" (Merleau-Ponty 1962: 91).

Whereas Bourdieu sees our immersion in our class habitus as limiting our ability to grasp it as a whole, Merleau-Ponty, like James, argues that our habitual responses to our world actually provide us with the means of gaining a fresh perspective on it. "Thus," Merleau-Ponty asserts: "it is by giving up part of his spontaneity by becoming involved in the world though stable organs and pre-established circuits that man can acquire the mental and practical space which will theoretically free him from his environment and allow him to *see* it" (Merleau-Ponty 1962: 87). Habits, on this account, do not mire us in the world or even in a given habitus; rather, they allow, in Deleuzian terms, new syntheses to be established between the body and its world, syntheses that are passive to the extent that they don't require our explicit awareness, but active to the extent that they express a dynamic engagement with the world. As Merleau-Ponty observes, "habit has its abode neither in thought nor in the objective body, but in the body as mediator of a world" (Merleau-Ponty 1962: 145).

That this world is always a social world, as Bourdieu argues, cannot be denied. However, significant changes in the habitus have implications at both the individual and the community level. Even Immanuel Kant, who sees the individual's rationality and autonomy as the defining feature of her or his humanity, also recognizes in his political writings the crucial role the community plays in all aspects of the individual's life.[7] Although, as the example of the events of September 11 illustrates, the impetus for significant change in the habitus may occur from without, the form that the changes themselves take as well as their effects are always worked out on an intercorporeal level, that is, through alterations in the daily interactions between bodies as well as within our own.

Merleau-Ponty's work highlights the importance of the specific bodily aims and projects that demarcate one person's habits from those of another. And, the *New York Times* profiles remind us of how one person's absence can completely undo the habits of so many others. Indeed, one of the most powerful and unforgettable images from the media coverage of the World Trade Center Towers after they were hit and before they collapsed on September 11, was of individual bodies falling to the ground after people had hurled themselves out of the windows to escape from the suffocating smoke and fire in the upper levels of the buildings. As collective witnesses to this final, horrifying exercise of individual freedom in the face of inevitable death, millions of us experienced the power of the body to affect our own bodies, a communication of the incommunicable.

Taken together, Merleau-Ponty and Bourdieu set the stage for a deeper understanding of the complex relationship continually unfolding between the individual and the larger social community.[8] I've focused on habit, in particular, because I believe, with Merleau-Ponty, Bourdieu, and James, that it is at the concrete, material level of our habits that we can best assess personal and communal commitments to genuine social change. Finally, if James is correct that an individual's character becomes "set" like plaster by the time he or she is thirty, this is not the fault of the habits he or she has acquired but rather, is due to a failure to seize upon the possibilities they offer for transforming the givens of our world.

Notes

A longer version of this essay appears in *Refiguring the Ordinary* (Indiana University Press, 2008: 75–97).

1. Habit, I would suggest, is as important as time and memory for Proust and it serves as one of the most pervasive leitmotifs in his work. While I do not have time to develop this argument here, I would also maintain that Proust's ambivalence toward habit seems to flow from his recognition that habit is a primary means through which time and memory are registered corporeally. And, if this is so, then we need to turn to the phenomenon of habit, in all of its ambivalence, in order to understand more concretely how time and memory function in everyday life.

2. I say adults here because children are often prone to lose their interest in the previous project if they are distracted from it. Indeed, one of the frequently heralded signs of adulthood is an ability to "stay on task" in the face of appealing alternatives. Today, it seems, the emphasis has switched from being able to "stay on task" to being able to "multitask." While the former involves being able to retain one's concentration on a single activity and to follow it through from beginning to end, an individual who is only able to focus on one project at a time and who cannot spread their interest and attention across several different activities simultaneously can also be seen as limited.

3. See Hubert L. Dreyfus and Stuart E. Dreyfus, "The Challenge of Merleau-Ponty's Phenomenology of Embodiment for Cognitive Science" for a more in-depth account of Merleau-Ponty's notion of the intentional arc. Dreyfus and Dreyfus argue that the functioning of neural networks as they have been observed and described by cognitive scientists, provides empirical support for the presence of an intentional arc. While it is beyond the scope of this essay to pursue this further, it would be interesting to explore the connections between James's view of the neural pathways that are responsible for the formation of specific habits and the activity of neural networks operating in the brain.

4. For Kant, volition is absolutely central to morality since one must will to do one's duty in order for an action to be considered moral. What is crucial for Kant, however, is not so much volition itself but rather the force that motivates the will. He asserts that both reason and the inclinations (emotions) have the power to propel the will to action but, on his account, an act is moral only if reason alone is the determining ground for volition. In a sense, Kantian morality and Jamesian morality may not be so far apart after all since morality for Kant doesn't hinge on the presence or absence of volition but on the presence or absence of rational intent, which will in turn serve as the motivating force for volition. Indeed, Kant would very likely have been sympa-

thetic to an exhortation to make an appeal to reason habitual in one's daily life though James would have argued, in a Humean vein, that it is the emotions that must propel one to be influenced by reason in the first place.

5. Of course, we must not forget that even as some people's lives were rendered visible and therefore mournable through these obituaries, there were many other lives that did not receive the same public recognition and commemoration. In *Precarious Life*, Judith Butler argues that the very "realness" of the lives of unmourned victims of violence is placed in question by their exclusion from public discourse. Insofar as "Those who are unreal have, in a sense already suffered the violence of derealization," she asserts that, "They cannot be mourned because they are always already lost or, rather, never "were . . ."" (Butler 2004: 33). While I agree with Butler that it is important to acknowledge those who were not deemed worthy of recognition in the first place, I am emphasizing the power of *The New York Times* obituaries to evoke the myriad ways in which life's meaning and value is expressed through the habitual.

6. Both James and Bourdieu, however, embrace to some extent the possibility for social change. David Hoy's excellent essay, "Critical Resistance: Foucault and Bourdieu" argues that individual political resistance to a given habitus is indeed compatible with Bourdieu's theoretical framework. And, one need only look to William James's work on multiple realities, freedom of will and its role in the formation of belief to see why, despite being a "bundle of habits," human beings have the potential on his account to draw on new experiences to create new associations that in turn can produce new meanings and new values. For both authors, however, it is difficult to reconcile the self-perpetuating or conservative quality of habits or the habitus respectively, with the spontaneity they nonetheless maintain is an essential component of everyday experience.

7. In "An Answer to the Question: 'What is Enlightenment,'" Kant distinguishes between the public and private use of reason and argues that the former rather than the latter must be the goal of the Enlightenment. Kant defines the Enlightenment itself as a movement out of "self-incurred immaturity" (Kant 1991: 54). According to Kant, while the enlightenment requires freedom, it can also involve restrictions on freedom if the individual's interests come in conflict with those of the larger society. In his words:

> The *public* use of man's reason must always be free, and it alone can bring about enlightenment among men; the *private use* of reason may quite often be very narrowly restricted, however, without undue hindrance to the progress of enlightenment. (Kant 1991: 55)

Kant's defense of freedom in the public domain (which he identifies as essential to the continued progress of enlightenment) even when it restricts freedom in the private domain is precisely the theoretical framework George W. Bush has implicitly (and most likely unwittingly!) appealed to to justify his controversial Presidential orders authorizing the denial of basic civil liberties to suspected terrorists. While, as many have argued, Kant seems to be articulating a very reactionary politics with potentially dangerous consequences on both a civil and individual level, what interests me here is his recognition that the single moral agent who is at the center of his own deontological ethics is not all that counts, and that the interests of the community always need to be reckoned with and addressed.

8. Although I am using the term "community" in the singular here, I do not mean to imply that there is only one community (e.g., a single, global community), or that an individual can belong to one community alone. Indeed, the majority of people are part of several different (and usually overlapping) communities simultaneously. Moreover, the significance of particular habits themselves clearly varies from one community to another and this further complicates attempts to fix their meaning and influence once and for all.

References

Bourdieu, Pierre (1977). *Outline of a Theory of Practice*. Trans. Richard Nice. Cambridge: Cambridge University Press.

——— (1990). *The Logic of Practice*. Trans. Richard Nice. Stanford: Stanford University Press.

Butler, Judith (2004). *Precarious Life: The Powers of Mourning and Violence*. London: Verso.

Deleuze, Gilles (1994). *Difference and Repetition*. Trans. Paul Patton. New York: Columbia University Press.

Dreyfus, Hubert L. and Dreyfus, Stuart A. (1999). "The Challenge of Merleau-Ponty's Phenomenology of Embodiment for Cognitive Science" *Perspectives on Embodiment: The Intersections of Nature and Culture*. Edited by Gail Weiss and Honi Fern Haber. New York: Routledge Press, 103–120.

Hoy, David Couzens (1999). "Critical Resistance: Foucault and Bourdieu" *Perspectives on Embodiment: The Intersections of Nature and Culture*. Ed. Gail Weiss and Honi Fern Haber. New York: Routledge Press, 3–21.

Husserl, Edmund (1962). *Ideas: General Introduction to Pure Phenomenology*. Trans. R. Boyce Gibson. New York: Collier Books.

James, William (1950). *The Principles of Psychology: Volume One*. New York: Dover Publications, Inc.

Kant, Immanuel (1964). *Groundwork of the Metaphysic of Morals*. Trans. H. J. Paton. New York: Harper and Row.

——— (1991). "An Answer to the Question: 'What is Enlightenment?' *Kant: Political Writings*. Ed. Hans Reiss. Trans. H. B. Nisbet. Cambridge: Cambridge University Press.

Merleau-Ponty, Maurice (1962). *Phenomenology of Perception*. Trans. Colin Smith. London: Routledge & Kegan Paul.

Proust, Marcel (1981). *Remembrance of Things Past: Volumes 1–3*. Trans. C. K. Scott-Moncrieff and Terence Kilmartin. New York: Random House.

Wittgenstein, Ludwig (1968). *Philosophical Investigations*. Third Edition. Trans. G. E. M. Anscombe. New York: MacMillan.

CHAPTER 14

The Borderlands of Identity and Culture

RASHMIKA PANDYA

> An old photograph in a cheap frame hangs on a wall of the room where I work. It's a picture dating from 1946 of a house into which, at the time of its taking, I had not yet been born. The house is rather peculiar—a three storeyed gabled affair with tiled roofs and round towers in two corners, each wearing a pointy tiled hat. 'The past is a foreign country,' goes the famous opening sentence of L. P. Hartley's novel *The Go-Between*, 'they do things differently there.' But the photograph tells me to invert this idea; it reminds me that it is my present that is foreign, and that the past is home, albeit a lost home in a lost city in the mists of lost time. (Rushdie 1991: 9)

When I first immigrated to Canada from Kenya in 1969 it was my present that was "foreign," a place where "they" did things differently. However, despite the initial culture shock and displacement I felt, I am at home now, though I am also strangely always at home in my memories of the world I left in 1969. In fact, my memories of the place I left do not remain on the "other" side of my present but intertwine with the present to create the world I *live* today. This intertwining, what Salman Rushdie calls a "cross-pollination," is not an assimilation of the past into my present but something unique between the cultural milieu I inhabit now and that other world I left so long ago but that still infuses my present (Rushdie 1991: 20). This chapter is inspired by my own experience of living within more than one language and tradition and by a strange claim Merleau-Ponty makes in the *Phenomenology of Perception*:

> [T]he full meaning of a language is never translatable into another. We may speak several languages, but one of them always remains the one in which we live. In order completely to assimilate a language, it would be necessary to make the world, which it expresses one's own, and one never does belong to two worlds at once. (Merleau-Ponty 1989: 187)

While Merleau-Ponty may be right that no language is fully translatable into another and that languages express particular "worlds," the notion that we only "live" in one world at a time does not describe the experience of inhabiting various localities, of "singing the world" in various ways, *at one time* (ibid.). In a footnote to this claim Merleau-Ponty cites the autobiography of T. E. Lawrence. The notion that despite immersion in multiple worlds we only ever inhabit one world at a time is supported by Lawrence's description of the incongruity between the Arab world he inhabited for ten years and the English world he was raised within. It is worth citing the whole passage as it informs Merleau-Ponty's claim that we only ever live in "one" world, *one linguistic, cultural, historical and social space*, at any one time.

> In my case, the effort for these years to live in the dress of Arabs, and to imitate their mental foundation, quitted me of my English self, and let me look at the West and its conventions with different eyes: they destroyed it all for me. At the same time I could not sincerely take on the Arab skin: it was an affectation only. Easily was a man made an infidel, but hardly might he be converted to another faith. I had dropped one form and not taken on the other, and was become like Mohammed's coffin in the legend, with a resultant feeling of intense loneliness in life, and a contempt, not for other men, but for all they do. Such detachment came at times to a man exhausted by prolonged physical effort and isolation. His body plodded on mechanically, while his reasonable mind left him, and from without looked down critically on him, wondering what that futile lumber did and why. *Sometimes these selves would converse in the void; and then madness was very near, as I believe it would be near the man who could see things through the veils at once of two customs, two educations, two environments.* (Lawrence 1997: 14)

When my attention was first drawn to these passages on the relation between language and world, I thought that they were expressing the uniqueness of various cultures, of various ways of being-in-the-world and so I did not give it much thought. However, something about this formulation of the relation between language and world did not seem quite right. First, it did not seem right in relation to my own experience as an immigrant since my experience did not suggest the either/or of "madness" or one world that Lawrence suggests and second, it did not seem philosophically in keeping with Merleau-Ponty's formulation of language as expression. If any particular language, as expressive, was open to revision and re-creation then it seemed that the relationship *between* languages should entail the same porosity and leakage and this put into question the notion of "worlds" as unique localities. No world could be free from contamination by other worlds if language functions as Merleau-Ponty claims. And, this "contamination" would recast in what sense the terms "identity" and "difference"/the "same" and the "other" should be understood. Perhaps the real philosophical issue is whether we accept the absoluteness of either identity or difference/the same or the other? Third, if we accept the claim that languages are indeed transformed *within* particular worlds but somehow resist outside influences, this does not seem in keeping with the universality of prereflective life or the prelogic of the world that Merleau-Ponty develops in the *Phenomenology*. Despite an inherent ambiguity at the heart of lived experiences, Merleau-Ponty seems to suggest a *common* basis for all our expressions—an interworldly world that underlies and informs any particular expression. These three questions led to a self-questioning: if Merleau-Ponty is right then I predominately *live* in one world and am at best a voyeur in the other but is this my experience? Am I, like Lawrence, only *affecting* belonging to a Canadian world while my real self, the one that came from an African East-Indian world, lies repressed somewhere in the "void"? Perhaps I am delusional, and my sense of belonging to the African East-Indian world is lost forever—a mere figment of a lost time and place—a nostalgic dream? Is the only alternative to this either/or madness or is it indeed possible to see the world through two veils at once, perhaps even multiple veils?

This essay explores these issues of identity and difference through the use of personal narrative.[1] I have appropriated anthropologist Arjun Appadurai's notion of "imaginary identities" to suggest a space created between cultures and traditions: this space is not only apparent in those of us who have left our ancestral homes to create new homes elsewhere but is increasingly the state of all of us in a global world (Appadurai 1997: 33). Appadurai points out that imagined worlds are both sites of resistance and sites of subjugation (Appadurai 1997: 27–47). Imagined worlds can be sites of resistance insofar as they resist the homogenization of difference and sites of subjugation insofar as they create nostalgia for a world that does not exist, privileging heterogeneity allergic to any sense of commonality or similarity.[2] Appadurai maintains that we must be as vigilant in resisting nostalgic views of our differences as we are in resisting forces of homogenization. Throughout this chapter, even where I do not explicitly mention Appadurai, it is this notion of mediating between maintaining "difference" and resisting the temptation to fall prey to "nostalgic" illusions of difference that motivates my analysis. Along with Merleau-Ponty, Appadurai claims that there is no purity of culture or language and this is perhaps because there never was. Even Lawrence, who throughout his autobiography struggles with his sense of identity, recognizes that the terms of this struggle, explicitly "Arab" and, perhaps more implicitly, "English," are constructs (or creations) to a certain degree (Lawrence 1997: 14).[3] I argue that despite the problematic relationship between language and culture in the *Phenomenology of Perception*, Merleau-Ponty's works, *including* the *Phenomenology of Perception*, can accommodate a thesis that negotiates a space between worlds, one that does not reduce the particularity or singularity of any world to some universal or generalized notion but also suggests that worlds are not hermetically sealed localities. In the following, I argue that the relationship between one world and another mirrors the relationship between consciousness and body, subject and object and self and other in Merleau-Ponty's thought. The "correlation" of the preceding terms suggests that these dualities are both irreducible and *related*. As correlated, both terms are paradoxically distinct and mutually inclusive. Neither of these terms operates without bringing in its wake its other: body is tied to consciousness in such a way that experience is impossible without their correlation, just as subjectivity is intrinsically tied to intersubjectivity (i.e., the linguistic, cultural, historical, and social world). And yet, the body is no more reducible to consciousness than is the subject merely an instance of the particular world she arises out of and within. The dual terms of Merleau-Ponty's philosophy maintain an odd tension between universality (i.e., generality) and particularity, transcendence and immanence and this tension is perhaps not so much a *problem* with his account as a possibility of moving beyond one sided or abstract philosophical accounts with their hierarchical privileging of one side of any duality. I suggest that the notions of flesh and reversibility, articulated in *The Visible and the Invisible*, both of which maintain a paradoxical proximity and distance (i.e., a "hyperdialectic"), are already at work in Merleau-Ponty's earlier corpus. The earlier works implicitly suggest an alternative account of the relationship between language as expression and the world it articulates. My claim is that the notion of intersubjectivity as articulated in the earlier works can be broadened in order to make a space for a notion of "community" that transgresses borders, whether these be metaphorical or real.

Part One suggests that Merleau-Ponty's claim that we only live in one world at a time is due to a self-proclaimed bad ambiguity in the *Phenomenology of Perception* (Merleau-Ponty 1964: 11).[4] Despite this "bad ambiguity," I contend that the *Phenomenology* already contains suggestions of Merleau-Ponty's later ontology, which offers an interesting resolution or mediation to the issues surrounding questions of identity and difference. While the ontological position of *The Visible and the Invisible* is only implied in the works preceding it, I think that the operative concepts of flesh, reversibility and écart are already at work not only in the works that follow the *Phenomenology of Perception*, but within that work as well. Part Two offers an analysis of Merleau-Ponty's broadening of language and expression, which suggests a transition to a multiworld viewpoint. In concluding, I suggest that latent in Merleau-Ponty's earlier works is an ethics of reciprocity and a politics of difference.[5]

Part One: Embodied Truth/Difference Embodied

In the *Phenomenology of Perception* Merleau-Ponty argues that we are born into particular social, cultural, and historical worlds and that these worlds to a large extent determine not only *what* but also *how* we know. Subjectivity is intersubjectively instituted. By arguing for the primacy of perception and privileging the body as a condition of knowledge, Merleau-Ponty also argues for a perspectival notion of truth. The social, cultural, and historical situation we find ourselves in to some extent determines *what* we know and *who* we are, even to the extent that through the body image it determines *how we are*.[6] While this does much to validate (and explain or problematize) experiences different from and outside of a Western or patriarchical paradigm, it also results in what Merleau-Ponty later refers to as a "bad ambiguity." In the *Phenomenology of Perception* the solution to this bad ambiguity usually suggests a measure of normativity by which to adjudicate competing claims of validity. In a late chapter of the *Phenomenology*, the measure of truth is clearly defined in terms of an intersubjective "norm," though the aim of the chapter is to illustrate an ambiguity at the heart of all experience (Merleau-Ponty 1989: 299–345). Using patients suffering from hallucinations as an example, Merleau-Ponty documents through various cases that the patients in question distinguish their hallucinations from similar experiences that are "real."[7] The conclusion drawn from this is that since the patient acknowledges a difference between experiences (i.e., the hallucination vs. the real experience) and since the hallucination cannot be intersubjectively verified, the patient must come to the conclusion that her hallucinations are unreal (or, I suppose, remain self-deceived).

While Merleau-Ponty certainly does not overtly claim that the patients' hallucinations are to be measured against an intersubjectively agreed upon view of reality, there is throughout this section of text a perceptual adequation at work—the patient is deceived not about experiencing what she does but about the adequacy of that experience and the possibilities of the world as it *is*.[8] And, since the world as it is, is the world as it is perceived by "normal" subjects, "the phenomenal world," normativity acts as a measure of truth(s). However, the examples used illustrate that this adequation is exactly what the patient *does not* acknowledge—for the patient there certainly is a difference between her hallucination and a similar experience that others share. For example, there is a difference between an imaginary powder only the patient sees and a real powder that others perceive, but *both* are equally real (though not the same) to the patient. Otherwise hallucinations would not be an issue or problem for the patient. If the perceptual adequation is removed, then hallucinations would be just another way to experience the world and are, according to Merleau-Ponty, no more deceptive than our experiences of our own past. For, "When I recall my past at the present time I distort it, but I can allow for these very distortions, for they are conveyed to me by the tension created by the extinct past at which I am aiming and my arbitrary interpretations" (Merleau-Ponty 1989: 337).

The adequation at work in memory appears to share the same kind of modality at work between reality and hallucination. If we relegate the world, self, others and even the past to a necessary contingency, as Merleau-Ponty does, then it seems that all we can count on are "arbitrary interpretations." Merleau-Ponty counters this "arbitrariness" by grounding truth within an intersubjective framework, any truths we can have are negotiated by the linguistic, historical, cultural, and social matrix within which those truths arise. If we apply this claim to the view that intersubjective communities are different from each other—unique localities—then there is no common measure or norm by which to judge differences of opinion when two worlds collide but, more disturbing, there does not seem to be any ground for communication or interaction *between* worlds. We must accept the inherent differences and both (or many) claims as valid and legitimate (i.e., there is an "immeasurability" to these types of claims). On the surface such a view suggests a healthy respect for differences. Certainly Merleau-Ponty wants to claim that we can move beyond our own point of view and try to encompass perspectives not our own. In his words, "I misunderstood another person because I see him from my own point of view, but then I hear him expostulate, and finally come round to the idea of the other person as a centre of perspectives" (Merleau-Ponty 1989: 337–338).

However, this encompassing gives us only a partial and limited understanding of others since we are to a certain extent determined and individualized by our own contexts: there is a solipsism rooted not only between individuals within a world but between worlds as well. If the solipsism between individuals in a given community is mediated by the inherence of any individual in a certain "style" or manner of being-in-the world that is influenced by the style of the community within which they become individuals (i.e., by the sedimentations of meaning that are historically instituted within the self-understanding of both communities and individuals), then it seems there is in Merleau-Ponty's system a counter to the accusation of solipsism.[9] But what of the solipsism between worlds, is there a similar resolution available? While it *seems* "natural" to see the relationship between an individual and her particular world as analogous to that between worlds, I think there is in the *Phenomenology* some resistance to carrying this analogy too far. First, the similarities that unite individuals to their particular communities are not analogous to the relationship between worlds where differences abound. While a community of language users who share a common history may express their world in relatively similar ways, this is definitely not the case between worlds, where even the most immediate form of expressions, gestures, are indications of a wholly different hold on the world. As Merleau-Ponty aptly notes, our gestures are unique to the world we find ourselves within. Anger is expressed by a smile in the Japanese context, while in the Western context, anger is expressed by a reddening of the face and stamping of the feet or hissing of words (Merleau-Ponty 1989: 189). How is it that the Japanese individual and the Western individual could ever understand each other if this is the case? Given Merleau-Ponty's claim that even if we speak various languages we only *live* within one language, one world, and his use of Lawerence's experience as an example of this "one world" view, it would seem that there are two related and equally problematic possibilities: First, we would be forced to admit that between worlds, as between individuals, there is an absolute difference that can never be transgressed, never transgressed because of the second possibility which suggests that our world always colors our perspective so thoroughly that we never can see the other except through the lens of our world. In other words, I can certainly learn other languages and over time even learn to interpret the "foreigner" *but* this interpretation will always reflect the language and culture, which is "mine." There is an inherent violence entailed in such "translations." The problem as I understand it is not in the inherent inadequacy of ever knowing or understanding others but in the absoluteness of identity this view seems to suggest. The epistemological question of knowing others is intrinsically tied to the ethical and political issues of *how we relate to others*. A position that endorses a view of an absolute difference between individuals and between worlds introduces violence into all social discourse and makes ethics impossible. However, my own experiences lead me to believe that the claim that one world dominates my perspective, is at best, spurious. The question of which self I most truly inhabit and which world inhabits me is not as easy to answer as Merleau-Ponty *seems* to imply.

The reality may be that rather than *choosing* one cultural world, I actually create a space *between* worlds. In my own experiences, this space *in between* is not a fixed place but a re-creative space where I remake my self. Merleau-Ponty is right to say that the horizon or background within which re-creation occurs is to a certain extent determinate but this determinate horizon is itself infused throughout with difference. The African plateau of Kisumu and the endless prairie landscape both constitute my horizon, as does the cultural diversity inherent in either of these places. Salman Rushdie aptly expresses my understanding of the transition and in fact the *translation* from one world to another.

> The word translation comes, etymologically, from the Latin for "bearing across." Having been borne across the world, we are translated men. It is normally supposed that something always gets lost in translation; I cling, obstinately, to the notion that something is also gained. (Rushdie 1991: 17)

I too cling obstinately to the hope that in having been borne across continents something valuable has been gained. This hope is that the individual I am today, in this present, embodies not so much the *collision or assimilation* of two vastly different cultural worlds, but rather the translation of two worlds into something unique between the world I left and the alien world I entered in 1969. It is the hope that home is an expression of *both* the worlds that are so intrinsic to *who I am*.

Who am I?

My first memory is rocking back and forth in a cloth cradle tied to the door jams—of course I could not have known it was a door or that I was in a cloth cradle then—but still—I recall clearly the feel of swinging back and forth and the comfort this induced in me.

My next memories are filled with the warmth of African summers, the sweet smell of dung fires and the shrieking of my siblings and cousins, the feel of a stolen mango and the muted colors of an arid landscape. Muted, because through the heat, I recall that no color vibrated with its original hues, instead the colors all took on a subdued texture. My body was a part of that aridness and not distinct from the mango, the breeze, the warmth.

My first memory of pain: I am lying beside an enormous anthill, fascinated by the activity of the colony. Huge wine-colored ants swarming around and over me, I am mesmerized because the contrast of the ants against the dry dirt, which is almost the color of turmeric, reminds me of one of my mother's saris. I am not a threat until I decide to eat some dirt (a habit of mine in childhood), instantly I am in agony, my tongue on fire with an indescribable burning. I have obviously eaten more than dirt. I remember clearly the feeling of betrayal at something I could not articulate then, the synesthesia of self and world had just begun to unravel.

My last memory of Africa is the feel of my new birthday dress, a crinoline that scratched at my knees and collar, and a sense of foreboding as my mother explained we were leaving for a foreign land soon. My fear made the night seem especially dark and foreboding and not even the warm orange glow of our cooking fire could drive out a feeling of dread. I was just beginning to realize the world around me was separate from the world within. It felt like falling in a dream.

I do not remember the flight from Kenya but clearly recall my sheer terror of the cold in England—no central heating and my first experience of snow—cold, wet, and squishy, unlike the warm monsoon rains, which I would run about in barefooted. I did not like the boots, the coat, the scarf, and felt constrained and tied down. My body abandoned me and I a big girl of five could not control my bladder, the cold seemed to make it rebel against any control my mind tried to enforce. I was sad, because everything I knew that was comforting centered on warmth and light and this new place seemed so cold and dark. My mind still dealt in fantasies of home, while my body, an alien thing, inflicted me with all sorts of embarrassments.

Landing at the Saskatoon airport in November 1969, before it was large enough to have landing portals—the door opens—I stand at the door and am struck with terror, I am facing a wild howling whiteness that cuts through my inadequate English coat, a biting at my face with invisible teeth. I cannot move and my father with my younger brother in his arms pushes me forward. I am convinced for the next two years that I am being punished, if I am very good we will return to Kisumu, which I daydream about constantly. I know instinctively to say nothing of my fear or the more obvious fact that I have completely lost control of my bladder. I feel trapped since it is too cold to play outside. My family of seven shares a tiny room in my uncle's home, my world has shrunk and for the first time I feel trapped by my own body.

These vignettes of my childhood are representative of my first memories. Like all memories, they are filled in with the retrospective knowledge of the adult looking back. Merleau-Ponty's claim that the body is the condition of all knowledge suggests the body is the condition for conscious thought and so action. In this view, the above vignettes are a reflective look back at the initial recognition of the distinction of self and body—a distinction that is made *only* in reflection. It is the initial recognition of self as self-consciousness. In a very real way I took the cold Canadian prairie landscape within me, and since then have not been able to view myself as separate from those initial memories. However, the above also illustrates that this was not a process that occurred spontaneously or that ever fully integrated with my initial memories of Kenya. In one view, I lost a certain modality of being in moving to Canada, not just in the way I approached my physical surroundings but in the way I adapted to the social and cultural world that is Canada. And yet, the above does not indicate a choice of the world I knew, over the new one I was thrown into, but rather two worlds, one that lived only in my memories and one that I lived within and still viewed as foreign—alien. This experience of living between worlds, where one is only a memory, reflects T. E. Lawrence's experience and perhaps also explains his feeling of being on the edge of madness. Perhaps there is some legitimacy to Merleau-Ponty's claim that in such situations we always make a choice between worlds? Certainly if I had remained as I was, caught between the world I longed for and a world that was so foreign to my experience that it made me feel a prisoner in my own body, I too would have felt like I was going mad. However, if I have made a home here does this mean that who *I was* has been lost or forced into the background of my present—a faint memory that I can access only through the distorted lens of a different world—a different language and time? This either/or seems too extreme, especially since today I long for the prairie landscape as much as the plateau of Kisumu as I sit here so far from both. I *live* as much through the odd mixture of Gujarati and Swahili that colored my early years (and still is the language in which my family operates) as I do through the English that has become my first language and in fact, there is a sense in which both languages have influenced each other, not only in how I *speak*, but also in how I *think*.[10] The past is not a foreign country so much as the ground upon which I constitute the present and while the past can never remain impervious to influences from the present, the present is also influenced by the past. Lived time is not objective time as Merleau-Ponty is at pains to point out.

Oliver Sacks offers a phenomenological account of what it would be like if our experience of the past did remain completely distinct from our present lives in "The Landscape of His Dreams" (Sacks 1995: 153–187). Implicit in Sack's case study is the notion of an intertwining of past and present (no doubt the future as well) within "lived time." Sacks describes a painter who is obsessed by the place of his childhood. Franco, the painter, is haunted by memories of the Italian village he was born in, Pontito. His memories are so vivid that they overwhelm his life here and now. Franco is trapped in a nostalgic past that overwhelms his present and determines his future possibilities. Sacks is clear that the past that Franco recalls is a past that to some extent is informed by "who" Franco is today—Franco's paintings reveal not just the static memories of the boy Franco but the longings and regrets of the man Franco. While the perspective of Franco's paintings remain that of a child, the mood of the paintings reveal the longing for lost time that could only belong to the man. However, Franco seems unaware of this contamination of his idyllic past by the present and it is this failure to recognize the influence of his present on the past that prevents Franco from fully living in the present. Franco's obsession with Pontito is so extreme that he remains locked within a world seemingly impervious to change. The Pontito of Franco's memory remains untouched by the passing of time, unlike the "real" Pontito that has been transformed by the ravages of war and the exigencies of industrialization. Franco cannot fully live in San Francisco (his current home) since his whole life is geared toward a time and place removed from the present. If we can only inhabit one world at any given time, then Franco is an example of what would happen in the transition from one world to another. The world that informs who we are would predominate any other world that we tried to inhabit, our future would be determined by our past and our present would remain a sterile monument to a time and place long gone. A place long gone because like Pontito no "place," no (living) language or culture, remains the same over time. It is because of our ability to unite even the most disparate moments of our lives into a coherent story that most of us, unlike Franco, can take our situation in hand and transform even the most traumatic events into the fabric of meaning that is *this* life.[11] As Merleau-Ponty acknowledges, it is due to our ability to transform the contingency of life into a semblance of continuity, which allows us to escape the limitations of the past and move towards a future. Part Two deals with how this transition relates to the expressivity of language.

Part Two: Escape

> Man is a historical idea and not a natural species. In other words, there is in human existence no unconditional possession and yet no fortuitous attribute. Human existence will force us to revise our usual notion of necessity and contingency, because it is the transformation of contingency into necessity by the act of taking in hand. All that we are, we are on the basis of a *de facto* situation which we appropriate to ourselves and which we ceaselessly transform by a sort of *escape* which is never unconditioned freedom. (Merleau-Ponty 1989: 170–171)

Escape

I do not remember *learning* English. I started kindergarten approximately one month after arriving in Canada and, in my memory at least, English was just *there*. What I do remember is that my family had moved into a world of chaos, my uncle's modest house contained eleven children and five adults and unlike Africa where we lived with three times as many children and adults, this *space* seemed *so* small. While English may have appeared out of nowhere, my adjustment to prairie winters was not so sudden. I remember clearly the feeling of injustice when my kindergarten teacher would not let me go to the bathroom before I answered a simple math question. I knew addition and subtraction at a level beyond my years because in Kisumu in prekindergarten if you could not answer the teacher's questions you were placed above a vat of hot milk until you could answer the question, *correctly*. In retaliation, and because I still had not mastered bladder control in cold climates, I peed on the entire class—for some reason the classroom slanted downward. This was my first victory in Canada. It was a victory of defiance.

For the next five years my family moved at an average of once a year, I developed a speech impediment, became pigeon-toed to the detriment of anyone near me, developed near-sightedness that went unnoticed for three years and disappeared into a silent world within myself. Other than my siblings, I made no friendships; recesses were painful stretches of time that dragged on for eternities. After school it was the same every day: I watched as boys, big and small, beat my brother, my sister and I would pick him up and carry him home humiliated and full of rage. We spoke only Gujarati at home as if in protest to this harsh world of violence and injustice.

I remember public school as a time of assaults against my dignity. I was nicknamed Sambo. Often the teachers were even more ignorant than my fellow students. One teacher pointedly told the class, staring at me to make her point, that the problems with over-population in India stemmed from a lack of control *and* intelligence on the part of Indians; I knew she was wrong but did not have the words to tell her so. I further idealized my memories of Kisumu and my four siblings and I begged my mother for stories from Indian mythology, which became in our minds much more than stories, in those stories we found heroes who were like us. We developed an identity that differentiated us from them, them became in our minds Canadians. Our understanding of being African East-Indians was radically re-created to compensate for this alien world where we were not at home. And yet, at some point, we all rejected this view of us and them.

Every time someone walked into my house, there I was, ready to serve, tea-maiden. I was constantly reminded that this was good training; someday I would make a good Indian wife due to all this subservience. After all had I not already begun to learn that it was infinitely wiser to accept my role than to reject it in favor of a Western ideal of individualism? Look what it had got me so far, cold, bitterness, and generally a taste for freedom that I had never had before. I still remember that I felt so lost at that time—I had lost a world—but found nothing to replace it with. There was nothing worth keeping, nothing worth giving up in favor of new chains, even if those chains promised so much freedom. At that time I realized something important, since neither world I knew could offer me a world I actually wanted to live within, I consciously gave up both.

I do not remember exactly when the shift occurred and, in fact, it may not have occurred at a specific time but slowly over the years. However, at some point the critical eye of distrust toward Canadians shifted and became instead a gaze of suspicion toward the stereotypes of Indianness. The Indian community I grew up within had insulated itself from all outside influence, in an attempt to preserve its distinctness it actually propagated a stereotypical view of what it was to be Indian—a view that had no *real* foundations. This insularity led to a narrow-mindedness and worse to a set of unspoken "principles" that I found it impossible to live up to. Now all the injustice I initially attributed to Canadians became equally the injustice of Indians. Neither stereotype was acceptable and I rejected both, I found a home between the two. I developed a style that incorporated my understanding of the best in either world.

In *Consciousness and the Acquisition of Language*, Merleau-Ponty makes a case for the relation of identity and difference by showing that children move from a perspective of otherness to one of self-identity. Consciousness of others precedes consciousness of self. The child identifies with others, before the recognition of his own individuality. "In effect, the self and others are entities that the child dissociates only belatedly. He starts out in terms of a total identification with others" (Merleau-Ponty 1973: 36).

In the *Phenomenology of Perception*, Merleau-Ponty makes the same case for adults relating to each other. We are not the Sartrean "for ourselves" as much as *with* others. The Cartesian models of objects and others as *for* consciousness are rejected as secondary functions. Reflections on things or other people as other than myself are preceded by the experience of others and things as *with* me. There is a common modality to the being of things, others and myself and I, as incarnate consciousness, appropriate the world as a shared world of meaning. Merleau-Ponty illustrates that in my lived experience it is the possibilities open to me as a member of an intersubjective community that allows me to understand others and to express myself. While the notion of reversibility is only used in later works, the idea of it is already present in Merleau-Ponty's early work, as is the notion of écart. Reversibility does not designate a *coincidence* of consciousness/body, self/self, self/other or self/world but rather a divergence that creates a space or distance that opens up the possibility for any of these experiences. There is a certain reversibility built into the "systems" of self-other and self-world, since these all participate in the common fabric of Being. I approximate the perspective of the other or that of the world. But even my hold of my own innermost self is mediated through this divergence and reversibility. If language is understood as an expression of this primordial relationality, its very articulation, then it must be able to transcend any particular world but it does so *only through particular (unique) expressions*. Merleau-Ponty's notion of style reflects this paradoxical transcendence/immanence of expression (Dillon 1988: 208–223).[12]

Style as a certain way of being-in-world gives me both my unique perspective and an opening onto the perspectives of others.[13] Language is one of the expressive ways in which we come to recognize another's style. Language as gesture and speech opens the other's *way* of Being. However, Merleau-Ponty also wants to show that language is the expression of unique worldviews. Every language is a unique way of "singing the world" (Merleau-Ponty 1989: 187). There is in Merleau-Ponty's formulation of language as a means of expression of *a* world a truth that cannot be denied. And yet, my experience tells me that what happened when English became my first language was not the choice of one world over another, but rather the creation of a new world between the linguistic and so cultural confines of either English or Gujarati. I learned to sing the world in a way that was unique to me *but this world was also a shared world*.

> Language is an act of transcending. One cannot consider it simply as a container for thought; it is necessary to see language as an instrument for conquest of self by contact with others. (Merleau-Ponty 1973: 63)

Intersubjectivity, as a relationship of the individual to her world, involves the various ways in which a community can be understood to express itself; it involves the variety of ways that we as human beings situate ourselves in a world that is always already there. World(s), as already there, reflect the institutions that define a community's self-understanding, but also the possibilities open to any particular world to move beyond its institutions and to redefine itself. It is the individuals who make up a community, initially at least, who differentiate themselves from their community—so that the community at large changes—becomes more than it was. As Gary Madison notes:

> Language is [a] cultural acquisition; and although it owes its existence to speaking subjects alone, it precedes them all, such that each and every subject becomes a speaking and thinking subject, not by constituting language, but by taking it up. To speak is thus to live in a reason or a logos which exists, not as a thing or an idea, but as the permanent and sedimented trace of subjectivities. Thus in the first instance language transcends me because it belongs to others just as much—or just as little—as it belongs to me. But language's transcendence is also vertical: it transcends the members of a linguistic community taken all together; it is a phenomenon which has its own history. (Madison 1981: 122)

In "Language, Thought, and Truth," Paul K. Jacobson points out that Merleau-Ponty "tries to unfold how language, institution, history, and intersubjectivity mutually implicate each other and require a comprehensive treatment" (Jacobson 1979: 145). I suggest that Merleau-Ponty's view that one world dominates our perspectives undergoes an alteration in his writings dealing with expression. Worlds are still the unique expressions of specific intersubjective communities but the song that we all sing shares in a common aim, which is "the co-existence of men within a culture and, beyond it, within a single history" (Merleau-Ponty 1964: 9). The tension between a human world that we all share and particular intersubjective communities is never fully abolished in Merleau-Ponty's works. However, the relation between individual and community or one cultural world and another is no longer portrayed as one of polarity or incommensurability. In "On the Phenomenology of Language" Merleau-Ponty tries to illustrate that languages can change and even "leak" into one another: this is obviously a position that differs in some respects from the position in the *Phenomenology* that claims one language dominates who we are (Merleau-Ponty 1998: 87, 92). While the position is never clearly articulated, I think his phenomenological approach to language as expression is promising. If there is any sense in which to talk about a human world it is because of and not despite our differences. It is because of our differences that we all tend towards dialogue, towards communication. Our every action is in a sense an expression of our humanity and no matter how different those expressions are or how reactionary, they all seem to lead towards what Merleau-Ponty calls an "equilibrium."[14] "All human acts and all human creations constitute a single drama, and in this sense we are all saved or lost together. Our life is essentially universal" (Merleau-Ponty 1964: 10).

We are paradoxically initiated into this universal life through our particular intersubjective communities, through the *specific* linguistic community into which we are born. However, by changing the focus of traditional philosophies of language from *la langue* to *la parole*, concepts appropriated from Saussure, Merleau-Ponty returns language to a lived world within which language *speaks*. Arguing against the "universal grammar" of Husserl in his *Logical Investigations*, Merleau-Ponty shows that it is not so much the structure of languages that define particular languages but the *use* of language in any particular linguistic community.

> It will be a question not of a system of forms of signification clearly articulated in terms of one another—not a structure of linguistic ideas built according to a strict plan—but of a cohesive whole of convergent linguistic gestures, each of which will be defined less by a signification then by a use value. (Merleau-Ponty 1998: 87)

In fact, as Merleau-Ponty points out in *Consciousness and the Acquisition of Language*, the child initially takes up language as a certain style of expressing the intersubjective world the child is born into. The privileging of *la parole* is based on Merleau-Ponty's disagreements with the philosophical tradition's conceptions of language, specifically the relationship of thought and speech. In both the *Phenomenology of Perception* and *Consciousness and the Acquisition of Language*, Merleau-Ponty defends a gestural theory of speech. Like gestures, speech is the embodiment of an intention, just as my gesture of anger *is* the anger I feel, my speech is not a representation of my thoughts but the thoughts "embodied." In these works, Merleau-Ponty is trying to illustrate that unlike the empiricist and intellectualist views of speech that make it a third person process, "speech-like" gesture indicates how the speaking subject transcends herself in the act of expression.

Throughout the *Phenomenology of Perception*, Merleau-Ponty argues that the dualities of traditional philosophy must be overcome if we are to understand how it is that human beings experience and know their world. In trying to overcome the abstractions of traditional philosophy, Merleau-Ponty shows that the relationship of consciousness and body cannot be as either empiricism or intellectualism have claimed. Chapter Six of Part One of the *Phenomenology* illustrates that body is the nexus of speech (Merleau-Ponty 1989: 174–199). By arguing for a gestural theory of speech, Merleau-Ponty is able to illustrate that gesture and speech both are natural and conventional, each arises from biological being and each also arises from a certain style of being-in-the-world. The philosophical dilemma here is that traditional philosophy, in its intellectualist incarnations, has abstractly conceived of a consciousness that is pure thought, whether of itself or of a world and others. Consciousness viewed in this way oversees the movements of an objective body and this leads to irresolvable problems. The gestural theory of speech allows Merleau-Ponty to posit a theory of language that arises from our incarnate consciousness of the world and others. My understanding of my world is informed by my particular hold on the world and, my hold on the world is as dependent on this body that gives me a perspective unto a world, as it is on a consciousness that is able to transcend towards the world to give *my* world a meaning. As Merleau-Ponty notes in *Consciousness and the Acquisition of Language*, the child in the initial stages of language acquisition learns to speak a language by first learning the style of a particular language, the unique melody that every language embodies (Merleau-Ponty 1973: 76–77).[15] This style owes its existence to the intersubjective world that a language persists within. Just as the gestures that are used in various cultural worlds are unique to the particular hold people have on their bodies, languages also embody a unique expression of a world.

> Speech is comparable to a gesture because what it is charged with expressing will be in the same relation to it as the goal is to the gesture which intends it, and our remarks about the functioning of the signifying apparatus will already involve a certain theory of the significations expressed by speech. My corporeal intending of the objects of my surroundings is implicit and presupposes no thematization or "representation" of my body or milieu. Signification arouses speech as the world arouses my body—by a mute presence which awakens my intentions without deploying itself before them. (Merleau-Ponty 1998: 89)

The relationship of thought and speech illustrates how it is that words are not secondary to thought but the embodiment of thought. Just as the body is the nexus from which consciousness throws itself towards a world—the condition for any hold on the world I can have, my words are essential to the constitution of thought. There is a correlation between words and thoughts that paradoxically suggests a distinction between the two and yet also maintains the inseparability of each term from its other.

Words are vehicles of meaning and through speech it is not just words as signifiers that I express but a certain style of being. In speech, my thoughts are taken up by a listener. If this were not the case, then how could she ever respond?[16] While Merleau-Ponty does not use the term "empathy" he seems to suggest a kind of empathetic understanding required, not merely in our discourse with others, but also in any philosophical dialogue and understanding. Language does not give us a correspondence between a word and the thought it articulates since this kind of a correspondence would assume the possibility of a universal language, a perfect expression. Instead language operates within a background of sedimented meanings, cultural and historical styles, which requires a hermeneutical effort on the part of the listener to understand the other's meaning. This also suggests an indeterminacy to language, an indeterminacy that cannot be avoided or fully overcome but also does not suggest that communication and mutual understanding are impossible.

> In understanding others, the problem is always indeterminate, because only the solution will bring the data to light as convergent, only the central theme of a philosophy, once understood, endows the philosopher's writings with the value of adequate signs. There is then, a taking up of others' thought through speech, a reflection in others, an ability to think *according to others* which enriches our own thoughts. Here the meaning of words must be finally induced by the words themselves, or more exactly, their conceptual meaning must be formed by a kind of deduction from a gestural meaning, which is immanent in speech. And as in a foreign country, I begin to understand the meaning of words through their place in a context of action, and by taking part in a communal life—in the same way an as yet imperfectly understood piece of philosophical writing discloses to me at least a certain "style"-either a Spinozist, critical or phenomenological one—which is the first draft of its meaning. (Merleau-Ponty 1989: 179)

In communication with others speech is the embodiment and the expression of thought, if we are willing to listen, to "think according to another." And, to think according to another is never to think exactly like another—a pure language that gives us totally determinate meanings is not possible.

Our bodies express themselves through gestures that are recognizable by others in our cultural setting but gestures are never reducible to explicit signs. Gestures express our feelings, even though they are never fully explicit, just as our words carry meanings that are not fully explicit in themselves but still carry forward what we intend to *say*. For Merleau-Ponty, "Language bears the meaning of thought as a footprint signifies the movement and effort of a body" (Merleau-Ponty 1993: 82). Unlike "logical language" that "has the relative advantage of being exact," living language has an opacity that allows it to express meanings that are contextual (Merleau-Ponty 1973: 62). Even the silence between words can change the meaning of my expression (Merleau-Ponty 1993: 82). Words are diacritical, since they signify as much by the relation between words, as they do by the silence of what is not said (Merleau-Ponty 1998: 88). The system of language is never fully sedimented, because of the expressive nature of any language; language always tries to say more than what individual words signify (Merleau-Ponty 1998: 89).

Language also always expresses much more than representations or correspondences of thought to the thinking subject, the world or others. By privileging speech or *la parole* over the structures of any specific language, Merleau-Ponty illustrates that the expressive function of language always transcends the purely structural aspects of a language. All language is dialogue, even the inner language of my private thoughts (Merleau-Ponty 1998: 97). This conversation that is language may be hemmed in by the particularity of the language at hand but I always have the possibility of learning different languages and so learning to sing the world in various ways. Even within the confines of a single language, it is the changes instituted by speaking subjects that ensure that a language will always be able to express the world it is meant to signify. However, this also suggests that communication and mutual understanding are not givens but are acquisitions to be won by effort.[17] A language that does not retain the ability to transform itself through use cannot stand the test of time and eventually finds itself forgotten (Merleau-Ponty 1998: 88).

Language is expressive and because of this it has an indeterminacy that underlies it. While Merleau-Ponty stresses the indeterminacy of language, he also points out that there is a sedimentation of meaning in language; language is determinate and indeterminate (Merleau-Ponty 1989: 190–194). The indeterminacy of language is why language is not a correspondence of words to thoughts but the expression of a certain style of Being. Jacobson points out that the later writings of Merleau-Ponty relate truth and language; in fact, language becomes a vehicle of truth (Jacobson 1979: 164). These later writings also stress that while language is susceptible to sedimentation, it is only "relatively motivated" in that it is open to new situations. "Language is then both accidental and rational, fortuitous and planned; a realm in which, through the operation of this blind logic, accidents are transformed into reasons, and conscious meanings are able to emerge" (Jacobson 1979: 160–161). This blind logic is similar to the pre-logic of the perceptual world in that it has a transparency and yet, is at the same time, transcendent in its expression. Truth as timeless adequation between thought and reality becomes impossible under this understanding because truth is always situated (Jacobson 1979: 162). Words are constitutive of meaning and this meaning emerges not from some static signification that a word holds but in the relations between words, the silence between words and, most importantly, the *use* of words by speakers.

The structure of language as subject to Jacobson's blind logic contains a certain opacity but it is this opacity that creates a background of possibility for ever clearer expressions. New meanings arise because the relation of thought and words is at times spontaneous and indeterminate. If this were not true then language would not be expressive of meaning. Truth is always going to be situated truth and always truth that will be taken up in new contexts. "It is in this way that our present continues the past and can fulfil its promises" (Jacobson 1979: 163).

The individual expression that is unique to me can only arise out of the background of an intersubjective world that first gives me my thought. However, this background is never given once and for all, it retains a generality that allows for particularity, and indeed calls for individual expressions—without ever revealing itself completely. The notion that we can discover a universal language that is the ground of all language, throughout the ages, is the hope for a resolution that can never come. As long as we take up a given language and, in using it, transform it through use, language will always escape any attempts to define it in terms of an unchanging structure. Merleau-Ponty suggests that as long we speak, we will always re-create language; we will always sing the world in our own unique ways. And, if it is true that even in my inner thoughts I am speaking, which is to say that even my inner thoughts are a dialogue, then all language is an act of re-creation.

While in the *Phenomenology*, Merleau-Ponty suggests that we cannot live in two cultural/linguistic worlds at once, in "On the Phenomenology of Language," he states that there is an "oblique passage" from one language to another. However, even here, different languages are only "contingently comparable," just as two individuals, once we know them, may have similarities but remain unique (Merleau-Ponty 1998: 87). I think that this notion of a passage—oblique or not—is promising in relation to my own transition from one linguistic world into another. It suggests that we can indeed transcend our own situatedness, not only as individuals within a "community," but in the passage between communities (or worlds).

The "oblique passage" from one language to another illustrates that this movement, as a momentum of expression, opens the possibility that we may be able to incorporate various worlds in our notion of self. While Merleau-Ponty never takes the further step toward a vision of worlds that can and do "leak" into one another, the possibility for it is already evident in his phenomenology of language.

> Speech, as distinguished from language, is that moment when the significative intention (still silent and wholly in act) proves itself capable of incorporating itself into my culture and the culture of others—of shaping others and me by transforming the meaning of cultural instruments. It becomes "available" in turn because in retrospect it gives us the illusion that it was contained in the already available significations, whereas by a sort of *ruse* it espoused them only in order to infuse them with a new life. (Merleau-Ponty 1998: 92)

In light of the above, we, the inheritors of Merleau-Ponty's phenomenology, can understand that the new life that is infused *between* languages and cultures may radically alter the notion of culture as a distinct entity. Like individuals, cultures are a unique blending of various influences. Cultures, like individuals, reflect the ability to retain identity while at the same time through expressions of freedom re-creating themselves. Cultures too absorb differences, only to reaffirm their uniqueness. We may well all start out in one world but nothing prevents our absorbing various worlds into ourselves. Unlike T. E. Lawrence we need not view the intersection of two cultures as a battleground in which both sides are lost. In a very real sense, the kinds of choices we make in our lives affects who we are, and in turn, who we are affects our world.

Conclusion

In concluding, I would like to briefly address some of the ethical and political ramifications of Merleau-Ponty's phenomenology of language. As I suggested in my introduction to this chapter, Appadurai's claim that imaginary identities should mediate between being sites of resistance and sites of subjugation informs my self-understanding but also influences my interpretation of latent possibilities for an ethics of reciprocity and a politics of difference in Merleau-Ponty's thought. While the initial claim from the *Phenomenology of Perception* suggested that Merleau-Ponty merely reverses the duality of identity and difference, the same and the other, the analysis of language as expressive has shown that this was not Merleau-Ponty's last word on identity and difference. It is not only in the use of language by speakers in a particular linguistic community that language is transformed but also in the interaction between linguistic communities. While we should be vigilant in maintaining our differences, our singularity, we perhaps need to be just as vigilant in assuring that we do not create an insular world devoid of difference in doing so. Merleau-Ponty's analysis of the inherence of the subject within an intersubjective "world" illustrates that outside of all relation there would not be a subject at all (i.e., an individual). We can no more leave behind our "cultured" selves than we can our sexuality. As Merleau-Ponty suggests these are dimensions of our being. But as Merleau-Ponty's critique of historical materialism and psychoanalysis in the *Phenomenology* suggests, to *read* our "culture" or our sexuality into all the dimensions of life, to give one dimension dominion over all others, would be a mistake since it would reduce all signification, all expression, to one aspect of our existence (Merleau-Ponty 1989: 171–173 n.1). A politics of difference that recognizes our inherence in a "style" of life, while still maintaining a space for self-critique and reevaluation would offer a politics truly open to ethics. Philosophically this suggests that one does not overcome the dualistic and hierarchical thought of traditional philosophy by merely reversing the terms of any particular duality (i.e., subject/object, body/consciousness, self/other). Instead we need to embrace what the notion of reversibility exemplifies—an intrinsic intertwining at the heart of all existence. There is no individuality outside of all community and rarely (if ever) are worlds hermetically sealed localities. There are many ways to sing the world and even the tone deaf can learn to sing a different song.

Notes

1. My use of narrative as a way to express identity is influenced by Paul Ricoeur's *Time and Narrative*.

2. A view that would be "nostalgic" in Appadurai's sense would posit a difference itself impermeable to change, to differentiation. This would be an absolute difference and with Hegel I would suggest that such a difference must collapse into its opposite. G. W. F. Hegel, *Science of Logic*, 408–427.

3. Lawrence is clear the designation "Arab" is highly problematic since it refers to a group of people who are not united by common practices (i.e., styles) or localities. By implication one could say the same of Lawrence's "England." One does not need to have traveled outside of London to realize that there is barely even a family resemblance between the various groups and communities that are loosely united through the term "English."

4. "The study of perception could only teach us a "bad ambiguity," a mixture of finitude and universality, of interiority and exteriority. But there is a good ambiguity in the phenomenon of expression, a spontaneity which accomplishes what appeared to be impossible when we observed only the separate elements, a spontaneity that gathers together the plurality of monads, the past and the present, nature and culture into a single whole. To establish this wonder would be metaphysics itself and would at the same time give us the principle of an ethics" (Merleau-Ponty 1964: 11).

5. I would distance myself from positions that understand a politics of difference as entailing not just a critique but also a rejection of the traditional notion of community. I suggest that my cultural being, like my gendered identity, is not something I can leave at the door so to speak, it colors my world through and through, though this does not imply that it is not open to revision, to re-creation.

6. See: Iris Marion Young, "Throwing Like a Girl: A Phenomenology of Feminine Body Comportment, Motility and Spatiality," 51–70. Gail Weiss, "The Abject Borders of the Body Image," 41–59.

7. It could be argued that the case studies Merleau-Ponty uses actually suggest that the patients do not acknowledge the "reality" of others insofar as that reality does not acknowledge the patient's experiences. The patients do not understand why others do not "see" what they do. However, this does not alter my argument that the patients

are aware that they see what others do not and that what they see is *as real* to them as what others see.

8. For discussion of a notion similar to my "perceptual adequation" see: Kerry H. Whiteside, "Perspectivism and Historical Objectivity: Maurice Merleau-Ponty's Covert Debate with Raymond Aron," 132–151.

9. This is of course the point Merleau-Ponty repeatedly returns to especially in *Consciousness and The Acquisition of Language* and "The Child's Relations with Others" in *The Primacy of Perception*. Maurice Merleau-Ponty, *Consciousness and The Acquisition of Language*. Trans. Hugh Silverman (Evanston: Northwestern University Press, 1973). Maurice Merleau-Ponty, "The Child's Relations with Others" in *The Primacy of Perception*. Trans. William Cobb (Evanston: Northwestern University Press, 1964), 96–155.

10. As my partner continually reminds me, there is something a little odd in my English, he is convinced that it has absorbed the "flavor" of my Gujarati. He claims the rhythm of my spoken English is unique, despite the fact that I, unlike both my parents, do not have even the slightest Gujarati accent.

11. Susan Brison offers a disturbing personal account of the process of living through the trauma of rape in *Aftermath: Violence and the Remaking of a Self*. Brison's account attests to our human ability to overcome even the most traumatic experiences, not by forgetting, but by understanding and finding meaning in events which defy all reason or rationale (Brison 2002).

12. Dillon offers an intriguing account of the analogy of body/perception to language/thought—there is a sense, though different for each pair of the analogy in which *both* are flesh (Dillon 1988: 208–223).

13. I would suggest that the reversibility at the heart of my experience of the other is not exactly that of my relation with the world: the world, strictly speaking does not "look" back as the other person does, though arguably it does indeed "touch" back.

14. The notion of an "equilibrium" is referred to throughout *Consciousness and the Acquisition of Language*, as well as other works. While it is never clearly defined it can be understood in its scientific sense as a condition of stability, a tendency toward a state of maximum stability. I think in Merleau-Ponty's usage equilibrium takes on teleological implications—human beings are geared toward optimum ends—however, these are not ends knowable except in retrospect. There is an idealism that is reflected in the notion of equilibrium in Merleau-Ponty's philosophy.

15. What Merleau-Ponty means by style here may be clarified through an example. When I first moved to South Korea in 1995, I was taken aback by the harshness of Hangul, the Korean language. Initially Hangul only presented itself to me as sounds that were not in any way harmonious, I heard a discordant stringing together of sounds—no doubt because I am slightly tone deaf. Try as I might, I could not imitate the rhythm of Hangul and so speak Hangul, as long as I heard it as harsh and unrhythmic. What is interesting is that I could read Hangul and so get around Seoul with little problem, but I could not *communicate* with Koreans. By my second year in Korea there was a reversal in what I heard, suddenly Hangul seemed full of soft sounds,

the melody of the language became apparent, and I could now try to *speak* the language. I think there is a similarity of my experience with Hangul and the initial institution of language in the child; the underlying harmony of a particular language initiates the child into a speaking world and eventually the meanings this world holds. This initial institution into language cannot be reduced to a grasping of the structure of a particular language, since this is exactly what the child does not yet have. It is rather the unique way of incorporating the rhythm and texture of a language, in short, it is learning to understand how a language *sounds*, as long as one does not master the peculiarity of the language, one cannot *speak* a language with any kind of proficiency.

16. Of course one can choose *not to listen* but this already is to acknowledge the other in some sense—it is already a response.

17. Gary Madison makes this point: "Indeed, in language conceived of as a diacritical structure, there are cracks, gaps, or weak zones which prevent it from being perfectly clear for the speaking subjects and which make for difficulties in communication" (Madison 1981: 123).

References

Appadurai, Arjun (1997). *Modernity at Large*. Minneapolis: University of Minnesota Press.

Brison, Susan (2002). *Aftermath: Violence and the Remaking of a Self*. Princeton: Princeton University Press.

Dillon, M. C. (1988). *Merleau-Ponty's Ontology*. Evanston: Northwestern University Press.

Hegel, G. W. F. (1999). *Science of Logic*. Trans. A. V. Miller. New York: Humanity Books.

Jacobson, Paul K. (1979). "Language, Thought and Truth in the Works of Merleau-Ponty: 1945–1953." *Research in Phenomenology* 9: 144–167.

Lawrence, T. E. (1997). *Seven Pillars of Wisdom*. Great Britain: Wordsworth Editions Limited.

Madison, Gary Brent (1981). *The Phenomenology of Merleau-Ponty*. Athens: Ohio University Press.

Merleau-Ponty, Maurice (1964a). "An Unpublished Text." In *The Primacy of Perception*. Trans. Arleen B. Dallery. Evanston: Northwestern university Press: 3–11.

——— (1964b). "The Child's relations With Others," in *The Primacy of Perception*. Trans. William Cobb. Evanston: Northwestern University Press: 96–155.

——— (1989). *Phenomenology of Perception*. Trans. Colin Smith. London: Routledge Press.

——— (1973). *Consciousness and The Acquisition of Language*. Trans. Hugh Silverman. Evanston: Northwestern University Press.

——— (1993). "Indirect Language and the Voices of Silence," in *The Merleau-Ponty Aesthetics Reader*. Trans. Richard C. McCleary. Ed. Galen A. Johnson. Evanston: Northwestern University Press: 76–120.

——— (1998). "On the Phenomenology of Language," in *Signs*. Trans. Richard C. McCleary. Evanston: Northwestern University Press: 84–97.

Ricoeur, Paul (1984–1988). *Time and Narrative* 3 vols. Trans. Kathleen Blamey and David Pellauer. Chicago: University of Chicago Press.

Rushdie, Salman (1991). "Imaginary Homelands," in *Imaginary Homelands: Essays and Criticism 1981–1991*. London: Granta Books.

Sacks, Oliver (1995). *An Anthropologist On Mars*. New York: Vintage Books.

Weiss, Gail (1999). "The Abject Borders of the Body Image," in *Perspectives on Embodiment: The Intersections of Nature and Culture*. Eds. Gail Weiss and Honi Fern Haber. New York: Routledge Press: 41–59.

Whiteside, Kerry H. (1986). "Perspectivism and Historical Objectivity: Maurice Merleau-Ponty's Covert Debate with Raymond Aron." *History and Theory* 25: 132–151.

Young, Iris Marion (1989). "Throwing Like a Girl: A Phenomenology of Feminine Body Comportment, Motility and Spatiality," in *The Thinking Muse*. Ed. Jeffener Allen. Indiana: Indiana University Press: 51–70.

CHAPTER 15

Entwining the Body and the World: Architectural Design and Experience in the Light of "Eye and Mind"

RACHEL McCANN

Introduction

In his examination of the Flesh and the reciprocal nature of vision, Maurice Merleau-Ponty repeatedly holds up painting as an exemplar. In "Eye and Mind," he examines painting as a dynamic act in which the painter sees a portion of the world, brings it inside the body through vision, mixes it with his or her embodied way of understanding the world, and expresses the mixture back into the world in the form of a painting. This act makes the painting a "carnal echo," a residuum of the dynamic mixing of the visible world and the painter's carnal schema. In exploring painting as carnal echo, Merleau-Ponty characterizes it in spatio-temporal terms of depth, dimensionality, interval, and movement—the fundaments of architecture.

This chapter examines the design and experience of architecture as creative, embodied acts that deeply intertwine perceiver and perceived. Working from Merleau-Ponty's idea of painting as carnal echo, it examines how an architect internalizes the perceived through multisensory movement. It explores the deep sense of immersion within the sensuous world that intertwines perceiver and perceived, reorients the architect in deep relationship with his or her sensuous surroundings, and compels the architect to create. It examines architectural design and experience as interrogation into both the larger world and the recesses of the self.

Painting as carnal echo in "Eye and Mind"

Merleau-Ponty criticizes traditional Western philosophy's idea of art as representation or index, a formulation that ascribes generative power only to the mind. He contends that painting is not "a faded copy" (Merleau-Ponty 1993:

132, 126) of the thing and undertakes a lengthy criticism of Descartes' *Dioptrics*, in which Descartes examines etching as a means of representing objects and places. Merleau-Ponty argues that Descartes' etchings, which present things in terms of form and outline, represent rather than resemble things in the world. He contends that they serve as linguistic "indices . . . for forming an idea of the thing" (1993: 132) as etched lines stand in conceptually for the things they represent. These visual indices praised by Descartes spring neither from the thing drawn nor from our embodied relationship with it, but from the linguistic depths of our rational minds, seeking, as does the larger Cartesian project, to lend clarity to perceptual experience.

In *Dioptrics*, Descartes discusses an object's primary qualities, which include quantifiable properties such as length, height, form, and outline. He distinguishes these from secondary qualities, which include unquantifiable properties such as texture, color, and luster and thus are conceptually "uncertain," unreliable, and prone to change. Merleau-Ponty contends that engraving "present[s] the object by its outside, or its envelope," thereby allowing Descartes to dodge a confrontation with any deeper opening onto the world that an object's "uncertain" secondary qualities, such as color, might communicate (133). He argues that an examination of painting would come closer to revealing the nature of things and our relationship with them.

Merleau-Ponty's focus on relationship inverts Descartes's categories of primary and secondary qualities. In Cartesian representation, form and outline are primary, constant qualities, qualities we can grasp and hold conceptually, opposed to secondary qualities such as color, which are constantly in flux. But in a world whose most fundamental characteristic is interconnected flux, these "secondary qualities" become central. We engage a thing's secondary qualities intercorporeally, accessing qualities we can never appropriate or instrumentalize through the mind. In contrast to the "rule-governed [and] projective relationship" Descartes seeks between measurable form and indexical representation, Merleau-Ponty seeks an occasion for coming face to face with "a conceptless universality [and] opening upon things," which we nevertheless understand with our larger being. Because of the interconnected nature of the world's wild being,[1] the "uncertain murmur of colors" can make present a host of things: "forests, storms—in short, the world." Painting's exploration of the complex and changing interrelationships among form, light, texture, and color sheds light on our interconnected state in a way that representation of form and outline can never achieve (Merleau-Ponty 1993: 133).

Merleau-Ponty proposes the idea of painting as carnal echo, a formulation that locates generative power within the active and intersubjective relationship between human beings and the surrounding world. In this formulation, a painter opens himself or herself up to the world through vision. Through the channel of vision, the world enters the painter, inhabits the painter's interior, and mixes with the painter's carnality—his or her embodied consciousness. In mixing with the painter until it is no longer clear which is the painter and which is the world, the things of the world achieve a sort of doubling, existing simultaneously in the world and "at the heart of vision." The resultant mixture of painter and world is then expressed, literally pushed out, back into the world as a physical artifact, a painting. Merleau-Ponty points out that the continual exchange between body and world naturally produces carnal echoes. "Things have an internal equivalent in me; they arouse in me a carnal formula of their presence. Why shouldn't these correspondences in turn give rise to some tracing rendered visible again?" (1993: 124, 126, 128–129, 136).[2]

The painting's formative process makes it no sterile representation of things in the world, but progeny, the offspring of our carnal union with the world and the things in it. Painting as carnal echo manifests this fundamental intermingling. A painting of a grape, then, is neither a second instance of the grape, nor a representation of the grape, but a third entity altogether—the relational Flesh made manifest. Painting as carnal echo ascribes generative power not to the mind, but to the body, the cauldron in which the part of the Flesh that is the painter and a visible part outside the painter are combined.

Architectural design as carnal echo

What if the creative process in question is not two-dimensional painting or etching, but three- and four-dimensional architectural design? In one sense, architecture and painting are alike: when enframed by dualistic philosophy, both are commonly viewed as representations, yet, when enframed by Merleau-Ponty's ideas, both are carnal echoes of the real.

Art as representation attempts to stand in for or produce a copy of what it represents and thus serves merely as a linguistic icon that calls to mind an idea of the represented thing. Architectural design can make the same attempts, reproducing form from historical precedents, organizing space through geometric manipulation, creating architecture through disembodied intellection. Painting, which explores the complex and changing interrelationships among form, light, texture, and color, allows us to open up to the wild being of things, where each uncertain quality holds a little of the entire world in it.[3] Architectural design can also explore these relationships, generating form and space from awareness of embodied experience. As expressions or carnal echoes, both painting and architecture intertwine the world and our own carnality in expressing their creators' experience of seeing or inhabiting.

Architectural design offers opportunities for intercorporeal engagement unparalleled in painting. Where a painter internalizes and then expresses visible qualities of the world, the architect manifests its temporal, embodied nature. Where the painter responds to the internalization of vision with overlaid strokes of paint that make visible something previously invisible, the architect's sketch or model bridges between the internalization of embodied experience and the capabilities of building materials, space, and light to bring forth the latent qualities of spatial depth.

To begin the process of architectural design as carnal echo, the world "sees itself,"[4] and also feels its own spatiality, in the embodied gaze of the designer. Through the channel of movement, the sensuous and spatio-temporal world enters the body of the architect and mixes with his or her embodied consciousness. The progeny of this mixture is architectural design that reveals our fundamental intertwining with the world, design that manifests our involvement as motile, sensate participants in a spatial, sensible environment.

In architectural design, we experience the world sensuously and spatio-temporally and then create from that experience something material, sensuous, spatial, and durative. These aspects of architecture resonate with the most fundamental aspects of our corporeity. As such, architectural design satisfies the Flesh's demand that the spatiality of the world be expressed "over and over again" (Johnson 1993: 51). This repetitive expression manifests the generous and abundant nature of the Flesh, which Merleau-Ponty repeatedly describes in terms of contingency, porosity, openness, and genesis.

The architectural carnal echo is in turn experienced sensuously and spatio-temporally by others in a progressive intertwining of carnal echo and wild being. Thus architecture transforms the world coming inside to a reemergence, a pouring back outside—of vision into visibility (of the process of seeing into something seen), of motion into spatiality (of the process of moving into something spatial), of time into temporality (of the process of spending time into something durative). The world is neither subject nor object, neither inside nor outside as boundaries blur between perceiver and perceived. The resultant architectural design is present, visible, and spatial, but is also a transformation of the architect's understanding of him/herself being present, visible, motile, and temporal. Thus the reciprocal relationship, the ongoing exchange, between self and world that becomes visible in painting, takes inhabitable form in architecture. Indeed, it is a reciprocal act, a taking in and giving out whose intertwining of touching and tactility, movement and motility is layered onto the same intertwining of vision and visibility achieved by painting.

Where, in painting, "the eye sees the world and what it would need to become a painting," in architectural design, the body feels the world and what it would need to become a place or a shelter. The eye sees "the colors awaited by the painting" as the body feels the textures, light, or enclosure awaited by the place (Merleau-Ponty 1993: 127). Where a painter looks at the world and perceives its color, light, and form, an architect sees a place, a set of materials, or a changing quality of light. Where vision interrogates the world and produces something visible—a painting, movement interrogates the world and produces something spatial—a dance, perhaps, or architecture. To the architect, it is not simply line, color, and form, but also sun, wind, gravity, materiality, and motility that gain expression. Both sets of perceptions "arouse [in the painter or architect] a carnal formula of their presence" and engender an artifact or a place that exists as a "carnal expression" of the primary experience (1993: 126).[5]

Merleau-Ponty writes, "Painting scrambles all our categories" of "essence and existence, imaginary and real, visible and invisible" (1993: 130). Architecture scrambles these categories and more, adding time, space, movement, inhabitation, touch, sound, surface temperature, and kinaesthesia to the mix of the imaginary and real, visible and invisible. The architect's motility, like the painter's vision, is receptive and reciprocal. Merleau-Ponty contends that, by seeing, the painter approaches what s/he sees and "opens onto the world" (1993: 124). Architecture, because of its double existence as carnal expression and as real place, scrambles the categories of world and self as painting does, but it does so in a profusion of ways, of which vision and visibility are only one small part.

In embodied spatial experience, form and outline are secondary in our dynamic interrelationship to a host of natural and architectural elements that stimulate every sensing cell in our bodies. The architect brings the world inside in a panoply of superimposed sensations until it is no longer clear where the world stops and the architect begins. In this porous state, s/he is prepared to uncover the hidden structure of spatial experience, in which the spatiality and materiality of the world achieve a sort of doubling, existing simultaneously in the world and in the depths of the body.[6]

The ecstatic nature of seeing (for the painter) demonstrates the ambiguity of the boundaries between self and world. As the world enters the painter, the painter becomes absent to self to be present to the world, as "the mind goes out through the eyes to wander among objects" (1993: 126, 128). Painting, then, comes from the world—or, more exactly, from a relationship between embodied consciousness and the world—rather than from the mind, as Descartes would advocate. In architecture, the mind goes out through the fingertips that touch architectural surfaces, through the skin surfaces that respond to temperature changes, through the ears that sense solidity or hollowness, vastness or intimacy through echo lag, through our kinaesthetic bodies—*and* through the eyes as they take in the visual qualities of architecture. In all these ways the mind goes out to wander among perceived things, through space. In painting, this wandering effects a doubling of sorts, wherein things are "both out there in the world and here at the heart of vision" (1993: 128).

The invitation within spatial experience takes place at the prepersonal or prereflective level. By attuning to the potential of his or her own spatiality to interact with that of the emerging design, the architect can become caught up in the sensuous and spatial to the point of becoming lost in it, absent to self within the exchange. We absent ourselves imaginatively as we design, becoming lost in the emerging spaces the same way we become lost in experiences of already existing spaces. Thus the act of design burrows unselfconsciously beneath the artificial subject-object divide of Cartesianism. It also affirms that we are of the same stuff as the world.

When we lose ourselves in spatial experience, we accumulate a deep knowledge that resides outside the conscious mind and can find its way back out intuitively in architectural design. Many of the unexplainable creative leaps in design may come from this deep level of knowledge, aided by the wanton intercourse between seemingly unrelated elements of the Flesh. Although the uncovering is at its root intuitive and inexpressible, the architect uses conventional and unconventional techniques of observation, analysis, and abstraction to further it in the same way that the painter relies on a number of established techniques to express painting as carnal echo. The resultant architectural design is the carnal echo of the architect's embodied experience: the relational Flesh made manifest.

The Embodied Experience of Space

Descartes and Merleau-Ponty construe space very differently. Descartes presumes that we understand space as an extension or "prolongation of [our] bodily members" (Merleau-Ponty 1993: 136). But Merleau-Ponty asserts that the space of the body is unlike the rest of space, in the same way as our body is an object unlike other objects. It is unknowable—we cannot experience that space any more than we can see the inside of our eyes—but it is never neutral. Merleau-Ponty refers to the space of the body as the "primary *here* from which all the *theres* will come," as a "place the soul [or mind] inhabits" (1993: 136). The body is the origin point of spatiality, irretrievably altering space by its location and movement within it (138). We are surrounded by space, which constantly adjusts in relationship to our bodies. As carnal echo, architectural design creates in accordance with the way space plays out in relationship to the origin point of our bodies. The architect wonders: How can I be pulled along this path? What will make me want to linger in this place? Where will my hands rest? My eyes? These questions animate a design as the emerging space beckons us into its depths.

Between other things and ourselves lies the "third dimension," or depth, which Merleau-Ponty contends we must call the first dimension because all other relationships spring from it and are contained within it. Our perception of planes, lines, forms, and colors stems from their distance from and orientation to our bodies. Merleau-Ponty eloquently describes the phenomenological experience of depth as "an overall 'locality' in which everything exists at once and from which height and width and distance are abstractions, of a voluminousness which we express in a single word by saying that a thing is 'there'" (1993: 140).[7]

In experiencing depth relationally as the distance between us and a perceived thing—an unfolding phenomenon and ontological equal whose body abides at some remove from our own, we experience the "reversibility of dimensions" that stems from the relational nature of the Flesh. This reversibility, or intertwining, which sensory experience manifests, is rooted in our recognition of the thing as an unfolding phenomenon in dynamic relationship with ourselves. The distance between us is charged, and the space between us possesses a thickness born of relationship and characterized by beckoning, opening, solicitation, interrogation, and fascination. In this relational structuring of space, form and outline, rather than color, become "secondary and derived" as we perceive things moving and modulating against other things (Merleau-Ponty 1993: 140). Form and outline are subsumed in a primary, enveloping spatial relationship that encloses and relates the things and the perceiver.

Merleau-Ponty's examination of painting and vision culminates in an exploration of movement—an area that at first might seem tangential to the visual field of painting. He uses a complex and sometimes conflicting array of spatio-temporal images to illuminate the relationship between movement and vision: movement prefigures vision, encompasses it, and is the sequel to and maturation of it (1993: 124). Vision both springs from movement and falls to rest again in it. The body itself is an intertwining of vision and movement, and movement may be considered a reciprocal act in the same manner as vision. An intercorporeal consideration of architectural design immediately suggests examining how we design architecture to be viewed and experienced while moving through it—the design of spatial sequence.

Merleau-Ponty writes at length about the reciprocal relationship between vision and visibility as concretized in the body, about the kinship manifested in the fact that our seeing bodies are also visible. The other side of looking is our visibility: we can look at something, and we can ourselves be looked at (1993: 124). A parallel relationship between movement and spatiality is also concretized in the body, and the same kinship is manifested in the fact that our moving bodies are spatial as the world is both dynamic and spatial. The outward motility of our bodies and its inner dynamic cellular processes resonate with and echo the spatiality and dynamic processes of the larger world. Movement is thus a reciprocal act, an intercorporeal give-and-take, in the same way that vision is. While vision brings the world inside the painter through the eyes, it is movement through space that brings the world inside the architect. Both vision and touch are grounded in movement, entwining us with the world, and the creative process of architectural design recognizes this fact.[8]

Vision as Interrogation into Kinship

Vision is the channel through which the world enters a painter. Merleau-Ponty characterizes vision as a question, an openness, an outwardly directed, relational, and participatory act. Vision manifests more than its object; through it we question and explore the fundamental intertwinement of the Flesh, its dynamic nature, and our place within it. Vision invades and animates our depths; Merleau-Ponty states that even our imagination "borrows from vision" as, through its mediation, depth and light unfold to us, both inhabiting and enveloping us.

Merleau-Ponty contends that painters experience an especially deep immersion within the world. He quotes André Marchand (inspired by Paul Klee), who writes, "I think that the painter must be penetrated by the universe. . . . I expect to be inwardly submerged, buried. Perhaps I paint to break out" (Merleau-Ponty 1993: 129).[9] The image of submersion offers a particularly vivid image of total envelopment in a milieu. We are generally not cognizant of our immersion in the earth's atmosphere, although it adheres to every surface on and within our bodies. But what of the painter, to whom the air is thick with relationship? In a thicker-than-air medium, such as water, submersion overwhelms us as we feel the medium envelop our exterior surfaces and threaten to invade our interior. Even being immersed in a constrictive milieu such as a thicket subjects our being—particularly our orientation—to the thicket's internal logic. Here we are overtaken by the surrounding medium to the point where normal, unselfconscious sensing and movement are impossible. Such a radical breaking down of subjective boundaries is the foundational condition for painting, as the painter is struck by the overwhelming presence of the perceived and is compelled by its immediacy to "break out" through creative activity.

In our submersion within the world, we open our subjective boundaries to the point of disappearing as a subject and becoming a relationship, which a painter then expresses in painting. Here the subject-object relationship, the conceptual shell constructed around our intercorporeal existence, shatters to reveal a deeper perceiver-perceived intertwining in which it becomes "impossible to distinguish between who sees and who is seen, who paints and what is painted" (Merleau-Ponty 1993: 129). In this milieu, it is also impossible to separate the world from the human body or human expression as all three integrate within the phenomenal unfolding of the Flesh (147).

This experience of entanglement with the world engenders a sense of kinship with it, a deep knowledge that we are part of the same Flesh and made of the same stuff. This knowledge is central to our understanding of the Flesh's communality, and for this reason Merleau-Ponty repeatedly emphasizes the visibility of the seer. The reciprocity and kinship between the world and ourselves is the springing point for all our relationships within the Flesh. Galen A. Johnson writes, "In interrogating the depths of the world, the seer and painter interrogate the depths of the self" (Johnson 1993: 54). When we explore the world, we explore that of which we are inextricably a part, a world that is more self than other.

"This extraordinary overlapping or envelopment," Johnson maintains, "is one in which seer and seen are capable of reversing their roles as subject and object" (Johnson 1993: 47). There is a chiasm, a constant fluxing of subjective boundaries between the seer and the seen, the toucher and the touched, as between two hands (ibid.). In the dynamic and reciprocal process of perceptual unfolding, the self loses all of its Cartesian isolation and exists as a self only through its intertwining as perceiver with the perceived. This self, "caught up in things," is not a constituting, thinking self, "but a self by confusion, [immersion, and] narcissism" (Merleau-Ponty 1993: 124).

The painter's vision and the painting it generates reveal the indistinct boundaries between the world and our embodied consciousness. Recognizing visibility as "the other side of [our] power of looking" (Johnson 1993: 47) allows a painter to recognize the potential of looking as the other side of things' visibility, and so better to understand the active nature of the solicitation of things within the interactive domain of the Flesh. Painting manifests our visual relationship with things in the world, an interactive process of beckoning and interrogation wherein we perceive things actively soliciting our involvement. In a reciprocal arrangement in which the painter attunes ecstatically to the surrounding world, a mountain "makes itself seen" while the painter "interrogates it with his gaze" (Merleau-Ponty 1993: 128). In support of this point, Merleau-Ponty quotes Klee's observation, recorded by Marchand, that the trees see him as powerfully as he sees the trees (1993: 129).

Merleau-Ponty's phrases display the active character of the perceived in this Fleshly relationship: things "beckon" us, "make themselves seen," "articulate themselves" in us, whether we be writers, painters, or architects, teachers, parents, or lovers seeking creatively to contribute. We reciprocate by opening ourselves to their solicitation and creatively responding to it. Max Ernst contends that "the role of the painter is to grasp and project what sees itself in him," (Merleau-Ponty 1993: 129) and Gary Madison writes that the painter expresses the "internal and underground commerce" between self and world. The defining aspect of a painter, to Madison, is his or her "astonishment in the face of" this commerce and the compulsion to express the relationship rather than experiencing it unreflectively (Madison 1981: 321, footnote 28).

A painter channels, takes dictation, lives, as Merleau-Ponty puts it, "in fascination" and in profound lack that s/he seeks to remedy (1993: 129).[10] This interaction goes to the very heart of being, and painting is an exemplar of the ecstatic process in which, through opening ourselves to the world, we can get beneath the traditional western subject-object division. A painting's viewer can partake of this same astonishment, as the painter's carnal echo communicates something of the painter's experience of the intertwined Flesh.

Architectural Design as Interrogation

While the painter interrogates the visible world through vision, the architect interrogates space and time with movement—or at least with the imaginary texture, the anticipation and memory, of movement. To the architect, a mountain does not make itself seen so much as it makes itself climbed or makes its rough surfaces or its verticality felt or makes its own particular conditions of boundary and enclosure experienced. The architect interrogates the mountain spatially and temporally with all her combined senses, with his body as a kinaesthetic whole—interrogating the beckoning world, allowing it to animate his depths and infuse her imagination.[11]

Architects' sketchbooks and notebooks provide rich evidence of their sense of being beckoned by—and, reciprocally, interrogating—the places they inhabit. Their sketches and notes record the particular character of their own embodied interaction with the surrounding environment as each architect mixes the mass, space, and sensuousness of a succession of places with his or her carnal schema to generate a coherent approach to designing architecture. One architect's sketches of the Parthenon might show an interrogation of—even a fascination with—its proportional relationships of form. Another architect, visiting the same place, would interrogate it differently—perhaps becoming fascinated by the rhythm of light and shadow in the Parthenon's colonnade—and might take from that experience a conviction that light and shadow qualities can overpower formal relationships (Lewis 1999: 155). The architect's embodied experiences of space and material give rise in turn to new architecture that reiterates habitual experiences of moving through, passing under, pausing, confronting, and a host of additional spatio-temporal experiences.

Samuel Mockbee's paintings and architecture reveal his continued fascination with the sensuous and spatial qualities of the natural and built landscape of the American Deep South.[12] His lived experience of patterns of light and shade, surface textures, elemental rhythms, and the saturated colors that resist perceptual bleaching in the region's bright sunlight, all find expression in his work. The Bryant House in Mason's Bend, Alabama, designed by Mockbee and his students at the Auburn Rural Studio, exemplifies how architectural design exists simultaneously as an expression of the architect's embodied experience and as the ground for its inhabitants' original spatial experience.[13]

The front porch of the Bryant House (figs. 1 and 2) is a reinterpretation of a traditional Southern porch that expresses the designers' embodied experiences of the traditional porch and its progenitor, the shade tree. It gives physical form to the lived experience of dynamic interactions between light and surface, measuring the passage of days and seasons as it tracks striated shadows across the porch floor and the surfaces of its columns. It also manifests the designers' lived experience of the region's frequent, heavy rains while heightening the experience for its inhabitants: the clicking sounds of raindrops striking a translucent acrylic roof and the blurred sweep of water down its sloping surface, along with decreased air pressure, cooling breezes, and the percussive sound of water sliding from the roof to the pebbled ground surface below, make each rainfall a multi-sensory experience affecting ears, eyes, and even pores of the skin.

The porch of the neighboring Harris House (figs. 3 and 4) expresses the same fascination with space and light and the same embodied experience of hot and humid Alabama summers. It explodes the traditional porch into a large, principal living space whose exuberant, sloping roof lines allow wind to penetrate, hot air to exhaust, and moving sunlight to track around the porchroom's interior surfaces. It too exists simultaneously as the expression of its designers' embodied experience and as the setting for its inhabitants' subsequent embodied experience, intertwining carnal echo with wild being.

In both houses, sensuous surfaces made of varied materials interact with us as perceivers by absorbing or reflecting light, by withdrawing or releasing heat, by giving off odors caused by dampness and oxidation, and by inviting our eyes to wander among their differently colored and textured surfaces. Their explicit and implied spaces invite movement around and through, fluctuating with position and point of view. The houses unfold perceptually, gradually revealing varied material and spatial relationships and manifesting their kinship with our own material and spatial bodies.

To Merleau-Ponty, the defining aspect of the painter—and, by extension, of the architect—is a compulsion to express the unspoken things s/he learns from the "internal and underground commerce" between self and world (Ernst in Merleau-Ponty 1993: 129). Architectural design is a way of opening the self that springs out of the architect's "fascination [and] infatuation" with color, light, movement, space, and potential action. In becoming absorbed within the creative act of designing architecture, the architect becomes lost within the world's abundance, joining spatio-temporal memories of other places with imagining of the designed space's future inhabitation. Thus, in

Figure 1. Bryant House ("Hay Bale House"), Auburn Rural Studio, Mason's Bend, Alabama, 1993–1994, view of house and smokehouse. Courtesy of Timothy Hursley.

Figure 2. Bryant House, view of front porch. Courtesy of Timothy Hursley.

Figure 3. Harris House ("Butterfly House"), Auburn Rural Studio, Mason's Bend, Alabama, 1996–1997, frontal view. Courtesy of Timothy Hursley.

Figure 4. Harris House, view of porch interior. Courtesy of Timothy Hursley.

designing, the architect loses any sense of a distinct past, present, and future and experiences vertical time—"simply being there in the world" in a deeply integrated way—or being in several times at once (Johnson 1995: 51). S/he brings forward past spatial experiences into the present-moment act of design as s/he envisions an emerging space that will incorporate these qualities in the future.

As architects, we become aware of the qualities of a place that exist only at the threshold of ordinary inhabitation, qualities that are not ordinarily experienced. We ask space what it does to suddenly cause a place to be and to be this place,[14] what calls us to participate in its spatial, material, and sensuous wild being. Then, in design, we use architectural elements and qualities either to respond to perceived qualities or needs of the site itself or to call forth other qualities we have experienced through countless previous acts of inhabiting and moving through space.

Architectural design concerns itself with the hidden geometric, proportional, light, material, and solid-void relationships—as well as the influence of natural forces such as sun, wind, and gravity—that support a space. It can also make intangible things, memory, or anticipation salient parts of a spatial sequence. In architecture, the wall or the window, the row of pilasters or the longitudinal space work together to "render visible" spatial character or spatial sequence, and these are the elements the architect uses to advance a design. Light, shadow, proportion, degrees of enclosure, axiality, columns, walls, windows, and other architectural elements modulate space below the level of perception in a way that resonates silently with the spatiality and motility of our own embodied existence.

Conclusion

When architectural design functions as carnal echo, the architect opens to the larger world, attuning to its sensuous content and "wild being." S/he engages the whole body with its larger environment through multisensory movement that interrogates the depths of the spatio-temporal world, and participates both consciously and unconsciously in an intercorporeal relationship with unfolding phenomena. S/he attunes to the hidden relationships that support and modulate perceived space, and lives in fascination in the face of these relationships, compelled by this fascination to design.

All architecture entangles its designer and its inhabitants with the larger world, blurring subjective boundaries and intertwining vision and visibility, sensing and sensuousness, movement and spatiality. By understanding the implications of Merleau-Ponty's work for both the design and experience of architecture, recognizing in particular the importance of movement and materiality, we can establish a relationship with architecture that reveals the intertwined and intersubjective nature of the Flesh. In both making and experiencing architecture, we escape the confines of subject-object dualism and arrive at an intersubjective realm where the self "is a self . . . by inherence of the see-er in the seen, the toucher in the touched, the feeler in the felt, [and the mover in the moved through]—a self, then that is caught up in things" whose visibility, tactility, materiality, and spatiality both echo and complete our own (Merleau-Ponty 1993: 124).

Notes

1. For a fuller exploration of this theme as it relates to architecture, see Rachel McCann (erroneously attributed to Rachel McAnn), "Receptivity to the Sensuous: Architecture as 'Wild Being.'"

2. This is a process of transubstantiation where the painter lends his/her body to the world and changes the world into paintings. Galen A. Johnson calls painting "a disclosure of the world in the form of a heavier, less transparent, less ductile body than language" ("Ontology and Painting: 'Eye and Mind,'" in Johnson 1993: 39).

3. Adapted from Maurice Merleau-Ponty, "Eye and Mind," 132–133.

4. Max Ernst in Merleau-Ponty, "Eye and Mind," 129.

5. Merleau-Ponty contends that we perceive certain qualities only because they and our bodies are complementary: "Quality, light, color, depth, which are there before us, are there only because they awaken an echo in our bodies and because the body welcomes them" (125).

6. Adapted from Merleau-Ponty, "Eye and Mind," 124.

7. Merleau-Ponty, "Eye and Mind," 140, in Edward S. Casey, "'The Element of Voluminousness': Depth and Place Re-examined," in M. C. Dillon, *Merleau-Ponty Vivant*, Albany, 1991, 20–21. Casey contends that depth in Cartesian thought has to do with measured distance.

8. If vision is wrapped up in movement, the two are yet bridged by touch. The "other side" of touch is illustrated in Merleau-Ponty's example of two hands touching, where one hand is simultaneously perceiver and perceived. Merleau-Ponty provocatively links vision with touch and motility, writing, "through [vision] we touch the sun and the stars; [we] are everywhere at once" ("Eye and Mind," 146). For the architect, vision, touch, and movement all collapse distance, but in distinct ways. Vision brings the distant thing to us; movement brings us to the distant thing, and with touch we meet in the middle. With all three modes of interaction within space, sometimes we act and other times we are acted on.

9. The larger quotation reads, "'In a forest, I have felt many times over that it was not I who looked at the forest. Some days I felt that the trees were looking at me, were speaking to me. . . . I was there, listening. . . . I think that the painter must be pen-

etrated by the universe and not want to penetrate it. . . . I expect to be inwardly submerged, buried. Perhaps I paint to break out.'"

10. Merleau-Ponty asserts that the painter's interrogation is not rhetorical, but consists of questions inspired by need. He further states that the painter's tracings "will be revelations to others [who] do not lack what he lacks." This notion of need and lack reinforce his idea (developed by David Abram into an ecological philosophy) that we are completed as subjects by interaction with the world.

11. An architect may also override experiential concerns with conceptual or functional imperatives, making architecture in which quick ideation short-circuits embodied experience. For a more detailed treatment of this short-circuiting, see Rachel McCann, "'On the Hither Side of Depth': A Pedagogy of Engagement."

12. They also reveal his lifelong passion for social justice, a theme outside the scope of this essay but central to Mockbee's work. This theme is developed in Rachel McCann, "Architectural Design and the Expression of Embodied Experience," presented at the 2004 International Merleau-Ponty Circle Meeting, Allentown, PA, 2 October 2004 (unpublished). For further examination of Mockbee's work, see Lori Ryker, ed., *Mockbee Coker: Thought and Process*, and Andrea Oppenheimer Dean and Timothy Hursley, *Rural Studio: Samuel Mockbee and an Architecture of Decency*.

13. Although Mockbee's role in this design is that of teacher at the Auburn Rural Studio, his ideas and convictions permeate both the process and the resultant design.

14. Adapted from Merleau-Ponty, "Eye and Mind," 128.

References

Casey, Edward S. (1991). "'The Element of Voluminousness': Depth and Place Reexamined." In *Merleau-Ponty Vivant*, ed. M. C. Dillon. Albany: State University of New York Press, 1–29.

Dean, Andrea Oppenheimer and Hursley, Timothy (2002). *Rural Studio: Samuel Mockbee and an Architecture of Decency*. Princeton: Princeton Architectural Press.

Johnson, Galen A. (1993). "Ontology and Painting: 'Eye and Mind,'" in *The Merleau-Ponty Aesthetics Reader: Philosophy and Painting*. Ed. Galen A. Johnson. Evanston, IL: Northwestern University Press, 35–56.

Lewis, David C. (1999). "The Aesthetic Experience of Ambiguity on the Athenian Acropolis," in *Architecture and Civilization*. Ed. Michael H. Mitias. Amsterdam: Editions Rodopi, 143–164.

Madison, Gary Brent (1981). *The Phenomenology of Merleau-Ponty*. Athens, OH: Ohio University Press.

McCann, Rachel (1999). "Receptivity to the Sensuous: Architecture as 'Wild Being,'" in *Architecture and Civilization*. Ed. Michael H. Mitias. Amsterdam: Editions Rodopi, 123–141.

——— (2004). "Architectural Design and the Expression of Embodied Experience." Presented at the International Merleau-Ponty Circle Meeting, Allentown, PA, 2 October 2004 (unpublished).

——— (2005). "'On the Hither Side of Depth': A Pedagogy of Engagement," in *Writings in Architectural Education: EAAE Prize 2003–2005*. Ed. Ebbe Harder. Copenhagen: From, 67–81.

Merleau-Ponty, Maurice (1993). "Eye and Mind," in *The Merleau-Ponty Aesthetics Reader: Philosophy and Painting*. Ed. Galen A. Johnson. Evanston: Northwestern University Press, 121–149.

Ryker, Lori, ed. (1996). *Mockbee Coker: Thought and Process*. Princeton: Princeton Architectural Press.

Contributors

Justine Dymond received her M.F.A. in creative writing and her Ph.D. in English from the University of Massachusetts, Amherst. Her other publications include articles on Virginia Woolf, Okanogan writer Mourning Dove, and Spokane/Coeur d'Alene author Sherman Alexie. Her poetry and fiction have appeared in the *Massachusetts Review*, *Pleiades*, the *Briar Cliff Review*, WomenWriters.net, and *Cimarron Review*, among other literary journals. Her short story "Cherubs" was selected for the *O. Henry Prize Stories 2007*. She teaches at Springfield College in Massachusetts.

Sally Fischer is a professor in the Philosophy Department of Warren Wilson College in Asheville, North Carolina. Her articles on Merleau-Ponty have appeared in *International Studies in Philosophy*, and in *Merleau-Ponty and Ecology: Dwelling on the Landscapes of Thought*. Edited by William S. Hamrick and Suzanne L. Cataldi. State University of New York Press, 2007. She is currently working on a book manuscript on Marcel, Irigaray, and Merleau-Ponty.

Elizabeth Grosz teaches in the department of women's and gender studies at Rutgers University. She has written widely on phenomenology and post-phenomenological philosophies of Lacan, Irigaray, Foucault and Deleuze. Her most recent books are *The Nick of Time. Evolution, Politics and the Untimely* (Duke University Press, 2004), *Time Travels. Feminism, Nature, Power* (Duke University Press, 2005), and *Chaos, Territory, Art: Deleuze and the Framing of the Earth* (Columbia University Press, 2008).

Annemie Halsema is assistant professor at the department of philosophy of the Vrije Universiteit Amsterdam. She has published in the field of feminist philosophy, especially on Irigaray (*Dialectiek van de seksuele differentie*. Amsterdam: Boom, 1998), edited a volume on Butler (*J. Butler, Genderturbulentie*, Amsterdam: Boom/Parresia, 2000) and together with D. Van Houten on humanism (*Empowering Humanity. State of the Art of Humanistics*. Utrecht: De Tijdstroom, 2002). She is currently working on a book with the provisional title: *The Otherness of the Self. Ricoeur and Feminist Theory*, in which she brings Ricoeur's notion of the self into dialogue with the work of Irigaray, Butler and Jessica Benjamin.

Maurice Hamington is associate professor of Women's Studies at Metropolitan State College of Denver where he teaches Feminist Philosophy and Gender

Studies. He is the author of *Hail Mary? The Struggle for Ultimate Womanhood in Catholicism* (Routledge, 1995) and *Embodied Care: Jane Addams, Maurice Merleau-Ponty, and Feminist Ethics* (University of Illinois Press, 2004) as well as coeditor of *Revealing Male Bodies* (Indiana University Press, 2002) and *Socializing Care* (Rowman & Littlefield, 2006).

Lawrence Hass is professor of philosophy at Muhlenberg College in Allentown, Pennsylvania, and associate general secretary of the International Merleau-Ponty Circle. The author of many articles on thinkers and issues relating to phenomenology and postmodern philosophy, he is the author of *Merleau-Ponty's Philosophy* (Indiana, 2008) and co-editor of *Rereading Merleau-Ponty: Essays Beyond the Continental-Analytic Divide* (Humanity Books, 2000).

Greg Johnson is associate professor of philosophy at Pacific Lutheran University in Tacoma, Washington. He has previously published articles on both Merleau-Ponty and Feminist philosophy. He is currently finishing a manuscript, *Elements of Utopian Thinking*, which develops a nonconventional understanding of utopian thought by appealing to phenomenology, hermeneutics, and feminist philosophy.

Patricia M. Locke is a tutor at St. John's College, Annapolis, Maryland. She works in the areas of philosophy of art and literature, primarily with a phenomenological approach. Her current book project is *Recollecting Architecture: A Phenomenology of Ambiguity*, which considers ancient and contemporary architecture through a Merleau-Pontian lens.

Rachel McCann is professor of architecture at Mississippi State University, where she teaches architectural history, theory, and design. Her essays on architecture have appeared in *Writings in Architectural Education: EAAE Prize 2003–2005* (From, 2005), *Dictionary of Jewish-Christian Relations* (Cambridge University Press, 2005), and *Architecture and Civilization* (Rodopi Press, 1999). Her research weaves Merleau-Pontian thought and architectural theory to investigate the intercorporeal experience and design of architecture.

Janice McLane is associate professor in and chair of the department of philosophy and religious studies, Morgan State University. She is currently completing a book, *The Red Rose of Passion: Women and Internalized Oppression*, forthcoming from State University of New York Press.

Kelly Oliver is W. Alton Jones professor of philosophy at Vanderbilt University, where she is also an affiliate in women's studies. She is the author of over fifty articles and seven books, most recently *Women as Weapons of War* (Columbia University Press 2007); *The Colonization of Psychic Space: Toward a Psychoanalytic Social Theory* (University of Minnesota, 2004); *Noir Anxiety: Race, Sex, and Maternity in Film Noir* (University of Minnesota, 2002), and

Witnessing: Beyond Recognition (University of Minnesota, 2001). She has edited several books, including *Recent French Feminism* (Oxford University Press, 2004) and *French Feminism Reader* (Rowman & Littlefield, 2000).

Rashmika Pandya has recently completed her Ph.D. at McMaster University in Hamilton, Ontario, Canada. Her dissertation (*From Narcissism to Schizophrenia*) focused on issues of phenomenological method and subjectivity in the works of Edmund Husserl, Emmanuel Levinas, and Jean-Luc Marion. Currently she is working on a phenomenological approach to multiculturalism and minority rights within a Canadian context.

Gail Weiss is professor of philosophy and human sciences at The George Washington University. She is the author of *Refiguring the Ordinary* (Indiana University Press, 2008), *Body Images: Embodiment as Intercorporeality* (Routledge, 1999), and co-editor of *Feminist Interpretations of Maurice Merleau-Ponty* (Penn State Press, 2006), *Thinking the Limits of the Body* (State University of New York Press, 2003), and *Perspectives on Embodiment: Intersections of Nature and Culture* (Routledge, 1999). She has published widely in phenomenology, existentialism, and feminist theory.

Talia Welsh is a U.C. Foundation assistant professor of philosophy at the University of Tennessee at Chattanooga. Her main areas of research are philosophy of psychology, nineteenth- and twentieth-century European philosophy, and Feminist Theory. In particular, she writes on the connection between phenomenology and psychology. Her translation of Maurice Merleau-Ponty's lectures on child psychology at the Sorbonne is forthcoming with Northwestern University Press.

Bruce Young taught philosophy in the University of Wolverhampton in the United Kingdom for many years, establishing philosophy as an independent subject there. The undergraduate degree program for the design of which he was responsible was, after a quality review by academic peers from other universities, ranked fourth in the country for teaching (after Cambridge, Oxford, and London). In spite of this the university dismantled it, and since then he has worked for the university solely in postgraduate supervision. He now devotes most of his time to research and writing.

Index

Abram, David, 206–7, 212, 280
affective attunement, 143
Africa, 248, 251
alienation, 53–57, 132–34, 144, 158, 196
alterity, 1, 32–34, 38–42, 73–74, 153–54, 180; radical, 32, 41, 133
An Ethics of Sexual Difference, 3, 64, 93–94
anger, 157, 162, 247, 255
anthropology, 1, 49, 51
Appadurai, Arjun, 7, 243, 260–61
Arendt, Hannah, 170–72, 175, 177, 180, 184–85
art, 1, 103–7, 112, 119, 229, as representation, 265; critic, 145; depth in, 101, 107, truth in, 4, 99, 105, 106
Autobiography of Alice B. Toklas, The, 112

Beauvoir, Simone de, 63, 71–72, 80, 146
becoming, 31, 71–72, 92, 179, 270
Being, 38, 105–6, 192–93, 195–96, 200, 211, 253, 258. *See also* wild being
Being and Nothingness, 131
Benhabib, Seyla, 6, 169–77, 184–85
Bergson, Henri, 2, 13–27
Bernasconi, Robert, 34, 42
Bigwood, Carol, 47, 54–56
binaries: active/passive, 88–89; body/consciousness, 261; dilation/contraction, 235; exterior/interior, 124–25; figure/background, 209–10, 213; foreground/background, 7, 04, 210–11; freedom/determinism, 228; identity/difference, 169, 179, 243, 244, 252, 260; inside/outside, 41, 118, 125; masculine/feminine, 49–51; mind/body, 20–21, 31, 206, 210, 217;

mind/matter, 13–14, 17, 22, 26; nature/culture, 26, 67–68 noetic/noematic, 235; otherness/sameness, 169; plasticity/fixity, 228; same/other, 179; self/other, 2, 5, 8, 32–33, 35, 38, 40, 69, 132–33, 143, 159, 244, 252–53, 261; sex/gender, 5; subject/object, 2, 17, 22, 26, 70, 73, 76, 118, 133–34, 166, 212–13, 244, 261, 270, 274, 279; transcendence/immanence, 244, 253; universality/particularity, 244
blind faith, 147
bodily intentionality, 154, 157, 159, 226, 235
bodily motility, 208
body: schema, 207; female, 3, 193; gendered, 3, 158; -subject, 5, 18, 70, 153–54, 156, 235–36; textual, 118
Bordo, Susan, 46
Bourdieu, Pierre, 7, 223, 228–39
Bryant House, 275–76
Butler, Judith, 66, 93, 95, 156–57, 249

care. *See* ethic of care
carnal echo, 8, 265–68, 270, 274–75, 278
carnal love, 64, 70
Cartesianism, 270
castration threat, 132
Categorical Imperative, 173
Columbine High School, 203
conscience, 34, 68, 76
consciousness, 14, 17–26, 111, 120, 136–37, 155, 209–10, 228–30, 235–36, 244, 252–56, 261; embodied, 65; 68–70; 73, 76, 161, 163, 267–69, 273; evolutionary development of, 38; self-, 131–32, 145–46, 249

Consciousness and the Acquisition of Language, 252, 256
corporeal perceptual system, 136
corporeal schema, 18, 31
corporeality, 17, 38, 135, 211

Darwin, Charles, 14, 38
Deleuze, Gilles, 13, 235–36
Democracy Begins Between Two, 77
Dennett, Daniel, 14
Descartes, Réné, 5, 135, 137, 266, 270
determinism: racial, 112
Deutsch, Hélène, 51
dialectic, master/slave, 103
Dioptric, 135
dualism, 36–38, 40, 206, 279; in Levinas, 36. *See also* binaries
duration, 15, 18–21
Durkheim, Emile, 5, 143

Eichmann in Jerusalem, 170
Eichmann, Adolf, 170, 183–84
Elemental Passions, 74, 138
embodied communion, 158
embodied knowledge, 206–7, 214, 217
embodiment, 3, 45, 47, 52–56, 64, 66–77, 111–14, 117, 125–26, 134, 141, 166, 178–79, 190–91, 210, 212–13, 215–16, 255–57; female, 3, 46–47
empathy, 173, 203, 214–15, 256
empirical realism, 155
empiricism, 38, 85, 255
emplacement, 118, 123
energy, 16, 39, 52, 138–45, 180; social, 5, 141, 142, 143, 145
enlarged thinking, 171–76, 185
epistemology, 7, 85, 204, 214, 216; corporeal-centered, 204, 206–11
eschatology, 37
essentialism, 3, 76, 176, 182; biological, 50; critique of, 64
ethics, 5–7, 25, 33, 36–37, 71, 75, 146, 153–56, 162, 164–65, 169, 172, 176, 185, 204–8, 216–17, 224, 244, 247, 260–61; of ambiguity, 146; of care,
204–5, 211, 215–16; communitarian, 163; embodied, 203, 206; intersubjective, 3; of difference, 164; of reciprocity, 169
evolution, 17, 24, 38, 138
expression: univocity of, 33
Eye and Mind, 8, 35, 137, 265, 279–80

feminine, the, 2–3, 26, 42, 49–51, 63–64, 74, 87–89, 95, 157–58, 193, 195–96, 200
femininity, 26, 50, 76, 195–96, 197
feminism, 13, 26–27, 200
Finding Time Again, 99
flesh, 2, 7–8, 16, 22–25, 28–29, 33, 35, 37–42, 56, 68–69, 73–74, 90, 92, 95, 101, 105, 118, 125, 133–35, 137, 140, 146, 154, 156, 178–84, 200, 204, 206, 211–17, 244, 262; reversibility of, 146, 213–14
Forgetting of Air in Martin Heidegger, 139
Forgetting of Air, The, 79
Four fundamental concepts of psychoanalysis, The, 132
Freud, Sigmund, 5, 132
Frye, Marilyn, 197

Gallagher, Shaun, 142
gaze, the, 5, 28, 31, 35, 105, 106, 132, 134, 135, 137, 139
gender, 45–47, 49–50, 54, 63, 68–77, 91–92, 114, 154, 156–58, 160, 164, 166, 216; difference, 46, 47, 50, 164
Geographical History of America, The, 111–12
gesture, 45–46, 74, 76, 100–5, 143, 155, 157, 159, 161, 190, 193, 195, 211, 253, 255–56
Gibson, J.J., 5, 136–39, 145
Gilligan, Carol, 205
Grahn, Judy, 198

Habermas, Jürgen, 92, 95
habit, 7, 18, 155, 204, 206, 208–9, 213, 223–28, 233–38, 248

habitability, 223
habitus, 228–39; class, 230, 232, 236
hallucinations, 245
Hamington, Maurice, 165–66
Harris House, 275, 277
Heidegger, Martin, 14, 32, 64, 78
heterosexuality, 51, 112, 125
Holland, Nancy, 165
Holocaust, 5, 147
horizons, 162, 206, 209, 228; intersubjective, 4
human development, 1, 47
human nature, 67
Humanism and Terror, 181
Husserl, Edmund, 1, 14, 27, 31, 57, 64–65, 140, 235, 255

I Love to You, 95
identity, 22, 36, 54, 71–72, 75–76, 92, 163–64, 169, 172, 179, 191–92, 243–44, 247, 252, 260–61; gender, 71
imaginary, the, 99, 269, 274
imagined worlds, 243
In a Different Voice, 205
In Praise of Philosophy, 15
In Search of Lost Time, 99, 102
information, 138–40, 208
inner witness, 5, 147–48
intellection, 15, 144, 267
intentional arc, 155, 157–58, 226, 238
intentionality, 64–67, 75, 157, 190, 194–95, 233, 235; bodily, 154, 157, 159, 226, 235; corporeal, 64; sexual, 64
intercorporeality, 118, 153–54, 156, 158–62, 165–66, 179, 181, 213; dialogical, 160
intercorporiety, 133
intersubjectivity, 2–8, 13, 25, 31–34, 38, 64, 70, 73, 76, 86, 103, 111–12, 133, 154, 157, 160–66, 169, 189–91, 196, 197–98, 200, 211, 213, 232–33, 244–46, 253–56, 259–60, 266, 279; embodied, 6, 75, 153, 164
intuition, 15, 16, 18, 20–21

Irigaray, Luce, 3–5, 8, 61, 63–77, 85–95, 133, 138–39

Jacobson, Paul K., 254, 258
James, William, 7, 27, 223–29, 233–39
Johnson, Galen A., 273, 279

Kant, Emmanuel, 38, 171, 173, 190, 205, 237–39
kinship, 25, 140–41, 271, 273, 275
Kohlberg, Lawrence, 205, 219
Kruks, Sonia, 165–66

Lacan, Jacques, 5, 16, 132, 135–36, 139–40
language, 1, 4–6, 8, 23–24, 32, 36–38, 40, 68, 74, 76, 89–91, 93, 102, 103, 112, 116–26, 135, 142–43, 155–59, 161–62, 164–65, 174, 176, 189–90, 192, 195–97, 200, 211, 233, 241–44, 246–47, 249–60, 262–63, 279; acquisition, 256; game, 233; and culture, 247; definition of, 37; difference as organizing principle of, 121; indeterminacy of, 258; mimetic function of, 118, 120; nonrepresentational, 117; of community, 40; system of, 258; use of by men and women, 68
Laub, Dori, 5, 147
Le visible et l'invisible, 86, 93, 95. *See also* The Visible and the Invisible
Lectures on Kant's Political Philosophy, 171
Levin, David Michael, 178
Levinas, Emmanuel, 2, 5, 31–41, 64, 133, 144–45
Liberal individualism, 163
liberalism, 163
Lifting Belly, 122–24, 126
logic of practice, 230
Logic of Practice, The, 232
Logical Investigations, 255
look, the, 117–18, 131, 135, 139
Lugones, Maria C., 215–16, 219

Madison, Gary, 254, 263, 273
Manning, Rita, 205, 215, 217

marriage, sentimental, 115–16
masculinity, 50, 95
materialism, historical, 260
Matter and Memory, 20, 27
Mead, Margaret, 57
mechanism, 15, 20
Meltzoff, Nicholas, and Keith Moore, 142
memory, 16, 20, 24, 99–100, 105–6, 190, 232, 238, 246, 248–51, 274, 278
menstruation, 47, 51–53, 57–58
metaphysics, 13–14, 17, 26, 169, 261
mirror, 132, 136, 142, 174, 198; image, 136; stage, 132, 142, 149
Mockbee, Samuel, 274–75, 280
moral philosophy, 204–5
motherhood, 53–56
Murphy, Marguerite S., 119–20
mysticism, 15, 20

Noddings, Nel, 205, 207, 210
nominalism, 176, 182
noncoincidence, 3–4, 23, 86–94

other, the, 1–3, 6, 11, 17, 23–24, 28, 32–41, 54, 63, 69–77, 86, 92–93, 114, 121, 125, 131–36, 140–48, 153–56, 159–77, 180–84, 191, 193, 198, 203, 207–8, 210–15, 224–28, 232–36, 243, 246–47, 253, 260, 273; relationship to, 32, 64, 71, 73–75, 85; the otherness of, 6, 32
otherness, 3, 5–6, 32–33, 74–75, 77, 85–88, 93, 116, 119, 148–49, 160, 163, 169, 174, 180, 182, 212, 252
Otherwise than Being, 39–42
Outline of a Theory of Practice, 230

parole, 76, 255, 258
particularity, 144, 172, 205–6, 211, 216, 244, 258–59
penis envy, 132
perception, 1, 7, 13–14, 16–19, 24, 48, 65–66, 70, 73–74, 99–103, 107–8, 112–13, 136–37, 139, 141, 143–46, 155–56, 161, 190, 196–97, 204, 206–10, 213, 217–18, 230, 261–62, 271, 278; primacy of, 16, 141, 245; receptivity of, 196; sensory, 212
perspective: reversibility of, 170, 175–76
phallocentrism, 87–88
Phèdre, 104
Phenomenology of Perception, 21, 28, 35, 45–46, 48, 64–70, 77, 103, 109, 154–57, 160, 178–79, 219, 241–46, 253–55, 259–60
Phenomenology of Spirit, 131
phenomenology: existential, 63, feminist, 153–54
plasticity, 226–28
Plato, 86, 94
Polanyi, Michael, 214, 218
politics of difference, 244, 260, 261
postural schema, 136
pregnancy, 47, 53–57, 114, 135, 178, 181
Preston, Beth, 158
Principles of Psychology, The, 224
Prisoner, The, 103
propositional discourse, 91
Proust, Marcel, 4, 7, 97, 99, 103, 107–9, 223–24, 238
psychology, 1, 3, 46–49, 51, 56, 137, 224; of women, 48, 51

rationalism, 85
reciprocity, 6, 17, 31, 34–36, 42, 153–66, 170, 174–77, 182–86, 200, 204, 206, 212, 244, 260, 273
recognition, 5, 75, 77, 103, 131–49, 166, 175, 184, 197–98, 238–39, 249, 252, 271
Remembrance of Things Past, 223
Remembrance of Things Past: Swann's Way, 4
Republic, The, 228
responsibility, 2, 5, 34, 36, 38–40, 141, 144–45, 147–48, 156, 199, 207; ethical, 144; in Levinas, 39
responsiveness, 103, 137, 139, 145
reversibility, 6, 31–32, 36, 41, 73, 134–36, 146, 153–54, 158, 169–86, 197–200, 212, 236, 253, 261–62, 271;

condition of, 170; fundamental phenomenon of, 124–25; of flesh, 22–24, 135, 146, 213–14, 244
Ricoeur, Paul, 181
Rushdie, Salman, 241, 247

Sacks, Oliver, 250
Sartre, Jean-Paul, 5, 14, 16–17, 19, 31, 34–35, 63–64, 68–70, 79, 131–34, 139, 145, 253
Schmidt, Anton, 170–71, 183
Schneider, 46, 109, 157, 226
Scott, Charles, 181
sensibility, 33–39, 112, 226
September 11th, 231, 234, 237
sexual difference, 3, 27, 50–51, 64, 66–68, 75–77, 132
sexuality, 45, 51, 64, 66, 68–73, 89–90, 101, 112, 117–22, 124, 155–57, 159, 260; lesbian, 119–20, 125
silence, 6, 93, 101, 189–96, 200, 257–58; of oppression, 195, 200
Situating the Self, 176
Sjöholm, Cecilia, 74
Soja, Edward W., 111
solipsism, 6, 31–32, 74, 76, 156, 164, 170, 176, 182, 246
spatiality, 111–12, 115, 137, 156, 166, 206, 268–71, 278–79
Speculum of the Other Woman, 63, 71, 74
speech, 68, 124, 155, 157, 159–60, 189, 192, 195, 253, 255–59; gestural theory of, 7, 255–56
Spelman, Elizabeth V., 215–16, 219
Stein, Gertrude, 4, 111–26
stereotypes, 3, 5, 47–51, 252; sexual, 50, 125
Stern, Daniel, 143
Stoller, Silvia, 46, 79
subject: body-, 5, 18, 70, 153–54, 156, 235–36; hermeneutical, 158, 161, 165; subject-being, 3, 85, 87–88, 91
subjectivity, 2, 5, 13–14, 17, 21–28, 32–33, 49, 52, 63–66, 70–74, 89, 117, 132, 139, 144–49, 153–64, 175, 182, 193, 207, 209, 210, 216, 244, 260; 272; embodied, 123, 125, 133, 148, 154, 156, 160; female, 63; gendered, 111–13; interior, 118; racial, 113; sexual, 122
Sullivan, Shannon, 45, 156, 216
surplus of meaning, 181
Swann's Way. See *Remembrance of Things Past: Swann's Way*
symbolic, the, 4, 49, 90–92, 161; masculine, 63

Tender Buttons, 112–13, 116–20, 122–25
Three Essays on the Theory of Sexuality, 132
Three Lives, 112–13, 115, 117, 119
To Be Two, 68, 74–75, 78
To the Lighthouse, 112
Totality and Infinity, 33–38, 41–42, 80
transcendence, 32, 36–38, 40–41, 67, 69, 75, 145, 157, 172, 177, 180, 227, 244, 253–54; in Levinas, 38; of reality, 85–86
transcendental idealism: critique of, 155
truth, 4, 13, 15, 22, 26, 33, 57, 99, 105, 106, 162, 177, 178, 196, 245, 246, 253, 258, 259. See also art, truth in

universal grammar, 255
universal language, 257
universality, 6, 132, 206, 243, 244, 266

visibility, 4–5, 8, 23, 28, 102, 118, 134–35, 268–69, 271, 273, 278–79
Visible and the Invisible, The, 6, 18, 22, 24, 64, 73, 105, 112, 118, 133–35, 142, 179, 190, 200, 219, 244. See also *Le visible et l'invisible*
vision, 5, 8, 22–23, 28, 35, 106, 132–46, 174, 192, 259, 265–79; anonymity of, 135
vision-touch system, 135–37
vitalism, 15, 20
voice, 90, 106, 119–23, 134, 147, 189–93, 198–200, 205, 207

Weiss, Gail, 55–56, 165, 206, 211, 216
wild being, 8, 179–80, 266, 275, 278
witnessing, 133–35, 142, 146, 147–48, 192
witnessing, structure of, 147–48

Wittgenstein, Ludwig, 91, 94
Woolf, Virginia, 112, 198

Young, Iris, Young, Iris Marion, 6, 46–47, 55, 66, 156, 163, 169, 174, 194, 200, 261

www.ingramcontent.com/pod-product-compliance
Lightning Source LLC
Chambersburg PA
CBHW030130240426
43672CB00005B/87